Reformed Thought
on Freedom

Texts and Studies in Reformation and Post-Reformation Thought

Reformed Thought on Freedom

*The Concept of Free Choice
in Early Modern Reformed Theology*

Edited by Willem J. van Asselt,
J. Martin Bac, and Roelf T. te Velde

IB
Baker Academic
a division of Baker Publishing Group
Grand Rapids, Michigan

Published by Baker Academic
a division of Baker Publishing Group
P.O. Box 6287, Grand Rapids, MI 49516–6287
www.bakeracademic.com

Printed in the United States of America

Library of Congress Cataloging-in-Publication Data
    Reformed thought on freedom : the concept of free choice in early modern reformed theology / edited by Willem J. van Asselt, J. Martin Bac & Roelf T. te Velde.
        p.   cm.
    Includes bibliographical references and index.
    ISBN 978-0-8010-3521-0 (pbk.)
    1. Liberty—Religious aspects—Christianity—History of doctrines. 2. Reformed Church—Doctrines.
I. Asselt, W. J. van. II. Bac, J. Martin. III. Velde, Roelf T. te.
BT809.R44 209
233′.70882842—dc22   2009012090

10   11   12   13   14   15   16   7   6   5   4   3   2   1

Contents

Contributors

DR. J. MARTIN BAC graduated in 2001 with a master's thesis on the debate between Reformed scholasticism and Cartesian philosophy and has defended a dissertation on the will of God in seventeenth-century theology and philosophy at the Protestant Theological University in Utrecht (2009).

DR. ANDREAS J. BECK is professor of historical theology, evangelical theological faculty, Louvain. He has defended a dissertation on Gisbertus Voetius' concept of theology and doctrine of God at Utrecht University. His present research focuses on the relation between medieval and reformed scholasticism.

DR. EEF DEKKER was formerly lecturer in philosophical theology, Utrecht University. He has written a dissertation on freedom, grace, and predestination in the theology of Jacobus Arminius and published extensively on the concept of freedom.

DR. T. THEO J. PLEIZIER is minister in Langerak, a parish of the Protestant church in the Netherlands and researcher at the Protestant Theological University. He is preparing a dissertation in practical theology and graduated with a master's thesis (2001) on Francesco Turrettini's concept of human freedom.

DR. MARINUS A. SCHOUTEN has a graduate of theology from Utrecht University and wrote a master's thesis on Gomarus' doctrine of original sin.

DR. ROELF T. TE VELDE graduated from the Theological University of Kampen (Broederweg) and is preparing a dissertation in systematic theology on the connection between method and contents in the doctrine of God. He currently serves as a minister of the Reformed Church (liberated) in Pijnacker-Nootdorp, the Netherlands.

DR. WILLEM J. VAN ASSELT is senior lecturer in church history, Utrecht University, and professor of historical theology, evangelical theological faculty, Louvain. He wrote *The Federal Theology of Johannes Cocceius (1603-1669)*. His present research focuses on the methodology of interpreting Reformed scholasticism.

DR. GERRIT A. VAN DEN BRINK is a PhD researcher in philosophy of religion at the theological faculty at Utrecht University. He published a book on Herman Witsius and

Antinomianism and, together with Willem van Asselt, an English translation of Johannes Maccovius' *Distinctiones et Regulae Theologiae ac Philosophiae* (1656).

DR. B. J. D. VAN VREESWIJK is a minister in the Reformed Church in Hattem, the Netherlands. He graduated with a master's thesis on the Anselmian concept of satisfaction.

DR. ANTONIE VOS is senior lecturer in systematic and historical theology, Protestant Theological University, and professor of historical theology, evangelical theological faculty, Louvain. He has written *The Philosophy of John Duns Scotus* and is presently preparing a book on the theology of Scotus. His research on Reformed scholasticism is primarily an exploration against the backdrop of medieval thought.

Series Preface

The heritage of the Reformation is of profound importance to our society, our culture, and the church in the present day. Yet there remain many significant gaps in our knowledge of the intellectual development of Protestantism both during and after the Reformation, and there are not a few myths about the theology of the orthodox or scholastic Protestant writers of the late sixteenth and seventeenth centuries. These gaps and myths—frequently caused by ignorance of the scope of a particular thinker's work, by negative theological judgments passed by later generations on the theology of the Reformers and their successors, or by an intellectual imperialism of the present that singles out some thinkers and ignores others regardless of their relative significance to their own times—stand in the way of a substantive encounter with this important period in our history. Understanding, assessment, and appropriation of that heritage can only occur through the publication of significant works (monographs, essays, and sound, scholarly translations) that present the breadth and detail of the thought of the Reformers and their successors.

Texts and Studies in Reformation and Post-Reformation Thought makes available (1) translations of important documents like Caspar Olevian's *A Firm Foundation* and John Calvin's *Bondage and Liberation of the Will*, (2) significant monographs on individual thinkers or on aspects of sixteenth- and seventeenth-century Protestant thought, and (3) multiauthored symposia that bring together groups of scholars in an effort to present the state of scholarship on a particular issue, all under the guidance of an editorial board of recognized scholars in the field.

The series, moreover, is intended to address two groups: an academic and a confessional or churchly audience. The series recognizes the need for careful, scholarly treatment of the Reformation and of the era of Protestant orthodoxy, given the continuing presence of misunderstandings, particularly of the latter era, in both the scholarly and the popular literature and also given the rise of a more recent scholarship devoted to reappraising both the Reformation and the era of orthodoxy. The series highlights revised understandings regarding the relationship of the Reformation and orthodoxy to their medieval background and of the thought of both eras to their historical, social, political, and cultural contexts. Such scholarship will not only advance the academic discussion, it will also provide a churchly audience with a clearer and broader access to its own traditions. In sum, the series intends to present the varied and current approaches to the rich heritage of Protestantism and to stimulate interest in the roots of the Protestant tradition.

Richard A. Muller

Acknowledgments

This book is the outcome of several years of scholarship of the research group *Classic Reformed Theology* ("Werkgezelschap Oude Gereformeerde Theologie"). *CRT* studies early-modern scholastic theology (late-sixteenth to early-eighteenth-century texts) to stimulate a fair interpretation of the Reformed tradition. We are convinced of its relevance for the present church and of the need to articulate its faith in continuity with the past. Because these sources tend to be unjustly neglected due to confusion about their theological content, we have initiated some theological excavations to reveal their value.

Hence, our group was founded in 1982 at Utrecht University by Antoon Vos with the aim to more precisely study Reformed scholasticism and its methodology. In general, research of Reformed scholasticism has tended to ignore the continuity with medieval scholasticism and to disavow the scholastic method itself. Trained in the philosophy of religion, which had a revival in the 1970s, Vos saw a similar approach and intent to utilize philosophical concepts and arguments for the sake of a theological clarification of Reformed doctrine. The pioneering work on Reformed scholasticism of Richard Muller concerning a methodologically accurate and historical approach has also helped us to get rid of traditional prejudices and some modern agendas concerning this kind of theology. By bringing together church historians, dogmaticians, and philosophers of religion, scholastic texts were studied within the expertise of their respective disciplines.

Our group has studied scholastic texts of different Reformed theologians for several years now, trying to understand them in their own terms, backgrounds, and methods. This required training in scholastic terminology—medieval and Reformation theology in general and a close reading of the studied texts in particular. Here again Antoon Vos needs to be especially mentioned as he in fact taught our group how to read scholastic texts. Mainly based on his insights, we will further clarify and account for some crucial methodological perspectives in the introduction. The need of this approach is especially clear in the study of topics which have a theological as well as philosophical nature, such as free choice. This book presents a translation and commentary of six texts on free choice of important post-Reformation theologians. We hope that the fruitfulness of this methodological approach is demonstrated in this volume.

Currently, the members of the research group are: W. J. van Asselt (chairman), J. M. Bac (secretary), A. J. Beck, G. A. van den Brink, A Goudriaan, K. Hage, T. T. J. Pleizier, M. A. Schouten, R. T. te Velde, P. A. Visser, A. Vos, and B. J. D. van Vreeswijk. The translations and commentaries of the following chapters were originally made by individual members as indicated below.

Chapter	Translation by	Commentary by
1. Introduction		W. J. van Asselt, J. M. Bac, R. T. te Velde, M. A. Schouten
2. Zanchi	R. T. te Velde	R. T. te Velde
3. Junius	W. J. van Asselt	B. J. D. van Vreeswijk
4. Gomarus	W. J. van Asselt	E. Dekker, M. A. Schouten
5. Voetius	A. J. Beck	A. J. Beck
6. Turrettini	E. Dekker, T. T. J. Pleizier	E. Dekker, A. J. Beck, T. T. J. Pleizier
7. De Moor	E. Dekker	J. M. Bac
8. Conclusion		R. T. te Velde, A. Vos

During the project, one or two persons provided a first translation of the original text. After intensive correction and discussion, the final translation and an initial commentary on the text was prepared, which was then discussed again. So, although the original translations and commentaries were made by individual persons, the outcome is definitely the work of a team. Concerning the translations of the Latin texts, special mention has to be made of G. A. van den Brink, who was willing to check and improve all translations. Many thanks are also due to K. Scott Oliphint, Westminster Theological Seminary, Philadelphia, who read through the penultimate manuscript and offered significant help in producing a correct English text. In this respect, we are grateful to some former members who made an important contribution to the final result. For several years Eef Dekker took a leading part in the work and our group has lost much by his absence. In the course of this project A. J. Kunz, B. Loonstra, and C. A. de Niet also supported the group.

We are pleased to mention that Professor Richard A. Muller attended our meetings during his stay as visiting professor at Utrecht University, February through June, 1999. We must express our gratitude for his counsel and for accepting this work in his distinguished series published by Baker Academic.

Willem J. van Asselt, J. Martin Bac, and Roelf T. te Velde

Abbreviations

BLGPN   *Biografisch Lexicon voor de Geschiedenis van het Nederlandse Protestantisme.* Edited by Doede Nauta. 5 vols. Kampen: Kok, 1983-2003.

CF   A. Vos, H. Veldhuis, A. H. Looman-Graaskamp, E. Dekker, and N. W. den Bok. *John Duns Scotus. Contingency and Freedom. Lectura I 39,* Dordrecht/Boston: Kluwer, 1994.

CHLMP   *The Cambridge History of Later Medieval Philosophy: From the Rediscovery of Aristotle to the Disintegration of Scholasticism, 1100-1600.* Edited by Norman Kretzman, Anthony J. P. Kenny, and Jan Pinborg. Cambridge: Cambridge University Press, 1982.

DC   Roberto Bellarmino. *Disputationes de controversiis Christianae fidei adversus huius temporis haereticos.* 4 vols. Ingolstadt, 1596.

DLGT   Richard A. Muller. *Dictionary of Latin and Greek Theological Terms. Drawn Principally from Protestant Scholastic Theology.* Grand Rapids: Baker Books, 1985.

DRCH   *Dutch Review of Church History.*

DDPh   *The Dictionary of Seventeenth- and Eighteenth-century Dutch Philosophers.* 2 vols. General editor Wiep van Bunge. Bristol: Thoemmes, 2003.

FC   *Fathers of the Church.* Washington, DC, 1946-.

GFC   Bernard of Clairvaux. *On Grace and Free Choice (De Gratia et libero arbitrio).* Translated by Daniel O'Donovan OCSO. Introduction by Bernard McGinn. Kalamazoo: Ciscercian Publications, 1988.

KN   Antoon Vos. *Kennis en Noodzakelijkheid. Een kritische analyse van het absolute evidentialisme in wijsbegeerte en theologie.* Kampen: Kok, 1981.

MMPh   Simo Knuuttila. *Modalities in Medieval Philosophy: Topics in Medieval Philosophy.* London/New York: Routledge, 1993.

MPL   J.-P. Migne, ed. *Patrologiae Cursus Completus Series Latina.*

MW   Lambertus M. de Rijk. *Middeleeuwse wijsbegeerte. Traditie en vernieuwing.* 2nd
             edition. Assen: Van Gorcum, 1981.

NE   Aristotle. *Nicomachean Ethics.* Translated from the Greek (with historical
             introduction) by Christopher Rowe; philosophical introduction and com-
             mentary by Sarah Broadie. Oxford: Oxford University Press, 2002.

NTT   *Nederlands Theologisch Tijdschrift.*

PRRD   Richard A. Muller. *Post-Reformation Reformed Dogmatics: The Rise and Develop-
             ment of Reformed Orthodoxy, ca. 1520 to ca. 1725.* 4 vols. 2nd edition. Grand
             Rapids: Baker Academic, 2003.

RM   E. Dekker. *Rijker dan Midas. Vrijheid, genade en predesinatie in de theologie van
             Jacobus Arminius (1559-1609).* Zoetermeer: Boekencentrum, 1993.

RS   *Reformation and Scholasticism: An Ecumenical Enterprise.* Edited by Willem J.
             van Asselt and Eef Dekker. Texts and Studies in Reformation and Post-
             Reformation Thought. Grand Rapids: Baker Academic, 2001.

1

Introduction

"We establish free choice far more truly than our opponents."[1] The Reformed theologian Francesco Turrettini (1623-1687) made this rather surprising contention against contemporary advocates of freedom, the Jesuits, Remonstrants and Socinians, who complained that the Reformed categorically deny free choice. The Reformed account of predestination and providence was held to imply "Stoic fate." Ever since, a deterministic interpretation of Reformed thought seemed obvious.[2]

The Reformed scholastics themselves, however, were not impressed by this critique. They certainly confessed a foundational involvement of God's will in creation and the history of salvation. Yet, for them this insistence on divine will precisely established a realm for human willing. Being constituted in freedom, reality is open for human freedom as well. God himself, acting freely, enables human beings—who are made in his image—to act freely alike.

This rather daring interpretation of Reformed thought on freedom is mainly complicated in two ways. First, the contemporary notion of freedom in an autonomous, libertarian sense does not allow any creational dependence or divine guidance in human acting. In this sense, divine willing must exclude human freedom. As we will see, however, the Reformed dismissed autonomy as a proper interpretation of freedom.

Second, the theological concept of freedom was taken in a normative sense in scholastic theology. Being faced with the choice between good and bad, only rightly willing was taken to be properly free. A will in bondage to sin was denied to be free, though it acted freely in its own choice to sin. This sometimes rather definite denial of human freedom has to be taken as an explicit endorsement of the Reformed *sola gratia*: only divine grace enables to do good. Underlying this theological concept of normative freedom, however, was a more basic

---

1. Francesco Turrettini, *Institutio theologiae elencticae,* X.1.iii (Geneva: S. de Tournes, 1688); trans. George Musgrave Giger, ed. James T. Dennison Jr., *Institutes of Elenctic Theology,* (Phillipsburg, NJ: Presbyterian & Reformed, 1997), 660. See the chapter on Turrettini for more details. Frequently, the debate between Calvinists and Arminians is conceived in terms of free will. Although the terms are intimately related, both parties distinguished between free will and free choice and especially discussed freedom of choice. So, we follow their terminology (compare section 1.3).

2. It has to be noted that the term "determinism" was not known in early-modern times but originated in its modern sense only in late eighteenth-century German philosophy. Cf. "Determinisme," in *Vocabulaire technique et critique de la philosophie*, André Lalande (ed.), 7th ed. (Paris: P.U.F., 1956), 221-224. Still, the concept of determinism was denoted by Stoic fate.

philosophical concept of freedom, which made it possible to articulate sin as freely choosing to do evil.

We are convinced that the sources of Reformed theology present a balanced view on human freedom. Accordingly, this volume offers translations and analyses of some important theological texts on free choice from the era of early-modern Reformed theology. These texts do not yield a complete survey of the theme, but they do give a representative overview of the contents and developments, the consensus and diversity, of Reformed thinking on free choice. In this introduction, we will account for the methodological approach of the book and render some general help in reading these texts.

In short, the distinctive approach in this book is the intended combination of a historical with an analytical interpretation. Indeed, we even believe that a historical approach *requires* an analytical examination. The selected theological texts are full of exact definitions, detailed distinctions and profound arguments. Close reading and historical contextualization have to be combined with a more technical analysis of the line of argument in the texts. A rather intuitive study would not do justice to the analytical genre of these scholastic texts themselves. Conversely, an analytical approach can only proceed by a historical contextualization of the argumentation in the texts. Their crucial technical terms have to be understood by historical definitions and again cannot be grasped intuitively. This is even more important because the Reformed took part in a long scholastic tradition. Many concepts cannot be understood apart from the medieval background from which they originated, although the Reformed often took their meaning for granted, not explaining time and again what was likely known to their contemporaries. So, the nature of these texts requires the interaction of a historical and analytical approach.

This approach has its background in the philosophical and scholarly work of Antoon Vos, a pupil of L. M. de Rijk in medieval studies.[3] In his philosophical dissertation *Kennis en Noodzakelijkheid* (1981), Vos combined systematic, analytical and historical methods in order to design a theory of the properties of God which is both consistent in itself and also proof against so-called atheological criticisms.[4] In this research project he turned to historical resources that were mainly taken from Christian medieval thought and, in particular, from Duns Scotus' theories of knowledge and science and ontology.[5]

In 1982, Vos applied this research model to the history of Reformed scholasticism by reading its texts in their medieval context. For this purpose, Vos founded two research groups in the 1980s, *John Duns Scotus* and *Classic Reformed Theology*, to rediscover the riches of the oeuvre of Duns Scotus and

---

3. On De Rijk, see A. Vos, *The Philosophy of John Duns Scotus* (Edinburgh: Edinburgh University Press, 2006), 198-204, 302-303, 511-512 and 558-565.

4. *KN*, i-xviii and 1-456.

5. See now Vos, *The Philosophy of John Duns Scotus*, i-xii and 1-655; cf. *CF*, 1-2; and Vos, H. Veldhuis, E. Dekker, N. W. den Bok and A. J. Beck, *Duns Scotus on Divine Love* (Aldershot: Ashgate, 2003), i-x and 1-235.

of the Reformed scholastic tradition.[6] Focusing particularly on the medieval heritage of contingency thought, his numerous publications show that the logic, ontology and doctrine of God in Reformed thought mainly rest on Scotian innovations. He has also argued that classic Reformed anthropology is an anthropology of contingency, freedom and grace. In the present book, the reader will certainly find the most important results of Vos' innovative research project.

In this introduction, we will start with an account of the historical and systematic importance of the doctrine of free choice for Reformed theology (section 1.1). Next, the backgrounds of our historical approach will be clarified (section 1.2) and specific methodological considerations regarding the treatment of the selected texts will be given (section 1.3). Subsequently, some crucial terms and concepts of these texts will be clarified to facilitate an analytical understanding of the texts in their historical sense, introducing also a few convenient modern analytical tools that can help us to understand these complex texts today (section 1.4); we will introduce the selected texts briefly (section 1.5).

The subsequent chapters are written so that they can be read, as much as possible, independently of the rest, although the interested reader may frequently find cross-references. Yet, in order to understand the historical genres and conceptual contents of these texts, respectively sections 1.3 and 1.4 are pivotal for the rest of the book. So, we earnestly advise impatient readers who hurry to the heart of the matter to study at least these parts of the introduction.

1.1 Free Choice: The Fate of the Reformed Tradition

The analysis of free choice in early-modern Reformed theology is important for various reasons.

First, the definition of free choice has direct consequences for the substance of major theological themes such as predestination, grace, conversion and sin. Although it does not come prominently to the fore everywhere, the specific articulation of the concept of free choice influences the tenets of all these theological topics.

Second, it was—as we have said—also a pivotal topic in the confessional debates of the sixteenth till the eighteenth centuries. Jesuits, Remonstrants, and Socinians accused the Reformed of "Stoic fate" (determinism), while they in turn feared "Pelagianism" (human autonomy) in their opponents.[7] The key problem

---

6. See Willem Jan van Asselt and Eef Dekker (eds.), *De scholastieke Voetius*, (Zoetermeer: Boekencentrum 1995), *RS*, and this book.

7. In the famous controversy of the Jesuits with the Dominicans and Jansenists in the Roman Catholic Church around 1600 about grace and free choice, both parties pretended to be the true offspring of Augustine. In this debate, the accusation of "Lutheranism" or "Calvinism" was equivalent to Stoic fate or Manicheian necessity, while the danger on the other side was Pelagianism. As will be indicated below (1.3), these accusations should not be interpreted in a historical way, but rather systematically. A good introduction to the Catholic debate is given by Leo Scheffczyk, "Gnadenstreit," in Michael Buchberger, Walter Kasper, Konrad Baumgartner (eds.), *Lexikon für Theologie und Kirche*, 3rd ed. (Freiburg: Herder, 1995), 4:797. For a more extensive review of this controversy compare the older edition of the latter work: F. Stegmüller, "Gnadenstreit," in: Josef Höfer and Karl Rahner (eds.), *Lexikon für Theologie und Kirche*, 2nd

was the relation of sin and grace to human willing, so free choice was debated in the context of soteriology. The intensive debate with other traditions reveals the "catholicity" of the Reformed, as they strive to win the other parties in their common search for truth. With the emergence of Cartesianism especially in Dutch theology, the debate widened from the freedom of the will to the faculty of willing as such and its relation to the human intellect. The Reformed theological convictions involved a philosophical anthropology, and—for most Reformed— Cartesianism was not suited to articulate the Reformed doctrine of man.

Third, traditional and recent scholarship has tended to follow the interpretation of the opponents of Reformed theology and neglected its own witness. Jesuits, Remonstrants and Socinians alleged that free choice cannot function in a theology which stresses total depravity, unconditional election, irresistible grace and saintly perseverance. Interpreting predestination as the fundamental "central dogma" of Reformed theology, later scholars likewise judged that no place is left for freedom in such a deterministic system.[8] In this way they follow the intuitions of the Jesuits and Remonstrants, but it is questionable whether they have allowed themselves both to hear the defense the Reformed gave against their contenders and to try to grasp their intuitions and intentions as well. Therefore a detailed analysis of the texts is necessary. Intuitively, the Reformed convictions of predestination, original sin and effective grace seem to rule out free choice, but these scholastic theologians were convinced that their interpretations of divine grace and human free choice were compatible So, the first requisite for a fair interpretation is trying to follow their own arguments. A fatalistic impression of the Reformed tradition is strange to those theologians themselves, and consequently should be avoided by us as well.

Free choice is thus an important theme regarding the content, the history and the interpretation of Reformed theology. Still, it has gained very little explicit attention by scholars. Such Reformed themes as faith, grace and predestination are well-researched topics, but there are few detailed studies of free choice.[9] The present volume is intended as an initial attempt to fill this gap.

As said, the authors of this book have a historical as well as a systematic interest in the issue of free choice in Reformed scholasticism. We hope that the presentation of these texts will dismantle some popular historical myths about scholasticism—for instance, that it was monolithic, rationalistic, rigid or purely

---

ed. (Freiburg: Herder, 1960), 3:1002-1007; and E. Vansteenberghe, "Molinisme," in E. Mangenot, A. Vacant, É. Amann (eds.), *Dictionnaire de théologie catholique, contenant l'exposé des doctrines de la théologie catholique, leurs preuves et leur histoire* (Paris: Letouzey, 1929), 12:2094-2187. An extensive documentation and positive appraisal of the Jansenist and the Reformed positions in relation to the controversy is given by Henri de Lubac, *Augustinisme et théologie moderne* (Paris: Aubier, 1965).

8. Compare for the "central dogma" theory section 1.2.

9. Positive exceptions are Richard A. Muller, "Grace, Election and Contingent Choice: Arminius' Gambit and the Reformed Response," in Thomas R. Schreiner and Bruce A. Ware (eds.), *The Grace of God, the Bondage of the Will.* Vol. 2. *Historical and Theological Perspectives on Calvinism* (Grand Rapids: Baker, 1995), 251-278; regarding Calvin, see Dewey J. Hoitenga, *John Calvin and the Will. A Critique and Corrective* (Grand Rapids: Baker, 1997);regarding Ames, see E. Dekker, "An Ecumenical Debate," in *RS,* 141-154.

speculative. The texts will also prove the lack of evidence for a deductive procedure by which the whole body of theology is deduced from a single predestinarian "central dogma."

In addition, we contest some other popular systematic myths about Reformed theology—for instance, that sin exerts such a bondage of the will that man completely loses his freedom, or that grace controlled and enforced by predestination reduces man to passive and senseless stocks and blocks. Reformed theologians tried to locate the freedom of creatures between the Scylla of an independent autonomy and the Charybdis of a passive shadow play, and their extensive distinctions were necessary to avoid both errors. We are convinced that the texts show that both sin and salvation in the Reformed perspective center around the free will of God and human beings, and that the merciful divine initiative does not exclude, but requires, human freedom.

1.2 Continuity of Medieval Method in Post-Reformation Reformed Theology

We have been arguing that post-Reformation Reformed theology is worth studying both for what it is and for what there is in or about it that differs from theology as usually practiced today. For the purpose of orientation a few words are required to inform the reader about new developments and directions in the study of Reformed theology of the sixteenth and seventeenth centuries. These can be characterized as the attempt to develop a new understanding of Protestant theology in the post-Reformation period, usually indicated by the term "scholasticism." The term "Reformed orthodoxy" is also used to place it in historical perspective, by referring to the period of institutionalization and codification following the Reformation. The theology of this period is partly the result of a theological interpretation of the Reformation within particular, confessionally determined bounds. This theology was taught in the new Protestant academies and universities with the help of the so-called scholastic method, which involved drawing on medieval models.

It is no simple matter to give a final definition of the term "scholasticism." In fact, "scholasticism" is a collective noun denoting all scholarly research and instruction carried out according to a certain method, which involves the use of a recurring system of concepts, distinctions, proposition analyses, argumentative strategies and methods of disputation.[10] The most important of the theses put forward by the new research is that the term "scholasticism" refers primarily to a method, rather than to any definite doctrinal content. Medieval and Protestant scholasticism are distinct from other forms of theology in their methods of disputation and their argumentative strategies. This is confirmed by the witness of the scholastics themselves. For Voetius, e.g., scholastic theology is distinguished

---

10. For this view of scholasticism, see the pioneering work of de Rijk: *MW*, 25. A French translation is present in L. M. de Rijk, *La philosophie au moyen âge* (Leiden: E. J. Brill, 1985). De Rijk's international fame is mainly based upon his text-critical editions of medieval logical works, but his work had the much broader scope of revealing the dynamics of medieval thought in contrast to ancient thought.

from other forms of theology, like catechetical or didactic theology, by its genre and its intended audience.[11]

The development of this perspective was stimulated especially by new approaches in the study of Reformation history, which pointed to the medieval background of the Reformation. Partly under the impact of the new approach in Reformation studies, a shift took place from a narrow dogmatic or idiosyncratic interpretation of Reformed scholasticism to a more contextualized historical analysis. Thus, in these two areas of research—the Reformation and the post-Reformation period—we find much methodological convergence. The work of H. A. Oberman drew attention to the continuities between the theology of the late Middle Ages and that of the Reformers.[12] David Steinmetz and Richard Muller pointed to continuities and discontinuities between the Reformation and Protestant scholasticism.[13] The study of the theology of the Reformation has been revolutionized, and a similar shift can be detected in the study of Protestant scholasticism.[14] In both cases, the simplistic oppositions so characteristic of the older research (whether Roman Catholic or Protestant) are being subjected to devastating criticism.[15]

Consequently, the observation that it is no longer possible to study Luther or Calvin without knowledge of the medieval background has by now been established as part of the *communis opinio* in Reformation studies. It provides a research model that can also be applied to the study of the relation between the Reformation and post-Reformation orthodoxy. In methodological terms, it means taking leave of the accepted division into clearly demarcated periods. At the same time, insight into the medieval roots of the Reformation raises the question of the reception and use of medieval traditions in post-Reformation theology. Studying this reception, one is struck by a complex pattern of methodological continuity and confessional discontinuity, which cannot be described in simplistic terms.

Methodologically speaking, this implies at the very least that two specific positions are no longer tenable: (1) a radical discontinuity model, which views the development of post-reformational theology as a break with the Reformers; and

---

11. See Gisbertus Voetius, "De Theologia Scholastica," in *Selectae Disputationes*, vol. 1 (Utrecht: J. a Waesberge, 1648), 12-29.

12. H. A. Oberman, *The Harvest of Medieval Theology: Gabriel Biel and Late Medieval Nominalism* (Cambridge, MA: Harvard University Press, 1963); idem, *The Dawn of the Reformation* (Edinburgh: Clark, 1986).

13. D. C. Steinmetz, *Luther in Context* (Bloomington: Indiana University Press, 1986); idem, *Calvin in Context* (Oxford: Oxford University Press, 1995); Richard A. Muller, *The Unaccommodated Calvin: Studies in the Formation of a Theological Tradition* (Oxford: Oxford University Press, 2000), 39-61. Cf. Muller, *PRRD*, vols. 1 and 2.

14. Compare the introduction of *RS* and Willem J. van Asselt, "Protestant Scholasticism: Some Methodological Considerations in the Study of Its Development," *DRCH* 81 (2001): 265-274; idem, *The Federal Theology of Johannes Cocceius (1603-1669)* (Leiden: Brill, 2001), 94-105.

15. The danger of oversimplified oppositions is also recognized by the study of the interaction between Reformed scholasticism and post-tridentine Catholic scholasticism (R. Bellarmine, M. Cano, L. Molina, F. Suárez). Studies by Carl Trueman and Eef Dekker have shown that, in methodological terms, these two theological traditions resemble one another closely. See C. R. Trueman, *The Claims of Truth: John Owen's Trinitarian Theology* (Carlisle: Paternoster, 1998), 9-19; *RM*, 157-161.

(2) an ahistorical continuity model, which assumes the identity of the Reformation and orthodoxy, while losing sight of the fact that orthodoxy drew not only on the theology of the Reformers, but also had recourse to patristic and medieval and renaissance sources, and consciously applied their methods.

Apart from the attention of recent studies to the medieval context for the sake of an accurate grasp of Reformation and post-Reformation theology, a shift has also taken place with regard to the relation vis-à-vis the humanism of the Renaissance. In nineteenth-century historiography, humanism and scholasticism were portrayed as diametrically opposed intellectual movements.[16] According to recent historiography, Christian oriented humanism should be seen in continuity with medieval, scholastic scholarship, rather than in opposition to it.[17] The opposition between humanism and scholasticism came to be exaggerated beyond all proportion in the light of the later appreciation of humanism, and under the influence of the modern aversion to scholasticism. So far, the influence of this new Renaissance research on the study of the relation between the Reformation and scholastic orthodoxy has been negligible.[18] The most important implication for the study of Reformed scholasticism is to counter the idea that the Renaissance as a field of research has no relation to post-Reformation Protestantism. In this respect, Reformed scholasticism cannot be explained by medieval scholasticism and Reformation theology alone, but the influence of the Renaissance is also to be observed.[19]

Finally, some comments should also be made on the above-mentioned nineteenth-century "central dogma" theory, developed by, among others, the Zurich dogma historian Alexander Schweizer (1808-1888), and taken over in the Netherlands by the Leiden professor Jan Hendrik Scholten (1811-1885) in his *De leer der Hervormde Kerk.*[20] Schweizer and those who followed him constructed (unjustifiably) the theory of a "central dogma" (a monistic and deterministic conceived predestination concept for the Reformed, and justification ideology for the Lutherans), which was then used to "show" either continuity or radical discontinuity between the Reformation and Reformed scholasticism.

In sum: in order to avoid the pitfalls of older research sketched above, explicit attention should be paid to the context of scholastic discourse and its semantics. Such research focuses primarily on the conceptual apparatus of the scholastic

---

16. Jacob Burckhardt, *Die Kultur der Renaissance in Italien* (Basel: Schwieghaufer,1860).

17. See Paul Oskar Kristeller and Michael Mooney, *Renaissance Thought and Its Sources* (New York: Columbia University Press, 1979); Erika Rummel, *The Humanist-Scholastic Debate in the Renaissance and Reformation* (Cambridge: Harvard University Press, 1995).

18. One exception is Muller, *The Unaccommodated Calvin*, 75: "The assumption of a conflict between humanistic rhetoric and scholastic disputation may not apply at all to Calvin's work."

19. See Richard A. Muller, *Ad fontes agumentorum: The Sources of Reformed Theology in the 17th Century* (Utrecht: Faculteit der Godgeleerdheid Universiteit Utrecht, 1999).

20. A. Schweizer, *Die protestantische Centraldogmen in ihrer Entwicklung innerhalb der reformierten Kirche*, 2 vols. (Zurich: Orell, Fuessli und Comp, 1853-1856); J. H. Scholten, *De leer der Hervormde Kerk in hare grondbeginselen uit de bronnen voorgesteld en beoordeeld*, 2 vols. (Leiden: Engels, 1848-1850). In 1861 and 1862, a fourth, revised and expanded, edition appeared in Leiden; it was reprinted in 1870.

tradition. In particular, semantic research relates to the words, concepts, ideas and doctrines with which Reformed theologians carried on their work, and which gave a specific shape to the Reformed confessions and the ecclesiastical communities oriented on them at the time. It is becoming increasingly clear from such research that the study of the semantic fields of terms and concepts employed in scholastic discourse is an essential prerequisite for gaining insight into the question of continuity and discontinuity.[21]

The combined weight of these comments results in our diagnosis that doing research into Reformed scholasticism today is indeed a significantly different and a more difficult enterprise than it was a few decades ago. In this book it becomes clear that a much broader contextualization of the Reformed scholastic tradition is needed than has hitherto been the case. Moreover, through this "re-sourcing," insights are developed that problematise the older research at several points. Unqualified references to "isms" ("Scholasticism," "Aristotelianism," "Thomism" and "Scotism") are, historically speaking, inaccurate, because they disregard the contextually determined use of these phenomena during the Renaissance, Reformation and post-Reformation periods. These are historical phenomena with a long historical tradition.

Keeping in mind this proviso, there is, however, increasing evidence available that Scotist tenets played an important role in Reformed scholasticism.[22] This is not to say that all Scotist topics are evidenced in Reformed scholasticism. But as this book will show, there is enough evidence to argue that Reformed theology and anthropology participated in a tradition articulating an overarching theory of synchronic contingency developed by Duns Scotus, in which the radical dependence and freedom of all creaturely beings was formulated. The point of this approach is not to produce a new "central dogma," but to allow for new and unknown connections as a result of the widening of the "traditional" theological horizon.[23] It may help us to formulate a Christian worldview for today.

1.3 The Nature and Genres of Reformed Scholastic Texts

Embedding Reformed scholasticism in its medieval background has important consequences for the assesment of this kind of theology.

---

21. Thus, Johannes Altenstaig's *Vocabularius theologiae* (1516), reissued in 1619 under the title *Lexicon theologicum*, was an important sourcebook for both Roman Catholic and Protestant theologians. It contained an alphabetical survey of the most important scholastic and authoritative definitions derived from the texts of Bonaventure, Thomas Aquinas, Duns Scotus, Gregory of Rimini, Henry of Ghent, Pierre D'Ailly and Thomas of Strasbourg. See Johannes Altenstaig, *Vocabularius theologiae* (Hagenau: H. Gran, 1516); idem, *Lexicon theologicum quo tanquam clave theologiae fores aperiuntur, et omnium fere terminorum et obscuriorum vocum, quae s. theologiae studiosos facile remorantur, etymologiae, ambiguitates, definitiones, usus, enucleate ob oculos ponuntur, & dilucide explicantur* (repr. Cologne: J. Tytz, 1619).

22. See A. Vos, "Scholasticism and Reformation," in *RS*, 99-119.

23. See for a debate on this point P. Helm, "Synchronic Contingency in Reformed Scholasticism: A Note of Caution," *NTT* 57 (2003) no. 3: 207-222; and A. J. Beck and A. Vos, "Conceptual Patterns Related to Reformed Scholasticism," *NTT* 57 (2003) no. 3: 223-233.

The nature of scholasticism can be best understood by the work of one of its founding fathers, Anselm of Canterbury.[24] Anselm forcefully stimulated medieval theology by his conviction that rational analysis is essential to the understanding of faith and so is a theological duty. The intended harmony of faith and reason can be discerned in his *Monologue* (*Monologion*, 1077) in which Anselm attempts to demonstrate the nature and existence of God by an appeal to reason alone, which is remarkably formulated in the form of a long prayer. So, theology could be conceived as "faith seeking understanding" (*fides quaerens intellectum*) and both medieval and Reformed scholasticism in all its nuances and shifts may be conceived as expressions of this Anselmian spirit.[25]

The theological quest of seeking understanding meant a search for arguments for the truth of faith. Whereas faith trusts in God for the truth of its belief, understanding can argue for the veracity of its belief. Therefore, this scholastic kind of theology decidedly utilized philosophical disciplines like semantics, logics and metaphysics to articulate the Christian faith with the help of philosophical analyses in order to stimulate faith and make it understandable.

Several indications affirm this "truth-driven" nature of scholastic theology. First, it explains why the core of the scholastic method, in every period, consists of the so-called *quaestio* technique, which is directed to discover rational truth.[26] A second indication is the conscious use of medieval dialectic and Renaissance rhetoric and logic in theological expositions. Third, in their prolegomena, divergent theologians like Thomas Aquinas and Francesco Turrettini frequently appeal to Paul's intention to "take captive every thought to the obedience of Christ," or as Turrettini formulated, "the obedience of faith" (2 Cor. 10:5), in order to show that an argumentative approach is fundamental for theology.[27] Fourth, sometimes the method is more explicitly present. For example, the prominent Dutch Reformed theologian Gisbertus Voetius (1589-1676), of whom a text will be discussed in chapter 5, started his career at the academy of Utrecht

24. On Anselm, see R. W. Southern, *Saint Anselm: a Portrait in a Landscape* (Cambridge: Cambridge University Press, 1990).

25. An exposition of the relation between faith and knowledge in Anselm's work in comparison with later medieval scholasticm (especially Bonaventure, Thomas and Ockham) is given by *MW* 5, 139-183. In this book, we follow the hypothesis that the basic rupture in the history of European thought is not caused by the Reformation or Renaissance, which left the theological worldview intact, but by the breakdown of scholastic thought and the rise of the Enlightenment in the eighteenth century. So, medieval and Reformed scholasticism show development and considerable discontinuity as well, but are expressions of the same systematic theological paradigm.

26. Muller, *PRRD*, 1:15, 21-39; 2:6-11. Muller discerns four elements in this technique: the presentation of a thesis or *quaestio*, a thematic question; the indication of the subjects that stand to be discussed in that *quaestio*, the so-called *status quaestionis*; the treatment of a series of arguments or objections against the adopted positions, the so-called *objectiones*; the formulation of an answer (*responsio*), in which account is taken of all available sources of information, and all rules of rational discourse are upheld, followed by an answer to the objections, which is as comprehensive as possible. Muller counts only works as scholastic that display this structure; cf. also: Willem J. van Asselt and Eef Dekker, "Introduction," in *RS*, 11-43, esp. 26.

27. Turrettini mentions the passage five times (!) in his prolegomena and may be inspired by Thomas who did it twice in his part "de sacra doctrina" in the *Summa*.

with an oration in the Anselmian spirit of "faith seeking understanding": *To Conjoin Confidence in God with Knowledge (De Pietate cum Scientia Coniungenda).*[28]

Methodologically, this faithful search for theological truth has two important consequences for the way Reformed scholastics did theology, which we define as the "literary" method of *reverent exposition* and the "logical" method of *conceptual analysis.*[29] As we will show, both methods are related by the one quest of theological truth.

1.3.1 Reverent Exposition

Reformed theologians did not read their sources of Scripture and tradition in a historical sense as parts of an ongoing tradition but as "authorities" of truth.[30] Both Scripture and tradition were not conceived historically, but viewed systematically as a self-evident entity, embodied in texts laden with truth.[31]

An "auctoritas" was originally a judicial term to denote documentary evidence that constituted a contract or commitment. In an intellectual sense, an authority is someone whose thought is authoritative on account of his (churchly or intellectual) position and is held to represent truth which can only foolishly be neglected. Moreover, authorities were not cited as an additional support for their own systematic position, but as representatives of systematic truth itself. Hence, medieval theologians frequently define an authority in their works as "manifested rational truth, which is laid down in writing for the sake of useful application by posterity" and even more often appeal to them.[32] Note that these people who are wont to give exact definitions do not define them as "testimonies" (to rational truth) or suchlike, but as rational truth itself (*rationis aperta veritas*).

---

28. The term "pietas" is hard to translate, but to translate it only as piety is confusing. Usually the Reformed distinguish "piety" from the "practice of piety" or worship, so it has to do with a spiritual condition which should be practiced in worship, service and mission. Richard A. Muller defines "pietas" as "the personal confidence in, reverence for and fear of God that conduces to true worship of and devotion to God. Thus, piety, together with devotion, constitutes true religion," *DLGT*, 228 ("pietas"). So, piety comes close to faith.

29. Obviously, this introduction can only provide a provisional survey, as a fair and sufficient treatment of the methodology of interpreting scholastic texts would require a separate exposition; compare *PRRD*, vol.1. As will be shown, the method of reverent exposition is systematical rather than literal (in the sense of exegetically establishing the meaning of texts), but we call it thus in order to underline that it was a proper literary method in the perspective of the scholastics. The Reformed method of conceptual analysis is much broader than strictly logical (including semantical and ontological analyses and more), but as a rough indication of its philosophical and analytical nature the term "logical" might be useful.

30. On the idea of authorities, the method of reverent exposition and the ahistorical character of scholasticism in this respect, see *MW* 4 (esp. sections 4.3, 4.4 on authority, 4.7 on *exponere reverenter*, 4.8 on ahistoricity), 108-138; L. M. de Rijk, *Logica Modernorum*, vol. 1 (Assen: van Gorcum, 1962), 13-178. On the merits of the work of De Rijk for interpreting medieval scholasticism (which also applies to Reformed scholasticism), compare note 5.

31. Cf. *MW*, 115-117.

32. *MW* 4.3, 115, 116. De Rijk traces the definition to John Scotus Eriugena in the ninth century and remarks that it is often found identically in later authors; he mentions two places in Albert the Great.

Therefore, these texts had to be explained with reverence (*exponere reverenter*)—that is, notably, not historically in conformity with a tradition or author-intention but systematically in conformity with truth: reverence in correspondence to established theological and philosophical truth. This method of reverent exposition involved a hermeneutical procedure which went back to the patristic period. Until the breakdown of scholasticism and the historical revolution (both in the medieval period and, consequently, in the Reformation and post-Reformation period) an authority, be it the Bible, Aristotle, Augustine or Thomas Aquinas, was not quoted in a historical way, trying to understand historically what its original author had meant, but was primarily read systematically, and so was easily incorporated in its own conceptual framework. Such an authoritative text contained truth, and could be used to elucidate the matter under discussion—but not with its original meaning.

To be sure, there was some kind of exegesis, but as De Rijk has noted, the scholastics used both a kind of philological exegesis and semantic criteria which focused on the right interpretation of the involved authority and the hermeneutical norm of objective truth (of the debated subjects: *veritas rerum*) which resulted in an incorporation of the authoritative text in their own conceptual framework.[33] Therefore, identical citations can be interpreted quite differently with various authors.

Although there was no awareness of history in the modern sense, we cannot blame those who lived before the historical revolution for their unhistorical way of thinking; in the same way, neither can we charge them with their outdated physics with respect to the scientific revolutions of Newton, Einstein and others.[34]

The ahistorical method of reverent exposition in Reformed scholasticism has intricate consequences for a proper historical interpretation of these theological texts. Both the broader tradition-historical assessment and the interpretation of particular terms and concepts is complicated in this way.

First, the method of reverent exposition makes it quite hard to demonstrate affinity to a certain theological tradition ("Augustinianism," "Thomism," "Scotism," "Nominalism" and so forth) or influence of a particular theologian or philosopher who is often cited. For instance, to an untrained eye, it might seem that the references to or quotations from Aristotle give these texts an Aristotelian, philosophical or rationalist outlook. This is deceptive, however, for one cannot and should not deduce from the references to an "authority" (that is, an authoritative text) that the author who refers to that text identifies himself in a historical sense with the philosophical or theological tradition he uses. Therefore, it should be clear that drawing conclusions from the historical meaning of given citations in these texts in order to assess the personal opinion of the author who cites them is incorrect and provides no helpful procedure. Ironically, it would be

---

33. Cf. *MW* 4.7, 133.

34. For a historical sketch of the emergence of historical thinking (the "historical revolution"), compare E. Mackay, *Geschiedenis bij de bron. Een onderzoek naar de verhouding van christelijk geloof en historische werkelijkheid in geschiedwetenschap, wijsbegeerte en theologie* (Sliedrecht: Merweboek, 1997), particularly 29-264.

rather unhistorical to interpret the pre-modern perception of these citations (of authoritative texts) in a modern historical sense.

Likewise, by citing various authors with divergent opinions, their theology should not be typified as "eclectic," because they "implanted" the truth of their own conceptual framework in the interpretation of these sources rather than drawing it selectively from divergent sources.[35] This might explain why theologians with opposite convictions often appealed to the same authors and sometimes even provided identical citations to defend their case, as all parties in the seventeenth century appealed to Augustine, Thomas, Aristotle and other authorities: all of them were convinced that these confirmed their own position. In this way an authoritative text was incorporated in one's own interpretation of philosophical and theological truth.

In this respect, it is important to note that medieval philosophy and theology developed especially by writing commentaries and expositions on only one or few "authoritative texts" amid the extensive canon of authorities.[36] So, initially the *Sentences* of Peter Lombard were the common handbook of theology for both education and research; later, the *Summa* of Thomas acquired this privilege. Yet, it would be a mistake to conclude from this that all medieval theologians shared the same theological convictions, all being inspired by the same sources. Medieval schools differently interpreted the common handbooks. Consequently, they had a different systematic position while appealing to the same source. Research into tradition-historical continuity or discontinuity, therefore, should be done by a careful analysis of the systematical and conceptual framework of the involved theologians. When this is done properly, they can be compared systematically, and continuities or discontinuities can be established. In the previous paragraph, we have hinted that such comparisons provide increasing support for the observation that Reformed theology participated in the broader tradition of Scotism.

Secondly, the method of reverent exposition does not only complicate the general interpretation of Reformed theology with respect to tradition-historical continuities or discontinuities but also the particular interpretation of terms and concepts. For example, the meaning of the term "deliberation" ($\pi\varrho o\alpha\iota\varrho\varepsilon\sigma\iota\varsigma$) with Aristotle might be completely different from the connotation it has for a Reformed author who cites the philosopher in the context of his own exposition.

As a rule of thumb, then, it is safer to assume that the author using the quotation or reference, cites an important text without any awareness of the original meaning of that text, than to look for the original meaning of the quoted text in order to clarify the intention of the present author. This is not to say that the text was quoted arbitrarily without reasoning, nor was it only an ornament in

---

35. On this point we differ from Richard Muller, who discerns "eclectic tendencies" towards the medieval schools of Thomism, Scotism and Nominalism and "Christian Aristotelianism," Richard A. Muller, "Reformation, Orthodoxy, 'Christian Aristotelianism,' and the Eclecticism of Early Modern Philosophy," *DRCH* 81, no. 3 (2001): 306-325. To be sure, Reformed authors cite various sources to prove their case, but we propose they interpret these passages from one coherent systematic undercurrent.

36. See *MW* 4.4, 117-124.

one's own discourse, but rather a text was cited which was considered to be intrinsically important because of its truth.

Therefore, a few words are required on the complicated issue of the translation of crucial Latin concepts like *voluntas* and *liberum arbitrium*. The difficulty here concerns not only the possible equivocity of the terms with respect to present philosophical and theological discourse or the possible equivocity of the terms used by theologians whose texts are presented in this book, but rather the temptation to define them by tracing their historical origin. We have to be aware of developments and stipulations of individual authors, so in the context of established connotations of a term, the specific connotation by a particular author has to be discovered by a conceptual analysis of his particular use of the term. On the basis of our analyses we have decided which translation of these terms is the most adequate. For the sake of convenience, we have tried to present uniform translations as much as possible, but sometimes we had to choose a different term with a particular author. So, mostly we have translated *voluntas* by "will" and *liberum arbitrium* by "free choice," but *arbitrium* variously denotes judgement, complacency, or choice. In brief, our translation of key terms interacts with our systematic analysis of the underlying concepts. Only in this way differences and developments can be detected and evaluated.[37]

1.3.2 Conceptual Analysis

In medieval and early modern times systematic theology was not confined to scriptural exegesis. The medieval and Reformed theologians extensively utilized logical methods of *conceptual analysis* to disclose the truth of their authoritative sources. More precisely, in treating a theological subject, they developed a systematic and conceptual analysis of the topic and also employed authorities in this framework.

In the general definition of "scholasticism" given in section 1.2, the conceptual and analytical character of it was already indicated by referring to "the use of a recurring system of concepts, distinctions, proposition analyses, argumentative strategies and methods of disputation."[38] The aim of this introduction is not to examine all the differences between the use of dialectic in medieval scholasticism and of Renaissance logic and rhetoric in Reformed scholasticism. It should be clear, however, that "logic"—in the sense of the philosophical discipline that studies the structure of propositions and arguments by investigating their formal validity—plays a major role in Reformed scholastic theology.[39] All Reformed theologians were educated in the liberal arts, including philosophical disciplines like logic, before they were admitted to the study of

---

37. For a further elaboration see section 1.5.

38. Compare note 10.

39. See William Calvert Kneale and Martha Kneale, *The Development of Logic*, 2nd rev. ed. (Oxford: Clarendon, 1975), esp. 198-319. The Reformed theologian Keckermann noted happily that "never from the beginning of the world was there a period so keen on logic, or in which more books on logic were produced and studies of logic flourished more abundantly than the period in which we live," *Praecognitorum Logicorum Tractatus* 3 (Hannover, 1606): 109-110.

theology. Naturally, this preparatory knowledge was utilized in theological education.

Regarding freedom, the subject of this book, the character of this conceptual analysis can be described even more precisely. In addition to general logical arguments, the Reformed also used some kind of what we, in modern terms, would call a form of modal logic. A modal term is an expression (like "necessarily" or "possibly") that is used to qualify the truth of a judgment.[40] Modal logic is, strictly speaking, the study of the deductive behavior of the expressions "it is necessary that" and "it is possible that." However, the term "modal logic" may be used more broadly for a family of related systems. These include logic for explaining the concept of faith, tense and other temporal expressions, as well as deontic (moral) expressions and the logic of willing. In this context, some understanding of modal logic is particularly valuable in undertaking a formal analysis of the philosophical arguments of the Reformed scholastics, in which the use of expressions related to the modal family was a common practice.

Now, in the Reformed perspective, the highly debated issue of freedom clearly belonged to the area of modal logic. Although the Reformed scholastics definitely did not develop a formally articulated modal logic like the modern types, they extensively discussed modal concepts like necessity and contingency in relation to freedom. At the same time, they investigated in which "modes" debated subjects like divine foreknowledge and human freedom could be compatible or were incompatible in a "modal" sense.[41] Their modal discussions espicially centered around the logical investigation of the use of the modal verb "can." Hence, the verb "*posse*" appears time and again in these scholastic discussions on freedom, and the concept of free choice is explored by logical explorations of its use.[42]

With such a modal type of conceptual analysis the Reformed drew on a long scholastic tradition.[43] In fact, modern modal logic has in many respects rediscovered what was known already in medieval philosophy. Twentieth-century inventions of symbolic logic and possible world semantics are, therefore, convenient tools to articulate more precisely what was formulated in a rather rudimentary manner in the Middle Ages. The Reformed scholastics were convinced of being able to overcome many conceptual difficulties in the doctrine of free choice by using this kind of modal analysis. As will appear in the texts

---

40. For the term "modal" see also the final paragraphs of the next section (1.4.1). Compare George E. Hughes and Maxwell J. Cresswell, *A New Introduction to Modal Logic* (London: Routledge, 1996).

41. When we use the term "modal logic" to describe the logics of necessity, contingency, possibility and freedom of the Reformed, we are well aware that there are substantial differences between this kind of logic and modern formal modal logics and the accompanying possible world semantics (see the end of 1.4.1). We only contend that their logical explorations regarding the verb "can" are a parallel kind of logic. For the sake of convenience we will call it modal.

42. See section 1.4.1.

43. A good introduction in the use of modal logic in medieval philosophy is provided by Simo Knuuttila, "Modal Logic," *CHLMP*, 342-357, and his more extensive *MMPh*. A helpful introduction to medieval logic in general is provided by Alexander Broadie, *Introduction to Medieval Logic*, 2nd ed. (Oxford: Clarendon, 1993).

presented in this book, it is especially the relation between various kinds of necessity and freedom that is of great import to an adequate understanding of the issue of free choice.

Due to the analytical nature of scholastic texts, some general acquaintance with medieval and Renaissance logic and methods of argumentation (and technical terms which indicate them) is indispensable. Consequently, we have provided a clarification of the most essential logical concepts in the next section (1.4.3). Because logic and ontology are intimately related, we will first clarify the meaning of the most crucial ontological and modal terms (1.4.1). In order to help the reader to understand the complex conceptual analyses of the Reformed scholastics, we incidentally have used formalizations of their arguments in the footnotes. In this way some significant propositions are simplified so that an internal comparison between the diverse propositions can be applied. For this purpose we used a simplified version of symbolic logic. Below we give a list of logical symbols that will be used in the next section and in the commentaries. In our opinion, the use of (simplified) symbolic logic is very helpful in clarifying, comparing and testing the positions stated by our authors.[44]

-	negation
$\rightarrow$	material implication
= >	strict implication
$\leftrightarrow$	material equivalence
v	inclusive disjunction
&	conjunction
p, q	propositional variables or variables of states of affairs
qt1	q is the case at moment 1
a, b	individual constants
d, e	act constants
P, Q	property constants
Pa	a is the bearer of (possesses) property P
M	possibility operator
N	necessity operator
W	will operator
K	knowledge operator

1.3.3 Different Genres

Scholastic texts commonly share a "truth-driven" nature, which is reflected in the use of reverent exposition and conceptual analysis. Yet, different genres and styles were utilized in the course of time reflecting historical developments; for example, the compilation of *loci* or topics shows the influence of Renaissance rhetoric.[45] Likewise, the academic context and purpose of the text stimulated a variety of genres. A general textbook for theological students did not treat a topic in the same way as was done in a particular disputation.

---

44. On their meaning and theological use, compare *CF*, 34-37.
45. Compare Muller, *Ad fontes argumentorum*.

The basic assumption of this book is that any interpretation of theological texts has to do justice to the genre or nature and purposes of the studied text. Hence, our analysis is led by the specific genre of each text. For example, the question (*quaestio*), the genre that most closely identified with medieval scholasticism, arose from the classroom exercises that typified pedagogy in the West from the twelfth century on: debate or disputation.[46]

1.4 Clarification of Terms and Concepts

Scholastic theology as exemplified in the texts presented in this volume utilizes a fairly technical language. Rather than exceedingly complicating the matter, this technicality provides a high degree of argumentative clarity. The modern reader, it is true, must take some pains in order to understand the crucial concepts and distinctions. Therefore we give an introductory clarification of the most significant terms, concepts and distinctions, that will pave the way for understanding the subsequent texts and commentaries.

This section deals with the relevant terms in three groups: first, ontological concepts; second, anthropological terms; third, logical distinctions. In addition to the terms and distinctions that occur in the scholastic texts, we give some terms that are common in modern philosophy of religion, since we find them useful in explaining Reformed scholastic thought. We intend to give a historical explanation of the terms that were used by the Reformed themselves. In this explanation of *their* terms, we incidentally will use modern devices like symbolic logic (as given above) or concise schemes.

The introductory treatment of the terms in this section will not exclude an interpretation of the same concepts within their own contexts in the commentaries below. It serves as a common framework in which individual variety can be accounted for.

1.4.1 Ontological Concepts

By *ontology* or *metaphysics* we understand the philosophical analysis of *reality*. Leaving aside the question of whether a full and adequate explanation of reality (including God) can be given, we notice the fact that all thinking requires some basic assumptions concerning the nature of reality. While the Reformed scholastics mostly did not elaborate an explicit philosophical ontology (they left this to their colleagues in the philosophy department), their theologies show the active usage of philosophical categories to articulate distinctive Christian assumptions concerning reality.

In this section, we will first try to illustrate how the Reformed made use of the important ontological concepts of cause and effect.[47] Next, the ontological concept of "necessity" has to be clarified, in which respect we will pay attention

---

46. The titles of the following chapters already reflect the genre of each translated and commented source.

47. Another important metaphysical device, the distinction of means and ends, is more intelligible in itself, and is only treated in the commentaries themselves in its use for the discussion of free choice.

to an important distinction that the Reformed use time and again in their discussions of freedom (the distinction between the necessity of the consequent and the necessity of the consequence). Finally, the different connotations of contingency and its relation to the term necessity will be discussed.

A fundamental Christian insight is the relation between God as the Creator and the world as his creation. In scholastic discussions, this relation is often framed with the help of the ontological concepts of cause and effect. A cause produces an act, and either the act or the state of affairs brought forward by the act is called the effect.

```
cause  →  effect
      act
```

Scheme 1: The ontological distinction of cause and effect

Now, different kinds of cause and effect were premised. Here a second ontological device utilized by the Reformed: the distinction between subject and attribute. Regarding causes, they distinguished between subjects with the attribute of freedom (free causes) and subjects without that quality (natural causes).

A natural cause was held to have such a nature that it could produce only one kind of act. So, it was also called a necessary cause: it could only produce that act, and not another. For instance, fire was held to act always by burning, or animals, though they act variously, were held to be driven by instinct, so their nature made only one kind of act possible in due time.

Instead, a free cause was held to be able to act variously, not only at different times, but also structurally at one and the same moment. In distinction to the effects of natural causes (which were called natural or necessary effects), the effect of free causes was called contingent or free.

The distinction between natural and free cause is given with the way they "determine" their act. This technical term "determination" should not be associated with the *modern* term "determinism," because that term did not exist yet; the concept of determinism was denoted by other terms like "Stoic fate."[48] Rather, determination means that a cause gets directed to one effect. A natural cause is determined by its *nature* to the act; a free cause determines itself by *freedom* to one of possible acts. Hence, determination refers to the state of a cause: being undetermined means that the (free) cause has not yet directed itself to a certain effect. A determined cause will produce its determined effect, but still the effect can be either contingent (determined by a free act) or necessary (determined by a natural act).

---

48. Compare note 2. To be sure, the referent of the modern term "determinism" was known before that time, and the issue of Stoic fate played a major part in discussions on free choice (as will appear in the texts).

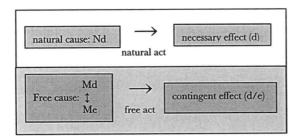

Scheme 2: The ontological distinction between natural and free causes and their (necessary and contingent) effects

In terms of the relation between God and man, both were held to be free causes. God as the *First Cause* (*prima causa*) and creatures as *secondary causes* (*secundae causae*) concur together in their acting to produce a contingent effect. We should be aware that this causal terminology does not imply a manipulative, causal relationship: God as the Creator initiates, sustains, empowers and governs all that exists, while leaving room for the causal activity of his creatures. God does not only stand at the beginning, but is present to every moment of time in providing life, powers, and possibilities for action. It should further be noticed that in this relationship God is *independent* of his creatures, while these are *dependent* on God. The secondary causes are contingent themselves, so they are dependent in their existence on him.

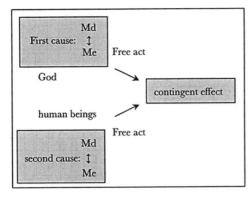

Scheme 3: The ontological distinction of First and second cause

Now, in regard to human freedom, the question might arise how the determination of the First cause to, say, effect d relates to the freedom of acting of the second cause. If the First cause chooses for d, does the second cause keep any freedom at all in its acting? Does the second cause keep a real freedom between different acts (both d and e), or does the determinate state of the effect leave only the option of d open?

Although an exact answer to this question would require a separate study, the basic answer is that the divine choice for d is realized by the free choice of the second cause for it. So, the second cause keeps both possibilities, but is guided to choose *by itself* for d.

Some clarification of this initial answer can be given by a closer look to the Reformed use of the terms "necessity" and "contingency." An important aspect of the Reformed view of reality is that a proper relation between necessity and contingency must be established. In the logic and ontology underlying Reformed theology, the distinction between "necessity" and "contingency" is irreducible, which means that both need to be respected and maintained.

Especially with respect to freedom this distinction is important, because freedom, necessity and contingency all are modal terms, which center around the modal verb "can."[49] Hence, the verb "*posse*" appears time and again in these scholastic discussions on freedom, and the concept of free choice is explored by logical explorations of its use. The verb has both the aspect of alternativity (*possibility* for willing) and ability (*power* to will something), and although it is sometimes hard to decide which nuance is meant or whether both figure together, in many places it clearly has a modal sense.

For instance, the terms "necessity" and "contingency" themselves are usually defined by the use of "*posse*" in common scholastic definitions:

(1) Things are *contingent* of which it is possible that they are or are not (*posse esse et non esse*).[50]

(2) Things are *necessary* of which it is impossible that they are not (*non posse non esse*).[51]

Likewise, the definition of freedom frequently invokes the verb "*posse*" and derivations of it (*potestas*) or supposes the verb by stating alternative possibilities for choice as an explanation of its freedom.[52]

---

49. For the term "modal" see 1.3.2 and the final paragraphs of this section (1.4.1).

50. The definitions combine "*posse*" with different verbs (to be, to become, to exist), but "*posse*" is the common denominator. Compare, for example, Turrettini, *Institutio*, III.12.x: "contingentia, quae possunt esse et non esse."; III.13.vi: "futuris (...) contingentibus (...) possunt esse et non esse." Comparable definitions are found with other authors, including Remonstrants and Catholics; for example, Simon Episcopius, *Institutiones theologicae* 4.II.xvii: "contingens, quod fieri possit ac non fieri" in his *Opera theologica* (Amsterdam: J. Blaeu, 1665), 2:301a.

51. Turrettini, *Institutio*, III.14.ii: "Necessarium duplex esse: aliud absolutum quod simpliciter et per se suaque natura *non potest aliter se habere*, ut Deum esse bonum, justum etc. Aliud hypotheticum, quod non ita est ex se et simpliciter tale, quin possit aliter se habere, sed tamen posito aliquo necessario sequitur, *nec potest aliter se habere*, ut si ponas Deum predestinasse Jacobum ad salutem, necesse est Jacobum salvari, nim. ex hypothesi decreti; quia alias potuisset non praedestinari, et non salvari." Again, Remonstrants and Catholics gave similar definitions; for instance, the Remonstrant Philip van Limborch: "Res enim in se et natura sua spectata vel est necessaria, vel contingens; id est, ejusmodi habet essentiam, quae vel potest non existere, vel non potest non existere," *Theologia christiana* (Amsterdam: B. Lakeman, 1686), II.8.xix.

52. The different kinds of human freedom with respect to doing good (the four states, compare 1.4.2) are stated by Turrettini, following Augustine's *Admonition and Grace* (*De*

So, in this clarification we must explain the way in which the Reformed used the concepts of necessity and contingency in their discussion of free choice. An often used didactical device to explain the relations between necessity, contingency, possibility and impossibility is the so-called Square of Opposition, which arose in medieval philosophy and theology to explain modal problems.[53] Squares of opposition can be found in later scholastic texts as well, but mostly these authors implicitly draw on the established tradition.

An example of such a modal square is given below:

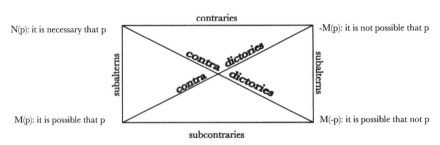

N(p): it is necessary that p — contraries — -M(p): it is not possible that p

subalterns — *contradictories* — *contradictories* — subalterns

M(p): it is possible that p — subcontraries — M(-p): it is possible that not p

Scheme 4: The Square of Opposition with respect to necessity and possibility

Each of the corners of this square has one modal term, and the lines between the corners indicate the possible relations between these options. It is important to note that for the sake of convenience we treat possibility and contingency as equivalents here.[54] The relations between them are not as exclusive and simple as might seem at first sight. Logically, distinctions have to be made between contradictory, contrary, subcontrary and subaltern relations:

(3) Two propositions are contradictory if they cannot both be true and they cannot both be false.

(4) Two propositions are contraries if they cannot both be true but can both be false.

(5) Two propositions are subcontraries if they cannot both be false but can both be true.

(6) A proposition is a subaltern if it must be true if its superaltern is true, although the truth-rule does not apply the other way around (the truth of

---

correptione et gratia) c.I, in terms of different kinds of "*posse*" (*Institutio*, VIII.1.ix): "*Libertas gloriae* in beatis est, *non posse peccare*, *libertas peccatorum* in statu peccati est *non posse non peccare*, *libertas fidelium* in gratia est *posse peccare et posse non peccare*, sed libertas Adami fuit *posse non peccare*" (italics from Turrettini).

53. A square of opposition with an extensive explanation and discussion of its historical origin is given in *MMPh*, 106-123; Simo Knuuttila, "Modal Logic," *CHLMP*, 342-357, esp. 342-343. Both works are helpful to understand medieval logics in general. A good introduction is provided also by Broadie, *Introduction to Medieval Logic*.

54. For the scholastics, contingency implied actuality and possibility did not, but both terms had the modal aspect of being able to be different (*posse esse et non esse*); compare the explanation of contingency in this section.

the subaltern does not imply the truth of the superaltern). Yet, if the subaltern is false, the superaltern must be false too.[55]

With this instrument, the scholastics utilized nuanced modal analyses in their theological works.

Their analyses show that necessity and contingency can be discussed on several levels. Especially with respect to freedom, the Reformed are cautious to note that something can be necessary in one respect, whereas it is simultaneously contingent in another respect. To clarify this point, Reformed theologians distinguish several kinds of necessity.

The basic distinction, occurring already from Vermigli onward, is between absolute necessity or necessity of the consequent (*necessitas consequentis*) on the one hand, and hypothetical necessity or necessity of the consequence (*necessitas consequentiae*) on the other hand.[56] We will explain this distinction in some detail, utilizing some formal logic (for the explanation of logical symbols, see section 1.3.2). We trust that this will help the reader to understand what is at stake here.

The necessity of the consequent/consequence distinction is based on the analysis of an implication. An example of an implication is:

(7) If I marry Sophie, Sophie is my wife.

This conditional assertion can logically be symbolized as:

(8) $p \rightarrow q$

In (8) we symbolize the conditional assertion of (7) by substituting its two parts by a letter (if p, then q) and substituting their implicative connection by the logical symbol for an implication ($p \rightarrow q$). In this symbolized proposition, we call p the "antecedent" and q the "consequent" of the implication $p \rightarrow q$. In Latin, the word for implication, or consequence, is *consequentia*.[57] Now, if we add a necessity operator (N) to the implication, we can construct different formulas.

---

55. So, something cannot be both possible and impossible or necessary while its opposite is being possible as well (contradictories); something cannot both be necessary and impossible, although it can be neither necessary nor impossible, that is, it can be possible (contraries); something cannot be possible while its opposite is not being possible as well, although it can be possible while its opposite is likewise possible (subcontraries); something that is necessary is also possible, whereas something possible does not have to be necessary (subalterns).

56. Peter Martyr Vermigli, *In Epistolam S. Pauli Apostoli ad Romanos commentarij doctissimi...* (Basel: P. Perna, 1558), 434-435. See Frank A. James, *Peter Martyr Vermigli and Predestination: The Augustinian Inheritance of an Italian Reformer* (Oxford: Clarendon, 1998), 81-82.

57. The English word "consequence" in a non-technical sense is a bit ambigious as it can denote both the *implication* itself ($p \rightarrow q$) and the *consequent* of the implication (q in $p \rightarrow q$). Yet, the Latin *consequentia* does not denote the consequent (that is the Latin *consequentis*), but the implication.

First, the implication itself can be necessary: if p, then q is always implied. Hence, the necessity operator is put in front of the whole implication:

$$N$$
(9) $N\,(p \rightarrow q)$ or $p \rightarrow q$

This kind of necessity was called the necessity of the consequence by the Reformed. It is important to note that this necessity applies to the implication between two states of affairs: in (9) the necessity operator N determines the whole of the consequence $p \rightarrow q$.

So, the relation of implication itself is necessary. Yet, neither p nor q have to be necessary, because p and q can be perfectly contingent. Referring to the example: it is contingent that I marry Sophie (I did not have to do so...), and it is contingent that Sophie is my wife (she did not have to be mine...); but the implication between both is necessary: it cannot be the case that I marry Sophie but that she is not my wife.

The Reformed stress that the necessity of the *consequence* is not equivalent with the necessity of the *consequent*. In formula (10), the necessity of the *consequent* obtains:

(10) $p \rightarrow Nq$

In (10) the necessity operator N is placed before the consequent of the implication and determines the consequent q. This proposition claims that the result of the conditional proposition is necessary. In terms of our example: it is necessary that Sophie is my wife (if I marry her). When the Reformed authors presented in this volume utilize the distinction between the necessity of the consequent and the necessity of the consequence, they point out that formula (9) does not imply formula (10): if the implicative connection between two propositions or events is necessary, this does not mean that either of both is necessary in itself.

In Reformed theology concerning freedom and grace, the distinction receives an important application in relating the doctrines of God and of human free agency. The opponents of Reformed theology state that God's infallible knowledge and effective will impose necessity on the acts of free creatures, thus destroying their freedom. According to them, necessity and contingency cannot be united. For instance, the Remonstrant Philip van Limborch stated:

> It is contradictory to say that something would both happen freely or contingently and happen necessarily. For that is free and contingent, which is possible not to happen (*potest non fieri*), but that is necessary, which is not possible not to happen. So, these two can be reconciled *in no way*.[58]

---

58. "Contradictoria sunt, libere seu contingenter quid & necessario fieri; nam libere ac contingens sit, quod potest non fieri, necessario autem quod non potest non fieri: haec itaque nullo respectu conciliari possunt," van Limborch, *Theologia christiana*, II.8.xiii.

Therefore, Remonstrants like Episcopius and van Limborch contest the validity of the distinction of the necessity of the consequence and the consequent for clarifying human freedom. The Reformed argued that by doing so the Remonstrants could not maintain divine foreknowledge and that they had to deny not only the divine decree and the providence that governs the world, but also divine omniscience. In their modal logic,

(11) N (GKp → p) (it is necessary that, if God knows that p, then p occurs)

implies

(12) GKp → Np (if God knows that p, p is necessary itself)

If God foreknows p, p shall surely happen, and in that sense, it is not possible that it does not happen. Yet, the Reformed were eager to show that this kind of necessity can be united with the contingency of p. This would only be impossible if we ignore the distinction between the necessity of the consequent and the necessity of the consequence: in that case there would be no difference between both kinds of necessity and p would be necessary in every respect.

So, by using this distinction, the Reformed made it clear that if God knows p, then the existence of p itself is not necessary; p is only necessary on the supposition of God's knowing. So God's knowing of p implies only the necessity of consequence and not the necessity of the consequent.

The same holds for God's will. In contrast to the will of creatures, God's will is always effective and is never frustrated. Again, the Reformed distinguish between

(13) N (GWp → p) (it is necessary that if God wills p, then p occurs)

and

(14) GWp → Np (if God wills that p, p is necessary itself)

One final clarification has to be made about this analysis of necessity. This can be done by exploring the structure of an implication. If the antecedent would be necessary in the relation p q, then also the consequent itself has to be necessary:

(15) Np → Nq

In that way the necessity of the consequent would still obtain after all. Especially with regard to divine foreknowledge, which perceives things as they are, problems arose. Since the Church Fathers the question was frequently debated whether God's eternal knowledge is necessary and especially how God can know the so-called "future contingents" if his knowledge is determined. In this respect the Reformed followed the medieval tradition of appealing to the pivotal function of the will: the divine will chooses freely, and its objects can be definitely chosen by it, without losing their contingency.[59] So, their starting point was the proposition:

(16) $M(GWp) \rightarrow Mp$

The application of the necessity of the consequence (with their belief in the effective will of God) shows in a nutshell the Reformed ontological convictions underlying their discussions of free choice:

(17) $N(M(GWp) \rightarrow Mp)$

In this ontology, the contingency of the effect can be united with a hypothetical necessity of the effect. Instead, the Remonstrant accusation of Stoic fate against the Reformed can only obtain if the divine will acts necessarily:

(18) $N(GWp) \rightarrow Np$

Yet, the Remonstrants would not accept that God's will acts necessarily, so their accusation is void. Their objections against the Reformed insistence on both decisive divine involvement in human action and decisive human freedom could only be explained by these distinctions. As we will see in the individual texts below, the distinction between absolute necessity (*simpliciter: necessitas consequentis*) and relative necessity (*secundum quid: necessitas consequentiae*) enabled the Reformed scholastics to point out how necessity and contingency/freedom are in certain respects compatible instead of squarely contradictory.

Instead, the Remonstrants simplified the issue by their rejection of the distinction. If necessity and contingency are absolutely opposite, you are forced to be either a libertarian or a determinist. The Remonstrants were content to uphold human freedom and were convinced of Reformed determinism. Yet the Reformed rejected both options as a far too simplistic scheme. Their firm conviction that they were unjustly charged with determinism can only be understood by a detailed logical analysis.

So, a neglect of modal categories in theology runs the risk of falling back into either a necessitarian, determinist worldview or an unstable, arbitrary ontology of mere contingency. The Reformed maintained a refined balance of necessity and contingency.

In the texts and commentaries below, we will further meet the following types of necessity:

---

59. It should be noted that they held divine foreknowledge to be contingent as well, by founding it on the free divine decree. Would the knowledge of God be necessary, the necessity of the events (p) would be unavoidable: $N(GKp) \rightarrow Nq$.

- natural necessity: necessity inherent in the essential nature of a thing. For example, it is necessary for a stone to fall downward, at least in the physics of that time.[60] Or, it is necessary for a lion to kill its prey.
- physical necessity: necessity deriving from an outward cause that forces someone or something. This is often called *coercion*.
- rational necessity: if the intellect judges an act to be good, it is rationally necessary that the will assents. This type of necessity presupposes the scholastic anthropology (see below).
- moral necessity: given someone's moral character (good or bad), it is necessary that she performs either good or bad acts. The Reformed scholastics employ this type of necessity to account for the different states of man (see the explanation of anthropological terms below).
- necessity of immutability: a necessity on supposition of God's decree and providence that encompasses all that happens in the world. The Reformed scholastics make it clear that this is a necessity of the consequence (if God decrees a to happen, a will happen), which imposes no (absolute) necessity on the thing itself.
- necessity of infallibility: a necessity on supposition of divine foreknowledge, which is again a necessity of the consequence which imposes no (absolute) necessity on the thing itself (it can be argued that in the Reformed view, this type of necessity depends on the former kind, but that would fall outside the scope of this introduction).

As the Reformed argue, of these six kinds of necessity only the first two are incompatible with contingency and freedom; the latter four, being examples of relative necessity, are fully consistent with contingency and rather enable the free agency of human beings.

The counterpart of necessity is contingency. In medieval and post-Reformation scholasticism, the concept of "contingent" always implies the actuality of the stated act. Thus, "p is contingent" means: p occurs, and p could occur otherwise.[61] The term "contingent" has had a long history, and conceptually it was used with profoundly different connotations. Here, we can only provide a basic outline of the history of the term in order to be able to clarify the possible connotations it might have had for the Reformed themselves. In order to do so, we will discuss the most important developments by paying attention to the concepts of contingency of Parmenides, Aristotle and John Duns Scotus.[62]

The history of philosophy reveals different accounts of contingency. As an extreme contrast to contingency we mention the view of Parmenides of Elea (b. ± 510 BC). His philosophy has partly survived in his didactic poem *On Nature*, in which the goddess of Right (Δικη) reveals to him the deceptive way of Belief and

---

60. Compare section 2.7, especially note 47.
61. Compare definition (1) above.
62. This explanation is dependent on *CF*, 23-33, and *MMPh*.

the right way of Truth. In the subsequent account of being and becoming, Parmenides resolutely (in the form of the revelation of the goddess) declared the oneness and unchangeableness of being. Hence, all becoming is only pretence. [63] According to Parmenides, all states of affairs are necessary, and there is only one possible course of events. Evidently, this philosophical account of reality is closely related to the worldview of ancient Greek polytheist religions, in which fate ultimately ruled.

Conceptually, the metaphysical articulation of contingency by Parmenides can be illustrated by the following time-chart of what happens in a certain period:

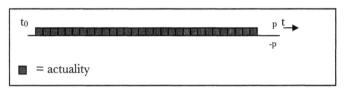

Scheme 5: Time-chart in relation to the conceptual pattern of Parmenides' metaphysics [64]

The upper part of the chart symbolizes the state of affairs p (for example, I walk), the part below the line the state of affairs ‑p. A filled square on the time-line symbolizes an actualization, while an open one symbolizes a not-actualized possibility. Remarkably, the metaphysics of Parmenides does not show any open squares: contingency is absent.

Historically, the metaphysics of Parmenides is important because it originated at the birth of philosophy itself. Parmenides was the "first full-blooded metaphysician," and he can be called in many respects also the founding father of logic as a philosophical discipline.[65] Christianity was confronted from its start with this necessitarian philosophy and its carry-over in different kinds of ancient Greek philosophy like Stoicism and Neo-Platonism.

Aristotle (384-322 BC) had an intense interest in physics. Hence, according to him, metaphysics must have room for the idea of natural change.[66] Therefore, in

---

63. For an account of the philosophy of Parmenides, compare: Edward Craig, "Parmenides (early to mid 5th century BC)," in *Routledge Encyclopedia of Philosophy* (London/New York: Routledge, 1998), 7:229-235; W. K. C. Guthrie, *A History of Greek Philosphy* (Cambridge: Cambridge University Press, 1965), 2:1-80.

64. This scheme can be conceptually deduced from Parmenides' ontological statements. Compare Robinson: "If what is is everywhere in contact with what is, it follows (according to Parmenides) that it can neither scatter nor come together. But Parmenides thinks of Necessity as a kind of force which prevents being from scattering or coming together, and this mode of thought is typical of the early Greek philosophers. We have seen it already in Heraclitus, who thinks of the logos not merely as the order of events, but as somehow enforcing that order (...)"; for further explanation, see John M. Robinson, *An Introduction to Early Greek Philosophy* (New York: Houghton Mifflin Company, 1968), 115. Compare also *KN*, 2-13.

65. For the first statement, see Jonathan Barnes, *The Presocratic Philosophers* (London: Routledge and Kegan Paul, 1979), 1:176. For his logical work, compare J. Mansfeld, *Die Offenbarung des Parmenides und die menschliche Welt* (Assen: van Gorcum, 1964), 107-121, esp. 121.

66. For a profound treatment of Aristotle's concept of contingency (which Knuutila calls a

his philosophy the idea of contingency was introduced and understood in terms of temporal change:

Scheme 6: Time-chart in relation to the conceptual pattern of Aristotle's metaphysics

Aristotle provided an improvement in a remarkable respect. Temporal change can be explained and states of affairs can differ. Yet, this alternativity figures only in a temporal sense. Structurally, on each moment only one state of affairs occurs without any alternative. Thus, open squares still lack and everything remains necessary. We call Aristotle's view of contingency "diachronic contingency": it equals contingency with change, and necessity with changelessness.

In his famous potency-act scheme, Aristotle interpreted possibility in the sense of something that is not yet realized. Yet, all potencies strive towards actuality and will be realized. This so-called principle of plenitude does not leave room for real possibility.[67] Many non-Christian thinkers and several Christian thinkers have held to Aristotle's view of contingency.

A radical alternative was established by John Duns Scotus around 1300. Central to his philosophy and theology is the concept of what we call "synchronic contingency." Synchronic contingency means that for one moment of time, there is a true alternative for the state of affairs that actually occurs. It can be argued that only this synchronic contingency can account for real freedom of choice, both on God's part and on our part. The reason is that without synchronic contingency there is no structural alternativity in reality, so neither can there be alternativity in acting, which is a requirement for freedom.

Scheme 7: Time-chart in relation to the conceptual pattern of Scotus' metaphysics

Our discussion of the concept of contingency here does not intend to force the subsequent interpretation, but to provide different understandings of the concept which we must be aware of in analyzing the texts of our Reformed

---

"statistical interpretation of modality") compare Lambertus Marie de Rijk, *Aristotle: Semantics and Ontology* (Leiden: Brill, 2002); *MMPh*, 1-44; *CF*, 23-33.

67. Compare Simo Knuuttila, *Reforging the Great Chain of Being: Studies of the History of Modal Theories* (Dordrecht / London: Reidel, 1981); A. O. Lovejoy, *The Great Chain of Being: A Study of the History of an Idea* (New York: Harper and Row, 1969).

authors. Moreover, the systematic relevance is that if the Reformed concepts of contingency must be interpreted as diachronic contingency, their account of freedom would be incomplete after all. Whatever nuances in the concept of necessity they may cherish, true alternativity in acting would still be missing. However, if these texts suggest a real conception of alternativity, they would provide a remarkably consistent and detailed articulation of freedom and the contention of Turrettini at the start of this chapter would become intelligible.

As noted before, in modern terms we would call the aspects of Reformed thought concerning necessity and contingency a form of "modal logic."[68] This is the branch of philosophy that studies the modal aspects of possibility, impossibility, necessity and contingency. In our view, elements of modern modal logics can help to elucidate the distinctions and concepts utilized by Reformed scholastic theologians concerning necessity, contingency and freedom. We use it as an extrapolation of Reformed thought from the sixteenth to eighteenth centuries. We should be aware that especially in questions of modality, ontology and logic are closely connected.

Of instrumental significance in modern modal ontology is the concept of "possible worlds": a maximal state of affairs that either includes or excludes any conceivable entity.[69] Possible worlds are alternatives to each other. In terms of possible worlds, it can be examined whether an entity is:

- possible: existing in at least one possible world
- impossible: existing in no possible world
- contingent: existing in one or some possible worlds, but not in all
- actual: existing in the actual world, and possibly existing in other possible worlds
- necessary: existing in all possible worlds[70]

---

68. Compare George E. Hughes and Maxwell J. Cresswell, *A New Introduction to Modal Logic* (London: Routledge, 1996); Alvin Plantinga, "Modalities, Basis Concepts and Distinctions," in Jaegwon Kim and Ernest Sosa (eds.), *Metaphysics: An Anthology*, 4th ed. (Malden, MA: Blackwell, 2003), 135-148; Alvin Plantinga and Matthew Davidson, *Essays in the Metaphysics of Modality* (Oxford: Oxford University Press, 2003).

69. This definition is derived from Alvin Plantinga, *The Nature of Necessity* (Oxford: Clarendon, 1974), 45. The standard introduction to possible worlds is: Raymond Bradley and Norman Swartz, *Possible Worlds: An Introduction to Logic and Its Philosophy* (Oxford: Blackwell, 1979). Modern analysis is divided regarding the metaphysical application of modal logic, which is reflected in the disagreement between defenders of actualist and possibilist models of possible worlds. According to actualism there is only one real world, whereas other "possible worlds" are abstractions, related to the actual world in being a possible alternative to it in one or more respects. Possibilism claims that all possible worlds are concrete (spatio-temporal) objects. Compare Peter van Inwagen, "Two Concepts of Possible Worlds," in Peter A. French, et al. (eds.), *Studies in Essentialism*, Midwest Studies in Philosophy 11 (Minneapolis: University of Minnesota Press, 1986), 185-213; James E. Tomberlin, "Actualism or Possibilism?" *Philosophical Studies* 84 (1996): 263-282. We follow the actualist model of Plantinga for its applicability in concrete analysis of divine and human action.

70. As mentioned above, the scholastic usage of "contingent" implies the actual occurrence of a thing. A parallel set of terms in scholastic Latin would run as follows:

Also, the distinction between the necessity of the consequent and the necessity of the consequence, explained above, can be further interpreted in terms of possible worlds. The necessity of the consequent states that the resultant proposition or event exists in all possible worlds (it is necessary). The necessity of the consequence can be expressed as follows:

(19) in all possible worlds in which p exists, q exists as well

Again, in this logic it is perfectly intelligible that both p and q are contingent entities. Moreover, the possible world semantics can be applied to properties of these entities:

* essential: in all possible worlds in which an entity exists, it possesses this property;
* accidental: in some but not all possible worlds in which an entity exists, it has this property.

We will see that the Reformed scholastic discussion of free choice presupposes these concepts; although they are not stated in the explicit, modern form, we will argue that they are structurally present in Reformed thought.

1.4.2 Anthropological Terms

As the theme of free choice is located in anthropology, it is important to understand the anthropological framework of Reformed scholasticism. It consists of two basic perspectives, which together yield the relevant consequences for human freedom.

The first perspective regards man's *essential* make-up. Here we encounter the following terms:

* mind-gifted nature (*natura intelligens*): man is basically viewed as a rational creature. This simply means that it belongs to man's essence to have the capacity of knowing, understanding and judging. Although Reformed theologians acknowledge the distortion of man's intellect by sin, they do not endorse an irrationalist view of man.

  It is helpful to notice that the authors of the texts in this volume sometimes use the term "nature" (*natura*) in different senses: basically, it should be understood as the whole of essential properties (of man); in a secondary sense, it can signify the accidental state of man (after the Fall, man's "nature" is corrupted).

1. possible	quod non est et potest esse
2. impossible	quod non potest esse
3. contingent	quod est et potest non esse
4. actual	quod est
5. necessary	quod non potest non esse

- soul (*anima*): to modern ears, it may sound strange to describe the soul as the principle of action. The scholastics did not intend to hypostatize the soul into a separate entity, but to indicate the relevant aspect of man's personality in the acts of knowing and willing.
- potency, disposition, act (*facultas, habitus, actus*): the Reformed scholastics follow the traditional Aristotelian "faculty psychology." The main capacities of the "soul" are knowing and willing. The scholastic analysis of knowing and willing distinguishes three levels, moving from the concrete to the abstract:
  - the concrete act (*actus*): "I know this person," "I want a cup of coffee," etc.
  - the disposition (*habitus*): a disposition is formed by repeated actions that result in a certain pattern of behavior; "I know how to drive a car," "I want the best for my neighbors," etc.
  - the potency (*facultas*): the capacity of knowing or willing, viewed apart from its concrete actions and possible objects.
- choice, will, judgment (*arbitrium, voluntas, judicium*): these terms are in the center of the texts studied in this volume. There are some differences between the authors in placing "choice" in relation to will and intellect. A common notion is that the will itself regards the ultimate ends (for example: being happy, striving for the good), while choice and judgment are concerned with the means (marrying in order to be happy, believing in God as the means to strive for the good). Moreover, all authors identify intellectual as well as volitional components in free choice (*liberum arbitrium*).

The second perspective is formed by the famous four-state model (in which *accidental* freedom is explained). It describes the different situations in which man finds himself in relation to God and the good. The basic components of the model occur in Augustine, while Bernard of Clairvaux gave it an influential elaboration. Whereas the model is based on the historical sequence of the biblical narrative, we focus on the structural differences it indicates in man's situation.

- Before the Fall (*ante lapsum; status integritatis*): this situation concerns only Adam (and Eve). He was created good by God, but had the possibility to choose the bad. In this state, man was endowed with all the gifts necessary to stay true to God, and at the same time had true freedom to obey or disobey God.
- After the Fall (*post lapsum; status corruptionis*): this state is exemplified in sinners who have not been renewed by God's grace. They can only sin, and have no possibility within themselves to do the good. Still, they have not lost the essential freedom of will and choice: although they are bound to sin, they sin willingly and by their own choice. The Reformed call this the *servitudo* (slavery) of man.
- Under grace (*sub gratia; status gratiae*): this state is chronologically also after the Fall, but is structurally characterized by God's grace of regeneration. Hereby, man is no longer a slave of sin, but receives a new

principle of life (the Spirit) by which he starts to do the good willingly. The Reformed realize that the obedience to God in this state is partial: next to the Spirit, there is the flesh (the old, sinful nature) that causes man to lapse into sin again.

• In glory (*in gloria; status gloriae*): after this earthly life, regeneration will be completed and the remainders of sin eradicated. In this final state, the habit of doing the good is so strong (by reason of God's preserving grace) the saints will no longer have the (actual) possibility of choosing the bad, but will be consistent in choosing the good.

In modern terms, we can describe the first perspective (man's soul and its faculties and acts) as the *essential* level of anthropology and the second perspective (man's states in regard to sin and salvation) as the *accidental* level. It is important to make this distinction in dealing with free choice.[71]

Concerning free choice itself, the following elements are common to most discussions in this volume:

• The ramification of freedom in terms of the freedom of contrariety (*libertas contrarietatis*, otherwise called "freedom of kind" [*libertas speciei/specificationis*]) and freedom of contradiction (*libertas contradictionis*, otherwise called "freedom of exercise" [*libertas exercitatis*]). This distinction can be explained again with the help of a square of opposition. For the nature of the relation between these four possible acts, compare Scheme 4 above.

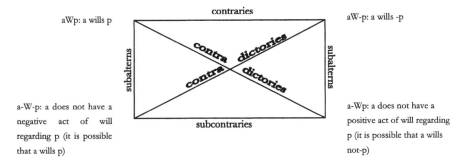

aWp: a wills p

aW-p: a wills -p

a-W-p: a does not have a negative act of will regarding p (it is possible that a wills p)

a-Wp: a does not have a positive act of will regarding p (it is possible that a wills not-p)

Scheme 8: The Square of Opposition with respect to the will

Frequent terms of Reformed scholastic discourse like the freedom of contrariety and of contradiction are explained hereby as follows. The

---

71. The importance of the distinction between essential and accidental freedom (in terms of formal and material freedom) is elaborated by Eef Dekker and Henri Veldhuis, "Freedom and Sin: Some Systematic Observations," *European Journal of Theology* 3 (1994): 153-161. An instructive modern extrapolation which discusses freedom in relation to (biological) psychiatrics is Guus Labooy, *Freedom and Dispositions*, Contributions to Philosophical Theology 8 (Frankfurt am Main: Peter Lang, 2002).

freedom of contrariety indicates the possibility of the will to choose *this* or *that* object. The different objects (walking or cycling) can be formulated as p and q, or for this sake also p and –p. So, the freedom of contrariety is symbolized by the upper line. The freedom of contradiction is the possibility of the will to either choose or reject a certain object. So, the freedom of contradiction is symbolized by the diagonal lines.

- The character of freedom as consisting of rational spontaneity instead of indifference. Our authors characterize freedom as "rational spontaneity": the will acts out of itself (*sua sponte*), not being driven by an inward or outward determining cause. This spontaneity is called "rational" inasmuch as the will is informed by the intellect and thus is not blind or whimsical in acting. The definition of freedom in terms of indifference was advocated by Jesuit and Arminian adversaries of the Reformed: they stated that, if all the requisites for acting were posited (rational judgment of the goodness of an action, God's decree), the will was still indifferent towards acting or not acting. The Reformed argued that this destroys man's dependence on God and even makes impossible all reasonable action. While most authors extensively argue for the untenability of conceiving freedom by indifference, some authors argue explicitly for a structural indifference or alternativity and make clear that this is factual contingency, which is also supposed in their conception of freedom as rational spontaneity.

- The relation of intellect and will. Despite some variations between our authors, it is clear that intellect and will work together in free choice: the intellect apprehends the object (attaches to it the true or false qualifier) and passes a judgment concerning the goodness or badness of the object or action; the will follows this judgment and makes its own choice. It is important to note that the will is *not determined* (*determinari*) by the intellect when it *follows* (*sequi*) the intellect: the will keeps its own task of choosing.

- The rejection of autonomy. While advocating a theology of contingency and freedom, the Reformed rejected a complete human autonomy as was propagated by contemporary Renaissance and early modern thinkers. They maintained the dependence of man on his Creator, and placed true human freedom within a larger framework. To be sure, true autonomy (sometimes indicated by the Greek word *autexousia*) is ascribed only to God.

1.4.3 Logical Distinctions

Many terms and concepts discussed above contained or implied logical distinctions already. We believe that scholastic texts cannot be understood without an awareness of their employment of logics. Therefore, we briefly explain some logical terms and distinctions that we meet throughout the texts in this volume.

- *Ratio*: We might be tempted to interpret the Latin *ratio* immediately as "reason" in the sense of our rational capacity. The scholastic usage of

ratio, however, is far different. The most common nuances of meaning are:
- argument
- aspect, characteristic
- concept
- ground, reason, account

It is important to identify in all cases the relevant meaning of this term.

• In the first act (*in actu primo*) / in the second act (*in actu secundo*): This distinction (used by Turrettini and de Moor) parallels the anthropological distinction between potency (*facultas*) and act (*actus*). Abstracted from a concrete volition, the will is capable of willing opposite acts (*in actu primo*); involved in a concrete act, the will cannot simultaneously will opposite things.

• In the divided sense (*in sensu diviso/divisionis*) / in the compounded sense (*in sensu composito/compositionis*). This distinction explains how two opposite acts are possible. A standard example is "Socrates sits and runs." As it stands, this proposition contains an apparent contradiction (sitting and running). Several solutions for this difficulty are possible. First, one could interpret the sentence diachronically: Socrates sits at t0 and runs at t1. However, our authors prefer an interpretation in terms of modality. A valid interpretation is in the divided sense: Socrates sits at t0 and it is *possible* that he runs at t0. The same is invalid in the compounded sense: it is not possible that (Socrates sits at t0 & Socrates runs at t0). The same point is made by distinguishing between the *simultas potentiae* (two alternative options at one moment) and the *potentia simultatis* (the possibility of two opposite acts at one moment). The former is affirmed and the latter denied by the Reformed scholastics.

The ontological analysis by logical distinctions like the necessity of the consequence /consequent, the volitional analysis by logical distinctions like first and second act or divided and compounded sense and the analysis of freedom by the distinctions of freedom of contrariety and contradiction all seem to suggest an ontology of synchronic contingency. These distinctions all presuppose that contingency is not a matter of temporal change, but of simultaneous logical alternatives. Among other things, the subsequent chapters will test in which respects this initial hypothesis is confirmed or questioned by textual evidence.

1.5 Survey of Chosen Texts

The Reformed tradition was not a monolith, nor was it articulated in an intellectual vacuum. Therefore it may seem quite audacious to present "the Reformed view" on free choice. Still, each theologian participated in the same confessional tradition, trying to preserve and improve the theological heritage. Offering six texts of Reformed theologians from different times and different universities, we hope to illustrate the general consensus and individual dynamics of Reformed thinking on free choice. In this way, these theologians might even provide us with a representative overview of the tradition as a whole. The authors are chosen for their important place in the Reformed tradition in general or because of their special contribution to this particular topic.

Girolamo Zanchi (1516-1590) experienced the transition from the initial Reformation stage to what is called Early Orthodoxy and became one of the formative theologians who codified Reformed faith to systematic theology.[72] Therefore he is the first author we have selected. Because Zanchi did not write a separate treatise on free will, we have chosen two texts, which provide the most independent and detailed account of Zanchi's thoughts on free will. The first text is taken from the treatises *The Works of God in Creation* (*De operibus Dei intra spatium sex dierum creatis*), which was first published in 1591. The second is taken from *The Fall of the First Man, Sin and the Law of God* (*De primi hominis lapsu, de peccato & de lege Dei*), published in 1597. The selected parts discuss free will before the Fall and free will after the Fall.

Next, the *Leyden Theological Theses* (*Theses theologicae*, 1601) of Junius are selected. Franciscus Junius (1545-1602) belonged to the third generation of Reformed theologians. The genre of the text, a disputation, indicates the profound extension of systematic theology.

Franciscus Gomarus (1563-1641) is among the most important Reformed theologians, but he is also associated with the Remonstrant debate on free will. We have selected an earlier text on free choice, when it was not yet a controversial topic: *Theological Disputation of Free Choice* (*Disputatio theologica de libero arbitrio*, 1603). For that reason we conclude that the theology about free will and free choice at the University of Leiden was already developed before the arrival of Arminius, who started his career in Leiden only in 1603. So, it can be stated that the selected disputations do not regard the position of Arminius or that of the later Remonstrants.

The fourth selected text is from the master of Dutch Reformed scholasticism, Gisbertus Voetius (1589-1676). From his extensive work we have selected a unique text. In 1995, Andreas J. Beck, the author of this chapter, rediscovered a disputation of Voetius that was held to be lost and consequently has never been discussed or even mentioned in modern secondary literature on Voetius until now. This *Philosophical-theological Disputation on the Freedom of the Will* (*Disputatio philosophico-theologica, continens quaestiones duas, de Distinctione Attributorum divinorum, & Libertate Voluntatis*) was written and defended by Engelbertus Beeckman with chairmanship of Voetius on June 25, 1652.

High Orthodoxy culminated in the work of Francesco Turrettini (1623-1687). He presents his thoughts on freedom of choice in *Locus 10* of his *Institutes of Elenctic Theology* (*Institutio theologiae elencticae*, 1679-1685). Like the whole work of Turrettini this *Locus* demonstrates the lucid mind of the author and his vast knowledge of the contemporary debates on free will. For our purpose we will only investigate Turrettini's own position.

---

72. For the usual chronological division of Reformed Orthodoxy, see Richard A. Muller, *PRRD*, 1:30-32.

The last selected text is from one of the latest major scholastic works of the Reformed tradition. Bernardinus de Moor presented a comprehensive description of theology in his huge, six-volume *Continuous Commentary on à Marck's Compendium of Christian Theology* (*Commentarius perpetuus in Joh. Marckii compendium theologiae didactico-elencticum*, 1761-1771). Free choice is not treated separately here, but in different *loci*. The most important discussion on free choice is found in chapter XIII, §13 of the *Commentary*. Here, freedom is discussed in the context of an explanation of the faculties of the human soul, intellect and will. We have selected two parts of this section: the first deals with the relation between intellect and will, and the other treats freedom itself, arising out of both faculties.

2

Always Free, but Not Always Good

Girolamo Zanchi (1516-1590) on Free Will

2.1 Introduction

Girolamo Zanchi (Hieronymus Zanchius) was one of the leading theologians in the second half of the sixteenth century.[1] He experienced and accompanied the transition from the initial Reformation stage to what is called Early Orthodoxy.[2] Born on the third of February, 1516 at Alzano (Italy), he lost his parents in his early youth, and at the age of fifteen he entered the monastery of the Augustinian Canons at Bergamo. Here, he received a thorough education in theology and philosophy, dominated by the works of Thomas Aquinas. In his later works, he shows the lasting influence of this scholastic training by the many references and allusions to "the angelic doctor."[3]

An equally decisive decade of his life was spent in the monastery San Frediano at Lucca (1541-1552). Zanchi happened to arrive at about the same time as Petrus Martyr Vermigli (1499-1562), who was already active in Reformation circles when he became prior of the San Frediano in 1541. Under Vermigli's direction, Zanchi was introduced to the writings of the Reformers, and gradually became convinced of the need of Reformation for church and theology. Whereas Vermigli was forced to leave the monastery in 1542 because of his Reformation sympathies, Zanchi could stay there until finally he too was expelled in 1552.

Zanchi stayed several months at Geneva, settling subsequently at Strasbourg, where he was appointed professor of theology and philosophy. After some years of quiet teaching and study, the climate became worse, due to the hostile activity of the Lutheran Johannes Marbach. The conflict escalated on the doctrinal differences between Lutherans and Calvinists concerning the Lord's Supper and

---

1. A bibliographic portrait is supplied by Christopher J. Burchill, "Girolamo Zanchi: Portrait of a Reformed Theologian and His Work," *Sixteenth Century Journal* 15 (1984): 185-207.

2. Compare section 1.5 above, "Survey of Chosen Texts."

3. For a careful analysis of Zanchi's relation to Thomas Aquinas' writings, see Harm Goris, "Thomism in Zanchi's Doctrine of God," in *RS*, 121-139. Goris does not mention the *auctoritates* culture (compare this volume, section 1.4), but remarks that Zanchi seemingly was not even aware that his doctrine of God differed from Thomas on the major point of divine simplicity (137). Goris says that in this respect "the similarity with the view of the *Doctor Subtilis* is striking" (139).

predestination. Although Zanchi at last agreed to sign a compromise formula on the debated issues, meanwhile it was almost impossible for him to live and work at Strasbourg any longer.

In 1563, Zanchi accepted the ministry in a local church at Chiavenna (Italy). Five years later, in 1568, he was appointed professor at the University of Heidelberg, where he participated for eight years in the theological education of future Reformed ministers and theologians. In 1576, the Elector of the Palatine, Ludwig VI, expelled all Reformed theologians from Heidelberg and restored the Lutheran religion in his country. From 1576 until his death, Zanchi worked at the newly founded academy of Neustadt an der Haardt (nowadays Neustadt a/d Weinstrasse). On the ninth of November, 1590, Zanchi died during a short stay in Heidelberg.

Much of Zanchi's teaching activities were in the field of biblical exegesis; the results are laid down in commentaries on the Epistles to the Ephesians, Philippians, Colossians, Thessalonians, the first Epistle of John and the Book of Hosea. Besides that, Zanchi wrote some extensive treatises on systematic theology, including *The Triune God, The Nature of God or the Divine Attributes, The Incarnation of the Son of God, Holy Scripture*, and *The Works of God in Creation during a Period of Six Days*.[4] In his *Compendium of the Main Points of Christian Doctrine* he summarized Calvin's *Institutes*. Further, he wrote several serieses of theses used for academic disputation. Lastly, in a brief exposition of his belief (*The Faith of the Christian Religion*) he intended to give a spiritual last will for his children. All his writings were collected by his sons and sons-in-law and published in eight volumes in 1605 (reissued 1617-1619).[5]

We may assume that all Zanchi's major writings originated in his academic lectures. We can easily recognize the scholastic *quaestio* structure: all topics are divided in different questions, to which Zanchi mostly replies with a concise thesis. Other opinions are briefly discussed, the thesis is explained and confirmed by testimonies from Scripture, tradition and further arguments, and objections are refuted. The prefaces to the different volumes of the 1617/1619 edition indicate that the actual order of publication reflects the order of origin.

2.2 Translation of the Texts

Zanchi did not write a separate treatise on free choice. The texts translated and commented in this volume are derived from two larger treatises. These sections were chosen because they provide the most independent and detailed account of Zanchi's thoughts on free will.

The first is *The Works of God in Creation during a Period of Six Days* (*De operibus Dei intra spatium sex dierum creatis*), which was published by Zanchi's

---

4. *De tribus Elohim, aeterno Patre, Filio et Spiritu Sancto, uno eodemque Jehova* (Heidelberg, 1572); *De natura Dei, sive de divinis attributis* (Heidelberg, 1577); *De incarnatione filii Dei* (Heidelberg, 1593); *De sacra Scriptura* (Heidelberg, 1593); *De operibus Dei intra spatium sex dierum creatis* (Neustadt,1591).

5. *Clariss. Viri D. Hier. Zanchii Omnium operum theologicorum tomi octo* (Geneva: Gamonet & Aubert, 1605; repr. Geneva: Samuel Crispin, 1617-1619).

sons and sons-in-law four months after Zanchi's death, in March of 1591. From this work, we selected the chapter on free choice before the Fall. This part treats the original nature and powers of free choice, of which we selected only the first section.

2.2.1 The Free Choice of Our First Parents before the Fall

[*The nature and powers of free choice*] [6]
[704] Since there are four states of man: before the Fall, after the Fall, under grace, and in glory; so it is customary to dispute on his free choice in a fourfold way, namely: how it was before the Fall, how after the Fall, how under grace, and how in heavenly glory. Here we have to speak only about free choice before the Fall, how it was in Adam and Eve; we will speak of the other states similarly, and that will be the proper *locus* on free choice.

However, I aim to present two questions far different from each other, one concerning the nature of free choice in itself; the other concerning its powers, how far they do extend. So we shall explain two questions on the free choice of our first parents before the Fall: First, whether man before the Fall was really endowed with free choice; second, of what kind were its natural powers, and whether it needed the grace of Christ and for what things it needed this.[7] What pertains to the first question, we respond briefly with this thesis:

Thesis I
Man before the Fall had truly free choice towards good as well as towards bad.

[*Explanation of the thesis*]
I. We have to explain here some points in order to understand better what we say, which even belongs to the treatment, in general, of free choice.

[*The term "free choice"*]
First of all, it should be seen what is understood by the term "free choice" (*liberum arbitrium*) in the Church, and whence this word is deduced. It is true, the term free choice is not found in Holy Scripture, no more than the Greek word αὐτεξούσιον that signifies the same. Yet, the things signified by these words are contained in Holy Scripture. And even these words are very frequent in the writings of the Fathers and were accepted in the Church. Thus we must not abhor these terms, but rather search for their meaning and true signification.
1. There are some, who understand by the term "free choice" a free faculty or power (*potestas*) of doing whatever good or bad; and this because of the fact that "choice" often signifies a power, as is clear with outstanding authors. Livy book 4 of the Macedonian War: "Of course, if you repeal the Oppian law, you will have no choice (that is, power) if you will forbid something that now

---

6. Girolamo Zanchi, "De libero primorum parentum ante lapsum arbitrio," in *De operibus Dei intra spatium sex dierum creatis*, lib. III, cap. 3, in *Omnia opera theologica*, tom. tertius, col. 704-710.

7. This translation only deals with the first question.

the law forbids."[8] So Ovid: "In your hands is the power (*arbitrium*) over our life and death." [9]

Thus, because some people see, firstly, that the impious cannot know or love God nor keep his commands, therefore they deny that they have free choice. They further see that even the pious cannot do what they want, although they know God and want to keep his law. For the flesh wars against the Spirit; since they do not realize whatever they will, [705] whence they deny even that the pious have free choice. And where they know that Adam could achieve whatever he willed, they say that only he really had free choice.

But they err, as we will show at its own place. Every man namely always has free choice, although not always a good one and capable of the good. When we say that man has free choice, the Fathers and the Church meant something else than that man has a free power to do anything, as we will soon say.

2. Others err even worse, when they extend this faculty of doing anything to the working-out of the things that one desires or intends. For they say that someone has free choice who has the faculty of accomplishing whatever he wills or intends. And because there is nobody who is not often frustrated in his intention by the fact that things happen otherwise than he intended, they want nobody except God to have free choice. For only God accomplishes whatever he wills.

But it is one thing to will and elect freely in virtue of your own discretion, but an other thing to work out in virtue of your discretion whatever you will. The former pertains to the nature of free choice; the latter to the powers of him who wills, which certainly only properly has place in God. Therefore this statement is not to the point.

3. Still others for that reason deny that there ever has been or is any man who has free choice, because they read that God works everything in everyone, and leads everyone by his own decision, and bends the hearts of men wherever he wills.

But they too hallucinate most shamefully. For the first cause does not exclude secondary causes. On the contrary, God leads whatsoever according to its own nature and character: he moves natures and wills, not by coercing but by bending; and from not-willing often makes them willing. Led by him they act, and that freely, without any compulsion. Therefore all these people have badly interpreted the term "free choice" and have defined it according to its worst interpretation; for it does not consist in the faculty of doing or achieving whatsoever, but in the faculty of freely willing or not-willing.

4. Next, there are some who reduce the term "choice" to the intellect, so that it signifies the judgment; but the term "free" to the will so that "free choice"

---

8. Livius, *Ab urbe condita*, book XXXIV, section 7.

9. We could not identify the exact quotation from Ovid. Most similar is the sentence "ius tibi et arbitrium nostrae fortuna salutis tradidit inque tua est vitaque morsque manu" from *Heroides* XII, Medea Iasoni.

would be nothing else but the judgment which, made by the intellect, the will chooses or rejects.

Although, concerning the matter itself, the will indeed chooses or rejects nothing, unless the intellect has judged it to be chosen or rejected, nevertheless I cannot approve of this interpretation of free choice, as if it were nothing but the judgment that the will freely follows and chooses, so that "choice" belongs to the intellect, but "free" to the will. For the adjective "*liberum*" is conjoined with the substantive "*arbitrium*"; and therefore "free" must refer to the same potency as "choice," in order to be "free choice."

[*Free choice means free will*]

So, what does the term "free choice" signify? It signifies the free agreement (*placitum*) of the will; for the will freely assents to and, so to speak, delights in anything proposed to it by the intellect; and by that, according to its free agreement, wills or wills not, chooses or rejects. This is the true meaning and etymology of "free choice."

"Choice" means agreement, arising from consultation and selection, because you choose, when two things are proposed by the intellect, the one and more desirable of them, leaving the other aside, in accordance with the free agreement of your will. That agreement is called "choice", as the verb *arbitrari* pertains to the courts, when it is decided which of both parties rests upon justice. So, Cicero often uses the phrase "to do in accordance with one's choice" instead of "to do something out of one's agreement." Aristotle calls it in the *Ethics* προαιρεσις. Hence, "free choice" signifies nothing but the free agreement of the will that follows the deliberation of reason or mind.

In short, nothing else is signified with this term in the Church but "free will" (*libera voluntas*). For the Latin Fathers wished to express with this term nothing else than the Greek with their αὐτεξουσιον. For what else does this term signify than free will? For the will is the only thing in man that is truly αὐτεξουσιος, that is, in its own right and its own power, which can be coerced by nobody. The intellect cannot be αὐτεξουσιος; for it is often forced to think and to do its duty. Therefore, the Latins, not only the sacred but also the profane writers, wanted to signify by the term "free choice" free will. Cicero in defense of Sextus Roscius says: "By the wink and choice of God all things are led," that is, by the free will of God. And concerning Brutus: "To feign and assimilate totally to someone's wink and choice," that is, to someone's will.[10]

Now, we can comprehend what is to be understood, with the Fathers and in the Church, by the term "free choice": namely, free will. Therefore, by saying that Adam had free choice we understand that he was endowed with a free will.

[*Common interpretation of free choice: it only deals with means, not with ends*]

II. Next, it should here in the second place be noted that the action of the will is twofold: the one concerning the self-evident ends, be they good or bad; the

---

10. Cicero, *Pro Sexto Roscio Amerino Oratio*, 131; *Tusculanae Disputationes*, lib. V, cap. XXVIII; *Orator*, VIII.

other concerning the means to be accepted in order to pursue good ends or to avoid bad ones.

The philosophers and even many theologians do not want the first kind of actions to belong to free choice. The reason: because [706] there is no consultation by us concerning self-evident ends; but as being immediately self-evident, naturally without any deliberation or consultation of the mind, we either accept them necessarily, if they are good, and the will is naturally drawn towards them, or we reject them if they are bad and unpleasant for us.

Free choice is properly the free agreement of the will that follows the deliberation and consultation of reason or the mind. So, they argue, only the second kind of actions properly belongs to free choice, and free choice properly deals [only] with them. The reason is that, as concerning self-evident ends, no errors can happen and therefore in them no deliberation of the mind is needed that the will would follow, yet concerning the means, we can easily hallucinate, and therefore deliberation and diligent consultation is needed. So, they argue, when free choice properly deals with the things about which there is consultation and deliberation (because in selection there can occur error), then the action of free will concerning means is the action of free choice properly spoken; likewise, when, to the contrary, the action is concerning self-evident ends, it is the proper action of the simple will, not of free choice: since free choice is the free agreement of the will following the deliberation of the mind.

I explain the matter with one or two examples. The intellect immediately understands that health is a good thing, and hence to be strived for and to be pursued; and therefore also the will naturally strives and wills for it without any consultation of the mind. However, because it is not really clear which is the way to go, either to regain or to keep health, therefore here much deliberation and consultation is needed. So they state that to the first thing, as being the end, properly the simple will belongs.

Hieronymus has a middle position. He argues that the free agreement belongs to the will (*voluntas*) in so far as it is called by Aristotle προαιρεσις. So, to be happy and to enjoy God and to live eternally, in itself everyone strives for without deliberation. For that reason, the will is led naturally to this end. But because the means towards this end, which are repentance towards God and faith in Jesus Christ as Paul says, are not self-evident for everybody, therefore about them there is deliberation and hence also free choice.

And this is what Aristotle teaches (*Ethics* book 3): "The will rather regards the end; the deliberation and προαιρεσις regard the things that lead to the end." So, Aristotle calls προαιρεσις (as I said above) what we call free choice. Likewise Thomas Aquinas defines it too (*Summa* part 1, question 83, article 4). And from this definition, it follows that free choice pertains merely to the means, as we said above. For it is apparent that the free agreement of the will moves around the means about which it properly deliberates. And in this regard, the words of the son of Sirach are properly understood (*Ecclesiast.* chapter 15): "He (God) created man from the beginning, and left him to the choice (*arbitrium*) of his own deliberation (*consilium*): if you will, you will keep my commands," and "Fire and water he presented to you: reach out your hand to which of both you will."

[Free choice pertains to both means and ends]

Although these things are all true, nevertheless I judge that in theology the term "free choice" is more broadly extended, namely when in an absolute sense it is accepted for the free will with which we will both the ends and the means. I am driven by these reasons:

1. Because often, even with profane writers, "free choice" is accepted for just the simple will, as is obvious for not ignorant people; for with the Fathers, in particular with Augustine, nothing is more certain than this. 2. Next, in Scripture we see openly that the will not only concerns the ends, but also the means, as it (expresses): if you will (namely, hear and keep the law), you will eat the goods of the earth. For Scripture does not use the term "free choice," but in its place always the term "will." 3. Even the Greek Fathers willed to signify by the term αὐτεξούσιος the whole faculty of rational appetite, that is the will, both of the means and of the ends. 4. You may add that even the blessed men in heaven and the angels are given free choice, although there is no more need of any deliberation and consultation. Indeed, they have truly more free choice than Adam had, as Augustine and Bernard show. Still, it is not so, as I said, that deliberation further precedes the action of their will. Why? Because nobody has a more perfect free choice than God? Still, everything he wills, he wills by his simple will that needs no consultation, by his infinite wisdom knowing everything most perfectly, both ends and means.

Therefore, not without reason do we understand and do we teach that the term "free choice" has to be understood in theology as the whole faculty of intellective appetite, which is called "will," and by which we will whatever we will, both means and ends, both ends and means. Therefore when the question is posed whether Adam was endowed with free choice, we ask concerning his whole will: whether it was truly free, or not.

[The threefold freedom of Adam]

III. Now, in the third place it is to be seen how Adam's will was free, and what is the proper freedom of the human will. The threefold freedom should be remembered [707], which Saint Bernard teaches in his treatise on *Grace and Free Choice*.[11] He points out a threefold freedom in Holy Scripture: One freedom from sin; the other from misery; the third from necessity. But by the term "necessity" he understands coercion, as clearly appears from his whole context, especially when he deals with us all.[12] For Adam was free from necessity, as we have shown.

But to the point, referring to the first kind of freedom is this word of Christ, "You will be truly free if the Son of man will have freed you."[13] And this word of the Apostle, "Where the Spirit of the Lord is, there is freedom." To this freedom

---

11. Cf. *GFC*, 61-64. Compare also Turrettini's use of the distinction, note 17 in ch. 6 and section 6.4.

12. Zanchi refers to *GFC*, 65, 66.

13. Scripture quotations are translated from the Latin in this chapter, since Zanchi frequently gives his own paraphrase instead of citing the Vulgate literally.

is opposed the slavery of sin, of which Christ says, "He who commits sin, is a slave of sin."

Concerning the second kind of freedom and the slavery opposite to it, is this word of the Apostle (Rom. 8): "The whole creation of God is subjected to vanity, not voluntarily, but due to him, who subjected it in hope: that it too is to be liberated from the bondage of corruption, into the freedom of the glory of God's children."

On the third kind of freedom are almost infinite testimonies of the Scriptures, such as that in Deut. 30: "I invoke heaven and earth as witnesses, that I have proposed you life and death. Choose life, so that you too may live." And that word of Peter to Ananias, Acts 5: "If you had kept it, would it not remain yours? And was it, being sold, not at your disposal?" Also, this freedom is confirmed by all places, in which sin is attributed to man, because he sinned voluntarily, not compelled. For this third freedom of the human will consists in this: that the will wills freely everything it wills, be it good or bad, and without coercion of anyone. And this is the innate and proper, natural and thereby eternal freedom of the human will, which was never lost, even after sin, and never will be lost.

All these kinds of freedom were natural for Adam, because he was created therein. But for our sake Saint Bernard calls the first freedom "freedom of grace," for by grace we are liberated from the slavery of sin. The second he calls "freedom of glory," for we will not be liberated from all misery until we will be in heavenly glory. The third he names "freedom of nature," for it is so conveyed to the whole human nature, that (while the other two were lost in Adam) it will never leave human nature.

So, when the freedom of Adam is discussed, all these kinds of freedom are in question. Hence, we argue, that he was free in all these ways, and that by his own nature, because he was created as such; whence also all these kinds of freedom were natural for him.

[Adam was free towards good as well as towards bad]

IV. Finally, it should be observed what we have said in the end [of the thesis]: that Adam truly had a free choice towards good and bad. For some people are free only towards the bad, such as those who are slaves of sin, the impious men and all devils. But this is rather slavery than freedom: for he who commits sin, is a slave of sin.

Others are free only towards the good, such as the blessed in heaven and God himself. This is the real freedom to which refers the word of the Apostle, "Where the Spirit of the Lord is, there is freedom." So, where the Spirit of the Lord keeps ground, there is perfect freedom and no slavery at all.

Others are so partly free towards the good that they nevertheless are also partly not free; free according to the Spirit, not free according to the flesh, which effects that we do not do whatever we will; to the contrary, it even effects, that we do what we do not will. These are the reborn men, still dwelling in this mortal flesh, about whom the Apostle writes in Romans 7 and Galatians 5. In them, the freedom of the will is not yet perfect, but they partly will the good, and partly do not will it. For he who has a full, true and perfect will, accomplishes everything he can accomplish by his powers. Hence, that someone does not effect what he can do, is due to the fact that he does not yet perfectly will what he seems to will.

Adam was in none of the three kinds: not in the first, because he was not confirmed in grace, as the blessed in heaven. Not in the second, because he had not yet committed sin, and therefore was not a slave of sin. Not in the third, because he did not stand, partly in the sinful flesh, partly in the Spirit, just as we who are reborn in Christ. He was totally ignorant of all sin and concupiscence.

So, there was a fourth kind of freedom in him, because he was free towards both good and bad. This was the proper freedom of Adam, as Scripture shows and the Fathers confirm. Therefore, in order to make a distinction between Adam before the Fall, and all the others after the Fall, be it without grace or under grace or in glory, we introduce this qualification: he truly had free choice towards good as well as bad. His choice was not truly simply free, for someone, who is free only towards the good is more free, as is the free choice of God and the blessed, but, we said, truly free towards good *and bad*, which was initially proper to the Angels and to Adam before the Fall.

Now it remains to confirm the thesis that is already explained.

[*Confirmation of the thesis*]

V. It stands firm that Adam (with whom I also comprise Eve) was endowed before the Fall with a truly free choice towards good and bad, in the three forms of freedom of which we have spoken [708] above.

[*Confirmed by the freedom from coercion*]

For, in the first place, his will was free from all coercion. If this is the nature of all men, even the impious, and that perpetually, that their will cannot be coerced, but that whatever they will, be it good or bad, they will it freely without any compulsion of the will (which everyone experiences in himself); how much more was the will of Adam endowed with this freedom!

So, his will was free both towards good and towards bad, and could not be compelled towards one of both, as also our will cannot. And this freedom of the will is properly the reason why sin is called, and truly is, voluntary: because although the impious cannot do otherwise than to will sin and, if they can, even fulfill it, nevertheless the fact that they will sin, they will it with the highest pleasure, agreement and free assent of the will.

[*Confirmed by the freedom from external and internal bounding*]

But add here that Adam had a will not only free from all coercion but even free from all necessity. For nothing there was for him, either externally or internally, by which he was bound to will or do either bad or good. About the external influences it is clear; for neither God willed to, nor the Angels (good or bad), nor the heavens could prompt him with any necessity either towards the good or towards the bad. That God did not will this, Scripture openly teaches, as we will soon show; that neither Angels nor heavens could, is manifest; because since they do not have such a power and authority over us, in a way that is usually demonstrated from the Scriptures as well as with efficacious arguments, and as was shown by us elsewhere; how could they have it over Adam the first man, created so perfect by God? We can conclude that from the things outside of him no necessity impelled him towards either bad or good.

But it is clear that he likewise had nothing *within him* that would infer on him any necessity either towards the good or towards the bad. For (as I will say later on the necessity towards the bad) he had been created totally righteous, right and good; and hence he was free of all sin, and in him there was no concupiscence at all by which he would be impelled or even attracted towards sinning; as it is now in us, both in the saint and in the impious. This concupiscence, which the Apostle calls "the law of the members, fighting against the law of the mind, and designating us to the law of sin and death," this concupiscence, I say, was not in Adam before the Fall; and therefore he did not have within himself this enemy by which he was attracted or pressed towards the bad. This is that other freedom of which we spoke above, the freedom from sin.

Likewise, he was even not subject to the corruption and the present vanity and misery by which we are compelled to take care of the things that pertain to the health or even the pleasure of the body. While being so busy with these things, it happens that we can make less time for the spirit, and often more than is suitable indulge in our body. Thus, even this misery of the body and the condition of present life is not unfrequently apt for sinning. For sure, due to this weakness of powers and due to this misery we often cannot bring forth the good we long for. Hence, that saying, "The body that is corrupted weighs heavy on the soul." But from this misery Adam was free, which was the third freedom. For he held his body strong and unhurt, bound by no illness or weakness, on the contrary subdued in everything to the soul, to all orders ready and quick and willing, so that due to the body he could no way be hindered to achieve the good.

[*Confirmed by the Scriptures*]

While these things are so, it is apparent that Adam had nothing to do with necessity of choosing or doing the bad, and was completely free. However, that he was even not bound to the good, although he was by his nature good and inclined at most to the good, but the least to the bad, this can no better be shown from Holy Scripture, which declares that Adam was endowed with such freedom of will that he could freely choose or reject both good and bad, both bad and good, if he willed.

Rightly Scripture teaches and urges it: in order to make clear that God was in no way the author of sin, but that the fact that Adam sinned resulted from his own free choice. Let us therefore hear the testimonies of Holy Scripture and the reasons deduced from them.

1. First, this is proved from the form of the precept by which God forbade Adam "to eat from the fruit of that tree." The argument deduced from the law, however, used to prove free choice in us, i.e. (as some interpret it) the free faculty of keeping or not keeping the mandates of God, has no value; because since we are by our nature bad trees, we cannot produce but bad fruits, i.e. to sin, and by this we are not free from the necessity of sinning unless we are

liberated by Christ; but by the precepts of God it is merely signified what we are held to do or not to do. On the contrary, concerning Adam there was an other state of affairs: for since he was created righteous, and the least inclined to the bad, that said law proves that he was free to keep or not to keep it freely. For the most just [709] Lord would not have given him the law if he was not by himself made free at observation or transgression thereof.

So, from the first mandate by which God ordered that Adam should not eat from the fruit of the tree of knowledge of good and bad, it is openly proved that Adam was so free, that he was not bound by any necessity to do either the bad or the good.

2. Second, the punishment added to the sin even more confirms the same: Otherwise (says God) "at the hour that you eat it, you will certainly die." But why this threat, if it stood not free to Adam to keep or not to keep the precept? Although we too are threatened with eternal death, if we do not keep the law; and unless he effects by his grace that we fulfill it, we cannot fulfill, yet there is a difference, as I said, between our state of affairs and Adam's. The fact that we cannot keep the law and on the contrary cannot but transgress it, adheres to us as guilt because we lost in Adam the freedom from necessity. For that reason, whether we can or cannot obey, the just punishment awaits us, and therefore God rightly adds his threats. But Adam was righteous and just so that he could obey the law of God if he willed; and consequently if he would not obey, the just punishment was promulgated. So even the punishment added to the law convinces that Adam was completely free from the necessity of doing or not doing good or bad.

3. Third, in Eccles. 7 it is found that God made "man righteous." To him, however, they have raised many thoughts or questions. He understands all these thoughts, sorrows and passions of life as deviating from this righteousness, and as turned off to the idle things of this world. But there are two things in these words: the first is that God himself made man righteous, i.e. just, good, without any vice, without any inclination towards the bad and the vanities of the world. The other is that these people Adam and Eve, declining by their own accord from the righteousness in God and turning off, both to give ear to Satan and to like the vanities of the world, have involved themselves in various questions, sorrows, solicitudes and passions. From this antithesis between God who made man righteous and men who by their own accord by themselves declined from the righteousness and involved themselves in various difficulties, is clearly proved the true freedom of Adam towards good and bad.

4. Fourth, the son of Sirach, interpreting in chapter 15 this place of Ecclesiastes, makes the matter plain. "He (God) created man from the beginning, and left him to the decision of his own deliberation." Or, as the Greek text has it, "left him in the hand of his own deliberation," ἐν χειρι διαβουλιου αὐτου. But this explains the freedom of choice of Adam. For he indicates first that to him was given the faculty of knowing what was good, what was bad, what was to be followed, what was to be fled, and of deliberation and consultation of what was needed to do, and he indicates this when he calls it διαβουλιον αὐτου, his

deliberation; and this pertains to the intellect which proposes to the will what it thinks to be avoided or to be done.

In addition the son of Sirach teaches that to the will was allowed the free will of assenting or not assenting, choosing or rejecting, willing or not willing. And he does this when he mentions the "hand"; saying "left him in the hand of his own deliberation." This is the free faculty of the will.

And what follows even more confirms the same; for he says "if you will, you will keep my commands," καὶ πίστιν ποιῆσαι, namely you will be able to give trust to your εὐδοκίας; so the observation of the mandates of God was in Adam's power, because it was placed in his will; for he says "if you will, you will keep my commands." (For he introduces God as speaking.) "And you are able to trust your own εὐδοκια," that is: you are able to give the right significance to your free agreement (*beneplacitum*) and your free will. How could Adam trust his free will and free agreement (*placitum*)? By choosing or rejecting. These words certainly teach that Adam was by no thing coerced or bound by necessity to will or do either good or bad.

He continues, with change of speaking person, "Fire and water he (namely God) presented to you: reach out your hand to which of both you will." By the names "fire and water" he understands opposites: fair and unfair, good and bad, life and death. Moses teaches this, who says, Deut. 30 verse 19: "I invoke this day as witnesses against you heaven and earth, that I have presented you life and death, blessing and curse. Now choose life." Yea, the son of Sirach himself explains it in the next verse saying, "Life and death together are presented to man; reach out your hand (says the son of Sirach) to which of both you will," i.e. use your own authority. So, Adam had it in his decision (*arbitrium*) to choose and to do good or bad. He says, "Life and death together are presented to man; which of both he pleases, will be given him." Those who extend these words of the son of Sirach to every man are erring; for not to whatever man is this power, about which the son of Sirach speaks, is allowed, but only to Adam and Eve before the Fall.

All these things teach that our first parents before the Fall had a free will; free, I say, not only from coercion as our wills are also; but even from all necessity because they were free, both from sin, and from misery, what certainly cannot be said of us.

So, we hold from the sacred [710] letters the confirmation of our thesis: *man before the Fall truly had free choice both towards the good and towards the bad*; furthermore that he had a will, free as well from all coercion, as even from all necessity of either sinning, or fulfilling the law, since he was free from sin and from misery, as it was stated; for he had no sin dwelling in him, nor something attracting to sin, nor a body bound to corruption that would weigh heavily on the soul or that would press down the mind, as it is read in Sapientia chapter 9.

And this suffices concerning the nature of free choice.

2.2.2 Free Will in Unregenerated Man after the First Sin

The second text[14] on free choice is taken from *The Fall of the First man, Sin and the Law of God* (*De primi hominis lapsu, de Peccato & de Lege Dei*), which was posthumously published by Zanchi's sons and sons-in-law in 1617. Selected from this book was the chapter on free choice after the Fall. This part treats the nature and powers of free choice in the state of sin, of which we translated only the first section.

[The nature and powers of free choice]

[87] The *locus* on original sin in both the reborn and non-reborn is immediately followed by the *locus* on free choice, both in the one and in the other sort of men. For, when we have demonstrated that, although human nature was not extinguished by original sin, nevertheless it is so corrupted that it can neither in the not yet reborn do good anymore by itself, nor is it perfectly renewed in the reborn in every respect.

Consequently, it is altogether to be discussed, what should be held concerning free choice in both the reborn and the not reborn. So, this *locus* will have two chapters: one, concerning free choice of unregenerated man, the other concerning free choice inasmuch it has been renewed in the reborn and is renewed, day by day. For, even in the choice of the saints, there always is something wrong from which they need to be perfectly liberated by Christ.

Next, there is not one, but a twofold question concerning free choice of any creature endowed with reason, as was stated by us more than once when we dealt with the free choice of the angels, and also when we discussed the creation of man after God's image and his free will towards both good and bad. One is about the nature of free choice in itself, the other about its powers, how far they extend. So, just as we then explained them as separated one from another, also at this moment the one should not be confounded with the other by us. Whence the first question will be about the nature of free choice, the other about its powers.

When this distinction of the question is observed, the whole discussion of the free choice of man becomes more lucid. It is clear that it is a true paradox what otherwise seems to contain contradictory parts, namely: that man even after the Fall does and does not have free choice.

For, if you regard its nature, free choice is always free in man, to which pertain almost infinite testimonies of Holy Scripture and the Fathers, by which free choice is stated in every man. That is why also Augustine says, "Free choice is always free, but not always good."

But when we consider the powers, how can be called free, what is a slave of sin, and by itself can do nothing but sin? For one is subjected as a slave to that, by which one is bound: and, "he who commits sin, is a slave of sin." Therefore,

---

14. Girolamo Zanchi, "De libero arbitrio in homine post ipsum non renato," in *De primi hominis lapsu, de peccato & de lege Dei*, lib. I, cap. 6, in *Omnia opera theologica*, tom. quartus, col. 87-94.

Augustine (*Enchiridion ad Laurentium*, vol. 3, chapter 30[15]) rightly states, "by using badly his free choice, man lost both himself and itself."

For this reason learned men teach, that it should be more truly called enslaved choice than free choice, although the same men unanimously write, that "free choice of every man, be it good or bad, always is so free, that whatever it wills, good or bad, it wills this always freely, always free from any compulsion." This is why Augustine says (*Against Julianus the Pelagian*, vol. 7, book 1, chapter 2[16]): "Free choice did not perish in the sinner, inasmuch as by it they sin most of all, who sin with delight, and agree (*placet*) by this love of sin in what they like (*libet*)."

So, in the different respects of both questions, both are true: that man even after the Fall is and is not endowed with free choice. This is why, in order to come to the explication of the first question, this is our sentence and thesis:

Thesis I
Man after the Fall, although he is made both slave of sin, and bound to many miseries, still has not lost altogether all freedom of choice, but he always retains one that is natural for him.

[Explanation of the thesis]
Because there is not needed much to explain and confirm this thesis, it is useful to repeat in short, [88] what we said more broadly in the *locus* on free choice of man before the Fall. And in the first place, something should be said about the term "free choice," and what is understood by it with the Fathers and in Theology.

[The term free choice]
What we call "free choice," the Greek Fathers called αὐτεξούσιον, as if they said "by his own and proper power and right." We do not deny that, with regard to the nature of our will, which is such that it cannot be coerced by anyone, this term applies even to our free choice. But yet it properly convenes [only] to the one God. For he properly and simply is αὐτεξούσιον, in his own right and power, because the will of God can be coerced by nobody and is governed and bent by nothing but itself. Our wills, however, although they can be coerced by nobody to will something involuntarily (and in so far they are of their own right), still because they depend on God, there is nothing they can will or not will but what by God's eternal decree was determined that they would will or not will; nothing

---

15. The reference "vol. 3" is to the Frobenius edition of Augustine's works (1528 or 1543); see note 16. Quotation from *Enchiridion ad Laurentium* IX, 30, to be found in *MPL* 40, 246.

16. This reference causes some difficulties. First, the "vol. 7" to which Zanchi refers is not a part of Augustine's writing, but indicates the volume in the Frobenius edition of Augustine's works (1528 or 1543), which Zanchi apparently had at his disposal. Second, the exact quotation could not be found in *Contra Julianus the Pelagian*, but instead in *Contra duas epistolas Pelagianorum*, lib. I, cap. II, section 5 (*MPL* 44, 552); and again in *Opus imperfectum contra secundam Juliani Responsionem*, lib. I, cap. XCIV (*MPL* 45, 1110).

they can will or not will, unless when by the hidden action and hand of God they are bent and moved towards willing or rejecting it.

Therefore, the term αὐτεξούσιον does very improperly fit for men, but most properly for God; and more justly the word ἑκούσιον than αὐτεξούσιον is stated of us; whence you find the one applied to man more than once in Holy Scripture, as in Philemon, in Hebrews chapter 10, and in 1 Peter chapter 5, but the other is never used.

And rightly we observe this distinction between free choice of God and of man. For although man is made after God's image and hence endowed with free choice as is God, still he is not made God and hence is not so free and αὐτεξούσιος as God is. So, it is needed that we establish a great difference between free choice of God and of man, not so much concerning the intellect (for there is some comparison between the knowledge of God and of man), as well as concerning the will: because God's will depends on no superior cause, but man's will on God's, so we rightly said that αὐτεξούσιον is properly attributed only to God.

The Latin word *liberum arbitrium* better fits man than the word αὐτεξούσιον, if its true meaning is held. For by the word "free choice" we do not signify the free faculty or power to do whatever, be it good or bad, as some people wanted; for in this sense even God himself would not have free choice, because he can not do the bad, which is sin; nor the angels and blessed spirits, because they can no longer sin; nor finally any of the men would be endowed with free choice, because neither the impious can achieve what is truly good, nor the pious work out any good they want, and none of both have the faculty of doing whatever.

Far less we signify by this word that faculty by which you can accomplish and bring into execution whatever you will or long for. For only God has this faculty, of whom alone we read in Psalm 115, "Whatever God wills, he does in heaven and on earth," whereas all the others, both angels and men, so depend on God's will and hand, that they can neither work out nor even will, but what the Lord wills them to will and work out; and conversely they cannot not will and not work out what the Lord wills and works them to will and work. So, it is clear that by the word "free choice" is not signified at all the faculty of doing and working out whatever.

So, this is the true signification of this term: "The faculty of freely willing or not willing, anything proposed by the intellect that you will or will not; or it is the free agreement [*placitum*] of the will [*voluntas*], which follows the deliberation of the reason or mind, and therefore it is the same faculty of freely willing or not willing, which is called the will."

Therefore, although by the term "free choice" the will itself is signified, still because the will follows the judgment of the mind, even the faculty of understanding itself is comprised. For *arbitrium* signifies in the Latin writers the agreement consisting of consultation and choice; namely, when two things being proposed by the intellect, you choose (after rejection of the one) the other as preferable in virtue of your own free will; whence also for Cicero to do something in accordance with one's choice is nothing but to do it in accordance with the agreement of one's will, which agreement Aristotle calls προαίρεσις; and Cicero often signifies the same free will with the term free choice.

In sum, by this term is signified by the Latins "the faculty of freely willing or not willing something, that is, the free will itself that in its willing and not willing follows the judgment of the mind, as well as the action of the will, that is, the free agreement of the will."

Next, when we theologians dispute about free choice we start a discussion not of any action of the will whatsoever, but of the will itself, the faculty of willing and not willing, whether it wills ends or means.

For the philosophers establish a twofold action of the will: one that moves around self-evident ends, be it good or bad; another about the means to be accepted in order either to pursue good ends [89] or to avoid bad ones. Well, the first kind of actions they signify by the noun "will," calling it ϑελησις, because the will is naturally without deliberation drawn into ends that are good in themselves; but the other they call προαιρεσις, because concerning the means deliberation is needed, which of them are to be chosen, or which to be rejected; and thus they want free choice properly to move around this second kind of actions.

In theology, however, as we have said before, we do not restrict the term free choice to προαιρεσις, but understand by it the whole faculty of willing and not willing, whether it wills the end or chooses the means. For what we call free choice the Holy Scriptures call the will. And this suffices concerning the signification of the term free choice, because we have already said many things elsewhere.

[Free choice is free from coercion]

However, in what sense do we say our will, even after sin, has remained free and has not been deprived from any freedom at all? In the second place, therefore, the threefold freedom is to be observed which Saint Bernard in his book on *Grace and Free Choice* wisely collected and observed from Holy Scripture. One he calls "freedom from sin," another "from misery," the third "from necessity," that is, "from coercion."

What is *freedom from sin* is known to all. The most free from it is God; free are the Angels and all blessed spirits; of which freedom Christ says in John, chapter 8, "You will be truly free, if the Son of man will have freed you." This perfect liberation will occur in the resurrection of the dead. Opposed to this is the slavery of sin, according to that saying, "He who commits sin, is a slave of sin." With respect to us, Bernard calls this freedom the "freedom of grace," because by grace we are freed from the slavery of sin.

Bernard says that the *freedom from misery* is that one by which Adam was free before sin; because he was not bound to death and any corruption; and that we all will be free from it when we will be in heaven; yeah, that even all creatures will participate in this freedom, according to that saying of Rom. 8, "The whole creation is subjected to vanity, not voluntarily, but due to him, who subjected it in hope: that it too is to be liberated from the bondage of corruption, into the freedom of the glory of God's children."

Therefore, Bernard calls it "freedom of glory"; to which is opposed the slavery of all misery which even God's children experience in this world. Further, inasmuch as the freedom from misery is referred to the will, only God's will is truly free from all misery because it is free from all subjection. For nothing prohibits him, but he can do whatever pleases him; and whatever he wills, he is prevented by no law nor any thing to achieve it. But the wills of all creatures are subjected to God's will, so that neither is it possible for them to will, unless what God wills and prescribes by his law, nor can they even achieve any of the things they will unless inasmuch as God provides them with the powers to complete what they will. And this way Adam's will did not fully enjoy this freedom before the Fall; far less does our will enjoy this freedom.

What is the *freedom from necessity*, is known as well. For he who cannot be coerced to any thing is truly called free from any coercion. But it is certain that the will, be it good or bad, is of such nature that it cannot be coerced to its own actions, that is to be willing or not-willing; for the implication of a contradiction would follow, namely that it willed something not willing or willing not. And thus this is the innate, proper and inseparable freedom of the human will, that, whatever it wills or not wills, be it good or bad, it wills or wills not this freely without coercion by any external principle.

Therefore, not unjustly Bernard calls this freedom the "freedom of nature," whereas he calls the first "of grace," the second "of glory." For it is inborn by nature to the will of the rational creature that it wills all things freely without any coercion; and hence he even has it as an eternal freedom of this nature.

[*Freedom from necessity is freedom from coercion, not from every necessity*]

And this is the reason, why all things, even the sins of the impious, which they cannot avoid, are called voluntary and are imputed to them; for although they cannot act otherwise than to sin, still because they will (*volunt*) their sin, they will it with the highest delight of the will and with free agreement and assent. To this pertain all those places in Holy Scripture in which sin is imputed to man, and he is proven to have voluntarily sinned. Acts 5, Peter to Ananias: "If you had kept it, would it not remain to you; and once given was it not in your power?" Christ clearly teaches "that a bad tree cannot produce good fruits, but only bad ones," but that still they all justly are to be punished because they sinned by their free will, coerced by no one.

For everyone the witness hereof can be his own conscience, so that it is not needed to seek for consultation far away. "While their own conscience (says the Apostle, Romans 2) renders them witness." "For sure, in the day of judgment everyone will be judged out of his own mouth," as Christ says, "because everyone's conscience will make himself manifest that he, whatever sin he has admitted, he has admitted freely and without coercion."

So, it is clear what we said in the Thesis, that man after the Fall, although he is made [90] both slave of sin, and bound to many miseries, still has not lost altogether all freedom of choice. For he retains and always will retain the natural freedom which is called the freedom from coercion, as was abundantly explained.

All Fathers subscribe to this doctrine, not to mention the Scholastics and the Doctors of our time. Augustine (*Enchiridion*, vol. 3, chapter 30[17]) says that by whom one is bound, up to him one is delivered as a slave. "When this statement is

---

17. See note 15.

right, I ask of what kind can the freedom of the bound slave be, unless when he likes it to sin; for he is freely enslaved who willingly fulfills his master's will, and so, he is free to sin, because he is a slave of sin." Here, Augustine nicely teaches how man after the Fall both became a slave and remained free. A slave of sin because he sins necessarily; still free because he sins freely and willingly. And *Contra Jul. Pelag.*, vol. 6, books 1 and 2:[18] "Free choice did not perish in the sinner, inasmuch as by it they sin most of all, who sin with delight, and agree by this love of sin in what they like."

Therefore, they err shamefully who for this reason think "that man after the Fall is no longer free, because he is tied to sinning by the necessity of his corrupted nature," and who therefore argue "that we take free choice away from man, because we say that impious men sin necessarily." For the freedom of our will does not consist in this that it is driven by no necessity to sinning, but in this that it is free from all coercion.

Indeed, "free" can be said in two ways: either as opposed to a slave, or as opposed to a coerced one. In the former way, the will after the Fall is not free; for it is a slave of sin, as Christ teaches in John ch. 8: "He who commits sin, is a slave of sin"; thus it is free in the latter way, because it cannot be coerced to sin but, whatever it does, it does so spontaneously. And the spontaneous is not opposed to the necessary but to the violated; because it can be both at the same time, necessary and spontaneous. For is not the will necessarily driven to its goal? But is it therefore unwilling and coerced? Surely not, for it wills the last end out of itself and willingly. So, also the impious man sins necessarily and cannot do otherwise but sin, because a bad tree cannot but produce bad fruits, and yet, he does not sin unwillingly and coerced but spontaneously and out of himself. So, in this controversy the distinction should be diligently held between spontaneity, which we call also freedom from coercion, and violation, which we call also coercion.

Spontaneous, and therefore free from coercion, is called that which, although it is moved by an external principle, still has such an internal principle that it is inclined to and agrees with that movement which is impelled by the external principle, just as when some friend takes me with his hand and leads me to an honorable meal. Be it that I am led by an external moving agent, am I therefore said to be drawn unwillingly and by coercion? No, because I do willingly agree with this coercion.

Thus, the will of the pious, although it is moved by God to the good, still is said to move itself spontaneously and freely because it does not resist the divine action, but by internal piety is inclined to this movement and willingly agrees. Hence that saying of John ch. 6: "No one comes to me, unless the Father drew him." He draws, not as coerced, but to the contrary as spontaneous. Contrarily the will of the impious spontaneously is inclined to sin, to which it is stirred up and drawn by Satan; hence no one can, when he agrees with sin, say that he sins out of an unwilling and coerced will, because he also moves himself towards sinning by an internal principle.

---

18. See note 16. It seems that here the volume number is wrongly 6 instead of 7.

Violated, however, and *coerced* is said to be that which is so moved by an external principle that it does not itself give aid to that movement, but does offer resistance; as is the movement by which a stone is thrown upwards. For in no way the stone moves itself by an internal principle to such a movement, thus the movement is merely violated. In the opposite case, if you move a stone downwards, the movement will be natural and spontaneous, because the stone will be moved downwards not so much by an external principle, as by its own proper internal principle; yet it is still moved necessarily both upwards, by a violated movement, and downwards, by a natural and spontaneous movement.

Thus, it appears clearly that, indeed, violated and spontaneous are opposed to each other, and therefore that which moves spontaneously, is not moved with violation, and that which is moved with violation cannot be called to move spontaneously and out of itself, but it also appears that the necessary is opposed to neither the spontaneous nor the violated, because something can at the same time be moved necessarily as well as spontaneously and free from all coercion and out of itself and naturally; also because the other way round we see that many things are moved at the same time necessarily as well as coerced and with violation.

By this observation and these examples our Thesis may be clear, namely: man after the Fall became a slave of sin and therefore he sins necessarily and is not able not to sin; yet he did not lose all freedom, since his will did not lose that freedom, which is called freedom from coercion; and this freedom is so natural to our will that we retain it forever, after the Fall under sin, as well as after the regeneration under grace; even no less [91] than when Adam had that freedom before the Fall; and therefore free choice in man always remains free, namely from coercion, although not from necessity in whatever state.

[*Confirmation of the thesis*]

I confirm this thesis with other testimonies from the Fathers and rational grounds.

[*Confirmed by Augustine*]

1. Augustine, *Retractationes,* part 1, book 1, ch. 15,[19] and the book *On the Two Souls, Against the Manichees*, part 6, ch. 10,[20] defines the will as follows: "The will is the movement of the soul, without coercion, towards either the avoidance of something, or towards the obtaining of it."

   In the first place you see here, what we said above, namely that the will is taken not only for the faculty of the soul by which we will, but also for the action and movement of the will. For Augustine here defines the will as "movement."

   Second, that this is attributed to it as proper and inseparable, namely that all movement of the will takes place without coercion, whether that

---

19. *MPL* 32, 609.
20. *De duabus animabus*, cap. X, 14. To be found in *MPL* 42, 104. Again, the reference to "part 6" in Zanchi's text could be to the Frobenius edition of Augustine's works (see note 15).

movement refers to keeping what you have, or to obtaining what you do not have. Thus the freedom from coercion is proper to the human will and inseparable from it.

Third, he silently teaches that necessity is not contrary to freedom from coercion; for he does not say: the will is the movement of the soul, happening while no necessity obliges, but merely: without coercion. Thus, by this reason the will is called free, not because it is held by no necessity, but because it cannot be coerced. Therefore, after this definition is given, Augustine immediately provides an explanation and conclusion, teaching that the will is free and how it is free, namely because it wills not unwillingly but spontaneously. "Why then," he says, "could I not define this way? Or is it difficult to see that 'unwilling' is contrary to 'willing,' just as we say that left is contrary to right?"

Next, below he concludes in these words: "Everyone who acts unwillingly, is coerced; and everyone who is coerced when he acts, does not act but unwillingly." It remains that the willing one is free from a coercing [principle], although one might think that he is coerced. So it was completely the same for Augustine to say "the will is not free, that is, not spontaneous" as to say "the will is no will." And it would be yet absurd to him to say "that the will is coerced to choosing what it wills not" and to say "that the will wills by not-willing." So, he shows that the willing is opposed to the unwilling and violated.

Therefore, this is the proper and inseparable freedom of the will, namely that it is free from coercion.

2. He makes the same point in the same part 6 on the events with Felix the Manichee, book 2, chapter 8. For when Augustine wants to prove against Felix that Christ was not cruel or unjust when he says to some who sinned yet necessarily as slaves of sin: "Go into eternal fire," he adduces an argument from free choice by which they freely and not by coercion rejected the mercy of God, and sinned freely, because voluntarily. Thus, he says, "if there is repentance, there is also guilt; if there is guilt, there is also will; if there is a will in the act of sinning, there is no nature that coerces." These things he says here.[21]

In short he teaches: although men, impious in their nature, cannot do otherwise but sin unless they are liberated by the Son of man from sin, yet it does not follow that they are coerced by nature to sinning. The reason is taken from the nature of the will. This is the reason: they sin voluntarily, for they have guilt; so they are not coerced to sin. For if it is a will, it cannot happen that it is coerced. Why so? Because it is repugnant to the nature of the will.

Hence, it is clear that the natural and perpetual freedom of the will is not the freedom from necessity, but the freedom from coercion. For the will sins necessarily while it is a slave of sin; still it does not sin by coercion because it does not sin unwillingly, but willingly, spontaneously and out of itself. For it does not sin by violated coercion, but by the most willing affection of the soul;

---

21. *MPL* 42, 541.

not coerced by an external principle but necessarily led by the movement of its own desire and the wickedness of its nature.

3. He concludes the same also in part 7 on the perfection of justice, against Coelestius, in argument 9.[22] Coelestius asked, "by what was man made sinful? By necessity of nature or by freedom of choice?" Coelestius wanted to conclude: if by necessity of nature, then man has no guilt; if by freedom of choice, then it can be avoided, because free choice, given by the most good God, is inclined more to good than to bad.

   Augustine answers and says, that it happened by freedom of choice, that he became sinful: "(for Adam sinned freely while he was able to not-sinning), but the subsequent penalty of wickedness of free choice (he says) made necessity out of freedom. Whence faith cries to God: lead me out of my necessities, Lord. Posed under these necessities, either we cannot understand what we will or we do not will nor are we able to fulfill what we understood."

4. In summary he concludes: "man after the Fall sins necessarily, but still the will is not coerced to sin." Largely sufficient, both in the places quoted before and in many, many others, Augustine showed to be always consistent in this matter.

[*Confirmed by Bernard*]

The opinion of the saint Bernard which we referred to above, is clear from the book on *Grace and Free Choice*. For he teaches, that this freedom, the freedom from coercion, is so natural to our will [92] that it cannot be separated from it; whence he also calls it freedom of nature.

[*Confirmed by Thomas Aquinas*]

Neither (to come to the Scholastics) is the statement of Thomas Aquinas different, part 2 of the great *Summa*, q. 6, a. 7 [sic].[23] He asks whether violence can be brought on the will. He answers: no way. The reason: because what happens by the will cannot happen by coercion. But concerning the actions of the will, he makes this distinction. Let me refer to his opinion faithfully:

"The action of the will is twofold: one that is properly of the will, because it is immediately elicited and produced by it. And this is to will or not to will. The other that is in fact imperated by the will, but delivered to execution by another faculty of man, as is to walk, talk, etc. For these movements, it is true, are imperated by the will but are completed by a moving potency each by its own instruments. Now, what concerns the acts imperated by the will, the will can suffer violence, inasmuch as the members can be hindered by external power to execute the command of the will, but what concerns that proper act of the will, which is to will and not to will, no violence can be inferred on the will. The reason is that the act of the will is nothing but some inclination, proceeding from an internal knowing principle, just as the natural appetite is nothing but some

---

22. *De perfectione iustitiae*, cap. IV, arg. 9. To be found in *MPL* 44, 295-296.

23. Here, Zanchi refers to the wrong article of *quaestio* 6 in the *Summa Theologiae*, part 2.1 (=Prima Secundae): it must be article 4 ("Utrum violentia voluntati possit inferri"), not article 7.

inclination, resulting from an internal, not knowing, principle.[24] However, what is coerced or violated, is from an external principle. Therefore, it is against the character of that proper act of the will to be coerced or violated, just as it is against the character of the natural inclination, say, of a stone, to move upwards. For a stone can be thrown upwards by power, but it cannot happen that this violated movement occurs out of its natural inclination. And similarly man can be drawn by violence; but what happens out of his will is contrary to the character of violence." All these things from the Father of Scholastics, Thomas Aquinas.

From these quotations it is more than sufficiently confirmed what we said, that this is the proper freedom of the human will, indeed perpetual, namely, that pertaining to its proper actions, which are to will and not to will, to choose and to reject, the will is always free from all coercion, although often what pertains to the imperate acts, they are not always brought forth by its power.

So, we see that nothing is more certain than what we said in the Thesis "that man even after the Fall did not lose his natural freedom of will, and that this is freedom, not from necessity, but from coercion."

[Freedom from coercion agrees with necessity of sin and immutable providence]

No arguments can be brought against this doctrine that can not easily be refuted because of what we have said. For this is the most important argument that usually is and can be used in this matter, deduced from necessity:

[*First objection*]: What happens necessarily by someone, that does not happen freely, and by that the agent himself is not free. For free is said to be, what can from two or more proposed things, choose at pleasure that which it wills. But the will of man (according to you) after the Fall necessarily wills sin, unless it is liberated by Christ from the slavery of sin. Thus it is in no way free after the Fall.

Answer: The fallacy is of homonymia in the term "free." For one is called free in a twofold sense, either inasmuch he is not anyone's slave, and free from all necessity, or inasmuch he does be a slave and is not liberated from the necessity of slavery, yet he still is free from all coercion, because what he does in service, he does with pleasing soul and spontaneously, although he does it necessarily.

Now we say that such is the freedom of the human will both before and after the Fall, both under grace and in glory. For (as was said above) to do freely whatever one does and still to do it necessarily, are not mutually repugnant. Is not God necessarily good, just, merciful? Is he then so by coercion and with violation? And is therefore God not free or truly endowed with free choice because he cannot will not to be God or to be such a God as he is? Do not also the holy angels in heaven and the souls of the blessed necessarily will what they will, namely only the good things that are in accordance with God's will? That is certain, because they are so confirmed in grace that they cannot will the opposite. Would you then say, because of this necessity, that they are not endowed with free choice? Not at all! As Augustine shows very well, they are endowed with a more perfect and more free choice than we who can sin. On the other hand, are not

---

24. "Sicut appetitus naturalis est quaedam inclinatio ab interiore principio et sine cognitione." The term "appetitus naturalis" refers to "instinct."

even the devils from such a nature that they always sin necessarily and cannot resist from sinning? Would we then say that they do not sin freely, and by that the sins cannot be held against them? Nothing less.

Thus, given that even on earth men after the Fall are so made slaves of sin, that they cannot not sin, and on the other hand, he who is born out of God does not sin, nor can he sin (as John says in the first epistle, ch. 2), namely wholeheartedly, persistently, and until death, hence neither for these nor for those the innate freedom of the will is removed which is the freedom from coercion. [93]

In the same way is answered to another argument that some use to deduce from the immutable providence of God by which all things are necessarily governed:

[*Second objection*]: What is governed by the immutable providence of God, that does not act freely. But the wills of all men are governed this way.

Answer: There are two sorts of things that are governed by God's immutable providence: there are some things that are destitute of all judgment and choice, as are the inanimate things and all animate things that lack reason. Concerning these beings the argument is conclusive, although even in them nothing happens from this providence of God with violation and against their natures.

There are other beings that are so governed by God that they still act even out of their own knowledge, deliberation and choice, as the angels and men, both good and bad. Concerning them the argument concludes nothing. For although with respect to the moving and governing God, whatever they do, they do it by immobile necessity, still with respect to their intellect and will, that is, their free choice, they do nothing knowingly and willingly unless out of free choice. But all of this must be named after the nearest cause, not after the remote cause.

And it is certain that God, although he does everything out of his own principle, still governs the creatures so that he maintains their natures and does not remove them. So the statement stands firm: that neither by the immutable providence of God, nor by any necessity of nature or of grace, the true and natural freedom of the will is removed: and that this freedom is the freedom from coercion, but not from necessity; and therefore even after the Fall man did not lose this freedom.

So, now I add a second Thesis, by which free choice is defined, what concerns its essence and nature:

Thesis II
Free choice is the faculty of the soul, free from all coercion, called "will" which, following the judgment of the intellect, out of itself either longs for or rejects all things proposed to it, both the desirable and the rejectable.

[*Explanation of the thesis*]
This is the general definition, by which the essence or nature of free choice is defined without any mentioning of its own powers, or the actions to which it

extends, or God's grace by which it is helped and bowed towards the good, but only the essence of the faculty is defined.

So also Origen, Περι ἀρχων, part 1, book 3, ch. 1, where he deals loosely[25] with free choice, defines only the nature of free choice when he says: "Free choice is the faculty both of reason to discern good and bad, and of the will to choose one of both." But let us briefly walk through our definition.

It is a faculty of the soul. This is the genus. For all potencies of the soul are called faculties, i.e. δυναμεις. And they are called *facultates,* because by them those things happen easily *(facile)* to which they were destined by the Creator. The intellect is in this way a faculty to understand, because we do understand. The memory is in this way a faculty to remember, because we easily remember the things past. So, the will is a faculty by which we easily will or not-will, choose or reject the things proposed by the intellect. This properly is what we signify by the term "free choice," although it does not will or not-will something without the intellect. Therefore Origen embraced both faculties in the definition of free choice, although what is properly called free choice is the will itself. For only the will is free. So we added for the sake of explanation:

Called "will." For Holy Scripture does not use the noun "free choice," but only "will."

Free. This is the quality proper to the will. So by this particle it is distinguished from all other potencies of the soul.

From coercion. For this is essential to the will and thus even perpetual, that it always be free from coercion; not, however, that it always be free from sin nor from misery; much the less that it be free from necessity, because when it is bad, it necessarily wills the bad, when it is good, the good, above all in heaven where it will be confirmed in the good. But it must always be free from coercion; otherwise to remove this freedom from it, it would no longer be a will, as Origen teaches very well, and after him Augustine and others. But from which coercion is it free?

From all. I have added this lest someone would perhaps think that it is in fact free from coercion by men and Satan but not from coercion by God. For also God does not ever coerce it; although "He bends and leads and turns everything where he wills it," as Solomon teaches. For even when he changes it and makes it good out of bad, and willing out of not-willing, he does not exert power onto it but persuasively leads it so that it, being led, spontaneously even moves itself immediately.

Which, following the judgment of the intellect. First, we do not understand by the term "intellect" [94] the *theoretical* intellect; for this, occupied only with the contemplation of the things, does not propose anything to the will as to be chosen or rejected; but we understand it as the *practical* intellect to which proper quality it is to think [*cogitare*] the things that belong to the *practice* and to propose them to the will. But let still no one think that the theoretical and the practical intellect are two mutually different faculties of the soul. For it is one and the same; but when it understands things pertaining to practice it is called *practical,* when it understands things pertaining merely to theory it is called *theoretical.* Therefore,

---

25. The text is difficult to read: it seems to give *duffuse,* which we interpreted as *diffuse.*

on its turn, the will follows the intellect because it is blind in itself. Thus God willed these faculties, intellect and will, to be different so that the former sees and knows instead of the latter and the latter in turn chooses and rejects instead of the former, and the one gives a hand to the other. However, I said: following the "judgment," but not the "consultation" or "deliberation." For consultation is concerning the means; but judgment is also concerning self-evident ends. For where the intellect sees these things, it immediately passes the judgment that they are to be rejected or chosen. Now, above we have said that free choice, according to the opinion of the Philosophers, moves merely around the means which need consultation, but that in theology we still understand by this term the will itself inasmuch as it wills or wills not both the ends and the means. So, this is the reason why we said "judgment" and not "consultation."

Hither also comes what we have said in the seventh place, *all things, both desirable and rejectable*. For even the ends are desired or despised, not only the means. Towards those all the will is brought and they are objects of the will.

Out of itself either longs for or rejects. Out of itself, spontaneously, i.e. as the Greek say ἐχουσιως; which word the Apostle uses in Hebrews, and Peter. The opposite is ἀχουσιως, unwillingly. But it is necessary if the will is free from all coercion, that it does will or not-will all things it chooses or rejects, wills or wills not, not ἀχουσιως but ἐχουσιως. If the will is truly free from all coercion, it is necessary that only the immediate and proper actions of the will be free from coercion; these are the actions which the Scholastics call elicited acts, i.e. to will and not to will. The other acts, which are called imperate acts, are not always such; for often the will commands tongues and hands to do something, which it commands still not simply ἐχων but also ἀχων, as when it commands to throw the ware in the sea in order to save life; as when it commands Peter's tongue to deny Christ for the sake of defending his life; but still the fact that it even wills this, it wills ἐχουσιως. So, it is proper only to those operations that are the immediate and proper actions of the will alone, i.e. to will and not to will, that they always happen truly ἐχουσιως.

[*Confirmation of the thesis*]

This explanation of the definition of free choice is so clear that it needs no demonstration, especially because it was proved sufficiently and often what is the most important in this question and definition, namely: that free choice is a faculty of the soul which is called will, so naturally free from all coercion that it cannot be a will, unless it be free this way, and that therefore this is the eternal freedom of the will. For this we have abundantly demonstrated with the first Thesis.

2.3 Structure of the Text

The structure of Zanchi's detailed discussions of free choice can be mapped as follows:

1. The nature of free choice before the Fall
   a. Thesis: Man before the Fall truly had free choice towards both good and bad.
   b. Explanation of the thesis
      i. The meaning of the term *liberum arbitrium*
         1. Wrong interpretations
            a. The power of doing whatever good or bad
            b. The ability to accomplish whatever one wills
            c. Free choice excluded by God's all-operating power
            d. Separation between "arbitrium" as belonging to the intellect and "liberum" as pertaining to the will
         2. Right interpretation: *liberum arbitrium* is the free complacency of the will, or, in short, the free will.
      ii. The object of free will
         1. Most current (philosophical) interpretation: free will concerns the means, not the ends; the ends are willed by the simple will
         2. Right (theological) interpretation: free will concerns both means and ends
      iii. The freedom of Adam:
         1. Adam possessed the threefold freedom distinguished by Bernard of Clairvaux:
            a. Freedom from sin = freedom of grace: lost by the Fall
            b. Freedom from misery = freedom of glory: lost by the Fall
            c. Freedom from necessity = freedom of nature: remains forever
         2. Different applications of the freedom towards good and bad:
            a. Free only towards the bad: impious men and all devils
            b. Free only towards the good: the blessed in heaven and God
            c. Partly free towards the good, partly bound to sin: the reborn men
            d. Free towards both good and bad: only Adam (and the Angels) before the Fall
   c. Confirmation of the thesis:
      i. By the freedom from coercion
      ii. By the freedom from all external and internal bounding
      iii. By the Scriptures

2. The powers of free choice before the Fall (not discussed in this commentary)

3. The nature of free choice after the Fall
   a. Thesis I: Man after the Fall is slave of sin and bound to misery, but still has retained the freedom of choice that is natural for him.
   b. Explanation of the thesis

    i.   The meaning of the term *liberum arbitrium*
1. Man is, unlike God, properly spoken not *autexousios*.
2. Wrong and right interpretations of *liberum arbitrium* (see 1.b.i.1-2 above).
3. Discussion is not about specific actions, but about the faculty of willing itself, concerning both ends and means.

    ii. The freedom of sinners is freedom from coercion
1. The threefold freedom of Bernard:
   a. No freedom from sin
   b. No freedom from misery
   c. Remaining freedom from necessity (i.e., freedom from coercion, not from every necessity)
2. Conclusion: Sinners are free, though they cannot avoid sin; they sin voluntarily, not coercedly.
3. The conclusion confirmed by Scripture, conscience and tradition

   iii. Freedom from coercion compatible with necessity of sin
1. Freedom from coercion is "spontaneity," as opposed to "violence"
   a. "Spontaneous" qualifies an internal principle, which, though being moved by an external principle, agrees out of itself with this movement.
   b. "Violent" qualifies an internal principle, which resists itself against a movement by an external principle.
2. "Spontaneous" is opposed to "violent," not to "necessary."
3. Sin imposes internal necessity, but no external violence.

c. Confirmation of the thesis
    i.   Testimonies from the Fathers:
1. Augustine: The proper freedom of the will is freedom from coercion; after the Fall, man sins necessarily, but free that is, not coerced.
2. Bernard: Freedom from coercion is natural.
3. Thomas: Imperate acts can be coerced, but elicited acts are always free.

    ii. Refutation of arguments against the doctrine
1. First objection from the necessity of sin
   a. Objection: What happens necessarily, does not happen freely.
   b. Answer: Freedom has a twofold meaning:
      (i) opposed to slavery
      (ii) opposed to necessity
      In the former sense, man is free; in the latter sense he is not free from all kinds of necessity.
2. Second objection from the immutability of providence
   a. Objection: What happens according to divine providence, does not happen freely.
   b. Answer:
      (i) What is necessary with respect to the remote cause, can be free with respect to the nearest cause.
      (ii) God's providence maintains the natures of his creatures: they act out of their own deliberation and choice.

   d. Final definition: Free choice is the faculty of the soul, free from all coercion, called "will" which, following the judgment of the intellect, out of itself either longs for or rejects all things proposed to it, both the desirable and the rejectable.
      i. Explanation of the elements of the thesis
      ii. Confirmation of the thesis (by reference to the previous thesis)

4. The powers of free choice after the Fall (not discussed in this commentary)

The main structure of Zanchi's treatment of free will consists of two levels. The first level is the distinction between the different states (*status*) of man: the state of righteousness (before the Fall), the state of sin (after the Fall), the state of grace (concerning the believers), and the state of glory (eternal life in heaven). The implications of this four-state-distinction will be discussed in section 8 of this commentary.

The second level concerns the distinction between the nature of free will in itself and the powers of free will in actual life.[26] For our present purpose, we will limit ourselves to Zanchi's treatment of the nature of free will in the different states.[27] In our commentary, five elements receive further consideration subsequently:

Terminological clarification (section 2.4)
Nature and object of free will (section 2.5)

---

26. *Omnia opera,* tom. tertius, col. 704. In our terms, we can describe this as the distinction between essential freedom and accidental, state-bound freedom (see section 1.4.2).

27. As we leave out the "powers" of free will from our discussion, we briefly indicate the contents of Zanchi's treatment of this topic. Concerning the powers of Adam *before* the Fall, Zanchi mentions the scholastic discussion about Adam's ability to persevere in obedience to God without the (supernatural) aid of grace. He states that, whereas knowing and loving God was natural for Adam, he needed God's auxiliary grace to stay faithful. This grace was indeed present, though not in the form of actually prohibiting Adam from the Fall: God left Adam in the possibility to sin or not to sin. From Zanchi's argument, it is clear that he rejects a separation between "nature" and "supernature." See *Omnia opera,* tom. tertius, col. 710-714. Regarding the powers of free will *after* the Fall (in unregenerate and regenerate man respectively), Zanchi remarks that this is a properly *theological* question, to be decided on the basis of Scripture. He distinguishes three classes of actions: natural (eating, sleeping), political/civil or moral (buying, fighting, learning), and religious (repenting, believing, obeying God). Of all these sorts of actions, man after the Fall is capable in the sense of *potentia passiva* (it is not logically impossible that man is their subject). Man still has the power (*potentia activa*) to perform natural actions, though not as perfectly as was intended by the Creator. Concerning civil and moral actions, man is so blinded that, in addition to God's general assistance, he needs the special light of God's grace to discern the right and good course of action. Zanchi further states that this moral ability is not in turn sufficient to prepare man's receiving God's grace of justification. So the third category, religious actions, is possible only through the grace of regeneration, by which man can perceive God and his benefices, and can choose and perform the right actions towards God. There is no active force in man contributing to regeneration; here, man is purely passive and God fully active. The remainder of Zanchi's lengthy exposition is devoted to controversial questions concerning the doctrines of grace, merit and perseverance. See *Omnia opera,* tom. quartus, col. 94-158. While it would be instructive for establishing Zanchi's theological position to examine the whole discussion, this would exceed the limits of the present volume.

Different kinds of freedom (section 2.6)
Freedom and necessity (section 2.7)
Free will in the different states (section 2.8)

The commentary will end with an analysis of the final definition of free will given by Zanchi (section 2.9) and with a brief evaluation on Zanchi's place in the Reformed tradition concerning free will (section 2.10).

2.4 Terminological Clarification

Zanchi's initial statement concerning free will runs as follows: Man before the Fall truly had free choice, towards good as well as bad. His explanation of this thesis starts with a clarification of the term *liberum arbitrium*. Zanchi discusses four possible interpretations of these words, which he judges incorrect and insufficient.

The first interpretation understands by *liberum arbitrium*: the free faculty or power of doing whatever is good or bad. Zanchi acknowledges that there are passages in classic Latin literature that use *arbitrium* in the sense of "power, authority." But he points at the consequences of this interpretation: since sinful man cannot do the good, he would in this view lack the *liberum arbitrium*. Only Adam before the Fall would in this case be endowed with free will. This consequence is firmly denied by Zanchi, who appeals to the common usage of the term in the Church and with the Fathers.

Although not made explicit by Zanchi, there seems to be a double problem with this first interpretation. First, the confusion of choice and power. Zanchi maintains that the capacity of choosing is not identical with the ability to actually perform the chosen act. The second problem is the fact that free choice does not necessarily imply the potency of choosing the good. Zanchi here anticipates his discussion of man's essential freedom as retained in the state of slavery of sin (cf. sections 2.6 and 2.8 below).[28]

The second interpretation goes one step beyond the first: *liberum arbitrium* is understood as the power to achieve whatever one desires or intends. In this view, it is not enough to have the freedom to will something, but in order to have *liberum arbitrium*, one should be able to accomplish one's goals. And since only God has the power to accomplish everything he wills, it is stated that only God properly has *liberum arbitrium*. Zanchi rejects the confusion of willing and working-out, that takes place in this interpretation.[29] However, Zanchi does admit that only God can properly be called *autexousios*. For this reason he prefers the Latin term *liberum arbitrium* to the Greek *autexousios*, because the former does not imply the connotation of independent power.[30]

A third view on free will takes its starting point in biblical passages stating that God works everything in everyone. From this statement, it is concluded that any free action from man's part is excluded by the fact that everything is caused by

---

28. *Omnia opera*, tom. tertius, col. 704-705.
29. *Omnia opera*, tom. quartus, col. 705.
30. *Omnia opera*, tom. tertius, col. 88.

God. Zanchi indignantly dismisses this conclusion: God as the first cause does not at all exclude the secondary causes. On the contrary, he acts in all his creatures according to their own nature, which is in no case destroyed by God's direction and government. So, in leading and bending man's will, which is by nature free from compulsion, God naturally leaves the *liberum arbitrium* intact.[31]

The fourth interpretation rejected by Zanchi consists of a distinction within *liberum arbitrium* between a rational (intellectual) and a volitional element. In this view, the two components of the term free choice are distributed among the two faculties of intellect and will. The word *arbitrium* then would refer to the rational act of the intellect that makes a choice for the preferable option on rational grounds, and the word *liberum* would refer to the volitional act of accepting or rejecting the option preferred by the intellect. Zanchi acknowledges the fact that intellect and will work together in harmony, so that the will always chooses the thing that the intellect considers the most preferable, but he refuses to allow for the separation of the two elements into intellect and will respectively. He argues that *liberum arbitrium* is one term, in which "free" should refer to the same potency as "will." In his view, *liberum arbitrium* is a free agreement, still arising from consultation and deliberation, but not including this deliberation in itself. This means that Zanchi holds that, when two things are proposed by the intellect as possibilities, it is the will that determines which of both is the most desirable. In contrast to other discussions of the *liberum arbitrium* (e.g., the one by Francesco Turrettini), Zanchi's definition of *liberum arbitrium* does not include the judgment of the practical intellect (but cf. also section 2.9 of this commentary).[32]

Zanchi's own opinion on the proper meaning of the term *liberum arbitrium* is that it signifies nothing but the free will. He holds that this interpretation is supported by the Church Fathers, both Latin and Greek. Concerning the Greek word *autexousios*, Zanchi argues that it does not properly apply to the intellect (which can be forced to think against its will), but solely to the will.[33]

So the result of the terminological clarification can be summarized:

(1) *Liberum arbitrium* is equivalent to free will.[34]

2.5 Nature and Object of Free Will

Zanchi's investigation into the nature of free will focuses on its object: the things that are willed or not-willed.[35] He mentions the traditional view held by many philosophers and theologians, that a distinction should be made between the action of the will concerning the ultimate ends and the action of the will concerning the intermediate means. This distinction parallels with a distinction

31. *Omnia opera*, tom. tertius, col. 705. This insight of Zanchi's is elaborated in section 2.5 of this commentary.
32. *Omnia opera*, tom. tertius, col. 705.
33. *Omnia opera*, tom. tertius, col. 705.
34. For this reason, the translation "free choice" is strictly speaking not applicable in Zanchi.
35. *Omnia opera*, tom. tertius, col. 705-706; tom. quartus, col. 88-89.

between the "simple will" (Greek *thelèsis*, Latin *voluntas*) and the deliberate choice (Greek *prohairesis*, Latin *arbitrium*).

This theory, going back to Aristotle's *Ethics*, is based on the supposition that there are ultimate goals that are self-evident because they are absolutely good and desirable (e.g., happiness, perfection, eternal life).[36] Whenever the will perceives these goals, it is naturally led to pursuing them, without hesitation or need of deliberation. In respect to these goals, the will is called "simple," which means: it acts purely out of itself, without being helped by other faculties of the soul (e.g., the intellect). Whereas the simple will is able to immediately assent to the self-evident ultimate goals, nevertheless it does not suffice to determine the way to attain the established goal. In the selection of the appropriate means, the will interacts with the intellect: the soul uses its rational capacity to survey the various possibilities and to weigh their respective merits; the will makes a decision on the basis of the intellect's ultimate judgment.

Zanchi acknowledges the philosophical utility of this distinction between the twofold action of the will. Still, he feels uneasy about the use of this distinction in the theological treatment of *liberum arbitrium*.[37] He presents an alternative interpretation, in which *liberum arbitrium* is consequently taken as the integral faculty of the will, concerning both ends and means.

It is important to see by which arguments Zanchi is driven. He provides four grounds for his view, three of which are based upon authority:

1. Profane and ecclesiastical writers in Latin often use *liberum arbitrium* as synonymous with the "simple will." Zanchi does not give exact quotations to prove this statement; he apodictically says that "not-ignorant people" do know this is true.
2. Holy Scripture does not have a separate word for the *liberum arbitrium*; instead, always the word "will" is used, even when it is clear that an action of the will concerning means, not concerning ultimate goals, is meant. Zanchi here argues from the contrary: since Scripture uses "will" to signify what the philosophers would call *arbitrium*, it is equally legitimate to interpret *arbitrium* as covering the whole range of actions that is covered by "will."
3. When the Greek Fathers speak of the will as *autexousios*, they do not distinguish between the action of the will concerning ends and means. This argument is important for Zanchi, since he had mentioned the fact that the Greek word *autexousios* is used to signify the same thing as the Latin *liberum arbitrium*. His reference to the Greek Fathers strengthens his claim, that the free will concerns both ends and means.
4. The last argument is taken from the situation of the blessed men and angels in heaven. Zanchi states that they are undoubtedly endowed with *liberum arbitrium*. Yet they do not, due to their state of perfection, need consultation or deliberation. One step further: even God is said to have a free will; but it cannot be said that he is engaged in ample deliberation before he chooses to

---

36. *NE*, book 3, chapters 6 and 7.
37. *Omnia opera*, tom. tertius, col. 706; tom. quartus, col. 88-89.

will something. From this argument, Zanchi concludes that deliberation by the intellect is not necessarily an element of *liberum arbitrium*. One might object that, although there is no discursive deliberation in God, there still is a co-operation between his will and his intellect; which is implicitly conceded by Zanchi when he argues that because of God's infinite wisdom he does not need any deliberation. Zanchi does not provide an answer to this objection.

From Zanchi's investigation into the nature and object of the free will follows the conclusion:

(2) *Liberum arbitrium* (or free will) indicates the whole faculty of intellective appetite, which is called will.

Let us try to trace the implications of this terminological statement. On the one hand, this interpretation of free will seems fit to ensure a broad view of human freedom: when it is accepted that freedom of the will belongs to man's nature, this freedom applies to the choice of both ends and means. So, it follows that when man chooses evil, he does so freely. This conclusion is explicitly drawn by Zanchi (see also section 2.6). [38]

Another consequence of the definition of *liberum arbitrium* as the whole faculty of intellective appetite might be, that the relation between intellect and will remains undecided. Whereas other authors (e.g., Turrettini) allow for a distinction between the intellective and the volitional aspect of free will, Zanchi ties them together with an indissoluble bond by declaring that the will itself is an *intellective* appetite (but cf. also section 2.7 concerning the judgment of the practical intellect).

2.6 Different Kinds of Freedom

Zanchi borrows a well-known distinction made by Bernard of Clairvaux to point at different sorts of freedom that should not be confused in the discussion of *liberum arbitrium*.[39] Bernard distinguished three kinds of freedom, for which he used two parallel sets of terms:

freedom from necessity (*libertas a necessitate*)   freedom of nature (*libertas naturae*)
freedom from sin (*libertas a peccato*)   freedom of grace (*libertas gratiae*)
freedom from misery (*libertas a miseria*)   freedom of glory (*libertas gloriae*)

The importance of this distinction is that it clarifies the various respects in which man is free or bound. Before the Fall, Adam was free in all three respects.[40]

---

38. *Omnia opera*, tom. tertius, col. 707, 708; tom. quartus, col. 89, 90, 91, 92.

39. *Omnia opera*, tom. tertius, col. 707; tom. quartus, col. 89. On Bernard's concept of freedom see Nico den Bok, "Human and Divine Freedom in the Theology of Bernard of Clairvaux: A Systematic Analysis," *Bijdragen, tijdschrift voor filosofie en theologie* 54 (1993): 271-295.

40. It is somewhat confusing that Zanchi calls this threefold freedom of Adam also "natural"; in this usage, the term is not equivalent to "essential." Zanchi displays an integral view of human

But by falling into sin, man lost an important part of his freedom: he now became a slave of sin, and was no longer free to do the good. This freedom from sin can only be regained by the grace of God: the forgiveness of sins by the blood of Jesus Christ and the renewal of the reborn by the Holy Spirit. Zanchi explains how different groups of people share in various portions of this freedom.[41]

First, the sinners who reject the salvation by God are totally slaves of sin and are in no way free towards the good. Second, the blessed men and the angels in heaven, completely filled with God's Spirit, are confirmed in the state of grace and are free only and completely towards the good; there is no possibility for them to commit sin. Third, the reborn men on earth are partly free from sin, inasmuch as the Holy Spirit works in them, and partly not free because of the sin remaining active in their flesh. A fourth, exceptional position is attributed to Adam before the Fall: he was completely free towards either the good or the bad. This initial freedom will never occur again.

As a consequence of the slavery of sin, men after the Fall are also subjected to many miseries. Zanchi explains how the sorrows of life and the weakness of the body prevent us from freely willing the good. Our attention is attracted to many things besides God, and our weaknesses provide a ready occasion for indulging sinful desires. Zanchi states that the effect of these miseries is a serious limitation of the human freedom, a limitation that will be removed when we enter the state of glory. Again, Adam before the Fall was not hindered by misery, and so he was truly free. The degrees of freedom taught by Bernard and Zanchi indicate the limits of the accidental exercise of the freedom of the will. The essential freedom that is basic to the next degrees remains undistorted, according to Zanchi. This statement is important in order to refute the charge that the Reformed doctrine of total depravity of man destroys his essential possession of a will.[42]

The real issue in the debate over the free will is the freedom from necessity. We will discuss the relation between freedom and necessity in the next section. Here, it is important to notice that Zanchi (following Bernard) speaks of a freedom of nature: this freedom is indissolubly connected with human nature, and remains unaffected by the Fall into sin.

Zanchi's discussion of the three kinds of freedom can be summarized as follows:

(3) After the Fall man has lost the freedom from sin and from misery, but he remains endowed with the natural freedom from necessity.

2.7 Freedom and Necessity

If freedom from necessity is, according to Zanchi, essential for man, it is important to reflect on the exact relation between freedom and necessity. From the previous section it is clear that the slavery by sin and misery does not destroy

---

nature in relation to "supernatural" things over against the early modern separation of the natural and supernatural realm.

41. *Omnia opera*, tom. tertius, col. 707.
42. *Omnia opera*, tom. tertius, col. 708.

the most fundamental freedom from necessity. Both Adam before the Fall and his posterity after the Fall possess this freedom of nature.

But what does Zanchi mean exactly by the word "necessity"? He does not provide one neat formula to express the meaning he attaches to necessity. Rather, his view of necessity is to be derived from the examples he provides and the explanation by means of other terms. He closely follows on Bernard of Clairvaux's definitions. It is clear from Zanchi's argument that he interprets the freedom from necessity basically as a freedom from coercion. Zanchi strongly holds that coercion is inconsistent with the nature of the will: it would be contradictory to speak of a coerced will.[43]

In this respect he refers to a helpful distinction made by Thomas Aquinas, between elicited acts and imperate acts of the will.[44] The elicited acts are *immanent* actions of the will, consisting in its inclination towards one of the existing possibilities: it is the will in action to will or not to will. In this category of acts, Zanchi, following Aquinas, firmly maintains that no coercion can be executed by any instance on the will: it is free from all coercion. The imperate acts, on the other hand, are *transient* actions of the will: the will chooses, but the execution of its decision is left to other potencies. For example: a prisoner can freely decide to escape, but he can be effectively hindered in the execution of this plan. The choice by the will itself is free from coercion, but the executive powers can be hindered by external agents or internal failures. So, concerning the imperate acts of the will, there can occur coercion.

(4) Freedom from necessity is freedom from coercion.

An additional clarification is provided by Zanchi's discussion of the terms "spontaneous" and "violent" in relation to both freedom and necessity.[45] The word "spontaneous," closely related to freedom, does not only indicate actions that are performed solely out of a free inner impulse, but also that category of actions in which two acting principles[46] are at work. Someone or something can be moved by an external principle and at the same time have an inner principle that consents with the movement by the external principle. Zanchi gives the example of a friend who takes one with his hand and leads him towards an honorable meal: then one is literally being led by an external agent, while at the same time there is no resistance but rather assent from one's own will. This action can, in Zanchi's view, be called "spontaneous" because the performed action is in accordance with one's own choice. This counts also in the area of religion: when God moves the wills of the pious towards the good, they still can be said to act

---

43. *Omnia opera*, tom. quartus, col. 91: It is the same to say (for Augustine, in Zanchi's words) "the will is not free, that is, spontaneous" as to say "the will is no will."

44. *Omnia opera*, tom. quartus, col. 92. The quotation from Thomas is taken from his *Summa Theologiae*, part 2.1, question 6, article 4 ("Utrum violentia voluntati possit inferri"). See our remark in note 23 above. The same distinction between elicited and imperate acts occurs in the text of Bernardinus de Moor (see 7.2, p. 1053).

45. *Omnia opera*, tom. quartus, col. 90.

46. "Principle" (*principium*) can stand for a personal agent or cause.

spontaneously because the inner principle of their will corresponds to God's purpose. And the other way around, evil men, when they are incited towards sin by the devil, still act spontaneously because they agree with the devil by virtue of their own desires. In short, "spontaneous" is not opposed to necessity arising from an external principle, provided that there still is an internal principle in agreement with the external necessity. The real opposite of "spontaneous" is "coerced," or "violent."

"Violent," the second word explained by Zanchi in this context, is called that type of action in which the movement by an external principle does not correspond with or rather is contrary to the internal principle of the object. Again, Zanchi provides an example to clarify his statement: when a stone is thrown upwards, this movement is called "violent," because the direction of the movement is contrary to the natural inclination of the stone.[47] This action can be called "necessary" as well, because it is necessary, given the fact that an upward power is exerted, that the stone will move upwards. On the other hand, if the stone is thrown downwards, the movement can be called "spontaneous" and "natural" (in accordance with the nature of the stone) and "necessary" as well, because it is necessary, given the external movement and the natural inclination of the stone, that it will move downwards.

The conclusion of this part of Zanchi's argument is that one kind of necessity is compatible with freedom of the will, namely necessity that leaves room for internal spontaneity of the will, while another kind of necessity is opposed to freedom of the will, namely coercion that destroys the natural or spontaneous inclination of the will.

(5) Freedom from coercion, that is spontaneity, is compatible with the necessity of sin.

The relation between freedom and necessity is further established by Zanchi in reaction to two objections raised against his view. In order to obtain a clear view of the conceptual framework from which he argues, it is important to look at his response in detail.

The first objection is: "What happens necessarily by someone does not happen freely, and by that the agent himself is not free. For free is said to be, what can choose at pleasure from two or more proposed things, whatever it wills. But the will of man (according to you [i.e., Zanchi]) after the Fall necessarily wills sin, unless it is liberated by Christ from the slavery of sin. Thus, it is in no way free after the Fall."[48]

In this objection, freedom is said to consist in the possibility of choosing between two opposite things. This could have given Zanchi the occasion to deal with the issue of alternativity. However, he neglects that question and instead

---

47. The background of this example is the common (Aristotelian) physics, the laws of gravity being still unknown. In this model, the downward movement of a stone is explained by an inward, natural tendency of stones to fall downwards, cf. J. A. van Ruler, *The Crisis of Causality: Voetius and Descartes on God, Nature and Change* (Leiden: Brill, 1995), 71-105.

48. *Omnia opera*, tom. quartus, col. 92.

points at a "fallacy of homonymia": the opponent uses the word "free" in an ambiguous sense. The opponent confuses the freedom from all slavery and all necessity with a more restricted form of freedom, consisting in acting willingly but still necessarily. Zanchi again maintains that freedom and necessity are not mutually exclusive, but that only necessity interpreted as coercion does destroy freedom. In addition to this fundamental insight, Zanchi argues from the perfect free will of God and the heavenly saints: although they are good by necessity, they still have a free will. And again he maintains that also the sinners act by their free will, although they cannot but sin. From this answer can be deduced an important aspect of Zanchi's position:

(6) Free will is not explicitly discussed by Zanchi as the possibility to choose opposite things, but as the unhindered movement of the will consenting in the performance of an action.

The second objection is taken from the doctrine of providence: "What is governed by the immutable providence of God, that does not act freely. But the wills of all men are governed this way."[49] In this argument it is supposed that, when God decides for an event, the freedom to act is destroyed. Zanchi denies this supposition.

He states that there are two categories of things governed by God's providence: first, things without a faculty of judgment and choice; second, beings endowed with rational and volitional capacities. The first class of things does not have freedom, so they cannot be said to lose it due to God's providence. Concerning the second class of beings, Zanchi holds that God's providence is indeed immutable and necessary in itself, but seen from the aspect of the human mind and will, there remains freedom of choice.

Zanchi here points at the distinction between the nearest and the remote cause (*causa proxima* and *causa remota*): the freedom of choice must be stated on the level of the nearest cause. In another context, Zanchi had already mentioned the relation between the first and the secondary cause (*causa prima* and *causa secunda*): the first cause (God) does not exclude secondary causes (human will).[50] In his governing all things, God preserves the nature of his creatures and leads them accordingly. In short, Zanchi states:

(7) Free will exists on the level of secondary causes and is not destroyed by immutable necessity on the level of the first cause.

Zanchi's treatment of the second objection is rather brief. From the overall problematic and hypothesis of the present study, we wish to have additional information on Zanchi's view of contingency in relation to the stated immutability of God's providence. This information is found in the fifth book of *De natura Dei*, dealing with providence and predestination. First, Zanchi

---

49. *Omnia opera*, tom. quartus, col. 92.
50. *Omnia opera*, tom. tertius, col. 705.

discusses the question of whether God's providence is immutable and, if so, whether it therefore imposes necessity on the things. To the first half of the question he responds with the thesis: God's providence is immutable indeed. The explanation of this thesis proceeds on the previous examination of God's immutability and will. As a part of the decree of God, providence is held to be immutable by Zanchi. Though he acknowledges that the things that happen under God's governance are mutable, he states that God's decree concerning the what, when and how of all events is eternal and immutable. The plurality of our human thoughts, which accounts for our mutability, is opposed to the unity or singularity of God's immutable decree. And the change of the concrete effects of God's decree does not imply a change of the decree itself. In discussing the example of Hezekiah, who was first said to die, and afterwards was granted fifteen more years of life, Zanchi comes to the conclusion that a change of things does not require a change of causes.[51]

Zanchi realizes that the second half of the question is the most difficult: does the immutable providence impose necessity on things? Does there remain contingency? Zanchi senses to proceed between accepting Stoic fate and making God's decree mutable. He responds with a lengthy thesis worth quoting in full:[52]

> Thesis II. God's providence, as the first and immutable cause of all things, does (it is true) impose necessity on all things, i.e. on the secondary causes, to work out this or that, and therefore also on the effects, to happen this way. However, it does not remove but rather conserves the nature of the things and the secondary causes, some of which are determined toward certain effects, but others undetermined. Therefore, it happens that, although in respect of the first cause all things happen with immutable necessity, still in respect of the secondary causes that work not coerced but according to their own natures, some things happen necessarily, but others contingently. While the divine providence stretches out from the beginning to the end, and disposes all things usefully.

This complicated thesis is followed by a lengthy explanation, of which we mention the most significant elements.[53]

First, Zanchi explains the term "necessary" by describing it as "that which cannot be otherwise than it is, or act otherwise than it acts." Examples: man is mind-gifted; the sun gives light. Of more interest is Zanchi's statement that something exists necessarily, because when it exists, it cannot be non-existent. Zanchi relates this necessity to God: all things that will be the case in the future, are present to God, and therefore have (as it were) reality already. *Coram Deo*, all future things are necessary. Zanchi here relies on Thomas Aquinas' explanation of God's foreknowledge.[54]

---

51. *Omnia opera*, tom. secundus, col. 447-448.
52. *Omnia opera,* tom. secundus, col. 449, Thesis II.
53. The whole explanation can be read in *Omnia opera*, tom. secundus, col. 449-452, followed by the "fontes rationum" in col. 452-456.
54. *Summa theologiae*, part 1, question 14, article 13 ("Utrum scientia Dei sit futurorum contingentium").

Contingent, the opposite of necessary, is called by Zanchi that which, before it happens, can happen or not happen, be or not be. He argues that contingency holds only *before* the actual occurrence, and appeals to a common saying of the Schools: everything that is, when it is, is necessary to be (*omne quod est, dum est, necesse est esse*). Similarly, a contingently working cause is such that it can produce or not produce an effect. Zanchi limits his definition to a *diachronic* understanding of *contingency*: it exists *before* the event's actual occurrence.

The necessity of things originates either in internal principles (the nature of the thing) or in an external inevitable cause (e.g., God's will and decree) or in both. In Thesis II, Zanchi distinguished between determined (*definitae*) and undetermined (*indefinitae*) causes. The sun is determined to give light: it cannot do otherwise. Man, however, is undetermined to activities as writing, walking, etc.: he can choose to perform or not perform these actions. For this distinction, Zanchi refers to Aristotle's *Physica*.[55] He makes it clear that the distinction holds only for natural, created causes. The supernatural ordination by God's eternal decree does always determine things towards a certain end or use. So we have to view things on two different levels. Zanchi elaborates the example of Judas' betraying Jesus: from his own nature, Judas was undetermined to doing this, his will was free and unforced; but seen as subjected to God's decree, Judas could not do otherwise, and thus was destined to his betrayal.

The conclusion is that one and the same thing can be both contingent and necessary: contingent in its secondary cause, and necessary seen from God's eternal decree and immutable providence. Moreover, a thing can be necessary in both causes: the sun gives light necessarily, because its nature is to do so and because God wills it. In both cases, the distinction of the two causes is fundamental for a correct understanding of necessity and contingency.

A number of examples make it clear what this position implies. Concerning Adam's fall in sin, Zanchi holds that on the one hand Adam was free to sin or not to sin. On the other hand, he was through God's foreknowledge, will and providence destined to sin, in order to manifest the highest good that God gave in Jesus Christ (this is a supralapsarian understanding of the Fall). The same holds for the death of Christ: he voluntarily gave himself into death, without being forced to. At the same time, the will and decree of the Father made it necessary that he would die. It did and did not impose necessity on Christ, in different respects.

Zanchi takes one further step. The necessity or contingency of secondary causes and effects do not stand on their own. They depend on God's providence: not only the events, but also their mode of existence is established by God's decree. Far from removing freedom and contingency, immutable providence is the source and foundation of contingency and freedom.

Behind Zanchi's interpretation of necessity and contingency lies a specific view of causality. He states that God is the "motor" of all actions and events in the created world. In a way that does not violate the creatures, God moves, reigns

---

55. On necessary (definite) and contingent (indefinite) causes, see Aristotle, *Physics* (Oxford: Oxford University Press, 1996), Book II, part 5.

and moderates everything. Considered as actions, events are set in motion by God through us; considered as good or bad actions, they are produced by our good or bad will.

In conclusion we can state that:

a. Zanchi considers events in the created world on *two levels* or in two respects: first, seen from the first cause (God and his providence); second, seen from the secondary causes.
b. Zanchi's explanation does not enter into the questions of (modal) logic, but is shaped by his theory of *causation*.
c. Zanchi gives a *diachronic* description of contingency: before something happens, it can happen otherwise; contingency is maintained here for the future, not explicitly for the present and the past.[56]
d. In Zanchi's view, the necessity arising from God as first cause is due to God's being the efficient and final cause of everything *and* to God's infallible foreknowledge and decree concerning the outcome of events.
e. Zanchi connects necessity with infallibility and immutability.
f. In Zanchi's view, the asserted immutability of God's providence *does* impose a necessity on secondary causes, while at the same time conserving their freedom and contingency according to the nature of secondary causes.
g. The *link* between the necessity and the contingency of events lies in the fact that God's providence comprises not only the outcome, but also the "mode of production" and the sort of causal relations of the creaturely events.

2.8 Free Will in the Different States

In introducing the subject of free will, Zanchi mentioned the fourfold state of man: before the Fall, after the Fall, under grace, and in glory. In his treatment of free will, the emphasis lies on the first two states: before and after the Fall. He does in fact provide a chapter on free will in the reborn man (under grace), but this chapter is not so much concerned with the basic structure of free will as with its practical significance for the way of salvation. We do not find in Zanchi a separate discussion of the free will in the state of glory, but in his discussion of the two former states, he regularly refers to the saints and angels in heaven. So we have to concentrate on free will before and after the Fall, which are indeed the most decisive points of view for establishing the nature of free will. The different sorts of freedom elaborate on Bernard of Clairvaux' distinctions mentioned in section 2.6.

The freedom of will before the Fall has two distinctive features: first, it is subjected to no necessity at all; second, it is freedom towards both good and bad.

---

56. This does not exclude a further explanation of diachronic contingency in terms of synchronic contingency. It can well be argued (as it is in the introduction to this volume) that diachronic contingency requires structural, synchronic contingency. The only thing stated in the text above is that Zanchi's formulation is limited to diachronic contingency, and that moreover his Thomist explanation of foreknowledge indicates that he did not consciously think in the Scotist way.

The freedom from all necessity is elaborated by Zanchi in three directions: there is no impulse by an inward sinful nature; there are no outward circumstances that compel Adam into one direction; and there is no necessity imposed upon him by God. This freedom from all necessity is one explicit step beyond the freedom from coercion common to all human beings. An important motive behind Zanchi's view is the need to avoid the conclusion that God is the author of sin. The question remains, however, how Adam could be excluded from the providential government of God (including necessity), which is generally accepted as basic for the relation between Creator and creature (see also the digression on God's providence and our freedom in section 2.7 above). Perhaps the safest conclusion is that by stating Adam's freedom from all necessity, Zanchi does not explicitly have in mind the relation between God's providential decree and Adam's decision to sin, but merely means: freedom from coercion (essential) *plus* freedom from sin and misery (accidental).[57]

The second feature of Adam's state is the *absolute* freedom to choose between good and bad. This ability, located on the accidental level of freedom, differs in Adam from all other subjects of free will: non-convert sinners only have the ability to act badly; the regenerate do partly the bad, partly the good; God, angels and the saints in heaven have a disposition merely towards the good. Thus, only Adam had an actual choice between good and bad. For Zanchi, this belongs to his being created after God's image, in a state of righteousness. Zanchi extensively deals with the precept given to Adam in paradise. In his view, the form of the precept and the punishment added to it implies that Adam had a real choice between keeping or transgressing the precept. In order to secure God from the accusation of being the author of (original) sin, Zanchi emphasizes that for God's part, man was created good and righteous. His eventual choice for sin originated not from his creation by God, but from his own inclination to follow the lies of Satan. Zanchi refers to a somewhat obscure place in the book of Jesus Sirach to confirm his statement that Adam was completely free to choose. The difficulty is not so much in the sentence that it was laid in Adam's hands to obey God's commands, as in the phrase that we translated as: "And you can make faith *eudokias*." Perhaps the best paraphrase is: by rightly using the free complacency of his will (*eudokia*), Adam could prove himself to be faithful to God.[58]

For the state of man after the Fall, the freedom of the will is maintained, but in a more limited sense. There is no longer a freedom from all necessity, but only from (violent) coercion. This is still an important kind of freedom, because it leaves intact man's responsibility for his deeds and because it secures God from the accusation of being the author of (actual) sin. In spite of this crucial freedom, there are three sorts of serious limitations: by the inward sinful nature of man, which impels him to commit sin; by the miserable condition of life, which puts constraints on man's choice and serves as an occasion for sin and selfishness; and

---

57. *Omnia opera*, tom. tertius, col. 708.
58. *Omnia opera*, tom. tertius, col. 709.

by the providential government of God, who determines with immutable necessity the course of events, including human actions.[59]

The second difference with Adam before the Fall is that man is no longer free to choose both good and bad. By the one decisive choice for sin by Adam, the possibility to choose the good was lost once and for all. Man as a sinner is considered a slave of sin. Still, this does not mean that he is free in no respect at all. For he does not commit sin against his own will, but, on the contrary, with his own full assent. So, the freedom of the will in the state of sin consists of spontaneity and agreement of the will.[60]

By extrapolation, the same holds for the state of grace: inasmuch as the principle of sin is still active in man, he does willingly sin; inasmuch as he succeeds to avoid sin and to do good works, his will is so changed that it willingly agrees with God's will. Zanchi describes the fact that man as a sinner is at the same time both enslaved and free as a paradox, which can only be solved when it is seen that the two qualifications apply in different respects. Zanchi refers to a short formulation by Augustine: "Free choice is always free, but not always good."[61]

We can conclude that Zanchi maintains the freedom of the will in all states of man, but that there are two important differences: Before the Fall, Adam was free from all necessity even from God's side, but after the Fall the freedom from necessity consists only of freedom from coercion. The freedom of Adam before the Fall included the possibility to choose both good and bad, whereas after the Fall man is only able to choose the bad out of himself, and to choose the good only due to the renewing work of God.

In sum, the essential nature of free will (free from coercion) has not been lost, but the accidental powers definitely have changed (bound by sin and misery).

2.9 Zanchi's Final Definition

Zanchi's insights into the nature of free will are summarized in a final definition provided by him in a second thesis in the chapter on free will after the Fall:[62] "Free choice is the faculty of the soul, free from all coercion, called will, which, following the judgment of the intellect, out of itself either longs for or rejects all things proposed to it, both the desirable and the rejectable." All elements of this definition are briefly explained by Zanchi, most of which we have already dealt with. We will look in more detail at some aspects not mentioned before.

First, Zanchi defines *liberum arbitrium* as a faculty of the soul. This is its *genus*. Zanchi exposes that the soul possesses potencies, which are designed by the Creator each to fulfill its proper task. This can be called a teleological understanding of the faculties. The propriety of the faculty of will is to will or

---

59. *Omnia opera*, tom. quartus, col. 89.
60. *Omnia opera*, tom. quartus, col. 89-90.
61. *Omnia opera*, tom. quartus, col. 87.
62. *Omnia opera*, tom. quartus, col. 93.

not-will, to choose or reject. Although Zanchi does not want to separate the activities of the soul, he yet emphasizes the proper task of both intellect and will.

Second, the will is characterized as "free." This cannot, according to Zanchi, be stated of the other faculties (e.g., the intellect). Zanchi had already explained that this freedom is essentially a freedom from coercion.

Third, Zanchi emphatically states that the will is free from *all* coercion. This includes not only coercion by men or by Satan, but even coercion by God. Zanchi frankly holds that even in the conversion of men, God does not use coercion, but only persuasion and flexion. Some decades later, the word "persuasion" became suspect because of the view of the Remonstrants who restricted God's activity in the conversion to "moral persuasion" (*moralis persuasio*). Zanchi cannot be accused of their heresy, for he explicitly speaks of a real change of the will by God.

Fourth, Zanchi clarifies his view on the relation between intellect and will by distinguishing between the theoretical and the practical intellect. He does not intend to separate them into two faculties, but only to distinguish two functions of the intellect. When it understands things that belong to the field of contemplation (*theoria*), the intellect is called theoretical. When it understands things pertaining to the field of practical activity (*praxis*), the intellect is called practical. This practical intellect provides help to the will, which in itself is blind. So the will makes a free choice on the basis of the actual possibilities understood and proposed by the intellect. Zanchi speaks of the *judgment* of the practical intellect to indicate that it is no mere consultation and deliberation concerning the means, but also decisive judgment concerning the ends (cf. section 2.5 of this commentary). Remarkably, Zanchi does not elaborate on his statement, that the will "follows" the judgment of the practical intellect. By that, his exact view on the relation between intellect and will remains somewhat unclear.

Fifth, by speaking of "all things, both desirable and rejectable," Zanchi once again expresses his opinion, that the ends as well as the means fall within the reach of free will.

Sixth, Zanchi refers to the distinction between elicited and imperate acts in order to restrict the maintained freedom of the will to the elicited acts, that are called the immediate and proper actions of the will.

2.10 Evaluation: Zanchi's Place in the Tradition

Since Zanchi is a prominent theologian of the transitional era from Reformation to Reformed Orthodoxy, it is important to assess his place in the tradition. This question has two aspects: Zanchi's relation to the preceding tradition of Church Fathers and scholastics; and his position in comparison to his Reformed contemporaries.

Concerning Zanchi's relation to the tradition of church and theology, we should note that he shows a positive attitude. He quotes some of the Church Fathers (Augustine, Origen and his namesake Hieronymus) with apparent approval. It is not surprising that Augustine is by far his favorite Father, as he is for all Protestant and Catholic theologians of that era. Particularly in the matter of free will, Augustine's treatises provide much evidence for the Reformed position against the semi-Pelagianism of much Roman Catholic theology. From the medieval theologians, Zanchi quotes Bernard of Clairvaux for his famous distinction of the threefold freedom, and twice he refers to Thomas Aquinas, whom he calls the Father of the Scholastics. Other strands of medieval thinking are not explicitly present in his argument, although we suggested that the structure of Zanchi's argument allows for a more far-reaching concept of contingency than occurs in Thomistic thought.

With respect to Zanchi's place in the Reformed theology of his day, it could seem remarkable that he provides a rather positive treatment of free will: he does affirm that there is still some basic freedom of the will in man after the Fall. Given Luther's fierce attack on the doctrine of free will (*De servo arbitrio*), it could be considered betrayal of the Reformation to allow it a positive place again. Furthermore, Calvin in his *Institutes* is rather negative on free will. He complains of the lack of clarity with the Church Fathers and states that the term "free will" is far too flattering for the miserable remains of freedom in man.[63] Yet, Calvin does not deny natural freedom, but the power to do good. Likewise, Melanchthon is much more nuanced than Luther, and Reformed theologians such as Petrus Martyr Vermigli and Zacharias Ursinus deal in a similarly balanced way with this doctrine. Although they perhaps provide more warnings against possible abuse of the doctrine of free will, they still give a positive treatment of the essential nature of free will. In the case of Vermigli, there even are striking similarities with the discussion provided by Zanchi.[64]

We can safely say that Zanchi helped to reintroduce the theme of *liberum arbitrium* to the agenda of Reformed theology, but he did so in accordance with other outstanding theologians of his day. Moreover, his foundational discussions leave open a more detailed investigation of the questions concerning necessity and contingency. In the next chapters of this volume, we will find a more elaborate conceptual apparatus being developed by Zanchi's immediate and remote successors.

---

63. John Calvin, *Institutes*, book II, chapters II and IV.

64. Melanchthon, "De humanis viribus seu de libero arbitrio," in *Loci praecipui theologici* (1559), *Melanchthons Werke im Auswahl*, vol. 2, part 1 (Gütersloh: Bertelsmann, 1952), 236-252; cf. also in *Loci communes* (1521), in ibid., 8-17.

Ursinus, "De libero arbitrio," in *Loci theologici*, *D. Zachariae Ursini Opera theologica*, part 1 (Heidelberg: Johannes Lancellot/Ionas Rosa, 1612), col. 633-664; cf. also "Theses de libero arbitrio," ibid. col. 739-740.

Vermigli, "De libero arbitrio," in *Loci Communes* (London: Ioannes Kynston, 1576), 184-210.

3

An Image of Its Maker

Theses on Freedom of Franciscus Junius (1545-1602)

3.1 Introduction

Franciscus Junius (François du Jon) belonged to the third generation of Reformed theologians.[1] He was born at Bourges on May 1, 1545, one of the nine children of a local nobleman. He studied law at Bourges and Lyons, and theology at Geneva during Calvin's last years (1562-1565). In 1565, he accepted a call to be the pastor of the Walloon congregation of Antwerp. Here, he was associated with Marnix of St. Aldegonde in a committee to spread political and religious literature—for which the authorities put a price of 300 guilders on his head.

After a short stay in Ghent (1566) he fled to Heidelberg where the Elector Frederick III commissioned him and Immanuel Tremellius to write a new Latin translation of the Hebrew Old Testament. Because of the restoration of Lutheranism at Heidelberg in 1576 he was forced to go to Neustadt an der Haardt where he became a professor of Hebrew. During his stay at Heidelberg and Neustadt, he had Zanchi as one of his colleagues. After the reintroduction of the Reformed religion in the Palatinate he returned to Heidelberg, and in 1584 he became a professor of theology there.

In 1591, he was requested by the French king Henry IV to come to France as his adviser in Protestant affairs. On his trip to France he visited Leiden where, in 1592, he accepted an appointment as professor of theology. In 1594 Gomarus arrived at Leiden to be his colleague, staying there until 1611. Together with Gomarus and Lucas Trelcatius Sr. (1542-1602), Junius made an important contribution to the development of the theological faculty of Leiden University. Moreover, it was exactly during this period—the last decades of the sixteenth century—that the "identifying paradigm of systematic Reformed theology" took shape.[2]

---

1. For Junius' biography, see *BLGNP* (Kampen: Kok, 1983), 2:275-279; F. W. Cuno, *Franciscus Junius der Aeltere, Professor der Theologie und Pastor (1545-1602)* (Amsterdam: Scheffer, 1896); B. A. Venemans, *Franciscus Junius en zijn Eirenicum de pace ecclesiae catholicae* (Leiden: Elve/Labor vincit, 1977); C. de Jonge, *De irenische ecclesiologie van Franciscus Junius (1545-1602)* (Nieuwkoop: De Graaf, 1980).

2. See A. Vos, "Scholasticism and Reformation," in *RS*, 99-119, esp. 110-111. With this "identifying paradigm," Vos means the structure of divine knowledge, the natural knowledge (*scientia naturalis*) of possibilities being in structural order before the decree of the divine will,

Junius was a prolific and many-sided author. He wrote on Hebrew grammar, exegesis, dogmatics and ecclesial law. In his *Theological Theses* (written during his time at Heidelberg and later at Leiden), he covered amply in short, numbered paragraphs the principal topics of theology.[3] Shortly after his arrival at Leiden, he published *Eirenicum, or the Peace of the Catholic Church among Christians* (1592), addressed to the Landgrave of Hesse, which took the form of "Meditations" on Psalms 122 and 133, warmly urging the cultivation of a spirit of peace and unity in the churches.

His irenical attitude, however, did not hinder him from articulating a clear theological position. For example: in the arising conflict between Arminius and Gomarus he rejected an intense polemic, but stuck to the traditional position and thus took the side of Gomarus.[4] He finished his career at Leiden in spite of invitations to be a minister in La Rochelle, a professor at Geneva, or at the new University of Franeker.

The *Theological Theses* contains disputations, which are subdivided in theses. So, these texts belong to the genre of the *disputatio*, the most celebrated genre of theological discourse on an academic level from 1250 onward. One of these disputations is translated and commented on in the rest of this chapter. In order to do justice to this text and its author, some comments should be made on the character of a disputation as well as on the issue of authorship.[5]

First of all, it should be remembered that the text we are about to analyze was written as a preparation for the public performance at which for two hours a student, or "respondent," defended his theses against three or six opponents while a professor was presiding the disputation. Consequently, the theses are quite lapidary and do not offer a comprehensive instrument to unravel the entire theology behind the theses. Nevertheless, the logical-semantic character of the disputation as a whole helps to give way to a plausible reconstruction of the theology that was defended by the respondent.

The academic background of the disputation was the scholastic method. Its history shows an increasing precision in determining the context and content of Latin terms by means of logical analysis.[6] In this way relevant distinctions could

---

whereas the free knowledge (*scientia libera*) follows the decision of the will. Vos argues that this model warrants the contingency of reality and distinguishes Reformed theology from the Jesuit and Remonstrant middle knowledge (*scientia media*) approach.

3. Franciscus Junius, *Theses theologicae, quae in inclyta academia Lugduno-batava ad exercitia publicarum disputationum, praeside D. Francisco Junio variis temporibus a Theologiae Candidatis adversus oppugnantes propugnatae sunt* (Leiden, 1592).

4. Later on, in 1609, Gomarus narrated Junius' warning against Arminius, issued on his deathbed; see G. P. van Itterzon, *Franciscus Gomarus* (The Hague: Martinus Nijhoff, 1930), 82.

5. For the development of the genre of the disputation in the Middle Ages, see *MW*, 123-132; *CHLMP*, 26-27. The history of the disputation and its relevance at Leiden University is analyzed by Margreet J. A. M. Ashmann, *Collegia en colleges. Juridisch onderwijs aan de Leidse Universiteit 1575-1630, in het bijzonder het disputeren* (Groningen: Wolters-Noordhoff, 1990). See also W. Otterspeer, *Groepsportret met dame*, vol. 1, *Het bolwerk van de vrijheid. De Leidse Universiteit, 1575-1672* (Amsterdam: Uitgeverij Bert Bakker, 2000), 236-242.

6. See *MW*, 130-132; *RS*, 99-119, esp. 107; G. R. Evans, *The Language and Logic of the Bible in the Earlier Middle Ages* (Cambridge: Cambridge University Press, 1984); Marcia Colish, *Medieval Foundations of the Western Intellectual Tradition 400-1400* (New Haven / London:

be made which were used as technical terms for drawing theological conclusions with respect to other theological claims. In Junius' *Theses* these distinctions are sometimes made explicit; at other times they are implicit and have to be discovered by further analysis. In either way, we have to explore their significance for Junius' way of making theological claims. That is what we consider to be our primary task in the systematic analysis of Junius' *Theological Theses*.

Secondly, some comments are necessary on the authorship of the disputations. Although it is difficult to establish a general procedure, it may be helpful to distinguish between formal and material authorship. As for the person who wrote the disputation in question, we may assume that the respondent was its author, i.e., the student who had to defend the theses during the disputation.[7] At the same time, there is enough evidence to assume that the professor presiding over the disputation was the author in a material sense, or the *auctor intellectualis*.

First of all, he was responsible for editing the theses. That the preparation of the text for editing took much of the professor's attention is indicated, for example, by Gomarus' observation that "professors who were presiding over disputations needed as much time for disputations as for preparing their lectures."[8]

Secondly, when in his text the student differed from the systematic thinking of his professor, he had to account for this, and in most cases such deviation would not be allowed.

Thirdly, it can be argued that even if the respondent was guilty of plagiarism, the public defense required a well-considered handling, for the respondent was always dependent on the opinion of the presiding professor.

Fourthly, in the case that other professors did not agree with the theses that were defended, they entered into a debate with the presiding professor, which suggests his involvement in the content of the theses.

Finally, it could be the case that there was a difference between the official text of the disputation and its public defense. During the public disputation the respondent could offer counter-theses that differed from the theological position defended by the presiding professor.[9] From such an unexpected procedure we can infer *e contrarie* that the printed theses were indeed in accordance with the theology of the presiding professor.

From all this information we can conclude that the theology implied in the disputations was indeed the opinion of the presiding professor. This allows us to

---

Yale University Press, 1997), 275-277; R. W. Southern, *Scholastic Humanism and the Unification of Europe*, vol. 1, *Foundations* (Oxford: Blackwell, 1995), 102-133.

7. See Ashmann, *Collegia en colleges*, 311-23. Ashmann's most relevant arguments for this are: the correspondence of some respondents manifests that they themselves drew up the theses; the dedications of the disputations are an indication of the respondent's opinion on his piece of work; the presiding professor had a more general task: he had to correct and to suggest literature and had to approve the theses before they were allowed to be printed; the theses sometimes showed plagiarism.

8. See P. Molhuysen, *Bronnen tot de geschiedenis van de Leidsche Universiteit*, vol. 1, *1574– February 7, 1610* (The Hague: Martinus Nijhoff, 1913), 91-92.

9. See van Itterzon, *Franciscus Gomarus*, 108.

reconstruct his theology by analyzing the disputations defended under his chairmanship. Moreover, the material authorship of the presiding professor is the more plausible as the disputations were published under his name, as is the case with Junius' text.

3.2 Translation of the Text

Junius devoted various disputations to the topic of free choice. In the *Theses Leydenses* defended at the University of Leiden in 1592, he discussed it in two disputations, the disputations xxi and xxii. The older *Theses Theologicae*, defended under his professorship at the University of Heidelberg, were published simultaneously with the Leiden theses in 1592 and contain only one disputation on free choice, entitled *De libero hominis arbitrio, ante & post lapsum* (On free choice of man, before and after the Fall). We have selected disputation xxii of the Leiden theses for translation, for it is in this disputation with its fifty-eight theses that Junius—perhaps under influence of Gomarus—presented his most elaborated discussion on the topic of free choice. Joannes Bouverius was the respondent of the disputation.

[Disputation] XXII: Free Choice

[The term free choice]
1. Free choice (*liberum arbitrium*) is not one thing (when we are addressing the denotation of the term), but manifold.[10] As it is composed out of two words, the one explains the other. The former pertains to an attribute, and the latter to a subject. By briefly speaking about the etymology of both and about the various meanings that seem to contribute to the present purpose, we shall provide ourselves an easier entrance into examining the essence of the thing we are dealing with.

[Choice denotes an election of the will]
2. The order of the things themselves as well as of doctrine postulates that in every discussion one starts with the subject: Choice (*arbitrium*) is derived from judging (*arbitrari*), when we believe Augustine, *Hypognost. 3,*[11] or (according to some grammar scholars) from judge (*arbiter*). Whatever one asserts, it all amounts to the same thing and each denomination indicates very clearly the genuine sense of this word.

An arbiter is such a judge, who has the power over a whole controversial case between contestants (as Festus states in book 1 of his *De verborum significatione*), i.e., someone who does not resolve a case according to a law or by strict rule, but by what he judges to be just and fair. Judging is to perform

---

10. As explained earlier in this book, we have chosen to translate "*arbitrium*" with "choice." In these theses we see that "*arbitrium*" also has the connotation of judgment: it is a choice based on deliberation and judgment.

11. Augustine's *Hypognosticon*, which Junius refers to, better known under the title *Hypomnesticon*. The quotation is from *Hypomnesticon*, lib. III, cap. IV; see *MPL* 45, 1623.

the task of a judge or to settle a controversy according to a free decision of the will. So it is for this reason that a sentence, which is pronounced by a judge, is commonly called an "*arbitrium.*"

3. Although the term "choice" is determined first of all by its forensic use (as we have said), later on they began to derive other uses from that use and began to apply it to all those things, which can relate to a deliberation or, especially, to an election based on a deliberation. With respect to the former it is usually ascribed to the intellect, but in regard to the latter it refers to the will.

4. The choice of the intellect (which is commonly called γνωμη by the Greek) is a mental act by which a mind-gifted nature distinguishes between intelligible objects and after deliberation judges which of those objects are true or false.

5. The choice of the will (which the Greek distinguish from the preceding kind of choice with the name προαιρεσις) is likewise the act, by which the will either chooses, because it is good, or rejects, because it is bad, the things distinguished, judged and set before the will by the intellect.

6. Thus, election (*electio*) in this way is called a choice (*arbitrium*), because it is as it were a sort of sentence and a last judgment of the will. For this reason we commonly say that this or that is in our choice, i.e. in our election and power.

7. These three are the principal meanings of "choice." The last one is the most usual and most suitable for our purpose and in this discussion (passing over the other meanings) we accept only this one [namely, choice as an election of the will].

[*Freedom from necessity attributed to choice*]

8. Freedom (*libertas*) is, as we said, the proper attribute of choice. Taken in general and καθολου, it is divided by theologians in two theses, namely [1] freedom from obligation (which others call freedom in attendant circumstances or freedom of means), and [2] freedom from necessity. The latter (*haec*) concerns the will by itself; the former (*illa*) concerns the events and consequences.

9. [1] Freedom from obligation or freedom in attendant circumstances we call the freedom according to which it is free for a willing person to do whatever he wills according to his own choice or movement, in accordance with the order congruent with his nature, without any adventitious restraints or impediments from outside.

10. [2] What is called freedom from necessity is stated in a twofold way, in virtue of two modes of necessity: for it is opposed either [a] to coercion or [b] to necessity proper (in which simple coercion itself is usually included).

11. [a] Free from simple coercion are those things, which, although they are done necessarily and it is impossible that they are not done, nevertheless are done willingly and ἑκουσιως. With respect to this kind of freedom our will must be considered to be free towards ends that are self-evident and good in itself: for those ends the will seeks freely, but nevertheless so, that it cannot not strive after them. For example: we are so willing to be happy, that in no way can we be willing to be unhappy.

12. [b] Free from necessity proper is said of those things which according to our judgment we can *will, will not, not will not, or not will*.[12] In this our own will is not hindered by any force of necessity, either the necessity of the consequent or the necessity of the consequence (necessity would be introduced by any principle, either internal or external, or by any cause). Our will merely relates to those things in a contingent and free way.

[*Analogous attribution of freedom to the will*]
13. Both kinds of freedom, for which we have used the general name "freedom from necessity," are attributed to the will by means of analogy, in relation to the status of the willing subjects, of the objects that we are willing and of the circumstances.
14. The *subjects* of freedom we consider in two ways: in themselves and as they are related to an object:

    Considered in themselves they are free from coercion only, not from necessity [proper]: For they are willing freely and according to their internal principle, but necessarily. This is by reason of their nature, according to which this free necessity of willing (*haec libera volendi necessitas*) is imposed on them.

    Considered in relation to the object, however, the individual subjects do not relate to the object with the same kind of freedom. For God is related to the election of the good in another way than creatures.
15. Some of the *objects*, according to their nature, are determined to one [alternative of both possible choices] such as those natural and self-evident ends (which we discussed in thesis 11). Other objects are not determined (as Nazianzus says in his *Apologeticus de fuga*), having an equal attraction to both [alternative possible choices]. Of this kind are all the means as well as some subordinate and unknown ends. The first ones exclude only coercion; the latter ones exclude every kind of necessity.
16. From *circumstances*, which are various and multiple, mostly causes arise, which change the mode of willing by their occurrence. For the freedom in the regenerate man differs from the freedom in the unregenerate man; the freedom belonging to Adam's state of integrity is another freedom than the freedom after the Fall or the freedom we shall possess in the state of glory, as we will elaborate in what follows.

[*Definition of free choice*]
17. Having said this, it should be possible to define free choice conveniently as the faculty of the discrete will (*voluntas discreta*), free from necessity, by which a mind-gifted nature chooses one thing above another from the things which are shown by the intellect, or, choice facing one and the same thing, accepts it as being good, or rejects it as being bad.[13]

---

12. For an explanation of this sequence, see section 3.4.2 below.
13. We translate the term "*voluntas discreta*" with "discrete will." According to thesis 19, by it is meant the will that chooses after the intellect has discerned (see theses 5 and 19).

18. In this definition, three points have to be examined: [a] the subject of free choice, [b] its object and [c] its act. The explanation of these things shall considerably contribute to the understanding of what follows.

19. [a] The *subject* is twofold, one being the whole subject, the other being the partial subject:

    The total subject is either uncreated, like God, or created, such as the angels and men, which we will discuss in due place.

    The partial subject is the will, not the natural will (for this will does not have a choice, because it relates to only one thing), but the discrete will, so called according to the common use by the Scholastics, because it acts on the basis of the discernment (to say it that way) and the judgment by the intellect.

20. If this will is moved from ordinate principles, through ordinate means, to an ordinate end, in an ordinate manner, it is called a *voluntas, προαιρετική*. But if this will is ill-informed and blindly allows itself to be abducted by particular causes (as very often happens to the sick: when the disease is getting worse they do what the physician prohibits), it is called a "will by cause or from cause."

21. [b] The *object* of free choice, when discussed in general, was assigned by us in the definition above when we said that the free choice is posited in the election of things which are the result of a consultation. These objects are either means or ends. About ends, however, because there is seldom deliberation, one seldom makes a choice either.

22. But if the discussion concerns the special object, we use a threefold distinction. For whatever comes before the discrete will is either good, or bad, or indifferent. Now, the same account pertains to the will and its choice.

23. [c] The proper *act* of free choice is election, but it can happen in two ways: either by selecting one thing from two or more opposites (this is usually called the freedom of contrariety [*libertas contrarietatis*]), or, only one thing being proposed, by accepting or rejecting this one (this is called the freedom of contradiction [*libertas contradictionis*]). Both ways we have described in thesis 17.

24. Thus far about the definition of the free choice and its parts. Now, we must see if this definition equally fits to all the species of the total subject enumerated above (for that element in this question is highly debated). Therefore, we shall discuss each individual subject in a single way, beginning from God, the highest and universal principle of all things.

[*Divine freedom*]

25. That God is uttermost free is confessed by everyone, for whom in their hearts there resides a sense of divinity. To detract freedom from God is equivalent to denying God, because this very thing belongs to his main attributes, from which not even the least one (if we may say so) can be taken away, without abolishing immediately the whole concept of Deity.

    This freedom of God is twofold, in so far as we distinguish initially a twofold relation: [a] freedom, namely, related to the *apprehension* of the will, and [b] freedom related to the *execution* of the thing apprehended and commanded by the will.

26. [a] According to the first aspect of freedom (which we especially discuss in this *quaestio*), freedom is attributed to God, but not universally, if freedom is understood as freedom from necessity proper. The reason why will be clearly evident from the distinction of the special objects of free choice, namely good and bad (for indifferent things are no point of debate here).

27. These objects are proposed to the will either by one singular act and as mutually opposed [good and bad], or they are proposed separately and absolutely, considered in themselves [either good or bad]:

If the objects are proposed in the first mode, God is related to them in a determinate and necessary way and he cannot incline himself to both parts.

But in the latter mode, a distinction has to be made again: in relation to the bad [object], he can be considered in no way to be free, unless understood as a freedom from coercion. This is detested by his free will not because it is unwilling, but because the condition of its nature requires this: it is utterly repugnant to its nature to prefer the bad to the good.

To the good [object], however, he is most free, if you consider either the freedom of contradiction or the freedom of contrariety. For he can choose or not choose, if there is a singular object; and he can choose this or that, if there are more objects.

28. [b] Regarding the other aspect [freedom of execution], there is no debate about the fact that this freedom belongs to God only and that it cannot be attributed to the creatures, unless in a very improper way and with greatest restriction. For he is the only αὐτεξούσιος, most free from himself, in himself and by himself, having every right and power over everything he has created, and his will neither depends on nor is governed by any external cause, but everything depends on his will.

29. Thus, this freedom existing in God in the most perfect way is most perfect and like a prototype (πρωτότυπος). All other freedom is only an image of it and just like a representative example (as they name it), therefore conceded to mind-gifted creatures that they, in as far as they are adorned with certain particles of divinity, somehow reflect the image of their maker.

[Created freedom before the Fall]

30. These creatures are of two categories: Some are immaterial, like the angels, other are material, such as mankind. The former participate only in the superior nature, the latter participate in both the superior and the inferior nature, and acknowledge them as a common principle of their actions.

31. To both kind of creatures God has imparted the light of the intellect and the faculty of will, as a singular principle of their own actions in themselves, by which they are moved freely by themselves to their actions, and by means of a voluntary act.

32. Furthermore, this principle in the creation being right, holy, not contaminated by any stain of inordinate desires, voluntary (αὐθαίρετος) followed the judgment of the intellect (which could not be deceived because of the innate

light of truth), in such a way that under its guidance, both angels and mankind, in accordance with the order that is congruent to their nature and in an intelligent way, were willing the ends and the objects shown by reason, and performed them by acting: although the angels acted in a more excellent way than mankind, because of the excellence and simplicity of their nature.

33. For in man, even before the Fall, the intellect could not raise itself by transcending the natural limits to supernatural knowledge, nor could the will apprehend those things, except supported and sustained by supernatural help.

34. For this reason, to this particular principle of his nature was added (*superadditus*) a singular principle of grace for Adam, by which his intellective will was acting, singularly moved, above its natural mode. Hence, those words of Genesis 2:23 announced by that prophetic spirit: "This at last is bone of my bones and flesh of my flesh." Hence also in the same place, verse 20, the imposing of names to every single animal and many other things, which the intellect would never have been able to exert by its own insight or by the powers of its natural will.

35. Although man was made in this holiness and in the integrity of all the parts of his soul and body, and endowed by his nature with such principles that agreed with the will of God in the most complete harmony; yet, because he was not so constituted that he was not mutable, he always retained a potency of willing or doing the opposite of what he willed and did, in this way that from the rectitude of his nature and "the very support of grace, he was able (*posset*) to desert when he willed so, or to remain in it, if he willed so," as Augustine very clearly teaches in *Admonition and grace*.[14] God had endowed him with the ability: but willing what he was able to [will] remained free to his own choice.[15]

36. That the first man was created mutable is clear, firstly, from the Word of God, Gen. 2:17: "The day you will eat, you shall surely die." Secondly, from the event, which (being miserable) was followed by the miserable condition of the whole human race. Thirdly, from an argument. For when only God in himself and by himself is immortal and immutable, he could not have made him immortal and immutable, unless he made him consequently God. But only Christ is the essential image of God the Father.

37. Still, in this mutability, the first man had choice, free from all necessity. First, this is demonstrated by the nature of the image of God to which he is formed, as mentioned in Gen 1:26. Nothing is more adequate to this [image] than a solid freedom; nothing is more incompatible with this than the fetter of necessity. Moreover, in a not obscure way the Lord has testified to the free condition of the human will by the proposition made to Adam in Gen. 2:16, 17 regarding the two trees, *the tree of life* and the *tree of the knowledge of good and evil*: the function of the first tree was only one of promising,

---

14. *De correptione et gratia*, chapter 11, section 32 (*MPL* 44, 935).

15. Junius has a wordplay which is hard to preserve in translation, therefore the original is given here: "*Posse* etenim ei dederat Deus: *velle* autem, quod *posset*, arbitrio suo reliquerat liberum."

whereas the function of the second tree was one of forbidding with a threat of death.

[*The Fall and its consequences*]

38. Therefore, being bound to the conservation of this innate rectitude by no necessity except of law and obedience, he squandered it by his own inner principle and most freely, when by consuming the fruit of the forbidden tree he declined from the norm of life prescribed to him. So, by using it in a bad way, "he ruined both himself and his choice" (as we say with Augustine in his *Enchiridion ad Laurentium*, cap. 30).

39. For by this singular fact (which God permitted and ordained to a righteous end, according to his eternal decree and counsel and without any guilt) the image of God was totally obliterated and was followed and replaced by an incredible disorder and corruption of human nature. A corruption both of the particular nature of Adam and of the common nature of all posterity, who sinned in him, being propagated according to their nature by him as their principal individual. For the same gifts which he had received for himself and his posterity, he lost for himself and his posterity by his deed.

40. Therefore, this mutation is followed by a necessity (which they call a necessity of the thing itself and of the effect). This necessity determines the potency which is free to either good or bad in a threefold way, in as much as it has a threefold relation to these two special objects, namely either to the good or to the bad or to both at the same time.

41. This threefold necessity, however, originates from a threefold consideration of the two adventitious forms existing in mankind, namely corruption and holiness (which the apostle calls the law of the flesh and the law of the Spirit, Romans 8:2, 3). For a necessity towards the bad follows from the innate corruption adjoined to our nature, a necessity towards the good follows from holiness; from both together follows a necessity towards the good and the bad.

42. Hence, a threefold condition of mankind after the Fall emerges, according to which a threefold account of free choice in man should be given: one according to the state of corrupted nature, hence called carnal ($\sigma\alpha\rho\varkappa\iota\varkappa\acute{o}\varsigma$), another according to the state of partly regenerated nature, hence called spiritual ($\pi\nu\epsilon\upsilon\mu\alpha\tau\iota\varkappa o\varsigma$), but only rudimentarily. The third condition concerns the state of his totally renovated and glorified nature, whence it is named perfectly and completely spiritual.

[*Carnal freedom*]

43. We confirm, however, that in this first state some traces of the freedom of choice of man are still visible, although they are totally corrupt. For in indifferent matters, the thing itself and the common experience of all people testify that the election of the will has remained free and indifferent to many things. But how it deals with good and bad things cannot be explained by a sole distinction.

44. First, it should be noted that good and bad are interpreted in two ways, namely in a narrow and a more extended sense:

In the narrow sense it stands for actions with respect to their own category (*genus*) and good and bad according to the essence of the deed (as it is called).

In the extensive sense it stands for actions that are such in every respect, whether in themselves and according to their nature, or accidentally by reason of their attendant circumstances. As the attendant circumstances of the actions I mention the principle, circumstances, means, object and end. When all these things are concurring in an ordinate way to an action, it is good; if inordinately, it is bad.

45. Thus, in respect of the good and the bad considered in the first [narrow] sense, the unregenerate is free to some extent. For although he is not directed to both in the same way—more to the bad than to the good because of his wickedness—yet in political, economical and moral actions, or in other affairs which are subjected to the senses and reason, we assert that the elective will, conjoined with its mode [of operating] doubtlessly has freedom of choice.

46. But when good and bad are taken [extensively] in general, the account is very different. For the unregenerate necessarily sins, not even being able to will or to do anything [else] (until by the grace of regeneration he does something that is not polluted by some fault). For he either wills and does an action, which is bad in itself, or when willing and doing actions, which are good in themselves, they change from good actions in themselves into sins by accident, because they are not derived from a good principle and are not directed towards a good end, by way of [being] a good means towards a right object: Matth. 7:18, "A bad tree cannot bear good fruits," and Augustine, "Duties are weighted by their ends and not by their actions."

47. Therefore, they err who grant to natural man some time, in which he is able not to sin or in which at least "he can morally do some good, not only without faith, but even without special help, if no temptation is pressing" (Bellarminus, *Controversiae*, book 3, chapter 9). For they oppose the Holy Spirit who declares in the Scriptures, Rom. 14:23: "Whatever does not proceed from faith is sin," and Genesis 6:5: "Every imagination of the thoughts of his heart was only evil continually."

48. Thus it is very certain that no choice towards supernatural actions has survived in carnal man, since according to 1 Cor. 2:11, 12 and 2 Cor. 3:5, and Rom. 1:7, his intellect and will do not own him naturally that choice of supernaturalcactions and that principle of grace: which choice, being bestowed by God to our first parent in creation to compensate this deficiency of his nature, was lost totally by sin.

49. So, the Pontificals disgracefully ramble when they assert that the free choice in those things which pertain to life and piety is only damaged and not totally extinguished through the defect of Adam and that other powers have been left even in corrupted nature: although it concerns powers which are sleeping and half dead (Bellarminus, *Controversiae*, book 3, chapters 11 and 15).

[*Initial spiritual freedom*]

50. The state of corruption is followed by the state of regeneration in the work of which *three* degrees of divine grace are to be observed. Although operating at the same time, some are yet prior to others and some are later than others, regarding the order of cause and effect.

51. The *first* degree is the one by which God out of mere pleasure in Christ vivifies us, who are dead in sins, by adopting us as his sons while by nature we were sons of wrath according to Eph. 2:3; and, thereafter, he vivifies us by inserting us into his communion, so that we are made participants of his death and resurrection, from Whom as our head the spiritual life floats down in us.

52. The *second* degree immediately proceeding from the first, is the one in which God equips us with the qualities necessary to establish rightly this way of life, while we begin to live again by the power of this adoption and the communion with Christ. Indeed, he ennobles us with a twofold righteousness: an imputed righteousness common to all the elect, which is usually called justification before God; and an inherent and personal righteousness which is usually called sanctification. Both are effects of this second grace (although the inherent righteousness follows the imputed righteousness). Therefore, this grace itself received a twofold name, the grace of justification and the grace of sanctification.

53. We define as grace of justification the grace according to which God regards us not in our own person but in the person of Christ, and makes his perfect righteousness, although it exists outside us, by imputation our righteousness, and incites the experience of it in our minds by faith.

54. The grace of sanctification is an internal operation of the Holy Spirit by which man, being already implanted in the communion with Christ through the mercy of God and clothed with his most absolute righteousness (which alone can exist before the tribunal of a supreme judge) is gradually transformed into that image of God that was lost through the first sin, while the Spirit himself (who is said by the apostle to be given as an earnest of our inheritance, Eph.1:14) creates a new and heavenly light in his previously obscured mind, rectitude in the will that was perverse and hostile to God, and further a true holiness in all affections.

55. The third degree of divine grace in the work of our regeneration is our conversion to God, or the action emanating from the new creature, both of the mind in acknowledging and of the will in embracing God in Christ. Everywhere in Holy Scripture this newness of life (Rom. 6:4 and Gal. 5:21) is called the fruits of the Spirit.

56. These three are the principal acts of our regeneration, in the first two of which we are nothing but passive, although not like trunks and stakes. For as natural man confers nothing to his generation, so carnal man does not contribute anything to his spiritual regeneration. However, in the third degree, which is properly the effect of the preceding ones, we begin to cooperate with the Spirit as principal agent, and acted upon by the Spirit we start acting. For that reason, Holy Scripture not rarely contributes to us in this state what is done by the Spirit.

57. Nevertheless, as long as we are dwelling in this world, the holiness of this renewal is only rudimentary, and even in the best ones there always remain remnants of a certain impurity, inasmuch as man is on this world both old and new. Hence, it occurs that in this state the freedom of the will is of a certain extent: partly to the good, partly to the bad, in as much as the will is driven by these two principles: flesh and Spirit which are conflicting with each other (the Spirit, however, being superior). Indeed, the will is driven in a free way by both principles, although in a necessary way according to the third sort of necessity.

[*Glorious spiritual freedom*]

58. In the state of glory, however, our condition will be most simple and therefore our will most free, but it will be disposed to that which is good only and this necessarily and eternally, although not coerced. For then our old man will be totally abolished, and being made like the angels, 1 Cor. 15:49, we shall perfectly bear the image of that heavenly man Christ, whom with the Father and the Holy Spirit be the honor and the glory, for ever and ever. Amen.

Corollary

The providence of God was not the cause why Adam fell, nor did it even bring any necessity upon him to act well, as long as he was in the state of integrity.

3.3 Structure of the Text

Before commenting on the text we present an overview of its structure:

1. The essence of free choice in terms of subject (*arbitrium*) and attribute (*libertas*) (theses 1-16)
    a. The etymology of the subject: threefold meaning of "*arbitrium*"
        i.   The *arbitrium* of a judge in a juridical process (thesis 2)
        ii. The judgment of the intellect (thesis 3)
        iii. The election of the will (theses 4-6)
        Regarding free choice, the latter meaning is meant.
    b. The etymology of the attribute: twofold meaning of freedom
        i.   Freedom from obligation (thesis 9)
        ii. Freedom from necessity (theses 10-12)
            1. Freedom from simple coercion: willed freely, but necessarily (e.g., self-evident ends)
            2. Freedom from proper necessity: willed freely and contingently; no necessity of the consequent or of consequence
    c. The willing subject, the willed objects and the circumstances
        i.   The willing subject: God, angels, man (thesis 14)
            1. Subjects in themselves free from coercion
            2. Subjects as related to objects: different freedom for different subjects
        ii. The willed objects: means and ends (thesis 15)
            1. Determined objects: choice is determined to it (e.g., self-evident ends)

> 2. Undetermined objects: choice has freedom towards both opposites: accepting or rejecting (e.g., means, subordinate ends)
>   iii. The circumstances: different freedom in different states (the state of integrity, the state of regeneration, the state of glory) (thesis 16)

2. Definition of liberum arbitrium: Free choice is "the faculty of the discrete will (*voluntas discreta*), free from necessity, by which a mind-gifted nature chooses one thing above another from the things which are shown by the intellect, or choice facing one and the same thing, accepts it as being good, or rejects it as being bad" (thesis 17).

   a. The subject of free choice (thesis 19)
      i. The whole subject: God, angel or man
      ii. The partial subject: the discrete will
   b. The object of free choice (theses 21-22)
      i. General: the things about which deliberation is possible: means and ends
      ii. Special: the good, the bad, the indifferent
   c. The act of free choice: election (thesis 23)
      i. Selecting one from two or more opposites: freedom of contrariety
      ii. Accepting or rejecting one proposed object: freedom of contradiction

3. Application of the definition to the various subjects of free choice: God, angels, man (theses 25-58)
   a. Divine freedom: most perfect, and prototype of created freedom
      i. Perfect freedom (theses 25-28)
         1. Freedom of willing: his perfect nature is only free towards the good.
         2. Freedom of execution: only God has the right, power and independence to accomplish everything he wills.
      ii. Prototype of all freedom: all other freedom an image of it, reflecting its Maker (thesis 29)
   b. Created freedom with regard to angels and man
      i. Both angels and man had a good will, freely following the light of the intellect (theses 30-33).
         1. Angels acted more perfectly than man, having only a [superior] immaterial nature.
         2. Human intellect could not transcend its natural boundaries to supernatural knowledge, therefore his willing principle was sustained by a supernatural principle of grace.
      ii. The free will of man made his holy state mutable (theses 35-37)
         1. Adam's good and holy will always retained a potency to its opposite [bad] choice .
         2. Consequent mutability is confirmed by the original precept, the Fall, and from divine immutability.
         3. Freedom from all necessity is confirmed by the image of God and the two trees of paradise.
      iii. By the Fall, man lost his freedom towards good and bad (theses 38-42).

    1. Man freely squandered the innate rectitude of his nature.

    2. Hence, his free potency towards good and bad is determined by a necessity to one of them, but differently according to the various states of corrupted, regenerated and glorified nature.

c. Human freedom after the Fall

    i. Human freedom in the state of corruption: a trace of original freedom (theses 43-49)

      1. Freedom in indifferent matters

      2. Freedom to the good in a narrow sense: moral and civil justice

      3. No freedom to the good in an extensive sense

        a. Either willing actions which are bad in themselves

        b. Or distorting actions which are good in themselves by a wrong principle and a wrong end

        c. No more free choice towards supernatural actions, the original principle of grace being rejected and lost by sin

    ii. Human freedom in the state of regeneration: freedom regained (theses 50-57)

      1. Three degrees of divine grace:

        a. Vivification by communion with Christ

        b. Justification and sanctification

        c. Conversion

      2. Human freedom and grace

        a. Man contributes nothing to his regeneration in the first two degrees, just like his generation.

        b. Man cooperates with the Spirit (being the principal agent) in his conversion.

        c. Freedom to the good only rudimentary, inasmuch as the principles of flesh and Spirit are conflicting.

    iii. Human freedom in the state of glory: perfect spiritual freedom (thesis 58)

      1. Our will shall be most free

        a. Free towards good only

        b. Free towards good necessarily and eternally, but not coerced

      2. This freedom is on account of perfect renovation

        a. Our old man being totally abolished

        b. We will be made like the angels

        c. We will perfectly bear the image of the heavenly man Christ.

From this scheme it becomes clear that the disputation has three main parts. After a clarification of terms, Junius provides a definition of the essence of free choice, which is subsequently applied to the various subjects of free choice. The last part, dealing with the similarities and differences of divine freedom and human freedom in its different states, is the most extensive. Our commentary will follow the main structure mapped above.

3.4 Terminological Clarification

From the start, Junius makes it clear that he wants to examine the essence of free choice. So, he investigates what always belongs to freedom, and in order to do so, he starts with a clarification of terms. Free choice denotes a subject (choice) the proper attribute of which is freedom. Before he gives a definition, Junius deals with the proper meaning of the words "choice" and "free" and how freedom is attributed to the will.

3.4.1 The Subject of Free Choice (Theses 2-7)

Naturally, a discussion of some entity starts with the subject and only after that investigates its attributes. The term "subject" will appear often in this disputation, and denotes either choice itself or a person who has free choice (God, angel or man). In the first part of his clarification of terms, Junius refers to choice itself. According to him, there are three different denotations of the term *arbitrium*. First of all, it can refer to the sentence of a judge in a controversial case. Secondly, it can denote a judgment of the intellect by which the intellect distinguishes between something being true or being false. Thirdly, it can denote a judgment of the will, by which the will decides that something is to be willed. In all three nuances, it is crucial that a person is *free* to decide.

In thesis 7 Junius explains why only the third meaning of *arbitrium* is at stake in the discussion of free choice. For it is a judgment of the *will* to choose or reject something. Initially, however, things which are the object of the judgment of will are object of the intellect, for it is the intellect that discerns these things and judges them to be good or bad. Then, the will proceeds to accept or reject them. Accordingly, Junius argues, the will does not choose at random, but has reasons for accepting or rejecting things. The reason why the will chooses something is that the intellect assesses it to be good. And the reason for the will to reject it is that it is judged to be bad. Therefore, the judgment of the will is an act of the will after a process of deliberation. It is a deliberated and argued choice.

In this way, Junius makes it clear that although the intellect plays an important role in this process of deliberation by discerning and judging, it is ultimately the will that makes the decision. The will does not automatically follow the intellect, because it has its own "sentence" and "judgment" (thesis 6).[16]

3.4.2 The Proper Attribute of Free Choice (Theses 8-16)

Subsequently, Junius discusses the meaning of the term "freedom." It is worth noting that here he is not yet referring to freedom in connection with the freedom of choice but to freedom in a general sense. Unlike Zanchi, Junius makes a distinction between the freedom of will in general (*voluntas*) and free choice (*liberum arbitrium*), and discerns more meanings of freedom than merely the freedom pertaining to free choice.

---

16. For reasons mentioned in note 10 of this chapter, we translate "*liberum arbitrium*" as "free choice."

According to its general sense, Junius distinguishes two kinds of freedom. The first general kind is freedom from obligation, the second is freedom from necessity, which, in turn, is divided as freedom from simple coercion and freedom from necessity proper.

Freedom from obligation (thesis 9) means that a person is free to follow his own course of action, because no obligation or any external impediment prohibits him from doing this. By adding "neither by any external impediment," Junius underlines that it is a condition for freedom from obligation that there are no external constraints that make the course of action impossible. Freedom from obligation can also be called freedom of circumstances or freedom of means: circumstances do not make a person's wishes impossible, and the means for carrying out his wishes are at a person's disposal. According to Junius (thesis 8), this freedom of circumstances pertains to the outcome (*eventus*) and consequences (*consequentiae*) of what someone is willing. So, we can conclude that the freedom from obligation does not regard willing itself, but only the executing of what a person wills, as he states in the last words of thesis 8.[17] For example, someone might be obliged by his boss to fly with a certain company for business trips, because the office has certain contracts with one airline only. So, the employee does have no freedom from obligation, and can only take these planes as a means to his destination. Instead, someone who is free from obligation can choose his means freely, whether he wants to fly this or that company or even go by train.

Freedom from necessity (thesis 11) is the second general kind of freedom discussed by Junius. This freedom consists of two types. In the case of freedom from simple coercion an individual is considered to "be free to act or choose voluntarily, although necessarily." The phrase "although necessarily" Junius adds for reasons made clear in thesis 14. For in that thesis he links freedom from coercion with a specific kind of objects to be willed, namely self-evident and good goals. Self-evident goals are goals of which it is self-evident that they are to be achieved. Junius gives the example of "happiness": it is self-evident that happiness is considered to be something to be aimed at and a good to be achieved. Happiness is necessary in the sense that it is not possible that an individual likes to be unhappy. However, it is important to note that, although these objects of will are necessary, we are not forced in any way to will them. We are free to will them and if we will them, we will them voluntarily.[18]

According to Junius, freedom from necessity proper (thesis 12) usually includes freedom from simple coercion. Zanchi, for example, presents the

---

17. In thesis 38 Junius mentions the *necessitas iuris et oboedientiae*. This necessity can be seen as an aspect of the *necessitas obligationis*. In that case, the opposite of a certain action is *impossible* because it is *forbidden*.

18. Note that to our modern mind something which is assessed to be self-evidently necessary to us can be assessed not to be so to others. Nonetheless, in order to understand medieval thought and Reformed scholasticism in depth, we have to be aware that free will and free choice are dealt with as rational faculties. According to our modern sense of life, we can will foolish and irrational things. We know that they are not true or even that they cannot be true. Nevertheless, we will them. In general, our authors do not analyze such cases.

traditional view that freedom from necessity proper is simply freedom from coercion.[19] The reason for this identification is that *necessitas* was etymologically derived from "coercion" or "constraint" (*ne-cedere*). Moreover, the original meaning of a term was generally held to be the proper meaning of it. Junius, however, realizes that this terminology, seen from the purely systematic point of view, is not very apt. In order to be fully free—not only in the case of necessary volitional objects but also in the case of non-necessary volitional objects—it does not suffice to be free from coercion. Accordingly, Junius states as the proper meaning of *necessitas* not its etymological meaning but the systematic meaning of the term which extends beyond freedom from coercion.

As Junius explains, an individual is free from necessity proper if the following four possibilities apply:

1. a person wills that   in formula: a W p[20]
2. a person wills that not   in formula: a W − p
3. a person does not will that not   in formula: a − W − p
4. a person does not will that   in formula: a − W p[21]

What is the difference between these four possible cases? The difference is that in the first two cases a person has an act of will, be it an affirmative (1) or a negative (2) act of will. In the latter two cases a person does not exercise an act of willing, i.e., she abstains from willing, whether that act of will would be a negative (3) or an affirmative (4) act of will. This latter pair can be understood as second-order acts of the will, namely the will-not-to-will.[22]

These four options correspond with the four corners of the famous technical and logical devise of the medieval square of opposition (see next page): (1) and (2) express positive acts of will that are located at both corners at the top, and (3) and (4) express negative acts of will that are located at the two corners at the bottom. The options opposing each other along the diagonals are called contradictions. Each of the options at the bottom of the square are implied by the respective options at the top of the square.

---

19. See section 2.7.

20. In these formulas, *a* is the subject of willing, *W* the act of willing, *p* the object of willing.

21. To our mind this sequence is not the logical one. The purely logical sequence would be (1), (2), (4) and (3).

22. *RM*, 113-122, explains that the category of second-order acts of will (or indirect will) is crucial for a correct theory of divine permission.

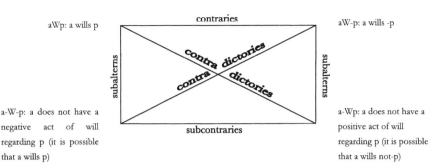

Scheme 9: The Square of Opposition with respect to the will [23]

According to Junius, the freedom from necessity proper is present when it is up to a person's own choice, and not to any other factor, to decide which of these four possibilities will be realized. Furthermore, it is important to note that Junius continues by saying that in choosing one or another of these possibilities the will is in no way hindered by the necessity of the consequent or even by the necessity of the consequence. By using the terms "necessity of the consequence" (*necessitas consequentiae*) and "necessity of the consequent" (*necessitas consequentis*) Junius refers to a technical-logical distinction that played a crucial role in medieval logic and philosophy, and in medieval theology as well.[24] Here he uses the distinction to explain why the will—if not hindered by the necessity of the consequent or the necessity of the consequence—does not have any kind of determination outside the determination by the will itself.[25]

Remarkably, Junius does not only exclude a necessity of the consequent, or proper necessity from free choice, but even hypothetical necessity has no place with regard to freedom. In order to understand this, we have to distinguish the final act of the will and the will itself in the process of willing. Later authors like Gomarus, Turrettini and De Moor are prepared to say that necessity of the consequence may apply to the acts of will. This kind of necessity has an implicative structure: on account of a, b is necessary:

$$N$$
$$(1) \quad a \rightarrow b$$

---

23. Compare section 1.4.2.

24. An extensive explanation of the distinction and its logical implications is provided in section 1.4.1 of this volume.

25. In Junius' days, the distinction was introduced into the debate on man's freedom in relation to God's will and decree. See, for example *RM*, 61-63. Dekker refers to *De Providentia Dei*, thesis 6, printed in F. Junius, *Opuscula selecta*, ed. A. Kuyper (Amsterdam: Muller, 1882), 159: "Eorum quae necessaria vocamus, duo sunt genera. Alia enim sunt per se et absolute necessaria, necessitate (ut vocant) consequentis; alia ex hypothesi, necessitate consequentiae."

Unlike other kinds of necessity, in this case both a and b can be contingent. For example, if Peter walks, it is necessary that he moves. Yet, walking is a contingent act, and this necessary implication does not make his moving itself suddenly necessary. So, a contingent act of human willing can be necessary on account of something else, e.g., that God has willed it by his decree and foreknown it. Yet God's decree, being a contingent act of his will, does not alter the contingency of the act. The crucifixion of Christ is a classic example to illustrate the necessity of the consequence:

(2) The soldiers freely crucified Christ.

(3) Hence, the crucifixion of Christ was a contingent act .

(4) The crucifixion of Christ was decreed (and foreknown and prophesied) by God.

(5) Hence, the crucifixion of Christ was necessary on account of God's decree (and foreknowledge and foresaying).

These propositions can be summarized as follows: the crucifixion of Christ (p) was both contingent in itself and also necessary by a necessity of consequence on account of the decree of God. The last proposition is symbolized by:

$$(6) \quad \overset{N}{GWp} \rightarrow p$$

In this way, it becomes clear how such a necessity is compatible with the contingency of the act. Regarding the final act of the will, Junius seems to allow the necessity of the consequence (for instance, on account of the Fall unregenerated man necessarily sins, as we will see). Yet, he clearly states that the determination of the will itself is free from all kinds of necessity: it is possible for the will to will, to will not, not to will or not to will not. So, it is of vital importance to distinguish the level of the final act from the level of the possible acts of the will. The will has many possibilities, but contingently chooses one of them. The fact that this particular act might be hypothetically necessary (on account of something else, which is in itself also contingent!) does not rule out the other possibilities as real possibilities for the will itself. On the level of possible willing, even the necessity of the consequence, which would be introduced by any internal or external principle or cause, does not apply. This necessity can only refer to the level of the final act.

3.4.3 Analogical Attribution of Freedom to the Will (Theses 13-16)

In thesis 13 Junius develops what may be called a very sophisticated theory of will. At this point, Junius does not immediately state which kind of freedom should be attached to the will. Rather, he argues that it is possible to ascribe each kind of freedom to the will "in an analogical way," that is to say, according to different categories. The different categories according to which both kinds of freedom can be attributed to the will are dependent on

a. the subjects who will;
b. the objects that are willed;
c. the circumstances in which a subject is willing an object.

a. The subjects of freedom

Regarding the subjects, or the beings which have freedom, Junius asserts that they can be viewed in two ways. In the first way the subjects are seen as they are in themselves. Considered in themselves the subjects are only free from coercion or external compulsion, but they are not free from necessity proper. Junius means that it necessarily belongs to the nature of a subject who has a will that it is willing. Such a subject cannot but will; he cannot stop being a willing person. The fact that he is willing, irrespective of what he wills, is necessary. Paradoxically, Junius calls it a "free necessity of willing" (*libera volendi necessitas*). Even in the case that a person abstains from willing, this abstaining is a (second-order) act of will.

In the second way the subjects are considered as related to the object. Here Junius makes a distinction between God and his creatures. He needs this distinction because God is related to the good as object of his willing in another way than human beings are. In theses 25-29 he will elaborate on this theme with respect to God, in 30-58 with respect to man.

b. The objects of freedom

In developing his theory of will taken in its general sense Junius proceeds to distinguish two kinds of objects. The first kind of objects Junius calls determined objects. These are objects of which the opposites cannot (rationally, cf. note 15 above) be willed. These objects are natural and self-evident ends. We note that in thesis 11 Junius has already introduced happiness as an example of self-evident ends by arguing that the opposite, unhappiness, is not a real option to choose. Therefore, in relation to these self-evident objects, only the freedom from coercion applies, not the freedom from necessity proper.

The second kind of objects are called undetermined objects. These objects have real opposites out of which a person can choose. Undetermined objects, therefore, refer to means and to subordinated and unknown ends or goals. Happiness, for example, is a determined goal, but the way ("the means") to achieve this goal is undetermined (for example, it is possible to achieve happiness by marrying or by not marrying; marrying in its turn can be seen as a subordinated goal to be achieved by other means). Regarding determined objects, choice is determined and there is only freedom from coercion. Regarding undetermined objects, choice has freedom to both opposites: accepting or rejecting. In this case there is freedom from any necessity. These objects are properly the object of free choice (thesis 21).

c. The circumstances of freedom

Junius distinguishes several kinds of circumstances referring to the four states in which man can be situated. Each of these states has its consequences for how freedom can be ascribed to man. At this point in the disputation, Junius only makes it clear that in different circumstances the will is willing in a different way, while in theses 33-58 he will show how these different states or circumstances change the mode of willing. The first state refers to the situation of man before the Fall (state of integrity), the second one to the situation after the Fall (subdivided into the state of corruption and the state of regeneration), and the third one to the future state of man (state of glory).

3.5 The Definition of Free Choice

Having explained the meaning of the term *arbitrium* and the concept of freedom, Junius proceeds by giving his definition of the *liberum arbitrium*. Again, it is important to note that Junius describes the essence or the unchangeable structure of free choice. The definition runs as follows: free choice is "the faculty of the discrete will (*voluntas discreta*), free from necessity, by which a mind-gifted nature chooses one thing above another from the things which are shown by the intellect, or choice facing one and the same thing, accepts it as being good or rejects it as being bad." In this definition he picks up several elements developed in the former theses. But at the same time he inserts some new elements, which he is going to discuss in the subsequent theses.

The definition picks up thesis 5 by the phrase: "by which a mind-gifted nature chooses one thing above another thing from the things which are shown by the intellect." But there is a difference. While in thesis 5 Junius is only speaking of free choice as "choosing or rejecting something," he now adds the phrase "chooses one thing above another." This is not without reason, for as we shall see in thesis 23, he relates these two ways of choosing to two kinds of freedom.

According to Junius, three points of this definition require further attention. First he examines the subjects of free choice, then its objects and finally its act. Earlier (theses 14 and 15) he had dealt with the subject and object of freedom in general; now he deals with the subject and the object of free choice in particular.

3.5.1 The Subject of Free Choice

Junius considers the subject of the free choice in two ways (thesis 19). First, the subject is considered as a whole and, secondly, the subject is considered as a partial subject. With the expression "the whole subject" he refers to the subject in its totality, namely a concrete being: God, angels and men. This distinction is important, because in each of these subjects free choice is not present in the same way.

With the partial subject Junius means a part or function of that person. In free choice, the relevant functional aspect (partial subject) is the discrete will. This discrete will must be distinguished from natural will, because natural will, in virtue of its nature, is the will as directed to only one thing. Natural will does not choose between different things, but is directed freely and without coercion to only one thing. As an example we can refer back to Junius' remarks in thesis 11:

116

by its nature the will pertains to happiness. Because the natural will does not choose between different things, it is not correct to view choice as belonging to natural will. Therefore, free choice is coterminous with the will viewed as "the discrete will." This discrete will is the will that discerns or chooses on the basis of the intellect's previous discernment and analysis of the object of willing.

This discrete will can *malfunction*, but if it is well *functioning*, that is, if the discrete will is moved by ordinate principles and ordinate means, to an ordinate end, in an ordinate manner, it is called "*voluntas proairetikè*" (thesis 20). In order to understand what Junius means by "ordinate," it is helpful to look at the alternative to "*voluntas proairetikè*" in thesis 20. The alternative is the "will by cause or from a cause" that occurs when the will is ill-informed and blind. Junius compares this deficiency with a disease that gets worse when the sick person acts contrary to the physician's well-informed advise. The patient is so sick that his will is no longer able to discern and to decide by itself. The sickness influences the patient in such a way that his will chooses, not what is truly good for him, but what he is longing for. In this way the sickness is the external cause by which the will of the patient is led astray.

3.5.2 The Object of Free Choice

Junius approaches the object of free choice in two ways (thesis 21). The first and general meaning of the object of free choice is anything that is possible for the will to consider. (These are the undetermined objects discussed in thesis 15.) These objects can be the means by which a person can achieve a goal, or they can be the goals themselves, although free choice seldom takes these goals into consideration, for most of the time these goals are self-evident. Self-evident goals are strived for without any consideration or deliberation.[26]

In the second and special sense, the objects of free choice are distinguished corresponding to their different moral quality: the good, the bad and the morally indifferent. In the process of deliberation and judgment the good, the bad and the indifferent can all three be an object of free choice of the subject.

Therefore, not all things are objects of free choice. Objects of free choice are only things between which the will can choose after a process of deliberation. In further analysis, these things can be bad, good or morally indifferent.

3.5.3 The Act of Free Choice: Explaining Freedom

According to Junius the act of free choice is called "election," which can be viewed in two ways (thesis 23). First, a person can choose from two or more things by preferring one thing above another thing. In this case he selects one thing from two or more opposites (for example: he can choose to go to university by bus or by bike). Secondly, a person can choose to do or not to do one and the same thing. In this case he accepts or rejects one proposed object (for example: he can choose to go to university or not to go to university). It should be noted that for the third time in this disputation on free choice Junius uses the technical

---

26. With some reservation, Junius follows Zanchi's view on means and ends as the object of free will (see section 2.5).

terminology drawing on the scholastic tradition with its distinction between freedom of contrariety (*libertas contrarietatis*) in the first case, and freedom of contradiction (*libertas contradictionis*) in the second case. In the following chapters of this book it will be clear that the freedom of contrariety can also be defined by the Reformed scholastics in terms of a freedom of specification (*libertas specificationis*), that is, the freedom to choose one object and to reject another on the assumption that the will itself is not predetermined or predisposed toward any specific object. The freedom of contradiction can also be stated as freedom of exercise (*libertas exercitii*), that is, a freedom to act or not to act.[27] So, when Junius argues that in a certain situation man has free choice we have to remember that both the freedom of contrariety *and* the freedom of contradiction are at stake.[28]

Furthermore, when these two kinds of freedom are combined with the freedom of the will from necessity proper which was discussed earlier, our conclusion is justified that free choice is maximally stated by Junius. The freedom from necessity does indeed apply to free choice, and this works out in the dual freedom of contrariety and freedom of contradiction. Given this structure, the thing willed is willed freely and contingently, and the following four cases do apply (cf. the opposition square given in section 3.4.2 above): the will is able to will, not will, or will that not or not will that not. Because the will is free from necessity proper, there is no other factor than the will itself which realizes one of these possibilities. From this argument we might get a hint of the kind of ontology Junius presupposes in his theory of will. But a final conclusion on this subject has to wait until the end of our commentary (3.8).

3.6 Application of the Definition to Various Subjects

At this point in his theses, Junius has developed the set of distinctions needed in order to formulate in which sense we can speak of free choice. A definition of the essence of free choice requires that it applies to all subjects of free choice. Yet, these subjects have different kinds of freedom, so it has to be investigated how this general definition particularly applies to free entities. As will be seen, Junius here examines the moral dimension of freedom, that is, how free choice is related to good and bad. Although different subjects are differently related to good and bad, Junius holds that they all have the same basic freedom, which is essential to them.

3.6.1 God as Subject of Free Choice (Theses 25-29)

Junius starts this section by discussing the freedom of choice respectively present in God, angels and men. Divine freedom is most perfect and the prototype of created freedom. It is an uncreated freedom and must be distinguished from the created freedom of man and angels. In order to clarify in which way God is free, Junius makes a distinction between the freedom related to

---

27. Compare sections 4.4 and 6.6 in the chapters on Gomarus and Turrettini.

28. Junius mentions the two aspects of freedom together without explaining their mutual logical relations. *RM*, 138 argues that the *libertas contradictionis* is the fundamental freedom which is presupposed by the *libertas contrarietatis*.

the *apprehension* of the will and the freedom related to the *execution* of the thing apprehended by the will.

By the apprehension of the will Junius means the performing of an act of will. God is not necessitated to his act of will. In this respect we can ascribe freedom to God, whereby freedom is understood as freedom from necessity proper, although it cannot be ascribed to God in all aspects. To explicate this, Junius considers the objects which God's will can apprehend, in two ways. In the first way the objects are taken together and set before the will, while being mutually exclusive. In this case God is not free to will all the objects, for God is not free to will contradictory things at the same moment. (For example, he cannot will that at the same time I am sick and I am healthy.) Here, it should be noted that Junius does not assert that one particular thing is a necessary object of God's will, but that he necessarily wills one object and not mutually exclusive objects. From a logical point of view it is impossible to will two things at once. In the second way the objects are considered in themselves and not related to other objects. In this case God is not free to will what is bad but he is certainly free to will what is good, according to both the freedom of contrariety and the freedom of contradiction. So, God has the possibility to choose between different good things; but he is not necessitated to choose good things, only because they are good. He can decide not to choose a good thing.

With regard to the second kind of God's freedom, the execution of the thing apprehended by the will, God is totally free: only God has the right, power and independence to accomplish everything he wills. This divine freedom is a prototype of all other freedom.

Created freedom is an image and reflection of uncreated freedom. In general, the concept of reflection plays an important role in the theology of Junius.[29] In his discussion of the nature of theology, he relates divine self-knowledge and revealed knowledge of God among human beings by the same concept. Divine knowledge is the "archetype," of which all other knowledge of God is derived. Human knowledge of God is an "ectype," a partial reflection which mirrors this infinite divine knowledge. Likewise, human freedom is an image of the freedom of its Maker. Junius is even prepared to say that man is adorned with certain particles of divinity in this respect. Therefore, human freedom is foundational for the characterization of man as the image of God. Freedom is expressly given to human beings by God to reflect his own glory. By this mark of its Creator, man reflects his Maker. Maybe that is one of the reasons why Junius discusses it so carefully and extensively in this theological disputation.

---

29. See Willem J. Van Asselt, "The Fundamental Meaning of Theology: Archetypal and Ectypal Theology in Seventeenth Century Reformed Thought," *Westminster Theological Journal* 64 (2002): 319-335; idem, "Natuurlijke theologie als uitleg van openbaring? Ectypische versus archetypische theologie in de zeventiende-eeuwse gereformeerde dogmatiek," *Nederlands Theologisch Tijdschrift* 57, no. 2 (2003): 135-152; idem, "De ontwikkeling van de remonstrantse theologie in de zeventiende eeuw als deel van het internationale calvinisme," in P. van Rooden and P. J. Knegtmans (eds.), *Theologen in ondertal. Godgeleerdheid, godsdienstwetenschap, het Athenaeum Illustre en de Universiteit van Amsterdam* (Zoetermeer: Boekencentrum, 2003), 39-54.

3.6.2 Man and Angels (Theses 30-58)

Earlier, in thesis 16, Junius had stated that the mode of freedom of the will varies on the circumstances in which it is situated. Therefore, Junius does not present one account of free choice, but four accounts that correspond to the four states of man. As we saw already, Junius uses the classical division between the state of man before the Fall and the state of man after the Fall. The state after the Fall is threefold: it concerns man in the state of corruption, man in the state of regeneration and, finally, man in the state of glory.

Junius deals with free choice in angels too, but he does so in combination with man before the Fall, since it is in this situation that free choice in man and angels are comparable. We omit a comment on free choice in angels and concentrate on free choice in man.

3.6.3 Free Choice of Man before the Fall (Theses 30-37)

Junius starts the discussion of free choice in the state of integrity by describing the constitution of man in this situation. In the state of integrity God has endowed him with the light of the intellect and the faculty of will. The will is a principle for all his actions, in virtue of which he can act freely and on his own initiative. Junius gives here a very clarifying explanation about the exact relation between intellect and will. The will is a singular principle of action, a principle of its own. Although it always follows the judgment of the intellect, this following of the will is independent (*authairetos*)[30] from the intellect: it freely assents to the intellect. So, the will follows the intellect, not because it is the slave of the intellect, but because it decides independently to do what the reason judges to be good. Undistorted by bad longings, the will decides to act, because it wills to do the good. It does not will the good because it is dictated by the intellect. The ends and means are shown to man's will by the intellect, according to the order of his nature (thesis 32), and man wills what is fitting for him. Junius refers to the faculty of will here and not especially to that of free choice. It is clear, however, that he means the discrete will pertaining to free choice, since this is the "part" of the will that chooses after the judgment of the intellect has been made.

Although both will and intellect are perfect by creation, they have their bounds. Contrary to angels, man cannot attain knowledge of supernatural things without the support of God's grace (thesis 33).

A last and important point in this section that has to be noted here is Junius' emphasis on the mutability of man. By his own will man has the ability to persist in the state of integrity (thesis 35). But at the same time he also has the possibility not to persist in this state. To persist or not to persist was left to his own free choice, free from any kind of necessity, although it was not free from the necessity of law and obedience. But this necessity of law and obedience did not force anyone to do anything. All this implies that the decree of God did not force man to sin. As Junius (citing Augustine) says: God endowed him with being able (*posse*), but willing (*velle*) what he could do was left free to his own choice.

---

30. Cf. H. G. Liddell and R. Scott, *A Greek-English Lexicon* (Oxford: Clarendon, 1996), 275

We conclude that in this section Junius argues that in the state of integrity free choice was totally free: free from all necessity (thesis 37), free from the necessity of the consequent and free from the necessity of the consequence. Furthermore, it has become clear that this freedom includes both the freedom of contradiction and the freedom of contrariety.[31]

3.7 The Three States after the Fall

With the Fall, many things changed. The Fall into sin implied the introduction of an incredible disorder and corruption in the nature of man (thesis 39). Junius does not clarify how this corruption is generated by misusing the will: Is it a kind of sentence imposed by God? Or does this corruption automatically arise after the free choice has been misused? In medieval scholasticism the term "nature" was developed into a technical sense and was considered as the sum of all the essential properties of man. But here Junius uses "nature" in its original meaning as "that into which something has grown." Nature in this original sense is the result of a process of development. The corrupted nature of man, therefore, does not point to a change in the essence of man, but it indicates what has become of man after the Fall.

At this point of his argument, Junius introduces a new kind of necessity in order to describe the situation of man after the Fall. This kind of necessity Junius calls the necessity of an existing reality and its effect (thesis 40). Hereby he means a specific reality in which something or someone is situated, which reality has necessarily a specific effect for something or someone. In brief, it is a *factual* necessity, not a *logical* necessity. The distinctive mark of each reality is the relation of man to the good and to the bad. First, there is a reality in which there is only corruption. This is the reality in which man does only the bad and Junius calls it the state of corruption. Secondly, there is a reality in which there is only holiness. In this reality man does only the good: it is the state of glory (of man in heaven). Thirdly, there is a reality in which there is both corruption and holiness. In this reality man does the good *and* the bad. It is the state of regeneration (of man after conversion).

These specific realities have their effect on the free potency to do either good or bad. Although it seems to be contradictory to say that necessity determines the free potency of man, this necessity does not exclude the free potency of man. It has to be explained in this way: the (accidental) state in which man is situated necessarily implies a specific relation to the objects of his choice, while man, nonetheless, remains essentially free in his choosing. This necessity arises from man's own nature and not from any factor from outside.

3.7.1 State of Corruption (Theses 43-49)

Now the following question arises: is free choice left after the Fall? According to Junius, it is not possible to give one answer. In some respects free choice is left; in other respects it is not (thesis 43). In one case free choice is left, namely when it

---

31. See the commentary on thesis 12.

concerns indifferent things or things without the value of good or bad.[32] In this respect there is no difference between free choice before the Fall and free choice after the Fall. But regarding good and bad things Junius certainly makes a distinction.

First, he notes that good and bad can be interpreted in two ways, namely in a stricter and in a broader sense (thesis 44). In the *strict* sense actions are good when seen as such and according to the substance of the work performed (*substantiam operis*). For example, to give a sick man medicine is a good action in itself. In the *broader* sense, however, actions are considered good according to the qualities that turn them into truly good actions with respect to their adjuncts (*ratione adjunctorum*). According to Junius, these adjuncts regard the principle, circumstances, means, the object and the aim of the action. If all these adjuncts are "ordinate" in the sense of being appropriate to the quality of the actions, then the actions are good; otherwise they are bad. For example, to give a slave medicine in order not to lose him for your production is not a good action, because the aim of the action is not good. Or, to give another example: if you free someone from his pains by amputating his leg instead of giving him medicine, the action is not good, because you do not use the good means. In the state of corruption man is able to do the good and the bad in the strict sense, although man, Junius comments, is more inclined to do bad things. Here Junius refers to political, economical and moral actions.[33] In this respect an unregenerate man can do good things, e.g., making good decisions for the benefit of the community, spending well his money and behaving as a good citizen.

To do the good or the bad in the broader sense, Junius argues, is impossible for man in the state of corruption. In this state he does only the bad, because in virtue of his corruption everything that is good in itself becomes bad, because all that is in man is bad. Junius does not mention a reason for this statement, but it is not difficult to guess what he means: man's aim (*finis*) is not good, because all that he does—though freely chosen—is not directed to God and so, in the end, all that he does is bad. Therefore, when Junius argues that in the state of corruption there is a necessity to do the bad, he does not mean that everything man does is totally bad, but it is said in view of his fundamental relation with God.

So we can conclude by saying that after the Fall free choice is left, although not regarding good things, whereby "good" means: directed to God. Free choice itself is not essentially removed (which is not possible because it belongs to the essence of man). But because of the corruption of man, he is not directed anymore to ultimately good things (these are called supernatural by Junius).

---

32. Later in the development of Reformed scholasticism (see the chapter on Turrettini) the term "*indifferentia*" played an important role. But we suggest it is wise not to interpret Junius' use of this concept in terms of later discussions.

33. Note that in thesis 45, the ability to do the morally good in the strict sense is affirmed, while in thesis 47, Bellarmine's statement that natural man can do the morally good is rejected. In the latter case, Junius must have thought of the "good" in the broader sense.

3.7.2 State of Regeneration (Theses 50-57)

After dealing with the function of free choice in the state of corruption, Junius deals with the function of free choice in the state of regeneration in which three degrees of divine grace can be discerned (thesis 50). Explicitly he points to the fact that these degrees are not to be conceived as an order of time, but as an order of cause and effect. They can operate at the same time. The first degree of divine grace he calls vivification, the second one justification and sanctification and the third one conversion. In the first degree God gives us new spiritual life. In the first part of the second degree—justification—the righteousness of Christ is reckoned to be the righteousness of man. Man himself has not changed but is only reckoned as righteous. In the second part of the second state of grace—sanctification—God changes man from within. In his intellect he receives heavenly light, so that, we conclude, he can understand what is good and is able to discern spiritual things. In his will he receives rightness, i.e., direction to God. In the third degree—conversion—man is able to change himself by his renewed intellect and will.

In relation to the first two degrees of divine grace man, though passive, is not a trunk or stake, but is personally involved. Whereas Junius does not explicate what precisely he means by this, he states that in the third degree of divine grace man is active and cooperating with the Spirit. It is in this third degree that man himself is acting and (we add) using his free choice, but on the provision that his acts are partially good and partially bad. The reason for this is that in this third degree of divine grace holiness is only rudimentarily present in man. Therefore free choice of man in this state has to be seen in a specific way: it is partially related to the bad, because of the remaining corruption, and it is partially related to the good, because of the received holiness. To both corruption and holiness two parallel principles are allocated: flesh to the corruption and Spirit to the holiness. But these principles do not impose necessity, although it is necessary that free choice is related to both bad and good (thesis 57, cf. the explanation of *factual* necessity in thesis 40). In sum: because of the sanctification of man after regeneration the ultimately good things are again within the reach of free choice.

3.7.3 State of Glory (Thesis 58)

Finally, in the state of glory in future life, the will of man will be most free, although it will necessarily be disposed to that which is only good without any external compulsion. The nature of man is so transformed that he only freely wills what is good. Junius spends only a few words on this state. Then man will only do the good, because his will is so transformed that it is only directed to God, which situation is (inversely) comparable with the situation in the state of corruption, where the will of man was so corrupted that he only longs for the bad.

It is worth noting that Junius—compared with his discussion of the state of corruption—pays little attention to the state of regeneration and the state of glory. Two reasons for this lack of attention can be given. First, the freedom of choice in the state of corruption was a matter of fierce debate in his days.

Secondly, after dealing with the state of corruption, it seems that not much more has to be said, when we assume that the sanctification of man has a similar but opposite effect on free choice as corruption had. What pertains to the state of corruption regarding the good and bad, also–though conversely–pertains to the good and bad in the state of glory. Because the state of regeneration is a combination of both, the situation of free choice in this state can be derived from the other two states.

After meditating on the state of glory, Junius gives glory to God: (Christ), to whom, with the Father and the Holy Spirit, be the honour and glory for ever and ever.

In addition to the proper disputation, Junius gives a corollary on the relation between God's providence and Adam's fall. Once again, this side remark clarifies Junius' position on necessity and freedom. God's providence did not force any necessity on Adam to do the good before his fall, nor did God make Adam fall, but God made Adam such that he could fall by his own choice.

3.8 Summary

In this disputation Junius has presented an elaborated account of free choice. In this epilogue we will give the main lines of his account and evaluate his place in the tradition.

First of all it is clear that free choice and will are not to be identified, for the will does not always operate in the same way as free choice does. The will does not always choose between things, nor does it always choose after a process of deliberation. Free choice, however, is a faculty of the discrete will. It is the choice of the will after a process of deliberation to choose something. Here, the intellect plays an important role. It sets before the will the objects between which the free choice can decide whether they are good or bad. It is however left to the independent free choice which possibility it chooses, although it chooses not at random, but on the arguments given by reason. It chooses something because it is assessed by the intellect to be good, or it rejects something because it is assessed by the intellect to be bad.

Free choice given to man in creation is a reflection or an image of the divine freedom of his divine Maker. Therefore, free choice in the state of integrity was totally free and not restricted by any necessity. In order to explicate this, Junius used the traditional technical terms "necessity of consequence" and "necessity of consequent." From thesis 37 we can conclude that the free choice was free from both necessities: nothing outside the will of man forces him to choose something. Junius explicates free choice further by using two technical terms from the scholastic tradition, the freedom of contradiction and the freedom of contrariety. Together with the freedom from necessity proper it becomes clear that for Junius it is in the power of free choice to realize or not to realize a state of affairs or to realize one state of affairs instead of another state of affairs.

In this way Junius presents a fine account of what after the Fall of man has changed regarding free choice. After the Fall of man, the essence of free choice has not changed and it is not forced by anything outside. After the Fall too it remains free from necessity proper. At the same time, however, Junius asserts that whatever free choice chooses, it cannot be good, because only things done with a will directed to God are ultimately good. In regeneration free choice is restored with respect to the ultimately good things, although the corruption with all its consequences is not taken away. In the state of glory free choice only chooses good things. Then "we shall perfectly bear the image of that heavenly man Christ." Then we will exercise free choice in freely loving God as our ultimate end. Every choice is then chosen in service to the triune God as the basis of our happiness.

Junius was a Reformed theologian. Reformers like Luther and Calvin downplayed the existence of freedom of choice after the Fall. Accordingly, Junius states that man in the state of corruption cannot do but evil, because the source of his deeds is not good. But this does not imply for him that man has lost free choice. Free choice still functions, but distinctions are needed to make clear in which respect free choice is free. In that respect he has a more sophisticated view of free will than Luther and Calvin. Furthermore, we have seen that he used many technical terms stemming from medieval scholastic theology. Junius belongs to those Reformed theologians who relate their theology to the theological tradition of the medieval church, and extensively used its technical terms and distinctions in order to state the Reformed case in the debate with opponents. If we discern, in medieval Christian thinking, an intellectualist approach and a voluntaristic approach,[34] we have evidence to see Junius more in line with the voluntaristic tradition of the Middle Ages. Junius sees free choice as a faculty or part of the will, not as a part of the intellect. Although he does not explicitly state which part has the supremacy, the intellect or the will, he clearly emphasizes the independence of the (not-irrational) will from the intellect.

Related to this, we draw some conclusions on the ontology of Junius. Junius uses two sets of distinctions that suggest a model of synchronic contingency. These two sets are: first, the distinction between the freedom from "the necessity of the consequence" and freedom from "the necessity of the consequent" and, secondly, the distinction between freedom of contradiction and freedom of contrariety. The first set of distinctions is often used to avoid determinism and to assert that the *implicative* necessity of, for instance, God's knowing my actions does not impose an *absolute* necessity on me that would destroy my freedom. The second set is used to assert the different, contrary, possible options of acting for man. One important distinction belonging to a synchronic-contingent ontology, *in sensu diviso* and *in sensu composito*, is not mentioned by Junius.[35] But the two crucial distinctions positively endorsed by Junius give sufficient evidence for claiming that Junius' account of freedom presupposes a real alternativity in reality, i.e., a synchronic-contingent ontology.

---

34. See *CHLMP*, 629-641.
35. See the sections 5.4, 6.6 and 7.7 in the chapters on Voetius, Turrettini and De Moor.

4

Undisputed Freedom

A Disputation of Franciscus Gomarus (1563-1641)

4.1 Introduction

Two years after Junius began teaching at Leiden University, Franciscus Gomarus became professor at the same institution.[1] He was born in 1563 and studied in Straatsburg, Neustadt an der Haardt, Oxford, Cambridge and Heidelberg under important exponents of the second and third generation of Reformed theologians, such as Zanchi. After his studies, he became minister in Frankfort an der Main and Hanau (1586) and in 1594, when he was hardly thirty years old, he was invited to become professor of theology at Leiden University.

With respect to academy and church, his position became very significant in the debate with Jacobus Arminius (1559-1609), in which he was rather unwillingly forced. His rather notorious reputation in church history depends mainly on this debate about predestination.

At that time however, Gomarus had already written the *Approval of the Orthodox Doctrine of the Providence of God* (*Conciliatio doctrinae orthodoxae de providentia Dei*, Leiden, 1597), a major book on the relation between divine and human freedom. Here, he elaborated the Christian view on divine providence, showing that the divine will is free in a complete sense and relates to all things, granting human beings their own created freedom. So, concerning the content of the debate, Gomarus had already mastered theology in an academic sense, and his logical and metaphysical accuracy promised success and influence.[2]

Yet, it would be quite unfair to depict Gomarus as a rigid scholastic predestinarian, whose faith was governed by speculative philosophy, squeezing the *viva vox* of Scripture in an arid dogmatic system. Gomarus had a profound interest in original languages and the new developments in the field of philological Bible exegesis, which had emerged in the fifteenth and sixteenth centuries.[3] This Renaissance movement *ad fontes* is usually contrasted with

---

1. For the biography of Gomarus, see: G. P. van Itterzon, *Franciscus Gomarus*, (The Hague: Martinus Nijhoff, 1930); Willem J. van Asselt, "Franciscus Gomarus," in Wiep van Bunge (ed.), *The Dictionary of Seventeenth and Eighteenth-Century Dutch Philosophers* (Bristol: Thoemmes, 2003), 1:340-341.

2. The published research on the theology of Gomarus is still slight. At Utrecht University several (unpublished) MA theses have been written on his doctrine of God, predestination and original sin by J. Knoop, A. J. Kunz and M. A. Schouten.

3. Cf. *CHLMP*, 797-807.

scholastic method, but Gomarus, like many others, kept both together.[4] His exegetical expertise was acknowledged in his appointment by the authority of the General States of the Netherlands as proofreader for the new Dutch Bible translation, from 1629 till 1637.[5]

After Leiden, Gomarus lectured in Saumur (1615-1618) and Groningen (1618-1641). He died in 1641 after a final period of fruitful and untroubled labor. His systematic elaboration of Reformed theology influenced such prominent and divergent theologians as Samuel Maresius (1599-1673) and Gisbertus Voetius (1589-1676).

4.2 Translation of the Text

Gomarus held three disputations on free choice during his career, of which we have selected the first one.[6] It was defended on June 28, 1602 by Gilbertus Jacchaeus.[7] Arminius was not appointed in Leiden until 1603, and the debate started in the course of 1604. In this disputation, Gomarus rather undisturbedly presents his original position. The main debate in this disputation concerns the Catholic Reformation, being represented in thesis IX of this disputation by Robertus Bellarminus (1542-1621), one of the most famous Roman Catholic polemicists of that time.[8] The disputation is divided into twenty-six theses, being indicated with a Roman numeral.

Theological disputation on free choice, which Gilbertus Jacchaeus proposes for public examination, on D.V. 28 June 1602, Franciscus Gomarus ... presiding.

[*A. Definition of free choice*]
I.   Free choice is the free power of a mind-gifted nature to choose from those [means] leading to a certain goal, one [means] proposed by reason above another, or to accept or reject one and the same [means].

[*Preliminary points: the subjects, acts and freedom of choice*]
II.   In order to have a precise grasp of this definition, we must know that free choice exclusively applies to the mind-gifted natures of God, angels and

---

4. Paul Oskar Kristeller has powerfully combatted the absolute contrast between scholasticism and humanism in *Renaissance Thought and Its Sources* (New York: Columbia University Press, 1979).

5. For Gomarus' work on exegesis as well as his proofreading, see Van Itterzon, *Franciscus Gomarus*, 254-260, 325-368.

6. The other disputations under the chairmanship of Gomarus are respectively: Samuel Gruterus, *Disputationum theologicarum decima-quarta de libero arbitrio* [19 Martii] (Leiden, 1603); and Hieronymus Vogellius, *Disputationum theologicarum quinto repetitarum decima-sexta de libero arbitrio* [24 Nov.] (Leiden, 1607). On the authorship of disputations, see the introduction on Junius (3.1).

7. Gilbert Jack (c. 1578-1628) was born in Aberdeen. Just three years after his dispuation on free will, he was appointed as extraordinary professor in logic at Leiden and from that time on he contributed greatly to the teaching of logic and metaphysics in Leiden. See Han van Ruler, "Jacchaeus, Gilbertus (c.1578-1628)," in *DDPh* I, 487-493.

8. For Bellarminus' view on free will, see Dekker, "An Ecumenical Debate," in *RS*, 141-154.

human beings. Since free choice does not differ from the will, any nature which is will-gifted must be taken to have free choice. For it is the same faculty: with regard to a goal it is called will (*voluntas*); with regard to the means, however, it is called free choice (*liberum arbitrium*), just as the one intellective potency is called intellect (*intellectus*) with regard to first principles, and is called reason (*ratio*) in so far as it draws conclusions.

III.   The term "free act" can be used in two ways: either with respect to the kind (*species*) of an act or with respect to the exercise (*exercitium*) of an act.

An act is called free with respect to its kind, if we embrace an object in such a way that we are able to (*posse*) reject it, or reject it in such a way that we are able to embrace it.

An act is called free with respect to the exercise, if the act is elicited in such a way that—the knowledge of the object remaining the same—it is also possible (*posse*) to be not-elicited. Free choice applies either to both acts, or at least to one of them, namely that of exercise.

IV.   Freedom is twofold: one from coercion and another from necessity.

Free from coercion is that which, although it is necessitated to its act, nevertheless is free in the sense that it is not coerced, but works spontaneously, like a stone falling down, or a dog hunting game.

Free from necessity is that which is by itself indeterminate, i.e., which determines itself by an intrinsic potency to elicit its own act. Free choice is free in both ways, not only in the sense that it is not coerced, but also in the sense that it is not necessitated.

[Unfolding of the definition]
V.   This being presupposed, I say that free choice is a *potency* or *faculty*, flowing forth from the essence of the soul, so it is certainly not an act or habit or something similar. For a human being has free choice even if he does not do anything, but an act exists only when it is being exercised.

Nor is it a habit, for every habit is determined to one [kind of acts], but free choice, being a free potency, is like a mistress of its own act and is able to produce or not to produce that [act], according to its choice (*arbitrium*).

VI.   I say: of *a mind-gifted nature*, since the principial "principle by which" (*principium quo*) of a free action [by which it is performed], is always the essential spiritual form, as is the rational soul in a human being.

VII.   I say: from those [things] *leading to a goal*, since the proper objects of free choice are formed by the means leading to a goal, and since its proper act relates to them most of all. For when reason presents various means to attain a goal and persuades to accept one or another according to the nature of the goal, then free choice relates itself to that means in such a way that it either chooses or rejects it, otherwise than the potency of intellect [relates to it]; for that is a necessary potency, which assents necessarily to the proposed object.

VIII.   I say: *choose one above another*, for sometimes there are more means, namely three or four, and in that situation free choice behaves in such a way that it chooses one means above another, which act is called the freedom of contrariety (*libertas contrarietatis*) in the schools.

Sometimes, however, there is only one means, which is accepted or rejected, which [freedom] is called the freedom of contradiction (*libertas contradictionis*).

IX.   I add: *in accordance with what reason deems best to fit*, not because the judgment of reason determines the will, as Bellarmine wishes, Book III, *Free choice and grace* chapter 8, but only because reason judges the goodness or badness of a means.[9]

[*B. Theological anthropology*]

X.   These things being presupposed, let us now consider what a human being was able to [choose] with respect to spiritual matters and concerning the Kingdom of God and the salvation of the soul before the Fall; what [it was able to choose] after the Fall and before conversion, what in conversion, and what after conversion.

[*The first state*]

XI.   Human beings before the Fall were made perfectly, without any stain or lack of either soul and body. For human beings did not only consist of soul and body as essential parts, but also of these added (*superadditis*) ornaments: namely, being endowed with original justice and holiness, the soul did not only direct the lower powers and potencies, but it also perfectly subjected the human being properly and personally (*verum et ipsum*) to God, so that he was able to execute whatever God would command, without additional grace.

XII.   The body, being endowed with immortality and a certain majesty in its ruling among the rest of the beasts, was perfectly subjected to the soul and was so apt to its call, that it promoted its actions rather than impeded them, as in short, there was such a harmony between all faculties and parts of man, that wherever the will would bend, they would adjust to it.

XIII.   Original righteousness perfected the soul to such an extent, that as long it remained, it was possible for the soul to perform nothing that was not

---

9. This is chapter 8, "De Libero Arbitrio et Gratia," in Book III of Bellarmine's famous (four-volume) *Disputationes de Controversiis christianae fidei adversus huius temporis haereticos* (Ingolstadt, 1596).

pleasing to God and really good [i.e., to perform perfectly good works]. For it was possible for her to choose the good and consequently live, or choose the bad (yet under the appearance of a good) and consequently die, as happened.

XIV. This original righteousness, however, has been natural in so far as it not only perfected nature, and elevated nature to its supernatural goal, but also in so far as it was given to man from the very first beginning. In this sense others call it supernatural, since it did not flow from the essence of the human being.
Thus far concerning the first state of the human being.

[*The second state*]
XV. A second and indeed very miserable one follows. Let us see what is taken by it from man and what has remained.

XVI. In the first place no sane person will deny that he remains a human being, although a wounded one. Namely, insofar he was before the Fall undisputably a mind-gifted animal (*animal rationale*), so also after the Fall. The necessity of a definition, namely, is so absolute that it cannot be altered without contradiction.

XVII. And not only do body and soul remain in a corrupted human being body and soul as partial substances, but also the faculties and potencies of them, which flow from them with material necessity, although now they are attrited. [The corrupted human being] has undeniably intellect and will, and also imagination and a twofold appetite [attraction and rejection], corresponding to it.

XVIII. The defect, however, is this, that a human being is bereft (*privatus*) from original righteousness. and holiness, the source of every good action; furthermore [is the defect] that his immortal body has become mortal and the lower appetite runs counter to reason to such an extent, that it throws off the yoke of reason and tries to attain dominion.

XIX. This being the case, nevertheless the faculties are able to do something remaining [good] in external affairs of both practical and theoretical nature. For although the intellect is clouded, it is able to investigate the nature of things, in order to measure their magnitude and proportion and to understand many things about God and his essence, albeit with difficulty. The intellect can even discuss the Trinity and the person of Christ when reading Scripture, but not as it is due, i.e., not out of a godly devotion and godly inclination towards God. This is also valid for morality, as the Apostle teaches in Rom. 2:14: "For the gentiles who do not have the Law, do by nature the things contained in the Law."[10] Concerning all these things we frankly teach that the unregenerate man performs them freely.

XX. However, this does not alter the fact that the doctors of our Churches justly assert that nothing can flow forth from an unregenerate human being but sin and damnable things, and [they justly assert] that in spiritual matters, like in repentance, justification, etc., not any free choice is left at all (except an idle name).

XXI. Since before the Fall original justice was the source and principle of every spiritual and truly good act, this [source] being taken away, no acts flow from there anymore—unless somebody would dare to claim that an effect can exist without a cause. And since a contrary habit succeeded it, there is no doubt that whatever corrupted human being does without grace, it is hostile and adverse to God. Because "the mind of the flesh (φρόνημα carnis) is enmity against God, for it is not subject to the law of God, neither indeed can be," Rom. 8:7; "every imagination and the thoughts of his heart was only evil continually," Gen. 6:5; "The natural man does not receive the gifts of the Spirit of God, for they are folly to him, and he is not able to understand them because they are spiritually discerned," 1 Cor. 2:14.[11] In Eph. 2:1 and Coloss. 2:13, the Holy Spirit declares that all human beings are *dead by nature*, and as there is in a dead man no potency to act unto life, so neither is in the unregenerate a natural potency to perform any good spiritual work, unless that which is above its nature fashions a new intellect and heart.

XXII. Although the unregenerate are not able to do anything but sin, they do it freely, for they elicit the exercise (*exercitium*) of an act in such a way that they are able not to elicit it, and they are in a way masters of their own acts. However, with respect to the kind (*species*) of act they are determined, since they are able to do nothing else but sin and have evil as their object, under the pretext of the good.
Besides, it is not otherwise for the good angels, who, confirmed in grace, are necessarily determined with regard to the kind of act, for they are able to do nothing else but good, even if [the exercise] to elicit an act here and now is totally free for them.

XXIII. Since good works follow justification and presuppose an infused faith and love, it is clear how the glorious deeds (as they are commonly entitled) of Scipio and other heathens must be judged. For they lack the pure source

---

10. We have reworded the RSV here more closely to Gomarus' text.
11. The citation from Romans is translated from the Latin to preserve Gomarus' wording of the "mind of the flesh" (RSV has "the mind that is set on the flesh").

(*fonte*), namely, faith (*fide*), and their goal (*fine*), namely the honor of God. How can anyone dignify these [works], I ask, to call them good?
This about the second state. Now, a third [state] follows.

[*The third state*]

XXIV. Concerning this [state], it is discussed whether either our will according to its natural and inborn faculty cooperates actively with the divine will in the first conversion towards God; or whether the will is rather passive in the first conversion, in such a way that the will concurs in no way [with divine will] at the first moment of conversion, but bears (*patiatur*) that this power (δύναμιν) of willing well is being infused to it? The first is claimed by the Roman Catholics; we claim the second, and this with Scripture.

XXV. [For instance:] Ez. 11:19: "I will take the stony heart out of their flesh and give them a heart of flesh." 1 Cor. 12:3: "No one can say "Jesus is Lord," except by the Holy Spirit." Ps. 51:10: "Create in me a clean heart, O God, and put a new and right spirit within me." John 6:44: "No one can come to Me, unless the Father who sent Me draws him." Philip. 2:13: "For God is at work in you, both to will and to work for his good pleasure."
This about the third [state]; on it follows a fourth.

[*The fourth state*]

XXVI. In this fourth [state], being renewed and made children of God which are led by the Holy Spirit, they act in such a way that they freely cooperate with divine grace. For since the new man is built up gradually, which means that the image of God, lost in Adam, returns little by little, it is not doubtful that they will freely, and devise their actions in shape with the divine Law. Indeed, the more sin is expelled and grace introduced, the more vigorous freedom gets, until they lay off sin completely, being shaped to [the image of] Christ. With Scripture I assert that what is started in man by prevenient grace, is made perfect and completed by concomitant grace.

4.3 Structure of the Text

In commenting on what Gomarus has to say about free choice, it is very important to realize that our text is a disputation, and texts of this genre tend to be very condensed. Gomarus' text is no exception to this rule. Since the text is so dense, it is worthwhile to consider its structure first.

1. Definition of free choice (theses I-IX)
   a. Definition: Free choice is "the free power of a mind-gifted nature to choose from those [means] leading to a certain goal, one [means] proposed by reason above another, or to accept or reject one and the same [means]." (thesis I)
   b. Demarcation of the discussion (theses II-IV)

- i.   Subjects of free choice: mind-gifted natures (thesis II)
- ii. Acts of free choice: called free with respect to their kind or their exercise (thesis III)
- iii. Freedom from coercion and from necessity (thesis IV)
- c.   Explanation of the definition (theses V-IX)
  - i.   Choice relates to means (thesis VI)
  - ii. Freedom of contrariety and freedom of contradiction (thesis VIII)

2. Theological Anthropology (theses X-XXVI)
   - a. Ability of free choice in spiritual matters in the four states of human beings (thesis X)
     - i.   First state: before the Fall (theses XI-XIV)
       Power to choose good and bad (thesis XIII)
     - ii. Second state: after the Fall but before conversion (theses XV-XXIII)
       No power to choose good, freedom of exercise only (thesis XXII)
     - iii. Third state: in conversion (thesis XIV-XV)
       Human will passive in first conversion
     - iv. Fourth state: after conversion (thesis XVI)
       Free cooperation with divine grace: the more sin is expelled, the more vigorous freedom gets

The disputation has two main parts: the definition of free choice and a theological anthropology. The things Gomarus wants us to know in his definition and subsequent clarification all apply to his theological anthropology, as we shall see later on.

Within the first part, we can distinguish between Gomarus' definition of what free choice is (thesis I), the preliminary points regarding what is and what is not indicated by the terms used in the definition (theses II-IV) and the unfolding of the definition (theses V-IX). The method of first giving a definition and then step by step unfolding or elucidating it, is common in scholastic discourse.

The very concise definition of free choice at the beginning is not an arbitrary formulation, as also Gomarus himself makes clear later on (in thesis XVI). The definition provides the essential characteristics of free choice, because choice always has these properties. Because Gomarus expects his readers to pay close attention to each and every term of his definition, he conscientiously makes some preliminary points to demarcate the real issue of freedom (theses II-IV). This section interrupts to some extent the scheme of giving a definition and commenting on its components, but we can easily see why such a section is needed. There is much confusion about the use of specific terms, and it is better to clarify beforehand the way in which they are to be understood. Having clarified the proper topic of the disputation, Gomarus explains his definition by elaborating on its terms.

The second main part of our disputation is on what we have called "theological anthropology." Here we find a discussion of the various "states" of a human being: (1) before the Fall, (2) after the Fall but before conversion, (3) in conversion and (4) after conversion. It is important to note that these are not the four proper states which are usually discussed with respect to free choice.[12] Instead, Gomarus leaves out the fourth state of the renewed in glory and treats the moment of conversion separately.[13] We suggest that he wanted to treat the most controversial points only, and therefore left out the state of glory and instead paid attention to the moment of conversion.

This might also make clear why the second state (the state of a person after the Fall but before conversion) is treated most extensively. Here, the power of free choice to do good is lacking, but still choice is free according to Gomarus. Catholics like Bellarmine granted free choice in the second state some power in spiritual matters and charged the Reformed with destroying freedom by their denial of it. Therefore, the Reformed opinion of free choice could be easily misunderstood and needed explanation concerning this state in particular.

It is important to mention once again that Gomarus wants us to keep in mind the distinctions made earlier, for in his discussion of the various "states" a human person can be in, he constantly presupposes these distinctions.

4.4 The Definition of Free Choice

Gomarus starts with supplying a definition of *liberum arbitrium*, of which he provides an extensive explication: "Free choice is the free power of mind-gifted nature to choose from those things leading to a goal, one thing proposed by reason above another, or to accept or reject that one thing" (thesis I). Such a dense definition can only be understood properly if one already knows its concepts and its explanation. In effect, it could rather be taken to be an extremely concise summary of the disputation.

Two issues especially deserve attention here: the relation of free choice to the will and its relation to the intellect. Gomarus alternately discusses both, but in order not to distract attention, we first comment on issues related to the will, and later on come back to the issue of the relationship between free choice and intellect (in commenting on thesis VI onward).

In thesis II we find Gomarus' way of connecting free choice to the will. Although some theologians, like Gomarus' teacher Zanchi, view free choice and will as synonyms, Gomarus makes a distinction here. Both concepts refer to the same power, but properly spoken the "will" (*voluntas*) refers to the potency as directed to a goal and "free choice" (*arbitrium*) denotes it in relation to the means which are to be chosen.

Perhaps an example will elucidate the matter. Suppose I am thirsty and want to quench my thirst; the quenching of my thirst is the goal I am willing. There are different ways to fulfill that goal. But that is to say that I may will different means.

---

12. These states (compare the other chapters) are usually qualified as "before the Fall," "after the Fall," "after conversion" and "in glory." They denote a moral state of the will, which is directed to either good or bad or both.

13. Gomarus only calls the first two explicitly a "state." Whereas the usual states convey the different moral states of the will, the moment of conversion is rather a transition from the second to the third state. Yet, both states and their transitions have to do with the moral powers of free choice with respect to spiritual matters, and these powers are the proper theme of Gomarus (cf. thesis X).

For instance, I could will to drink water or juice or another appropriate beverage. Another example: If a person wants to live to God's honor, he can accomplish that by willing to look after the poor or by devoting his life to the study of theology, or whichever other ways there are to fulfill the willed goal.

Because will and free choice are the same faculty, but seen from different angles, Gomarus' disputation is about free choice; the issue is not the freedom of the will with respect to the goals, but with respect to the means.[14] In this respect of the means, he says that the choice of the will is free.

In thesis III, a further specification is added. This specification is in fact already an elucidation of the definition, and therefore we see it recur in thesis VIII. Discussing the range of free choice, Gomarus mentions two types of freedom. In the first place, freedom to choose the one means above the other. He calls this with a traditional term, freedom of contrariety (*libertas contrarietatis*, or, with an equivalent term, freedom with respect to its kind [*libertas quoad speciem actus*]).[15] It is the freedom to choose from various means to attain a goal. For example, one could choose either car or bike to get home. In the second place, Gomarus discusses freedom of contradiction (*libertas contradictionis*, or, again with an equivalent term, freedom with respect to the exercise [*libertas quoad exercitium*])[16]. Here we encounter freedom of the volition itself. For example, I could will to go home or not will to go home. Although free choice applies to both types of freedom, Gomarus explicitly states that the freedom with respect to the exercise of act is the basic one. The other type can be lacking, but free choice is still there.

Thesis IV brings us a final elucidation regarding freedom. Free choice is both free from coercion and free from necessity. The first one, freedom from coercion, regards the fact that if a person makes a decision, he is not coerced from outside to do that. This means that a person's choice is spontaneous, not "against his will." Such a choice, however, could still be necessitated from the inside, as it were. This type of necessitation is ruled out in the second type of freedom mentioned in this thesis, the freedom from necessity. We should be aware of the fact that, according to Gomarus, free choice determines itself, and therefore, is free from necessity. Indeed, this is a most important contribution to the elucidation of what exactly we mean by "free choice." For if we had only the former elucidations of the concept, it would still be possible for circumstantial factors to determine which actual choice free choice would make. But here Gomarus explicitly refers to a free act as being "from itself indeterminate, i.e., which determines itself out of intrinsic potency." There is no power which can necessitate the actual choice. There is only the intrinsic potency of the will itself, which determines the actual choice of the will.

---

14. Gomarus makes it clear (thesis VII) that all objects of free choice are directed to the goal, so the freedom of the *arbitrium* is seen in the context of the will itself: if the will has an evil goal, a good choice is impossible from the outset, because the whole motivation is wrong. Gomarus does not discuss the freedom of the will with regard to the goal, but being the same faculty, the qualifications of the *arbitrium* must bear on the *voluntas* as well.

15. In logical terms: $aWp \wedge aW\text{-}p$. In turn, $aW\text{-}p$ can be taken to mean: aWq.

16. In logical formula: $aWp \wedge a\text{-}Wp$.

We now come to the point at which Gomarus actually starts to unfold his definition. In thesis V, he first comments on the proper place of free choice. Its proper place is in the soul. Gomarus actually says "that free choice is a potency or faculty, flowing forth from the essence of the soul," by which he means to say that having free choice is essential to being human. Gomarus then specifies that free choice is a potency and not an act or a habit. For we only have an act if something is being done. Free choice, however, is an essential property, a power which exists also if man does not use it. It is not a habit either, for a habit is a disposition which by definition is related to one thing only. Since free choice is actually a free potency, which is related to two or more possible alternatives (as Gomarus made clear in the former thesis and is restating it here), it cannot be a habit.

We did not yet comment on the fact that Gomarus attaches free choice to mind-gifted natures. This concept raises the question of Gomarus' opinion on the relationship between intellect and will. In his definition, he makes use of the term "mind-gifted nature" (*natura intelligens*) to express cognitive power. He also uses another term, reason (*ratio*) to express argumentative power. So, reason is the form of the intellect which is used if an argumentation of some kind is to be performed. "Intellect" in a restricted sense seems to relate to those things which can be known intuitively, without having to argue for them.

In this context, Gomarus draws a parallel between the potencies of knowing and willing. Just like the intellect proper (*intellectus*) perceives the truths which are known in themselves and reason (*ratio*) concludes what can be deduced subsequently, so the will proper (*voluntas*) desires the goals which are good in themselves and free choice seeks the appropriate induced means.

Both times when Gomarus speaks about mind-gifted natures, he immediately introduces the concept of will (theses II and VI). So, this term does not report a rationalistic anthropology. Also the term "reason" (*ratio*) can easily be misunderstood. In this context, it does not mean "reason" as it came to be understood since the Renaissance and Enlightenment: referring to reason as the only source of knowledge, possessed by the autonomous human being, living without God. In Gomarus' usage it functions in an anthropology in which man is regarded as living before God (*coram deo*). Here, reason is "argumentative power," and it is a power in service of faith, not at war with it.

So, Gomarus' usage of the term "mind-gifted natures" displays an intimate relation between intellect and will. If free choice is to function at all, reason is a *conditio sine qua non*: reason supplies information about possible choices and their relative advantages. A goal cannot be reached without weighing the different means, nor without the choice of the right means. Reason plays a major role here.

Therefore, it is precisely in free choice where intellect and will combine. We cannot will anything without knowing what there is to be willed, nor can we choose anything without having a will in the first place. For, as Gomarus makes explicit, free choice makes a *free* choice. It is not the case that the will just slavishly follows reason. On the other hand, it is also not the case that the will just chooses at random. Gomarus seems to make an addition to the original definition when he adds (or at least clarifies himself): "in keeping with what reason deems best to execute" (thesis IX). There is a direct relation between intellect and will. Although reason's judgment is not supposed to *determine* free choice, it nevertheless *guides* it.

This relation between intellect and will (or precisely, reason and choice) straightforwardly applies to the case of means (thesis VII). Reason judges the various means to a goal; free choice elects or rejects them. The intellect's potencies would not be able to elect or reject, for as Gomarus has it, "the intellect necessarily assents to the proposed object." In a harmonious situation free choice will choose the right means to reach the goal. A human being knows whether a means is good or bad by its argumentative power.

In summary: by defining free choice as a free power of a mind-gifted nature, Gomarus situates the task of free choice to choose the right means within the context of a goal-directed will and a means-assessing intellect.

4.5 Free Choice in Its Four States

What does Gomarus' exposition mean in terms of a theological anthropology? That is the subject of the second part of the disputation. Especially the question about the capabilities of man in spiritual matters is important for him. There is another Leiden disputation in which Gomarus extensively discusses free choice in natural matters like eating and drinking and in moral matters.[17] These are almost completely kept out of consideration in the present disputation (an exception is thesis XIX). Gomarus concentrates upon free choice in spiritual matters. So in a way, we cannot say that in the present disputation we find Gomarus' complete doctrine of free choice. However, the subject of free choice in spiritual matters is of course the culmination point of the theological debate: what capabilities does man have in spiritual matters?

In what follows, Gomarus answers this question. In order to do so, he first introduces a fourfold distinction (thesis X): we should ask our question with respect to the potencies of human being (1) before the Fall, (2) after the Fall and before conversion, (3) in conversion and (4) after conversion. We have noted already that these four moments are not the usual states of common theological anthropology, as Gomarus' third moment is in fact the transition from the second to the third state.[18]

This fourfold distinction will prove to be crucial for the interpretation of Gomarus' doctrine of free choice. As we shall see, there is a great difference between the way free choice functions before and after the Fall, as there is a great difference between the functioning of free choice before and after conversion. In a way, these distinctions give a salvation history structure to this second part of our disputation. Let us see how free choice functions in each of the "states."

---

17. *De libero arbitrio*, 19 maart 1603. Respondent: Samuel Gruterus.
18. Compare note 11.

4.5.1 Free Choice before the Fall

In the first place, there is the situation before the Fall. Gomarus posits that human being is created perfectly by God, without any stain or lack of body and soul. Body and soul form a twin which is essential for mankind.

In addition to these essential properties, human being had accidental properties as well. Gomarus speaks about "added ornaments" (thesis XI), an expression we take to be a metaphor of accidental properties. These ornaments consist in original righteousness and holiness for the soul, and in the power not to die for the body. Especially original righteousness and holiness are important for the functioning of free choice. They constitute as it were the source from which reason draws and proposes various means to free choice.[19] Original righteousness and holiness, however, are accidental properties. So, if man loses this original righteousness, he remains man, as Gomarus reminds us later on (thesis XVI). The same thought follows from Gomarus' remarks on perfection: original righteousness perfects nature (theses XIII and XIV). So it is a perfecting property, not contained in the essence. It is indeed God's gift. Gomarus can say that original righteousness is "natural," but then he takes it to refer to the fact that it was given from the very first beginning. Nevertheless, it is an accidental property—an ornament, to use Gomarus' description. He is aware of others[20] who, for that reason, prefer to speak of original righteousness as a supernatural rather than as a natural property.

It seems to be the case that Gomarus wants us to understand the discussion about original righteousness as the "source" of good things as being connected with the goal of our will. If we do not choose as our goal the glory of God, or if we want to undo the directness toward God, then by that very fact we lose our righteousness and become sinners.

In his exposition of original righteousness in thesis XIII, Gomarus precisely distinguishes the structural level of Adam's possibilities from his actual acting. It was possible for him to choose the good and it was possible to choose the bad. So on a structural level, both were possible for Adam. Here, the verb "can" (*posse*) seems to be used by Gomarus in the sense of possibility.[21] In the first part of the thesis he seems to denote the ability of Adam instead. By original righteousness, Adam was perfectly able to obey God. He could act in such a way that he did nothing that was not pleasing to God. The double negations in the sentence are a bit confusing, but Gomarus positively means that Adam was able to obey (that is, do nothing that is displeasing to God).

Therefore, the structural level of possibility should not be interpreted in a neutral sense.[22] Adam was able to choose good and bad on the level of means,

---

19. This metaphor is Gomarus' own; see thesis XXI.
20. We do not know who they are.
21. Compare sections 1.3.2 and 1.4.1.
22. Cf. *DLGT*, 177: "In the Reformed view, an original indifference to good or evil would have been a defect in the creature. Adam was not therefore indifferent to good and evil, but created good and upright, with the ability to continue in the good. Adam's freedom was a freedom to be obedient, not a freedom to obey or refuse to obey." The issue of how the

but the goal of his will was good as well. So, it was natural for him to choose the good on the level of means. So, free choice is not neutral, as if it were the case that man, before the Fall, could indifferently choose between two alternatives: obey God or disobey him. Disobedience is unnatural for a good creature, who is directed unto God from the creation of his being onward. This is indicated by Gomarus when he says that original righteousness elevated human nature to its supernatural goal. As long as original righteousness was present, man was directed to God as his goal.

Yet, the possibility level did not only apply to free choice regarding the means, but also to the level of the goal itself. The will could choose to live without the enjoyment of divine Goodness as its highest goal. So, this balanced distinction of ability and possibility, both on the level of goal and means, makes it possible to state that Adam was created good and directed to the good, and still had freedom to choose the bad.

What applies to the soul, also applies to the body. It was endowed with the power not to die. The body obeyed the soul in doing the good; body and soul worked together in doing the good.

In sum: free choice in man before the Fall functioned as it was meant by God. Human being was able to choose the good, because reason could draw from a good well: original righteousness. This made it possible to choose the right means to attain the goal: to live a life to God's honor.

4.5.2 Free Choice after the Fall and before Conversion

What remained of free choice after the Fall? This question has been answered in very different ways in the course of the history of theology. Probably because of this very fact we find Gomarus giving much attention to it (nine out of twenty-six theses). So: what has been lost and what remained after the Fall?

Gomarus starts by explicitly stating what is at first sight fairly obvious: human being remains human being, however wounded (thesis XVI). The Fall does not turn human being into a devil, just as man was no angel before the Fall. Indeed, man remains a sentient and mind-gifted being, for that is part of man's essence. An essence cannot be changed.[23] If we take a closer look, however, the fact that man is said to remain a human being implies that both will and intellect are to some extent still there. This is not only derivable, as we have seen, from earlier theses, but Gomarus also explicitly states it in thesis XVII. Moreover, if human being has will, it follows that he also has free choice—again an inference that Gomarus himself makes (see thesis II).

The disputation continues by spelling out what is absent: original righteousness. By recalling our suggestion that the loss of original righteousness is to be connected to the loss of the right goal of man—God—it is possible to appreciate that Gomarus can say in thesis XX that regarding free choice in

---

alternativity of the will and its purposiveness agree with each other is not explicitly discussed by Gomarus, but later authors like Voetius and Turrettini precisely treat it.

23. Gomarus wants to say this by his expression "a definition cannot be changed." Of course we can change a definition—but we cannot change the essence of that to which a definition refers. An essence we take to consist of the set of essential properties a being has.

spiritual matters nothing at all is left. At first sight this contradicts Gomarus' earlier contention that free choice is an essential part of human being, and therefore cannot be lost. Free choice seems to be intact, but idle with regard to the will's proper goal. The will has a wrong goal, so now, it functions only in those areas in which the highest goal is not immediately involved. Regarding these specific areas which are specified in thesis XIX as common morality, the will can do some good.[24] But these areas are not connected to God anymore. So, the intellect can also come to know a lot about God by itself, but not as it is due, that is, with reverence and worship. Reason and will are in the same boat with regard to sin. Both have structurally as much power as they had before the Fall, but on the account of the wrong goal chosen at the Fall, man directs his power for the sake of a bad goal. Therefore, the powers of (the intellect and) the will to do good are severely damaged, not by some outward lot or an external yoke of sin upon the will, but by the wrong direction of the will itself. The saying "end good, all good" is reversed here in a frame of act-theory.

So, after the Fall man has become an opponent of God (*adversarius*), a rebel. This is almost a point of definition again: we do not call man a sinner because of a wrong actual deed in particular, but we call him so since he chose in general against him in the first place. Original sin and the state of sin is not judged on the level of means, but on the level of goals. Since man has deliberately taken away his proper goal, he can only be called a sinner. With respect to this willful prejudice, Gomarus can say that no free choice is left at all concerning spiritual matters.

It is worthwhile to consider once more the connection between the two types of freedom mentioned before. Gomarus said that in order to have free choice, a person has to have minimal freedom with respect to the exercise of the act. In thesis XXII, Gomarus states that the not-reborn actually *have* precisely that freedom—despite his statement in thesis XX. It is, therefore, not difficult to point out that sinners are responsible for their actual sins, just as they are responsible for *being* a sinner in the first place. Sinners have the freedom with respect to the exercise of the act. So, although they cannot produce but sinful acts, they produce them freely. They could have not produced them.[25] They cannot but produce sinful acts, because they have abandoned their good goal—and in this sense we can understand Gomarus when he says that free choice is only an idle name (thesis XX). Nonetheless, this particular, "unfree" freedom with respect to the exercise of the act is more than spontaneity: in the case of spontaneity (thesis IV)

---

24. In his disputation of 1603, Gomarus supplies details on the powers of man after the Fall. Thesis XI of that disputation: "In statu vero corruptionis alia est ratio: Nam homo voluntate sua a bono aversus et ad malum conversus, se et liberum arbitrium perdidit. Ut autem hoc recte intelligatur, inter actiones naturales, morales et spirituales distinguendum est. Naturales sunt quae ad animalem tantum vitam pertinent, ut edere, dormire. Morales, quae externam obedientiam et conservationem generis humani. Spirituales, quae ad vitam hominis spiritualem, et ad veram eius beatitudinem spectant." So in natural and moral perspective man after the Fall still possesses freedom of goal. In spiritual cases this freedom is lost.

25. The opposite is the case with the good angels (see thesis XXII). They are determined to the type of act by the good. They cannot but produce good acts, but possess just like human beings, the freedom with respect to the exercise of the act. They are free to produce the good act.

the act can be necessitated, while in the case of an act of free choice it cannot. Free choice is intact, but it does not function. Sinners still presume that their object is a good object, but it isn't. Gomarus adduces a host of quotations from Scripture as evidence for his case.

Another point must be mentioned with regard to thesis XXI. Gomarus is very clear about the inability of a human being to free himself from being a sinner. There is an asymmetry here: while man can choose to become a sinner, he cannot help himself to find God again. God has to come to him: "unless that which is above nature builds their heart and intellect again."

In sum: a human being after the Fall and before conversion, although he is free, cannot produce spiritually good acts just by himself.

4.5.3 Free Choice in Conversion

In only two theses Gomarus treats the topic of free choice in conversion, or rather, he alludes to it. Here, the basic structure of the *quaestio* clearly shows: is this, or rather that, the case? In the medieval period, a lengthy argumentation would normally follow. Gomarus just points out that whereas the Roman Catholics see some activity initiated by the human will in conversion, the Protestants do not. So, he holds that in the first moment of conversion, human will is completely passive. This follows from what Gomarus said in the previous sections on the wrong goal of the will, for there is no natural return to God. So, there is no activity of free choice involved in the restoration of the proper goal of the will. By conversion it is divine benevolence itself which directs a human being again to its infinite goodness. Being liberated on the level of goals, man himself again has proper freedom on the level of means. Now, he is not only able to choose wrong, but also the right. Again, the level of possibility and actual willing have to be distinguished. Structurally, man always has the *possibility* to choose the good. Therefore, he is responsible and justly to be blamed if he chooses the bad. Yet, by the direction of his own will to the wrong goal, man rules out his own *ability* to choose the good. So, his will has to be redirected first before the possibilities can be really actualized.

4.5.4 Free Choice after Conversion

After conversion things seem to be quite simple, for Gomarus needs only one thesis to explain this state. It comes to this. After conversion the will is made free. The new man is built gradually, and one can say that the righteousness and holiness return little by little in a human being. Gomarus here refers to the language of man being the image of God: the image is returning, since the proper object of man's will is returning.

However, we need to comment a little bit more on the use of "freedom" here. For we have seen that, strictly speaking, freedom was never lost in all senses. Gomarus specifically means to address the return of the proper object of the will, without which a person can only will bad things. With the return of the proper object of the will, what Calvin and many others called "Christian freedom" comes into the picture. Christian freedom is precisely the proper functioning of free choice concerning the good object, or the beginning restoration of freedom of goal. Spiritual growth of the new man means a growth in freedom. The more the proper object of the will is recognized, the more freedom there is.

Gomarus probably refers to the eschaton when he says that there will be a state in which man lays off sin completely. Again, the distinction of the two nuances of the involved term "*posse*" is helpful to explain the growing freedom of man, if also the goal of the will and the relation of free choice to the means are taken in. The direction of the will to its proper goal is not restored once and for all, but built up gradually. In this process, the people of God are said to cooperate freely. In the process of conversion, the will struggles between its old goal (of the old man) and its new one (of the new man in Christ). Likewise, choice receives an initial ability to choose the good, but this has to be strengthened by choosing good acts. In that way, the right direction of the will shall be confirmed more and more. Gomarus seems to indicate that finally, the direction of the will to God as its goal will be thus steadfast, that man is even unable to sin anymore. In this respect, the freedom of the blessed surpasses the original freedom of Adam. This perfect freedom on the level of ability still supposes the possibility of the opposite, and yet, by his nuanced distinctions Gomarus is able to make his readers confident that sin will not have to be feared at all in glory.

4.6 Evaluation: Gomarus' Place in the Tradition

During his study in Neustadt (1580-1582) Gomarus was taught Hebrew by Junius, New Testament exegesis and theology by Zanchi. After Neustadt he went to England where he studied in Oxford (1582) under John Raynolds and in Cambridge (1583) under William Whitaker. At the beginning of 1585 Gomarus returned to the continent in order to finish his studies at the university of Heidelberg under the tutelage of, again, Junius. According to Van Itterson, Gomarus considered Zanchi and especially Junius—he became his son-in-law— as his principal teachers.[26] Together with them Gomarus can be seen as one of the founding fathers of the phenomenon known as "scholasticism" within the developing Reformed theology. Regarding the issue of "free choice" we can say that Gomarus, compared with his teachers and their prolix discussions on the subject, presented a very concise but clear and balanced view on human free choice by elaborating on the distinctions he found in Junius and others, for example, the specification of the objects of free choice as the means towards a goal, thus utilizing the crucial end-means (*finis-media*) tool of the medieval *will* tradition. The ultimate goal of man's life is not a matter of deliberation and choice, but is immediately given and desired.

We also note his distinction *between libertas contradictionis* and *libertas contratietatis*, which he equated with the distinction between *libertas exercitii* and *libertas specificationis*. Although free choice applies to both types of freedom, Gomarus explicitly states that the freedom with respect to the exercise of act is the basic one. The other type can be lacking, but free choice is always present and intact, and yet it does not always function. Freedom was never lost in all senses. It

---

26. Van Itterzon, *Gomarus*, 23-32.

is due to his precise distinctions that he is able to state that in order to have free choice, a person has to have minimal freedom with respect to the exercise of the act. Accordingly, Gomarus distinguished between the level of possibility and actual willing: structurally, man always has the *possibility* to choose the good. Therefore, he is responsible and justly to be blamed if he chooses the bad. Yet, by the direction of his own will to the wrong goal, man rules out his own *ability* to choose the good. Therefore, his will has to be redirected first before the possibilities can be really actualized.

To present Gomarus' position regarding "free choice" as some sort of determinism, therefore, would be a serious misinterpretation of his argumentation. The fundamental structure of his anthropology differs significantly from a deterministic structure that overlooks the different kinds of freedom. In many ways Gomarus can be seen as a prominent representative of the new generation of Reformed theologians who aimed at a professionalization of the theological enterprise on an academic level. He was the main teacher of Gisbertus Voetius, who considered Gomarus a *"theologus fide dignissimus"* (a very truthworthy theologian) whose grateful disciple he remained until the end of his life. [27]

---

27. See Gisbertus Voetius, *Selectae Disputationes* (Utrecht: Joannes à Waesberge, 1648), 1:465; cf. *Selectae Disputationes* (Utrecht: Anton. Smytegelt, 1669), 5:100: "Cum d. Gomaro numquam contendi, nec contra eum defendi, nec scriptum aliquod ipsius, aut disputationem oppugnandam mihi sumsi; [...]. Quam gratus ipsi discipulus usque ad finem vitae fuerim, quamque ego *euthumiai* en honori venerandi et veterani theologi ac praeceptoris mei studuerim, testari possent epistolae *amoibaiai* (mutual correspondence)." This correspondence also shows Gomarus' great appreciation of Voetius' work.

5

The Will as Master of Its Own Act

A Disputation Rediscovered of Gisbertus Voetius (1589-1676) on Freedom of Will

5.1. Introduction

Gisbertus Voetius was certainly the most important and influential pupil of Francisus Gomarus. Born during the Dutch Revolt on March 3, 1589, in the fortress town of Heusden at the border of the Dutch Republic, Voetius' excellent talent soon came to the attention of his teachers. In 1604, the Heusden magistrates sent the young Gijsbert to the Leiden State College. There he studied during the years of the Arminian crisis at the University of Leiden until 1611. Voetius attended among others lectures of Jacobus Arminius and Petrus Bertius, but he was especially influenced by Gomarus whom he deeply admired.[1]

In 1611, Voetius became Reformed minister in Vlijmen and Engelen, and 1617 in Heusden. From there he was delegated to the Synod of Dort (1618-1619) despite his unusually young age. In 1629-1630 he was involved in the reformation of 's-Hertogenbosch, which led him to an extensive debate with the famous Catholic scholar Cornelius Jansenius. When in 1634 the new Illustrious School of Utrecht was founded, Voetius became its first professor of theology, Hebrew and oriental languages. Soon after this school was promoted to a full university in 1636, Voetius combined his professorate with the position of part-time minister of the Reformed Church of Utrecht. Voetius held this influential double function, repeatedly complemented with the rectorate of the university, almost until his death in 1676. During these long years he trained promising theologians such as

---

1. See note 27 of chapter 4. The standard biography of Voetius is A. C. Duker, *Gisbertus Voetius*, 4 vols. (Leiden: Brill, 1897–1914; repr. Leiden: Uitgeverij Groen, 1989). Additional bibliographic materials can be found esp. in J. A. Cramer, *De Theologische Faculteit te Utrecht ten tijde van Voetius* (Utrecht: Kemink en Zoon N.V., 1932); D. Nauta, "Voetius, Gisbertus," in *Biografisch lexicon voor de geschiedenis van het nederlandse Protestantisme* (Kampen: Kok, 1983), 2:443–449; J. van Oort (ed.), *De onbekende Voetius: Voordrachten wetenschappelijk symposium Utrecht 3 maart 1989* (Kampen: Kok, 1989); W. J. van Asselt and E. Dekker (eds.), *De scholastieke Voetius: Een luisteroefening aan de hand van Voetius' "Disputationes Selectae"* (Zoetermeer: Boekencentrum, 1995); Joel R. Beeke, "Gisbertus Voetius: Toward a Reformed Marriage of Knowledge and Piety," in Carl R. Trueman and R. Scott Clark (eds.), *Protestant Scholasticism: Essays in Reassessment* (Carlisle: Paternoster, 1999), 227-243; Han Van Ruler, "Voetius, Gisbertus (1589-1676)," in *DDPh*, 2:1030-1039; Andreas J. Beck, *Gisbertus Voetius (1589-1676): Sein Theologieverständnis und seine Gotteslehre*, Forschungen zur Kirchen- und Dogmengeschichte 92 (Göttingen: Vandenhoeck & Ruprecht, 2007), 35-142.

Johannes Hoornbeek, Andreas Essenius and Matthias Nethenus, with whom he molded Utrecht into the academic center of the *Nadere Reformatie*, a religious renewal movement inspired by English Puritanism and committed to the progress of the Reformation.

The significance of Voetius' practical-theological work, however, should not tempt us to underestimate his importance for dogmatic theology.[2] It is true that he did not write a dogmatic textbook, but he collected his extensive disputations on selected subjects in five sturdy volumes (*Selectae Disputationes*, 1648-1669) that by far surpass that which is offered in popular textbooks in his time, both in scope and depth.[3] Had Alexander Schweizer studied the systematic-theological oeuvre of Voetius, he could not have maintained his pantheistic-deterministic interpretation of Reformed scholasticism, as J. H. A. Ebrard correctly observed.[4]

Voetius' *Selectae Disputationes* include three disputations that are of special importance for his concept of human free will and its relationship to divine agency: two disputations associated with the doctrine of creation and one extensive disputation discussing divine middle knowledge.[5] Moreover, in the fifth volume of the *Selectae Disputationes* his important treatise *De termino vitae* (*On the End of Life*) was reprinted.[6] There are still other relevant parts of Voetius' oeuvre, including a lengthy dissertation co-authored by Matthias Nethenus that has only recently been retraced.[7]

---

2. Contra Wilhelm Goeters, *Die Vorbereitung des Pietismus in der reformierten Kirche der Niederlande bis zur labadistischen Krisis 1670* (Leipzig/Utrecht: J. C. Hinrichs'sche Buchhandlung, 1911), 61; and Karl Reuter, *Wilhelm Amesius, der führende Theologe des erwachenden reformierten Pietismus*, Beiträge zur Geschichte und Lehre der Reformierten Kirche 4 (Neukirchen: Neukirchener Verlag, 1940), 10.

3. Gisbertus Voetius, *Selectae Disputationes [theologicae]*, 5 vols. (Utrecht [vol. 4: Amsterdam]: Joh. à Waesberge [vol. 5: Ant. Smytegelt], 1648-1669) (hereafter *Sel. Disp.*); and cf. Van Asselt and Dekker, *De scholastieke Voetius*, 12-33 and Appendix II. Other important works include *Exercitia et bibliotheca studiosi theologiæ* (Utrecht: Wilhelmus Strick, 1644); *Politica ecclesiastica*, 3 parts in 4 vols. (Amsterdam: Joannes à Waesberge, 1663-1676); *Syllabus problematum theologicorum. Pars prior* (Utrecht: Aegidius Roman, 1643); *De praktijk der godzaligheid (TA AŠKHTIKA sive Exercitia pietatis—1664)*, 2 vols., ed. C. A. de Niet, Monografieën van Gereformeerd Piëtisme 2 (Utrecht: De Banier, 1995).

4. Johannes Heinrich August Ebrard, *Christliche Dogmatik* (Königsberg: August Wilhelm Unzer, 1851), 1:XI–XII, 53, 72–74. Cf. further Andreas J. Beck, "Gisbertus Voetius (1589-1676): Basic Features of His Doctrine of God," in: *RS*, 205-226, esp. 205.

5. Voetius, *Sel. Disp.*, 1:831-850, esp. 835-850 ("Appendix ad disputationes de creatione secunda," defended in 1643 by Cornelius Bruynvisch); *Sel. Disp.*, 5:229-241, esp. 229-230 ("Problemata aliquot de creatione, pars decima," defended in 1660 by Godefridus Deys); *Sel. Disp.*, 1:285–339, esp. 293-295 ("De conditionata seu media in Deo scientia," in 4 sections; the original [co-]author is Matthias Nethenus, who defended this disputation in 1643).

6. *Dissertatio Epistolica de Termino Vitae ad Amplissimum Clarissimumque Johannem Beverovicum* (sent to Beverwijck in 1634 and published in 1641), esp. 109-116. For an analysis of this passage, see Andreas J. Beck and Antonie Vos, "Conceptual Patterns Related to Reformed Scholasticism," *NTT* 75 (2003): 223-233; and Andreas J. Beck, "Zur Rezeption Melanchthons bei Gisbertus Voetius (1589-1676), namentlich in seiner Gotteslehre," in Günter Frank and Herman J. Selderhuis (eds.), *Melanchthon und der Calvinismus*, Melanchthon-Schriften der Stadt Bretten 9 (Stuttgart: Froomann-Holzboog, 2004), 319-344.

7. *Disputatio theologica de concursu determinante, an determinabili?* 3 parts (Utrecht: Joannes à Waesberge, 1645-1646). This disputation is usually mentioned as being lost, but it can

The text we discuss in this chapter is taken from a disputation that was written and defended in 1652 by Engelbertus Beeckman under chairmanship of Voetius: *Disputatio philosophico-theologica, continens quæstiones duas, de Distinctione Attributorum divinorum, & Libertate Voluntatis.*[8] This text was never mentioned in modern secondary literature on Voetius, until it was "rediscovered" in 1995 by the author of this chapter.[9]

Although Voetius may not have been the direct author of this disputation, he can still be considered as its *auctor intellectualis* who supervised the preparation of the theses, presided over the disputation and approved it before publication. This was the common procedure in Voetius' days and it allowed for collecting disputations in volumes such as the *Selectae Disputationes* under the name of the presiding professor.[10] In-text references to writings of the *praeses* like the one in the last sentence in this disputation were thereby typically rewritten by the *praeses* as references to his own writings. It is true that the disputation in question—like many others—had not been included in the *Selectae Disputationes.* However, there is another disputation of the same respondent that has been defended one year later and reprinted in the fifth volume of the *Selectae Disputationes.*[11]

We do not know much about Engelbertus Beeckman—not to be confused with his famous contemporary Isaak Beeckman. He seems to have been (partly) raised in Nijmegen, the capital city of the Gelderland Province in that time.[12] Beside the two disputations defended under Voetius there are preserved two other disputations, presided by J. Hoornbeek and A. Essenius.[13] In 1656 Beeckman became Reformed pastor first at *Genniper Huis* (Kleef) near Nijmegen, and then in Nijmegen itself. He died on September 8, 1708.

Before we turn to the text of the second part of the disputation, it might be useful to note that Beeckman used extensively the chief work of the Scottish scholar Samuel Rutherford (1600-1661) that had been published one year earlier

---

be consulted at the *Universitäts- und Stadtbibliothek* of Cologne, the *Bibliothèque de la Riponne* at Lausanne and the *Württembergische Landesbibliothek Stuttgart* (only the first section). Cf. also Voetius' *Thersites heautontimorumenos hoc est, Remonstrantium hyperaspistes, catechesi, et liturgiae Germanicae, Gallicae, et Belgicae denuo insultans, retusus* (Utrecht: Abraham ab Herwiick & Hermann Ribbius, 1635), 83-94. For a discussion of all these texts, see Beck, *Gisbertus Voetius*, 401-425.

8. Utrecht: Joh. à Waesberge, 1652, A4r-B1v. This disputation was defended on June 25.

9. Andover-Harvard Theological Library, Cambridge, MA, call number: H74.851. The disputation is included as no. 38 in the rare if not singular volume, Gijsbert Voet, *Disputationes: A Collection of Theological Treatises in Latin by Various Authors, Defended before Gisbert Voetius of the University of Utrecht.*, 38 pam. in 1 vol. (Utrecht, 1637-1652). See for more details, Beck, *Gisbertus Voetius*, 238, note 139.

10. To increase readibility, we will always use the name "Voetius" in the rest of the chapter rather than using a double-name like "Voetius/Beeckman" or "Beeckman/Voetius." On the authorship of disputations, compare the introduction on Junius (3.1) and the chapter on Gomarus (4.2).

11. *Sel. Disp.*, 5:136-147 ("Notae et exercitationes ad *Thomae part. I qu. 27-44* de personis divinis, pars prima," defended on June 29, 1653).

12. The title page of the disputations mentions "Neom[agium].-Gelr[ia]."

13. Defended under Hoornbeek: *Disputatio theologica de efficacia providentiæ Dei circa malum* (Utrecht: Joh. à Waesberge, 1652). Defended under Essenius: *Disputatio theologica de induratione* (Utrecht: Joh. à Waesberge, 1653).

in the Netherlands.[14] This Puritan divine and Covenanter was highly esteemed[15] by Voetius, and his important *Examination of Arminianism* was published posthumously in Utrecht and prefaced by Voetius' pupil Samuel Nethenus.[16]

5.2. Translation of the Text

The present text makes up the second part of a Philosophical-theological Disputation, Containing Two Questions, the Distinction of the Divine Attributes and The Freedom of the Will (Disputatio philosophico-theologica, continens quœstiones duas, de Distinctione Attributorum divinorum, & Libertate Voluntatis). These quaestiones are followed by some corollaries, which belong to both parts, so they are not translated and commented on here.

The Freedom of the Will

Thesis I
This controversy about the freedom of the will is a commonplace in the books of the scholastics. The genuine definition of the freedom of will has been debated at length, often between the orthodox and the papists, and is still being disputed. The pelagianizing papists define "free" (*liberum*) as follows:

> A free potency by which, all things requisite for acting being posited, someone can act or not act

and "[can act] this or that," as Arriaga adds. This definition also does not satisfy Franciscus de Oviedo [in this regard] and he adds his own [corresponding] addition too (see both in their *cursus philosophicus*).[17] And thus in the end they both hold that the definition has to be understood about both the freedom of contrariety and the freedom of contradiction.

Now these authors claim an indifference of the free potency to both components not only in a divided sense but also in a compounded sense, which implies a contradiction in terms. Likewise they ask regarding the essence (*quidditas*) and integrity of a free nature for a twofold immunity, that is from coercion and from necessity, and indeed not only from intrinsic, absolute and natural necessity (to which we agree), but also from extrinsic, hypothetical necessity, which we deny. Thus we need to deal with these two issues: We have to

---

14. *Exercitationes apologeticae pro divina gratia, In quibus vindicatur doctrina orthodoxa de divinis decretis, et Dei tum aeterni decreti, tum gratiae efficacis operationis, cum hominis libertate consociatione et subordinatione amica [...]* (Franeker: Johannis Dhüiringh, 1651).

15. Cf. *Sel. Disp.*, 1:280, 292, 335, 336, 371; 5:124-125.

16. Samuel Rutherford, *Examen Arminianismi* (Utrecht: ex officinâ Antonii Smytegelt, 1668).

17. See Rodrigo de Arriaga, *Cursus philosophicus* (Antverpiae: Ex Officina Plantiniana Balthasaris Moeti, 1632); and Francisco de Oviedo, *Integer cursus philosophicus ad vnum corpus redactus: in summulas, logicam, physicam, de cælo, de generatione, de anima, & metaphysicam distributus* (Lugduni: Sumptibus Petri Prost., 1640).

investigate the concept of the essence (*quidditas*) of freedom, and we have to demonstrate its compatibility with necessity.

Thesis II

Therefore, freedom (viz. created freedom) means:

> The faculty that can out of itself and according to a mode of acting that fits its nature (*connaturalis*), choose and not choose this or that, by virtue of the power of its internal, elective and vital command (*imperium*).

I expound what I propound.

The faculty that [can choose] out of itself as the formal eliciting principle of its acts: Although God is the efficient cause of the acts of this faculty, he nevertheless is not their formal cause or even partial formal cause (*concausa*), namely inasmuch as these are free acts, since otherwise it would not be the will of man who wills, but God in it, which is an absurdity in theology. Note that this mode of acting of the free potency that fits its nature requires a twofold indifference: (1) *Objective* indifference, viz. indifference of the means that is displayed by the intellect as something that can be chosen (*eligibilis*) and does not have a necessary connection with the intended end as such (*absolute*). And (2) *Vital, internal and choosing* indifference, which belongs to the free potency that is not yet finally determined by the practical judgment.[18]

I briefly prove what I have said.[19]
[Major premise]: The essential structure of freedom is that by which is left to the will such a mastery of the act as a created entity can have.
[Minor premise]: Now by these two indifferences [is left to the will such a mastery as a created entity can have].
[Conclusion]: *Ergo* [these two indifferences constitute the essential structure of freedom].

The opponents grant the major premise. I prove the minor premise: Given these indifferences, no external agent, not even God, can overturn freedom in its natural mode of acting. Thus the ownership of the will's own acts is permanently left to it.

I prove the antecedent. The essential structure of choice is the objective union of the good, that is displayed by the intellect as non-necessary, with the intended end. Now freedom itself is the intrinsic, vital and sole formal cause of this union. For although God contributed to the actual existence of Cyrus' volition by

---

18. We read "per Iudicium practic*um* nondum ultimo determinatae" instead of "per Iudicium practicum practico nondum ultimo determinatae."

19. Starting at this point, the remainder of this second thesis is an almost literal transcript from Rutherford, *Exercitationes apologeticae*, 10.

stirring up his spirit (Ezra 1:1), the formal cause or formal partial cause of Cyrus' volition did not cease to exist, viz. as being a free volition.[20]

Thesis III

Let us hurry to the other points. The Jesuits put three things (which I almost would have called monstrosities) in opposition to a threefold necessity. (1) Against the necessity that originates from the decree, they oppose that insane fiction of a middle knowledge (*scientia media*); (2) against the necessity that originates from the physical premotion to act, they oppose the indifferent *precursus* and *concursus*, a horrible, huge monstrosity; (3) against the necessity that originates from the determination of the deliberated practical judgment they oppose that chimerical indifference, by which someone who is determined to one component remains at the same instance indifferent to two, or perhaps more components.

For an understanding of the first point these things should be noted:

(1) God works in us to will and even to accomplish by virtue of that power which operates in us very strongly and at the same time very wisely, Phil. 2:13.

(2) The end point (*terminus ad quem*) of both God who decrees from eternity and the creature who operates in time in a rational way, is the same.

Proof: God determines by virtue of his absolutely free and independent dominion the volition, which is in that instance indifferent to all eligible objects, to choose object B out of the successively eligible objects A, B and C, thereby removing the indifference in the compounded sense to A and C. The created will wills by virtue of its own, albeit dependent, freedom (what supposedly the opponents would not deny) the very same object B, thereby removing the indifference to the remaining objects that it did have in the preceding instance. Thus, when it comes to the connatural mode of acting, the will is not more necessitated by the decree than by itself. For although these necessities are diverse with respect to the starting point (*terminus a quo*), they are nevertheless the same with respect to the end point (*terminus ad quem*) and remove certainly the same indifferences. Indeed, the will itself removes in time the very same objects, that by virtue of the absolute divine decree could not be actualized, and, conversely, establishes these objects, that were to be actualized by virtue of the same decree under such a difference of time, because the decree causes from eternity [their] being "future" (*futuritio*). Hence it becomes clear how foolish it is when it is stated that the will that freely wills in time would be the cause of the eternal being "future" (*futuritio*), which nevertheless is done by the fiction of the Jesuits.[21]

---

20. Ezra 1:1: "Now in the first year of Cyrus king of Persia, that the word of the LORD by the mouth of Jeremiah might be fulfilled, the LORD stirred up the spirit of Cyrus king of Persia, that he made a proclamation throughout all his kingdom, and put it also in writing."

21. Cf. for this paragraph Rutherford, *Exercitationes apologeticae*, 106-109, 129.

Thesis IV

For an understanding of the second point it should be noted that the physical premotion to act is nothing else than *the applied power of God that awakens the creature that has a potency to the second act.* According to a double understanding this applied power is either as principle, namely an awakening principle, to be distinguished from our [willing] principle; or as action that is virtually passing over to us, it is to be identified with our action as it is considered. It is called *precursus* or *premotion* in so far as God in the first structural moment moves us and awakens the same power (*virtus*) that, by virtue of his conserving power (*vis*), exists in us—though slumbering, as it were. It is labeled *concursus* in so far as it accompanies our action and actualizes the effect as first universal cause.

Note, then, that the predetermination of our will is moderated by the all wise God in his ingenuity. For the predetermination of a *free cause* is not to such an extent one of necessity as it would be the case in a *natural cause*, e.g., fire, that is predetermined to burning. This indeed would be incompatible with both the nature [of a free cause] and God who operates wisely in nature.

Moreover, this predetermination—with the words of Rhaetorfortis[22]—is only ascribed to someone who wills this [predetermination] in order to have it, namely who wills it negatively, in as far as it is not not-willing, that is to say, not struggling, not resisting, not itself determining itself to the opposite component. Thus it is in vain if it is claimed here that our will could be forced, since "being forced" and "will" are contradictories; such a thing is neither established by us nor does it follow [from what we say]. Indeed, for something to be forced, it is not only required that what is said to be forced behaves merely passively towards what it is thus said to have been forced to. But as Ferrius[23] rightly notes, it is over and above all required that something that is forced exerts a contrary power to the opposite. Thus the predetermination turns the will sweetly and nevertheless strongly to that very end (*terminus*), to which it—certainly being moved and premoved by God—would have turned itself. So the opponents shall keep their indifferent *concursus* for themselves, a monstrosity that is devoid of any light.

Thesis V

Here follows the third necessity, which takes its origin from the practical judgment of the intellect. Some papists such as the Thomists defend this necessity together with us. From our [Reformed] theologians, some grant it together with

---

22. Samuel Rutherford [= Rhaetorfortis], *Disputatio scholastica de divina providentia, variis praelectionibus, quod attinet ad summa rerum capita, tradita s. theologiae adolescentibus candidatis in inclytâ Academiâ Andreapolitanâ, [...]* (Edinburgh: George Anderson, 1649), 414: "Nam quia praedeterminatio non datur nisi volenti eam habere, et contemperatur libertati, [...]." Cf. also Rutherford, *Exercitationes apologeticae*, 363-395, 477-502.

23. From Paul Ferry, Voetius possessed the work *Pauli Ferrii Vindiciae pro scholastico orthodoxo, adversus Leonardum Perinum Jesuitam* (Lugduni Batavorum: apud Wiardum Jelgerum, 1630); cf. *Bibliotheca variorium et insignum librorum, theologicorum et miscellaneorum, reverendi et celeberrimi viri D. Gisberti Voetii,* 2 vols. (Utrecht: Guilielmus Clerck, 1677-1679), I T 8° 300 and II T 8° 308.

Thomas, Sylvius and other of Thomas' followers;[24] others deny it together with the modern Jesuits. But let us note these things in passing: The will is effectuated by the ultimate practical judgment of the intellect—not by a physical influx that would flow into it in a real way, but sweetly by an effective motion, as it is determined by that with which it agrees (*ab accedente*). The necessity that arises from this source does not destroy freedom but is even essential to determined freedom. It is a free necessity, indeed, since it comes forth from a free principle and it removes from freedom only indifference in the compounded sense. Thus it is the case that the will does not only depend on the practical judgment, but is also determined by it, both as to the specification of the act (to which Thomas wishes to limit it, *Summa Theologiae* I-II, q. 9, a. 1), and as to the exercise of the act. Rivetus[25] and Maccovius[26] defend this also, and it is demonstrated by the Scriptures Ps. 9:11[27]; Joh. 4:10.[28] What the learned *praeses* and revered instructor thinks about this question can be learned from his disputations about creation.[29]

5.3. Structure of the Text

The structure of the disputation in question can be mapped as follows:

1. Introduction of the current definition of the Jesuits (thesis I)
   a. Definition: "A free potency by which, all things requisite for acting being posited, someone can act or not act [, act this or that]"
   b. Interpretation of this definition
      i. Indifference of the will toward contrary and contradictory acts (freedom of contrariety and contradiction)
      ii. Indifference not only in divided sense but even in compounded sense
      iii. Therefore, the essence of freedom requires a twofold immunity
         1. From coercion

---

24. The printer missed a comma after "Thomâ." This comma is required since Voetius does not refer to an alleged Thomas Sylvius, but to François Du Bois (1581-1648), also called Sylvius. See his *Commentarii in totam primam secundae partem S. Thomae Aquinatis* (Douai: Gérard Patté, 1635), ad I-II, q. 9, a. 1, and cf. Jacob Schmutz, "François Du Bois," *Scholasticon: Ressources en ligne pour l'étude de la scolastique moderne (1500-1800): Auteurs, textes, institutions*, ed. Jacob Schmutz (http://www.scholasticon.fr/nomenD.htm #dubois, accessed April 28, 2008).

25. For Andreas Rivetus, Voetius refers in *Sel. Disp.*, 1:839, to Rivetus' "*disp. de libero arbitrio*, anno 1631.7.Februarii."

26. From *Sel. Disp.*, 1:839, it becomes clear that Beeckman/Voetius probably refers to Johannes Maccovius, *Collegia Theologica quae extant, omnia* (Franeker: Ulderickus Balck; Joannes Fabianius Deûring, 1641), collegii sexti, disp. Miscellanearum quaestionum 6, 455 (454-455).

27. In *Sel. Disp.*, 1:839, Voetius also refers to Ps. 9:11[=10]: "And they that know thy name will put their trust in thee...," and he comments: "If therefore knowledge would not determine the will, it could happen that those who know the name of God would not trust in him."

28. In *Sel. Disp.*, 1:839, Voetius also refers to John 4:10: "If thou knewest the gift of God, and who it is that saith to thee, Give me to drink; thou wouldest have asked of him, and he would have given thee living water." Voetius comments: "So if the intellect would not determine the will, the Samaritan woman could have known the gift of God and still not asked living water from God, and then Christ would have said something wrong."

29. Cf. *Sel. Disp.*, 1:831-850 (esp. 838-850).

        2. From necessity
           a. Intrinsic, absolute and natural necessity
           b. Extrinsic, hypothetical necessity (cf. theses III-V)
      c. Conclusion: two issues: the essence of freedom and its compatibility with hypothetical necessity

2. Essence of freedom: Introduction of own definition (thesis II)
      a. Definition: "The faculty that can out of itself and according to a mode of acting that fits its nature, choose and not choose this or that, by virtue of the power of its internal, elective and vital command."
      b. Interpretation of this definition
           i. Will of man is formal cause of the acts of will
           ii. Twofold indifference
               1. Objective indifference
               2. Vital, internal and choosing indifference
           iii. Proof that twofold indifference constitutes the essential structure of freedom

3. Compatibility of freedom with hypothetical necessity
      a. Compatibility with three kinds of necessity (thesis IIIa)
           i. Necessity arising from the divine decree (contra middle knowledge)
           ii. Necessity arising from the physical premotion (contra *indifferent precursus* and *concursus*)
           iii. Necessity arising from the ultimate practical judgment of the intellect (contra chimerical indifference)
      b. Explanation of compatibility with each kind of necessity
           i. Necessity arising from the divine decree (thesis IIIb)
               1. God works in us very strongly and very wisely
               2. The end point of what God decrees and the creature operates is the same
                   a. God determines the indifferent will to a certain volition
                   b. The indifferent human will determines itself to the same volition
                   c. By (a) and (b) the same indifference is removed, and indeed only in the compounded sense
                   d. The will is not more necessitated by the decree than by itself
           ii. Necessity arising from the physical premotion (thesis IV)
               1. Definition: "the applied power of God that awakens the creature that has a power to the second act"
               2. The *precursus* of divine power and *concursus* of divine action
                   a. Understood as awakening principle, the applied power is distinct from our willing principle
                   b. Understood as action that is virtually transferred to us, the applied power is identical with our action
                   c. It is called *prec*urrence (*precursus*) as principle awakening our power (cf. a.; in the first structural moment)
                   d. It is called *con*currence (*concursus*) as accompanying action (cf. b.; in the second structural moment)
               3. Predetermination is moderated wisely according to the nature of a free cause
               4. Predetermination is only ascribed to a will who wills, or, does not resist
                   a. The will is not forced

        b. Predetermination turns the will sweetly and strongly to that very end to which it would have turned itself
    iii. Necessity arising from the practical judgment (thesis V)
        1. Will is sweetly moved by ultimate judgment of the intellect
        2. It is a "free" necessity that does not destroy freedom but removes indifference in the compounded sense only
        3. In that sense the will is determined both as to the specification and to the exercise of the act.

As we can easily see from this outline, Voetius' disputation is structured in a clear and logical way. He starts with an introduction of the highly debated definition of the Jesuits and adds some interesting and revealing remarks, culminating in the conclusion that there are two main issues at stake: (1) the essence of the freedom and (2) its compatibility with necessity (thesis I). The first issue is treated in thesis II, and the second issue is treated in theses III-V.

5.4. Definition of Freedom by the Jesuits

Voetius starts this part of his "philosophical-theological disputation" with the observation that the question of the freedom of the will was "a commonplace in the books of the scholastics." This was a hotly debated issue in Voetius' days, especially in the aftermath of Louis de Molina's *Concordia* or *Harmony of Free Will with the Gifts of Grace* (Lisbon 1588) and the controversy between Molinism of the Jesuits and Banezianism of the Thomists.[30] As recent research has pointed out, this controversy was resembled to a surprising level of detail by the famous controversy within Reformed Protestantism between Arminius and orthodox theologians like Gomarus.[31] Moreover, there was an ongoing debate in Voetius' days between Reformed and Jesuit theologians about the freedom of the will.[32]

The disputation translated in this chapter can be read as a contribution to this debate with the Jesuits. It is not by chance that Voetius takes the definition of the Jesuits as a starting-point. The definition cited by Voetius comes very close to the famous definition in Molina's *Concordia* and the definition in the work of other Jesuit theologians, like the highly influential *Disputationes Metaphysicae* of Francisco Súarez:

---

30. Cf. Luis de Molina, *Liberi arbitrii cum gratiae donis, divina praescientia, providentia, praedestinatione et reprobatione concordia*, ed. Johannes Rabeneck, Societatis Iesu selecti scriptores: Ludovicus Molina (Oña/Madrid: Collegium Maximum/"Sapientia," 1953); and cf. the excellent introduction and translation of Alfred J. Freddoso in Luis de Molina, *On Divine Foreknowledge (Part IV of the Concordia)*, translated with an introduction and notes by A. J. Freddoso (Ithaca/London: Cornell, 1988). The label "Thomists" is misleading since the Thomistic party was in fact fairly influenced by the work of John Duns Scotus.

31. Cf. *RM*, Eef Dekker, "Was Arminius a Molinist?," *Sixteenth Century Journal* 27 (1996): 337-352; and Richard A. Muller, *God, Creation, and Providence in the Thought of Jacob Arminius: Sources and Directions of Scholastic Protestantism in the Era of Early Orthodoxy* (Grand Rapids: Baker, 1991).

32. See, e.g., Dekker, "An Ecumenical Debate," in *RS*, 141-154.

(1) "Free" denotes a free potency, by which, all things requisite for acting being posited, someone can act or not act.[33]

There are three important elements in that definition. First of all, the definition speaks about the human potency to act or not act. Acting and not acting are contradictory to each other, and thus there is at stake the so-called *freedom of contradiction*.[34]

Secondly, the will as a free potency is understood as being *indifferent* to acting or not acting, even if all requirements for acting are settled. There was full agreement between Jesuit, Thomistic, Reformed orthodox and Arminian theologians that human will could not possibly act without the fulfillment of such prerequisites like the divine decree and *concursus* and the practical judgment of the human intellect. The point of discussion was whether and in which sense these prerequisites would strictly imply a specific human act (of will) or not.

It is noteworthy, thirdly, that this definition focuses on the potency to act or not act rather than on the potency to will or not will. Thus it explains freedom not on the level of the acts of will and in terms of *willing* options, but on the level of the *effectuation* of acts of will and in terms of *acting*. This distinction between willing and acting is important, because someone can be completely powerless in effectuating options and thus deprived of freedom in a *material* sense, and still be *formally* free in willing them.[35]

Having cited this definition, Voetius immediately reminds us that some Jesuit theologians such as Rodrigo de Arriaga and Francisco de Oviedo would add an important element to this definition and have it run something like this:

(2) [Free will is] a free potency, by which someone can act or not act, *act this or that*, all things requisite for acting being posited.[36]

The added element guarantees the so-called *freedom of contrariety:* there is not only freedom to act or not act (freedom of contradiction), but also freedom to

---

33. Voetius, *Disputatio*, A4r (italic in original): "*potentiam liberam,* qua *positis omnibus ad agendum requisitis, quis potest agere et non agere.*" Cf. Molina, *Concordia,* q. 14, a. 13, disp. 2, sec. 3 (ed. Rabeneck, 14) : "Quo pacto illud agens liberum dicitur, quod, positis omnibus requisitis ad agendum, potest agere et non agere, aut ita agere unum, ut contrarium etiam agere possit." And cf. Francisco Suárez, *Disputationes metaphysicae*, disp. 19, sec. 4, n. 1 (vol. 25 of the *Omnia opera* [Paris: Vives, 1866], 706): "nam causa libera est quae, positis omnibus requisitis ad agendum, potest agere et non agere."

34. Cf. the square of opposition as charted and explained in the introduction of this volume. Applied to the act of will, the contradiction at stake could be expressed in this formula: aWp & a-Wp.

35. For the distinction between formal and material freedom see Eef Dekker and Henri Veldhuis, "Freedom and Sin: Some Systematic Observations," *European Journal of Theology* 3 (1994): 153-161.

36. Voetius, *Disputatio*, A4r: "[...] *hoc vel illud* [...]."

perform act p or q.[37] Thus free will is defined as indifference toward both contrary and contradictory acts.[38]

In its wording this definition is characteristic for the Jesuits, but it has clear medieval roots going back, for example, to Duns Scotus.[39] Would Voetius reject this definition? Not necessarily so. Although the slightly polemical style of its presentation—"pelagianizing papists"—does not sound favorable, the real problem seems to be that the Jesuits claim an indifference not only in divided sense but even in compounded sense. Accordingly, they would want to immunize freedom from all kinds of necessity.

The distinction between a divided and compounded sense is part of the syntactical tools of the scholastic method.[40] The relevant part of the definition in question would read in the divided sense[41]:

(3) Given all requirements for performing p, it is possible for Engelbertus to not perform p.

In the compounded sense, it would read as follows:

(4) It is possible: Given all requirements for performing p, Engelbertus does not perform p.

The point is that the modal operator "possible" governs only the second part of the proposition in the first case—the proposition is divided into two parts—whereas in the second case the same modal operator governs both parts together forming the combined proposition.

Voetius would not deny (3), but he does reject (4) because according to him this rendering would imply a contradiction in terms.[42] But why assume that (4) would imply a contradiction?

The answer has to do with the range and content of the requirements. According to Voetius, these requirements include the divine decree (thesis III), the

---

37. Applied to the act of will, the contrariety at stake could be expressed in this formula: aWp & $aW\text{-}p$. Cf. the square of opposition and explanation in the introduction.

38. For the debates among Jesuits about the best definition of free will cf. Tilman Ramelow, *Gott, Freiheit, Weltenwahl: Der Ursprung des Begriffes der besten aller möglichen Welten in der Metaphysik der Willensfreiheit zwischen Antonio Perez S. J. (1599–1649) und G. W. Leibniz (1646–1716)*, Brill's Studies in Intellectual History 72 (Leiden: Brill, 1997).

39. Duns Scotus, *Quaestiones in metaphysicam* 9, q. 15, n. 22 (*Opera philosophica*, 4:680-681): "[voluntas] non est ex se determinata, sed potest agere hunc actum vel oppositum actum; agere etiam vel non agere." See also *CF, passim*. Other examples would include Gregory of Rimini (c. 1300-1358), Marsilius of Inghen (ca. 1340-1396), John Major (1467/9-1550) and Bartolomé de Medina (1530-1580); cf. Jacob Schmutz, "Du péché de l'ange à la liberté d'indifférence. Les sources angélologiques de l'anthropologie moderne," *Les études philosophiques* (2002): 172-173.

40. See *CF*, 118-123, 126-129; and Simo Knuuttila, *MMPh*, 118-122, 139-149.

41. For reasons of readability, we modify the wording and replace the term "someone" with a concrete person.

42. Cf. Beck and Vos, "Conceptual Patterns," 223-233, and Beck, "Zur Rezeption Melanchthons," 339-343.

physical premotion (thesis IV) and the practical judgment of the intellect (thesis V). Moreover, these three requirements strictly imply their intended outcome or object: Given the divine decree, the physical premotion and the practical judgment of the intellect with regard to Engelbertus' performing *p*, Engelbertus *will* perform *p*. But if these requirements strictly imply the performance of *p*, then (4) implies a contradiction. Engelbertus cannot both perform *p* and not perform *p*.

According to Voetius, the Jesuits deny the implicative relation between these requirements and the performance of *p*, or what Voetius calls an extrinsic, hypothetical necessity towards the performance of *p*, given these requirements. That is why they do not see the problem underlying proposition (4). Voetius objects to that denial, but agrees with them that there is no freedom of the will without immunity from both coercion and from intrinsic, absolute and natural necessity. Thus the will is neither coerced nor necessitated in the strict sense of the word. Moreover, there is a non-necessary, i.e., contingent relation between the will and both its acts and the objects of will.[43]

It is noteworthy that in his treatise *De termino vitae* Voetius found a way to accept the definition of the Jesuits even in the compounded sense.[44] There he took "all requirements" in a loose way and restricted their range such that it would include only those requirements that are *temporally* prior to the act of will.[45] These requirements thus would not include the divine acting involved. For this divine action is not temporally, but only structurally, prior to the human action, and "it is so intimate to the act of the creature that it cannot be separated or excluded from it."[46]

The problematic side of the definition of the Jesuits and especially their understanding of it prompts Voetius to investigate the essence of the concept of freedom (thesis II) and its compatibility with necessity (theses III-V).

5.5 Definition of Freedom by Voetius

Voetius now introduces in thesis II his own definition of freedom and specifies that it applies to created freedom, i.e., human and angelic freedom:

(5) [Created freedom is] the faculty that can out of itself and according to a mode of acting that fits its nature, choose and not choose this or that, by virtue of the power of its internal, elective and vital command.[47]

---

43. Cf. the explanation of different kinds of necessity in the introduction to this volume and in the next chapter.

44. Voetius, *De termino vitae*, 109 (italic in original): "[Libertas] definitur *facultas activa in homine, quae ex se et sua intrinseca ac particulari natura non est determinata ad unum tantum, sed indifferens ex se ad hoc vel illud operandum, et ad operandum, et non operandum positis omnibus requisitis ad agendum.*" Cf. also *Sel. Disp.*, 1:734-735.

45. Ibid.: "Intellige ergo in definitione libertatis, omnia requisita quae priora sunt et praerequiruntur tempore. Jam vero motio et praemotio Dei prior est natura, atque ita praerequiritur tantum, non tempore."

46. Ibid.: "quia Dei actus creaturae actibus tam intimus est ut ab iis separari aut excludi non possit." Cf. Beck and Vos, "Conceptual Patterns," 227-228.

47. Voetius, *Disputatio*, A4r (italic in original): "Est igitur libertas (creata sc.) *Facultas, quae*

In comparing this definition with the definition of the Jesuits, we first observe that the problematic element "all things requisite for acting being posited" is left out. Secondly, Voetius' definition explains freedom on the level of the acts of will and in terms of choice and *willing* options, rather than on the level of the *effectuation* of acts of will and in terms of *acting*. Thirdly, this definition comprises both *freedom of contradiction* ("choose or not choose") and *freedom of contrariety* ("this or that"). In this respect, it is in line with the definition as cited above in proposition (2). Finally, Voetius' definition is much more explicit in explaining how the will has the power to choose out of itself.

This last aspect is the starting-point when Voetius unpacks this definition. He clearly states that the will is "the formal eliciting principle of its acts." It is true that God is the efficient cause of the acts of human will—in that sense the divine action has to be included in the prerequirement for human will and action as explained above. But when it comes to the formal level, the divine action is not even a partial cause of the human act of will.[48] Otherwise it would be God *in* the will of man and not the human will itself which wills and chooses its acts. According to Voetius, that would be "an absurdity in theology." [49]

Despite the prevalent Jesuit usage of the term "indifference," Voetius does not try to avoid it. He rather insists that the specific way of free operation, as it is inherent in the essential nature of the will, requires a twofold indifference. It requires both

(6) *objective indifference*

and

(7) *vital, internal and choosing indifference.*[50]

Objective indifference is the indifference of the will in relation to its object. Voetius explains this kind of indifference in terms of the contingent relation of the means to the intended end. There are many ways to Utrecht, for example, and the means are not implied by the end. The ultimate end for the will is what is good in itself, and ultimately God as the *summum bonum* is the only appropriate

---

ex se, et respectu connaturalis agendi modi, tam hoc quam illud, potest eligere, et non eligere, ex vi interni, Electivi, et vitalis sui Imperii." For Voetius on angelic freedom see *Sel. Disp.*, 1:258-259.

48. For the distinction between total and partial causes cf. William A. Frank, "Duns Scotus on Autonomous Freedom and Divine Co-Causality," *Medieval Philosophy and Theology* 2 (1992): 142-164, and note the resemblance with Voetius in this regard.

49. Voetius, *Disputatio*, A4r (italic in original): "*Facultas quae ex se* tanquam principio formaliter elictivo suorum actuum, quorum licet Deus sit efficiens, non tamen est Causa vel concausa formalis eorum, qua scil. liberorum, nam ita voluntas hominis non vellet, sed Deus in ipsa; quod absurdum in Theologia."

50. Voetius, *Disputatio*, A4r-v (italic in original): "[...] Connaturalis agendi modus potentiae liberae duplicem requirat indifferentiam; *Objectivam,* [...]. Et *Vitalem, Internam, Electivam,* [...]."

end.[51] But there are many different means that are displayed by the intellect as something that can be chosen.

Vital, internal and choosing indifference is the indifference that the will as free potency has by virtue of its own nature and essential structure. Voetius adds that this indifference "belongs to the free potency that is not yet finally determined by the practical judgment" of the intellect.[52] In this sense, indifference is restricted to the structural moment "before" the determination by the practical judgment. As it will become clear in thesis 5, however, this restriction only refers to indifference in the compounded sense and has to be understood in terms of the interaction of practical judgment and will in which the element of freedom is interwoven in irresolvable ways.[53]

Voetius now continues with a syllogistic argument.[54] Without giving the reference, he in fact follows almost literally Samuel Rutherford in his recently published *magnum opus*.[55] Following Rutherford, Voetius wants to show that these two indifferences constitute the formal ground or essential structure of freedom. In the context of the debate with the Jesuits his point is that the alleged indifference to the prerequisites in the compounded sense is not a part of the essence of freedom. Thus the denial of hypothetical necessity in relation to the will would be redundant.

The syllogism runs as follows:

(8) Major premise: The essential structure of freedom is that by which the will has a mastery of the act that is maximally appropriate to a creature.

(9) Minor premise: These two indifferences grant to the will such a mastery of the act that is maximally appropriate to a creature.

(10) Conclusion: These two indifferences constitute the essential structure of freedom.

Formally this argument is surely valid: given the premises, the conclusion follows. The salient point, of course, is the minor premise (9). Do the two indifferences (6) and (7) really grant such a mastery of the act as is maximally applicable to a creature? Voetius is sure of his ground. He argues that no external agent, including God, could affect or overturn freedom as it functions according to its own natural mode of acting (= the antecedent in the argument for the minor premise). This is a strong statement, since the natural mode of acting at stake comprises precisely both the *freedom of contradiction* ("choose or not

---

51. Cf. Voetius, *Sel. Disp.*, 3:79-91 ("De amore Dei"), esp. 81.
52. Voetius, *Disputatio*, A4v: "quae est potentiae liberae, per Iudicium practicum nondum ultimo determinatae."
53. Cf. also the revealing conclusion of Voetius' extensive discussion on this question in *Sel. Disp.*, 1:848-850 (as referred to by Beeckman at the end of this disputation).
54. We use the term "argument" rather than "proof" because the verb "*probare*" is less strong in scholastic language than "*demonstrare*."
55. See note 19.

choose") and the *freedom of contrariety* ("this or that"), as is outlined in the definition (5). Voetius accordingly concludes that "the mastery of the will's own acts is permanently left to it" (= the consequent in the argument for the minor premise). Voetius follows here common medieval language by referring to the will as the master of its own acts.[56]

As a following step, Voetius supports the antecedent in the argument for the minor premise by another argument. He argues that freedom cannot cease to exist since it is intrinsically bound to choice. The essential characteristic of formal ground of choice is the union of a proposed good with the end. The intellect displays such an object to the will, but as being non-necessary. Moreover, the good is contingently related to its end (see above). Therefore nothing else than freedom or free choice can be in charge of the union of the displayed object with the intended end.[57] Otherwise the whole concept of human choice would be completely redundant.

Voetius illustrates this point by a biblical example: The Persian king Cyrus once published an influential proclamation. It was him who chose to do this, and he did it by virtue of his own volition. Nevertheless, a complete explanation of this event would ultimately include God who stirred up the spirit of Cyrus, as Scripture reveals to us. But that does not mean that Cyrus' own free volition would have been uninvolved or even abolished.

5.6 Compatibility of the Essence of Freedom with Hypothetical Necessity

Up to now, Voetius has dealt with the first of the two issues in the controversy with the Jesuits about the freedom of the will. Thereby he has shown that the essence of freedom consists in an objective and vital, internal and choosing indifference. Given this twofold indifference, the human will is the formal cause of its own acts of will (thesis II). According to Voetius, this is sufficient to guarantee the integrity and freedom of will. As a consequence, the will is free from coercion and "from intrinsic, absolute and natural necessity" (thesis I).

The second issue concerns the question of the compatibility with hypothetical necessity. Voetius encounters this question in theses III-V. Such hypothetical or external necessity has to be sharply distinguished from absolute, intrinsic or natural necessity.[58]

Natural necessity is the necessity inherent to the nature of something. Due to this necessity, a cause is determined to one specific effect. Fire, for example, has a natural necessity to burn every burnable object that is thrown into it (given the required conditions for burning such as sufficient oxygen, etc).[59] In his treatise *De*

---

56. Cf. Thomas Aquinas, *Summa Theologiae* I-II, q. 10, a. 1, ad 1; and esp. Duns Scotus, *Ordinatio* III, d. 17, q. un., n. 4 (ed. Vivès, vol. 14, 654b): "omnis voluntas est domina sui actus."

57. Voetius, *Disputatio*, A4v: "atqui Libertas est Causa intrinseca, Vitalis et sola formalis hujus unionis."

58. This distinction is closely related to the modern philosophical distinction between *de dicto* and *de re* necessity as, for example, advocated by Alvin Plantinga, *The Nature of Necessity* (Oxford: Clarendon, 1982).

59. Cf. Voetius, *De vitae termino*, 105, and *Sel. Disp.*, 1:842.

vitae termino, Voetius emphasizes that God can by no means impose such a necessity on man without transforming him first into a non-human being.[60]

Intrinsic necessity is the necessity that is given by the very definition of a subject. Being gifted with rationality, for example, is an intrinsic necessity of every human being (given the standard definition in Voetius' days). The denial of such an attribute would imply a *contradictio in adiecto*.

Absolute necessity is, strictly speaking, the necessity that something has irrespective of something else. Voetius also uses the term in a broader sense that would justify the translation as "real necessity" or "necessity proper."[61]

These types of necessity are irreconcilable with human freedom. Moreover, they are juxtaposed to hypothetical and extrinsic necessity, which is, according to Voetius, compatible with freedom. Such hypothetical, extrinsic, or—as Voetius sometimes calls it—relative necessity, boils down to the necessity of a strict implicative relation. It has as its basic form:

(11) Necessarily (if *p*, then *q*)

Thus the necessity at stake is the necessity of consequence (*necessitas consequentiae*) between antecedent and consequent, which is to be strictly distinguished from the necessity of the consequent or absolute necessity (*necessitas consequentis*).[62] As has been explained in the introduction (section 1.4.1), the decisive point of this distinction is that the necessary or strictly implicative relationship of two propositions (events, entities) does not make two separate propositions (events, entities) necessary themselves or impose any real necessity on them.[63]

In concreto, Voetius argues for the compatibility of three cases of hypothetical necessity with human freedom: Necessity arising from the divine decree (section 5.7), from physical premotion (section 5.8) and from the ultimate practical judgment of the intellect (section 5.9).

5.7 Hypothetical Necessity Arising from the Divine Decree

In order to understand the hypothetical necessity arising from God's decree in relation to the freedom of the will, Voetius in thesis III first refers to a Scripture and, secondly, gives an argumentative explanation. The scriptural reference is to Philippians 2:13: "For it is God which worketh in you both to will and to do of *his* good pleasure." Since the Church Fathers, this Scripture has been a *locus*

---

60. Voetius, *De vitae termino*, 105: "[...] hanc [necessitatem] libertati voluntatis non minus repugnare, quam coactionem nobis certum est. Eam ne Deus quidem per absolutam potentiam imponere potest homini, nisi prius in non hominem illum transforma[ve]rit."

61. Cf. Voetius, *De termino vitae*, 105-106.

62. Cf. Voetius, *De termino vitae*, 105-106.

63. The strict implicative relation between the antecedent and the consequent does not imply the necessity of the consequent. In case of an antecedent that is itself necessary, however, the necessity of the antecedent is transferred to the consequent, given a strict implicative relation between antecedent and consequent.

classicus for the interplay of divine grace and human will.[64] Moreover, by referring to such Scriptures the Reformed scholastics simultaneously pointed to contemporary biblical commentaries and the state of the art of exegetical methods.[65]

When quoting Phil. 2:13, Voetius adds a remarkable characterization of the divine agency: God works in us "by virtue of that power which operates in us very strongly and at the same time very wisely."[66] Probably Voetius wants to say that this wisdom to the highest degree (*sapientissime*) enables God to work in us without manipulating our will.

After this scriptural reference, Voetius presents an interesting argument for the compatibility of freedom with necessity arising from the divine decree. The gist of this argument is that there is one and the same end point (*terminus ad quem*) of both God who decrees from eternity and man who operates in time in a rational way, i.e., according to his or her own intellect and will.[67] This argument has to be understood against the background of the traditional distinction of God and man in terms of a hierarchical order of causes. Both God and man are free causes who concur in bringing about one and the same contingent effect, whereas God is the First Cause and man the subordinated second cause.[68] Inasmuch as they both freely bring about the same effect, there is no competition, rivalry or manipulation involved. The hypothetical necessity arising from the decree does not endanger freedom in any way.

Voetius supports this argument by further explaining the relation between first and secondary causes in regard of free creaturely acts. He now focuses on the different starting points (*termini a quo*) of the contingent effect that is brought about.

Suppose Gisbertus decides to visit his son Paul right now (= object B).[69] He also could continue editing his newest book on his desk (= object A) or go to bed (= object C), but he cannot do these things simultaneously. What is the relationship between God's and Gisbertus' own involvement concerning Gisbertus' volition to visit Paul?

Voetius argues that the basic structure of both involvements is exactly the same. He explains this common structure by analyzing the involvements in terms of structural moments.[70] On the divine level, the first "starting point," the involvement could be analyzed this way:[71]

---

64. See for example Augustine, *De natura et gratia*, 32 (*MPL* 44, 264).

65. See Muller, *PRRD*, 2: 507-508.

66. Cf. Thomas Aquinas, *Summa Theologiae*, I, q. 25, a. 6: "Quidquid enim Deus facit, potentissime et sapientissime facit."

67. For the sake of simplicity we render Voetius' references to "(rational) creature" as "man."

68. See also the introduction, section 1.4.1.

69. In this example, "visiting Paul" would be Voetius' object B.

70. Voetius' argument is phrased in terms of "earlier" and "later" "moments" (*instantia*). In such contexts, these moments usually have to be understood in a structural or logical sense. His usage of the distinction between a divided and compounded sense points into the same direction. Cf. Beck, "Gisbertus Voetius," 213-215, and Beck and Vos, "Conceptual Patterns," 224-225.

71. Cf. the similar passages in Rutherford, *Exercitationes apologeticae*, 108-109; and Rutherford, *Disputatio scholastica de divina providentia*, 588. Note also the similarity with Duns

First structural moment:	There are possible objects A (Gisbertus edits his newest book), B (Gisbertus visits Paul) and C (Gisbertus goes to bed), and *God* is indifferent to all of these.
Second structural moment:	In his absolutely free and *independent* dominion, God decides to select B, thereby eliminating the indifference of his volition towards A and C (in the compounded sense).

The human involvement has a similar structure:

First structural moment:	There are possible objects A (Gisbertus edits his newest book), B (Gisbertus visits Paul) and C (Gisbertus goes to bed), and *Gisbertus* is indifferent to all of these.
Second structural moment:	In his *dependent* freedom, Gisbertus decides to select B, thereby eliminating the indifference of his volition towards A and C (in the compounded sense).

In itself, both the divine and human will are indifferent to different volitions. But "once"[72] the will of both God and man determines itself to one volition, the will can no longer be held to be indifferent to alternative volitions, namely *in the compounded sense*. The qualification "in the compounded sense" is vital here. It points to the elimination of:

(12) It is possible: The will decides to select B and it decides to select A or C.

Thus, both God (by his eternal decree) and Gisbertus (by his will in time) decide that Gisbertus visits his son *rather than* editing his newest book or going to bed—the decision for the first event excludes the simultaneous decision for the two alternative events. They both remove the same indifferences. Understood in the divided sense, however, the will is indifferent and remains open towards alternative possibilities:

(13) The will decides to select B, and it is possible that the will decides to select A or C.

Scotus' theory of the neutral proposition; and cf. Andreas J. Beck, "'Divine Psychology' and Modalities: Scotus's Theory of the Neutral Proposition," in *John Duns Scotus (1265-1308): Renewal of Philosophy*, ed. E. P. Bos (Amsterdam: Rodopi, 1998), 123-137; and idem, "God weet wat Hij wil. Duns Scotus' theorie van de neutrale propositie," in *Geloof geeft te denken: Opstellen over de theologie van Johannes Duns Scotus*, edited by Andreas J. Beck en Henri Veldhuis (Assen: Van Gorcum, 2005), 135-152.

72. We put "once" in quotes because it should be understood in a structural rather than a temporal sense.

Voetius' main point in this connection is that God's decree and man's will arrive, each on its own level and in its own manner, at the same result: object B. This brings Voetius to the remarkable conclusion:

(14) The created will is no more necessitated by God's decree than it is by itself.

The structural indifference that holds for both in the structural moment prior to the choice of one option rather than another is removed for both by nothing but the choice itself.

Of course there are important differences between the divine decree and the human will. A decisive one was already mentioned by Voetius: God is independent in his decree, while man is dependent in his act of willing. A further difference is phrased in terms of eternity versus temporality. Man's will decides in time what God decrees in eternity to happen. For Voetius, it is beyond doubt that the future being of an event is eternally established by God in his decree. The preceding argument makes it clear that this does not imply the denial of created freedom. Instead, the human will acts out of itself and has a twofold indifference (see section 5.5), but its acts run parallel to God's eternal decree, without thereby ceasing to be free acts. If we drive the issue home in terms of hypothetical necessity, the following statement expresses Voetius' position:

(15) Necessarily: If God (eternally) decrees man to choose B, man (in time) will choose B.

According to Voetius, the Jesuits "oppose that insane fiction of a middle knowledge (*scientia media*)" against this necessity originating from the decree. Voetius here points to the Molinistic concept of middle knowledge.[73] Middle knowledge is the prevolitional and contingent divine knowledge of how any possible free agent would act given certain circumstances. It is called middle knowledge because it stands in the middle between Gods prevolitional natural or necessary knowledge of all possibilities and his postvolitional free or contingent knowledge of all actual events.[74] Whereas Voetius endorses both divine natural and free knowledge, he rejects middle knowledge as being a superfluous and absurd concept. It is superfluous because human freedom, rightly understood, can be safeguarded without it, given that the hypothetical necessity originating from the divine decree does not endanger free will. And it is a fiction because it would imply that human will would so to speak confront God with its decision

---

73. It is interesting that Voetius sees Petrus Fonseca (†1599) as the inventor of that concept rather than Luis de Molina (1535-1600), see *Sel. Disp.*, 1:255, 265; and Beck, *Gisbertus Voetius*, 277-280.

74. See Molina, *On Divine Foreknowledge;* Eef Dekker, *Middle Knowledge*, Studies in Philosophical Theology 20 (Leuven: Peeters, 2000); Muller, *PRRD*, 2:417-424; and Beck, *Gisbertus Voetius*, 281-284.

"before" God has decreed anything at all.[75] That way, human will in time would cause an eternal "being future" or, in other words, an eternal actualization of a temporal event.[76]

5.8 Hypothetical Necessity Arising from the Physical Premotion

In the preceding section, we have sketched the contours of Voetius' conceptual framework: God and creature operate each on their own level, and therefore the decree of God cannot damage human freedom or vice versa.

The next type of hypothetical necessity to be addressed is the one arising from "physical premotion" (thesis IV). This term may sound misleading to modern ears: we are inclined to understand it as if God were involved in "normal" physical causality in order to give the "first impulse" by which everything sets into motion. Against this intuitive misunderstanding, we should recall the framework of dual causality in which Voetius thinks. It is in this framework that Voetius elaborates his view of premotion and the sort of necessity it induces.

The terms "physical premotion" or "physical predetermination" (*praemotio* or *praedeterminatio physica*) originated from the Molinistic controversy and were probably coined by Domingo Báñez (1528-1604) and Francisco Zumel (1540-1607). During the "Congregatio de auxiliis" (1597-1607) these terms evolved into the distinctive marks of the neo-Thomistic, anti-Molinistic doctrine of grace, especially within the Dominican school. The adjective "physical" asserts that this divine action is not merely a moral-persuasive impulse, but efficacious and real.[77] Both the terms "premotion" and "predetermination" are not bound to a necessitarian framework nor related to absolute necessity. Moreover, the term "predetermination" simply refers to the truth-value of a proposition.[78]

Voetius defines this premotion as "the applied power of God that awakens the creature that has the potency to the second act." This compact definition needs to be unpacked. First, the premotion is the power *(virtus)* of God not as it is in itself, but as far as it is *applied* to the creature. Second, what this power does is *awaken* the creature. Third, the creature is awakened as far it has a *potency* to the second act. With "second act" is meant what we usually would call a concrete act of an operative faculty such as the intellect or will, e.g., a concrete act of will. Thus the will is *in actu secundo* provided that it is actually willing something, that is, it has an actual volition or a certain act of will. The scholastics generally held that the *faculty* which is operating the act is not totally wrapped up in the act but distinct from it and has its own being. So if we consider, for example, a volition and we abstract from the act *qua* act (i.e., the *actus secundus*), we precisely retain the

75. Cf.. Voetius, *Sel. Disp.*, 1:264-339.

76. From the divine point of view, the "being future" of an event means that the event will be actual at a certain time. From the point of view of man, such an event could occur in every "difference of time," i.e., in the past, presente or future.

77. See Wolfgang Hübener, "Praedeterminatio physica," in *Historisches Wörterbuch der Philosophie*, ed. Karlfried Gründer, Joachim Ritter and Gottfried Gabriel (Darmstadt: Wissenschaftliche Buchgesellschaft, 1989), 7:1216-1226.

78. Cf. the introduction of this volume (section 1.4.1, note 48); and *CF*, 45.

faculty of the will as it is *in actu primo*, viz. in its own being.[79] It should be noted that both the volition and its faculty exist simultaneously at the same moment of time. Thus the distinction between the primary and secondary act does not in itself involve a temporal distinction of two moments of time. What it does involve in our case is a distinction between two structural moments within one and the same temporal moment.[80]

Next, Voetius explains that the applied power of God can be understood in two ways. First, it can be considered an awakening *principle* in the first act of human willing. Second, the term "applied power" can designate the *action* that is virtually passing over to us, and thus, one might add, it refers to the second act of human willing. The expression "virtually passing over" *(virtualiter transiens)* is opposed to "formally staying within" *(formaliter immanens)* and points to the *effect* that can be produced by a cause.[81] Thus the divine power is externally denominated as far as it is represented by its effect. This effect is identifiable with the *human* action or volition.

Human will in the first act (*in actu primo*), the will as will, is related to the divine will in such a way that the divine will is the awakening principle of the human will. In this structural moment, two different wills are considered who are to produce a common effect. The human will in the second act (*in actu secundo*) is identified with the effect of the divine willing—not in the sense that they are formally identical, but as being inseparably united.

Expressing the same relation, Voetius now distinguishes *premotion* from *concursus*. The prefix "pre-" in *premotion* expresses that the creature's powers of activity are structurally preceded by God's influence on that power. More precisely, the applied power "is called *precursus* or *premotion* in so far as God moves us in the first structural moment," i.e., on the level of *actus primus*, and awakens our potency to acting. Thus our potency not only exists by virtue of divine creation and conservation, but it is also awakened by God to acting. Moreover, the divine applied power also goes along with the arising human act by actualizing the effect in the second structural moment, i.e., on the level of *actus secundus*. This divine activity is called *concursus*.

But would not this concept of physical premotion or predetermination endanger human free will after all? Voetius promptly tries to meet this question, tying in with his earlier paraphrasing of Phil. 2:13.[82] Using Zumel's term "predetermination," he comments that "the predetermination of our will is moderated by the all wise God." By way of explanation, Voetius introduces the

---

79. Cf. Rudolph Goclenius, *Lexicon philosophicum quo tanquam clave philosophiae fores aperiuntur* (Frankfurt, 1613; repr. Hildesheim: Olms, 1980), s.v. "*actus*," 52; Muller, *DLGT*, s.v. "*in actu*," 150-151; Felix Alluntis and Allan B. Wolter (eds.), *John Duns Scotus: God and Creatures: The Quodlibetal Questions* (Princeton: Princeton University Press, 1975), s.v. "*in actu primo, in actu secundo*," 513-514.

80. Also Turrettini and De Moor use the distinction in this sense, cf. sections 6.6 and 7.7.

81. Cf. Goclenius, *Lexicon philosophicum*, s.v. "*virtualiter*," 321; and Jorge J. E. Gracia (ed.), *Suárez on Individuation: Metaphysical Disputation V, Individual Unity and Its Principle* (Milwaukee: Marquette University Press, 1982), 279.

82. I.e., "by virtue of that power which operates in us very strongly and at the same time very wisely" (thesis II).

important distinction between the divine predetermination of natural and free causes. Applied to a natural cause such as fire, the predetermination indeed necessitates the cause, resulting in an effect that is completely predictable if its cause is known. The nature of a free cause, however, allows for alternative effects: a free cause can freely choose and not choose out of itself this or that.[83] This nature of the free cause is not compromised by the divine predetermination but remains intact when God wisely awakens it.

It is important to see that Voetius is really serious about the compatibility of divine predetermination with human free choice. The framework of synchronic contingency and alternativity is presupposed, and there are numerous indications for this such as the twofold indifference (thesis II), Voetius' understanding of the difference between indifference in divided and compounded sense, his understanding of the difference between first and second act and the Scotian distinction of different structural moments.[84] Moreover, Voetius explicitly excludes the possibility that the divine predetermination could thwart the preference of the human will. Following Rutherford again, Voetius emphasizes that man's will does not determine itself to the opposite of the predetermined effect, nor would it choose the opposite effect if there was no predetermination. Thus it is not forced since the main criterion for being forced is not met at all. In addition, Voetius takes one more step that is highly interesting:

(16) Predetermination turns the will sweetly and strongly to that very end to which it would have turned itself.

As a matter of course, the will is always moved and premoved by God. But God does that in such a sweet and strong way that the result is exactly the same as it would be, were the will to act without this premotion. Therefore the Jesuits err when they reduce the divine involvement in time to an *indifferent concursus*. Such an indifferent *concursus* would amount to:

(17) It is possible: God concurs to Gisbertus' will willing p and Gisbertus wills ¬p.

In this case, not only hypothetical necessity arising from divine premotion would be rejected, but also a contradiction would be implied. According to Voetius, the divine *concursus* is necessarily effective, though it is contingent in itself since God could concur to a different effect than he does.

5.9 Hypothetical Necessity Arising from the Practical Judgment of the Intellect

The last type of hypothetical necessity is discussed in thesis V. Unlike the other two kinds of hypothetical necessity, this necessity does not arise from God but from the human intellect. Voetius discusses now the relationship between the

---

83. See thesis II, and cf. Voetius, *Sel. Disp.*, 1:842.
84. Cf. note 70.

human faculties that are responsible for freedom: the intellect and the will. They both work together in free choice. Roughly spoken, the intellect presents the eligible objects to the will, and the will chooses or rejects these objects. A more precise account would distinguish on the side of the intellect between the apprehension of the objects, a merely theoretical judgment that attaches truth qualifiers, and an element of preference, the practical judgment that attaches value qualifiers. This discursive process could involve multiple repetitive steps, finally resulting in the *ultimate* or final practical judgment.[85]

The question at stake is now in which way the will follows this final practical judgment of the intellect. Voetius considers three possibilities: (1) The will presupposes the final practical judgment, but is not determined by it; (2) the will is determined by it, but only as to the specification of the act; and (3) the will is determined by it, as to both the specification and the exercise of the act.

As Voetius correctly notes, all three possibilities have found advocates not only among Roman Catholic theologians but also among Reformed theologians. Moreover, in his disputation *De creatione*, which is referred to in the last sentence of our text, Voetius discusses at length arguments pro and contra the determination of the will by the final practical judgment. Then, despite his own clear preference, he accepts both options as defensible points of view and emphasizes that neither option would lead to the denial of either the essential freedom of will or the efficacy of divine grace.[86]

The first of the three possibilities was defended by most Jesuits and would imply a "chimerical indifference, by which someone who is determined to one component remains at the same [structural] instance indifferent to two, or perhaps more components."[87] Here again we encounter the indifference in the compounded sense:

(18) It is possible: The ultimate practical judgment of the intellect judges that object B is good, and the will chooses object C instead.

Both the second and third option reject proposition (18). The ultimate practical judgment determines the will, but, again, in such a sweet way that the freedom of human will is not compromised. The hypothetical necessity involved could hardly be called necessity at all since it originates from a free principle— Voetius even calls it "free necessity" in paradoxical fashion. His more detailed disputation clarifies this point. There Voetius favors a complex theory of the relation between intellect and will in which the will finally moves the intellect to the final determination.[88] Thus "the will does not behave as a merely passive and

---

85. Cf. Voetius' detailed discussion in *Sel. Disp.*, 1:831-850; and see also section 1.4.2 of the introduction.

86. Voetius, *Sel. Disp.*, 1:846: "Nos, neutram tanti ponderis esse putamus, ut propterea per alterutram negemus stabiliri naturalem voluntatis libertatem, et gratiae divinae efficaciam contra Pelagianos."

87. See thesis III. "Component" refers to one proposition within a pair of contradictory propositions *p* and *-p*.

88. Voetius, *Sel. Disp.*, 1:846.

determinable potency, neither with respect to the intellect nor to any other agent."[89] The determination of the will by the practical judgment of the intellect is not a case of intellectual determinism in the modern sense of the word.

Given the "free necessity" arising from the practical judgment, indifference in the compounded sense is indeed rejected, but not indifference in the divided sense:

(19) The ultimate practical judgment of the intellect judges that object B is good, and it is possible that the will chooses object C instead.

Up to now we have focused on what the second and third option have in common. The difference between them concerns determination to the specification of the act only (option 2) *versus* determination to both the specification of the act and its exercise (option 3). In the third option, defended by Voetius, the practical judgment not only determines the will to choose object B rather than object C (specification). It also determines to the act of choosing object B rather than rejecting this act (exercise).[90] Thus the ultimate practical judgment of the intellect plays a vital role in both the "freedom of kind or contrariety" and the "freedom of exercise or contradiction."

5.10. Conclusion

In this forgotten disputation, presided by Voetius and defended by Engelbertus Beeckman, the human will is characterized as the formal cause of its own acts, being endowed with a twofold indifference. The will is first endowed with an indifference in relation to its object (objective indifference). Second, the will is a free potency that is indifferent to choose by virtue of its own nature and essential structure (vital, internal and choosing indifference). Voetius argues that this twofold indifference constitutes the essential structure of freedom and is compatible with three kinds of *hypothetical* necessity: (1) necessity arising from the divine decree; (2) necessity arising from the physical promotion; and (3) necessity arising from the ultimate practical judgment of the intellect. Thus Voetius does not reject these three kinds of necessity—this would be the position of the Jesuits. But he also does not deny the freedom of human will in the face of these kinds of hypothetical necessity—this would resemble a position which is sometimes called hyper-Calvinism but surely differs from the considered conviction of the Reformed scholastics treated in this volume. Moreover, Voetius agrees with the Jesuits that the human will is neither coerced in any way nor necessitated by intrinsic, absolute or natural necessity. He sharply denies, however, that the human will could be autonomous and control the required divine contribution, which would be little more than a general and indifferent *concursus* to the human act of will.

---

89. Voetius, *Sel. Disp.*, 1:850: "Nec habere se voluntatem, ut potentiam pure passivam et determinabilem, ratione intellectus, aut cujuscunque alterius agentis."

90. Cf. the square of opposition in the introduction (section 1.4.2).

If we compare this disputation with the texts of Zanchius (ch. 2), Junius (ch. 3) and Gomarus (ch. 4), it is striking that Voetius gave a clearly more technical explanation of free choice and its relationship to the divine action. Beyond doubt, Voetius' position is generally in continuity with that of his forerunners and especially his teacher Gomarus whom he admired throughout his life since his studies at Leiden University in 1604-1611. On the other hand, Voetius' explanation is not only technically enhanced but also more explicitly in interaction with the Jesuits. This is remarkable, indeed, given that the position of the Catholic or Counter-Reformation was prevailing already in the end of the sixteenth century. Obviously Reformed theology had become more professional and contextual—a more appropriate term than polemical—in the work of Voetius. This development continued in the work of Francesco Turrettini (ch. 6). It might be the case, however, that the underlying ontological framework has been worked out by Voetius even more clearly and consistently.

6

Beyond Indifference

An Elenctic Locus on Free Choice by Francesco Turrettini (1623-1687)

6.1 Introduction

Francesco Turrettini is well known as one of the major representatives of Reformed orthodoxy in the aftermath of the seventeenth century.[1] He was born in 1623 in the city of Geneva. From 1647 he ministered in an Italian congregation and from 1653 until his death he also served the academy in Geneva.

His *Institutes of Elenctic Theology* (*Institutio theologiae elencticae*), first published in 1679-1685 in three volumes, has been very influential as a textbook for orthodox Christian theology. For it did not only present the Reformed doctrine, but also included a detailed expounding of the rejected opinions.[2] This *opus magnum* was written at the end of his life and at the dawn of the eighteenth century for educational purposes in order to be used in the classroom at the Genevan Academy.

According to Turrettini and his contemporary orthodox associates, theology ought to be engaged in opposition against heretic and idiosyncratic opinions in order to defend the true catholic faith of the Christian Church. The main assignment of Christian schools is the positive explanation of doctrine and negative rebuttal of error and heresy. Turrettini himself distinguishes between different tasks of theology as an academic discipline, and one of them is about refuting error and heretical opinions including the positive elucidation of doctrine. A combination of doctrinal and polemical theology was called "elenctic theology" (*theologia elenctica*).[3]

Still, this kind of theology must not be interpreted as intolerant and narrow-minded, pursued by panic-stricken firebrands who are possessed to find error with

---

1. About his life, see E. de Budé, *Vie de François Turrettini, theologien genevois (1623-1687)* (Lausanne: Bridel, 1871); Gerrit Keizer, *François Turrettini. Sa vie et ses oeuvres et le Consensus* (Lausanne: Bridel, 1900). A translation of the *Institutes* is present in: *Institutes of Elenctic Theology*, trans. George Musgrave Giger, ed. James T. Dennison, Jr., 3 vols. (Phillipsburg, NJ: Presbyterian & Reformed, 1997), which also provides a good biography: James T. Dennison Jr., "The Life and Career of Francis Turretin," 3:639-658.

2. "Deadly opinions" as Turrettini says in the preface to his *Institutio*.

3. See *Institutio*, I.2.xi (references respectively to the locus, question and section) on the various modes of teaching or the manner of treatment in theology. See, for these different modes of theology, *PRRD* 2: 217-220.

everyone. Turrettini opposes time and again the same kind of theology: that of the Socinians, Remonstrants and Jesuits, holding their position to be a "pelagianizing" deviation from mainstream "catholic" Augustinianism.[4] So, the issue is not a rather marginal point of faith, but the Reformed confession of divine grace (*sola gratia*).[5] In this respect, he is well aware that many Catholics equally object to such a Jesuit soteriology, and not only does he refer to the tradition of the church, but also to contemporary Catholics in order to defend his case.

Moreover, the dispute with his opponents is quite fair. Turrettini adopts a high level of argumentation, never resorting to slander or distortion. After carefully describing the involved issue and the different opinions on it, he tries to argue his case and to refute counter-arguments. In this scholastic text, the questions are often structured along the following lines:

1. An exposition of the precise issue at hand, and thus, what the issue is not (*status quaestionis*);[6]
2. A specification of who the opponents are, and what they precisely believe;
3. A discussion of the opponent's arguments, accompanied by Turrettini's counter-arguments;
4. A concise summary of Turrettini's own opinion (called "sources of solution"), which resembles the medieval *determinatio magistralis* and which is often a very handy check for the reader to see if the discussion is understood.

Recognizing this fair procedure, a modern Remonstrant researcher has remarked that Turrettini approaches his opponents courteously and well-informed.[7]

The academic or scholastic "Sitz im Leben" of the *Institutes* is reflected in the method which Turrettini uses to present his theological opinions. A well-known method in those days utilized to organize the subject of a disputation in academic discourse was the method of *loci communes*, which became popular in Protestant scholarly theology by the example of Phillip Melanchthon's *Loci*

---

4. Regarding free choice, Turrettini holds that his opponents diminish divine grace by extolling free choice as an "indifferent" faculty, as if it were not enslaved by sin, whereas they charge the Reformed position with introducing necessity in the doctrine of free choice. See, e.g., X.1.i, X.2.i.

5. Although we surmise that this orthodox characterization of (respectively) Socinianism, some types of Roman Catholicism and Remonstrantism is frequently correct, and we think the issue to be of considerable theological-historical and systematic interest, in this chapter we will not dig deeply into questions concerning the adequacy of the orthodox's views in positioning their adversaries. Our main concern will be to sketch the systematic outlines of Turrettini's doctrine of free choice.

6. For example X.4.ii: "the question is not about...," and v: "Therefore the question returns to this..."

7. E. P. Meijering, *Klassieke gestalten van christelijk geloven en denken. Van Irenaeus tot Barth* (Amsterdam: Gieben, 1995), 190. See also E. P. Meijering, *Reformierte Scholastik und Patristische Theologie. Die Bedeutung des Väterbeweises in der Institutio Theologiae Elencticae F. Turrettins unter besonderer Berücksichtigung der Gotteslehre und Christologie* (Nieuwkoop: De Graaf, 1991).

Communes.[8] Turrettini used this device for presenting his theological opinions in his *Institutes*, and put different *loci* together, moving from the prolegomena of theology (*locus* I) to the doctrine of the last things (*locus* XX).

In Turrettini's system of *loci*, selected topics are discussed in a specific format, the technique of *quaestiones*. Each question is divided into several members, like definitions, the demarcation of the question, sources of argumentation, polemics and counter-argumentation.

We have to bear in mind that the placement of a *locus* does not alter its doctrinal contents,[9] but it does have implications for the selection of the topics under discussion. For instance, a placement of the *locus* of free will in the context of eschatology would probably focus the interest of the *locus* in discussing free choice in the state of glory. A placement of the *locus* in the context of creation directs the discussion of free choice to its functioning in the original state of righteousness. Turrettini, however, discusses the basics of anthropology in the context of the Fall and the nature of sin (*locus* IX) rather than in the context of the state of man before the Fall (*locus* VIII). Human freedom is therefore dealt with in relation to sin. The question therefore is: how is the human will affected by the Fall or the turning away from God by the human race. The first systematic point to be noted is that Turrettini does not alter his definitions of "freedom" (*libertas*), "necessity" (*necessitas*) and "will" (*voluntas, arbitrium*) because of the placement of the *locus*, but applies these definitions to the situation (*status*) of the relationship between God and man as affected by sin.

The arrangement of Turrettini's book has a salvation-historical core, which is apparent in the way he structures his *Institutes* with respect to the different ways human beings can be related to God (*status*). This is of particular interest for the topic of free choice. After dealing with creation in general, the creation of man in particular and the state before the Fall (*ante lapsum*), Turrettini turns to the topics of sin (*peccatum originale* and *peccatum actuale*) and free choice in a state of sin. So, the various ways or states by which the relation between God and man could be described are reflected in the ordering of the *loci* of Turrettini's *Institutes*.

6.2 Translation of the Text

Although Turrettini touches on human freedom in several places, his main discussion is *locus* X on free choice in the state of sin. Freedom is most controversial in relation to human sin, so in his treatment of the actual debates of Christian theology, Turrettini discusses the several opinions on free choice in this place.

Locus X has five questions. The first deals with the term free choice, the second and third with the essence of free choice, and the last two with the (accidental) powers of free choice in the state of sin to do good. We have chosen

---

8. See, for the method of *loci* in scholastic theology, *PRRD* 1:177-179.

9. For a discussion on placement and definition, see Richard A. Muller, "The 'Placement' of Predestination in Reformed Theology: Issue or Non-Issue?" *Calvin Theological Journal* 40 (2005): 184-200.

and translated the first three questions, which are in turn divided again in several theses.[10]

Tenth Topic (*locus*): Free Choice of Man in the State of Sin

[726] *First question: Whether the term "free choice" or self-determining power (αὐτεξούσιος) should be retained in the Christian schools. And to what faculty of the soul does it properly belong—the intellect or will?*

I.   The greatness of the corruption brought upon the human race by sin we have already shown. We have seen the source of evil in original sin and the muddy streams thence flowing in actual sins. Now more properly the miserable state of man and the most degrading servitude of free choice under sin must be considered. I confess it is a sad spectacle, but still most useful and highly necessary, in order that we may fully know the greatness of our misery and the more certainly understand the necessity of healing grace and the more earnestly seek it.

Yet this [spectacle] is even more diligently to be followed by arguments because the gravest controversies have been stirred about it by various adversaries almost from the very beginning and are even now urged in our day (in the discussion of which great talents have been and are now employed).

For not to mention here the most futile errors of heathen philosophers who (ignorant of the corruption of nature) contended that man could be the builder and architect of his own fortune and by making men free made them sacrilegious:[11] who is ignorant of the gigantic attempts of the Pelagians and semi-Pelagians on this subject! They deny either wholly the impurity of nature or extenuate [727] it most astonishingly to extol the powers of free choice. Neither the authority of various councils, nor the labor and industry of the brightest lights of the church (Jerome, Augustine, Prosper, Hilary, Fulgentius and others) broke these attempts so much as to prevent their renewing and causing to sprout again the very same things in succeeding ages; so that you would rather say that these enemies had triumphed over the fathers instead of being entirely conquered by them.

Nor do the Jesuits, Socinians and Remonstrants of our day on this subject (as also in various others) labor for anything else than to bring back (either openly or secretly and by burrowing) Pelagianism and semi-Pelagianism and

---

10. The page numbers of the original text are from the 1688-1689 edition, published in Geneva by Samuel de Tournes. They are indicated by references between brackets in the translation. We have extensively and thankfully used the Giger translation, but especially with respect to several technical terms, it was sometimes inadequate.

11. The last part of this sentence is derived from Augustine, who accused Cicero of this sacrilegiousness, because he denied divine foreknowledge on account of its threat to human freedom; Augustine, *The City of God* V.9 (*MPL* 41, 150). The sentence got proverbial character and was cited by almost every author in the early seventeenth-century controversies between Jesuits and Dominicans and Reformed and Remonstrants on free choice.

to place the idol of free choice in the citadel.[12] This is the Helen whom they so ardently love and for whom they do not hesitate to fight as if [they fight] for altars and firesides.

It is of great importance, therefore, that the disciples of true and genuine grace oppose themselves strenuously to these deadly errors and thus build up the misery of man and the necessity of grace that the entire cause of destruction should be ascribed to man and the whole glory of salvation to God alone. To this belongs the doctrine of free choice, concerning which we now dispute.

Whence the term "free choice" is derived[13]

II. However, because an accusation is usually stirred against us here by the papists (as if we could not accept the term "free choice" any more than the thing itself), a few remarks must be premised concerning the term.

The word "free choice," as also "self-empoweredness" (αὐτεξούσιος) used by the Greek fathers, does not occur in Scripture. Yet, it was received by the Christian schools as suited enough to designate that faculty of the mind-gifted soul by which the soul spontaneously does what it pleases, a judgment of reason going before. For they are mistaken who think they have found it in what Paul calls *the power of his own will* (ἐξουσίαν περι του ἰδίου θελήματος, 1 Cor. 7:37). For him, ἐξουσία does not mean freedom of choice, but facility of executing; nor does το θέλημα signify an act of the will, but an object (as often elsewhere). Therefore, the origin of this word seems rather to be drawn from the Platonic school, the followers of which several of the fathers were before they were converted to Christ. For what the Peripatetics called "free decision" (ἐλευθέρα προαίρεσις) and the Stoics "that which is our own" (τὸ ἐφ᾽ ἡμιν), the Platonists called "self-empoweredness" (αὐτεξούσιος).

III. Yet this name seems too arrogant, if considered precisely in itself, as if man would be in his own power; what belongs properly to God alone, who therefore is truly perfectly self-empowered (αὐτεξούσιος) and self-authorative (ἀνυπεύθυνος). He thus has his own right that he absolutely does not depend upon anyone nor can he depend so. Man, however, is always under authority (ὑπεύθυνος) and under power (ὑπεξούσιος).

For this reason, some have desired it to be removed from the use of the church to take away the abuse of the Pelagians who have spread their poison under it. Still, because it has now been received in the church by a long usage, we do not think it should be dismissed to the philosophers from whom it seems to have been derived, but that it can be retained usefully, if its right sense is taught and its abuse avoided.

Hence, it cannot be charged upon us without calumny that we can accept neither the term "free choice" nor the thing itself. For as we are about to

---

12. The word "citadel" (*arce*) might refer to the Capitoline hill in Rome, which was the center of pagan idolatry; at least Turrettini seems to censure an—in his eyes—idolatrous exaltation of free choice in his opponents.

13. In the margin of his text, Turrettini regularly gives a summary of the following part; we have used them as subtitles.

demonstrate later on regarding the thing itself [728] that we establish free choice far more truly than our opponents, so the writings of our men abundantly teach that we by no means repudiate this term, when it is properly understood.

IV. The subject of free choice is neither the intellect, nor the will separately, but both faculties conjointly. As it belongs to the intellect with regard to the choice or decision (προαίρεσις), so it belongs to the will with regard to freedom. Hence, you may rightly call it a mixed faculty or a wedlock (*connubium*) and meeting (συνκυρια) of both—the intellect as well as the will.[14] Nevertheless you would not properly say it rather consists in both faculties; for as the choice of the intellect is terminated in the will, so the freedom of the will has its root in the intellect. Hence, the philosopher [Aristotle], leaving this an open question, says that it is either the "appetitive intellect" (νους ὀρεκτιος) or the "intelligent appetite" (ὀρεξις διανοητικη), *Ethics* 5.2.[15]

V. Nor ought this to seem unusual since the intellect and will are mutually connected by so strict a necessity that they can never be separated from each other. Nor does there seem to be a real and intrinsic distinction here, but only an extrinsic distinction, with regard to the objects. One and the same faculty of the soul both judges by understanding, and embraces by willing what it judges to be good. It is called "intellect" when it is occupied in the knowledge and judgment of things, but "will" when it is carried to love or hatred. Thus "what is affirmation and negation in the intellect, that is desire and avoidance in the will," as the philosopher says (ὅπερ ἐν διανοια καταφασις και ἀποφασις τουτ᾽ ἐν ὀρεξει διωξις και φυγη).[16]

VI. In the soul, besides its essence, there are only three things: faculty, habit and act. In the common opinion, choice (*arbitrium*) denotes an act of the mind; but here it signifies properly neither an act nor a habit because both of them can be separated from man and also because they determine him to only one of contraries. Hence, "choice" signifies a faculty, not a vegetative and sensitive faculty (common to us with the animals, in which there is no place for virtue or vice), but a rational faculty, from which we are not indeed good or evil, but from which it is possible for us to be good or evil by its act and habit.

Second question: Whether every necessity is repugnant to freedom of choice. We deny against the papists and Remonstrants.

I. Before speaking of the nature and essential structure of free choice, we must first discuss the mentioned question on account of the opponents. For this is their capital error (πρωτον ψευδος) upon which they erect their erroneous doctrine [729] about the essence of freedom being placed in indifference, namely [the error] that "necessity of every kind is opposed to freedom of choice and necessity and freedom are diametrically (ἀντιδιηρημενως) opposed;

---

14. The Latin text has *connubium*, but *conubium* is the more proper spelling.

15. This seems to be VI.2 (compare next note) instead of V.2, *NE* 178, translated by Rowe with "intelligence qualified by desire or desire qualified by thought."

16. *NE* VI.2, 177.

nor can free choice be conceived or understood together with a determination to one [act out of alternative possibilities] or together with a necessity determining it antecedently." Their aim is no other than to take the will of man away from the necessity of divine determination and government and to make it uncontrolled (ἀδεσποτος) and the mistress of her own acts.

Not every [kind of] necessity is repugnant to freedom, but only certain ones

II. To this assertion of Pelagians is opposed the orthodox truth which maintains that not every necessity is at variance with freedom, nor that every necessity agrees with it; but that one is incompatible (ἀσυστατος) with it, while another cordially unites with it (which has been noticed before in passing, Topic VIII, Question 1). It must now be explained a little more distinctly.

III. Freedom is variously distinguished. Some, like Bernard, *On Grace and Free choice* (*Tractatus de Gratia et Libero Arbitrio*) 3.7 and due to him Lombard, Book 2, Dist. 25 make freedom threefold: first from necessity; second from sin; third from misery.[17] He [Bernard] calls the first "freedom of nature," which he grants us in the condition of nature; the second "freedom of grace," because we are restored to it in grace; the last "freedom of glory," because it is reserved for us in glory. By the first, we excel other living creatures; by the second, we subject the flesh; by the third we subject death. The first is so natural to man that it cannot be wrested from him in any way. The other two were lost by sin. This distinction we readily receive, provided that we understand by the word necessity a physical as well as a coactive necessity, which are incompatible (ἀσυστατος) with the nature of freedom.

IV. But to make the whole subject clearer, we distribute freedom and necessity into six heads: namely, as the will can be considered either with respect to: [1.] the external agent, or [2.] [human's bodily] matter and internal sense, or [3.] with respect to God, or [4.] the practical intellect, or [5.] the goodness or wickedness of the object proposed, or [6.] with respect to the event and existence [of the act]. Hence a sixfold necessity arises:

The first [kind of necessity] is a necessity of coercion arising from an external agent, where he who is compelled, contributes nothing.

The second is a physical and instinctive (*bruta*) necessity occurring in inanimates and animals who act from a blind impulse of nature or an animal instinct and innate appetite, however, without any light of reason, as the necessity in fire to burn, a combustible object being supplied; the necessity in a horse to eat, grass or hay being supplied, [the horse being] without any decision (προαιρεσις).

The third is a necessity of dependence in the creature on God, [a creature being dependent] both in respect to the *right* and the law established by him, and in respect to the *fact*, namely [in respect to] the government of

---

17. *GFC* 62, 63; Petrus Lombardus, *Magistri Petri Lombardi Sententiae in IV libris distinctae*, 2 parts in 3 vols. (Rome: Coll. S. Bonaventurae ad Claras Aquas, 1971-1981), part 1, vol. 2, II.xxv.8, 466-469.

providence: 1. in the antecedent decree; 2. in the subsequent execution. This necessity [of factual dependence] is called a hypothetical necessity, as well as a necessity of infallibility with respect to prescience and a necessity of immutability with respect to the decree and actual concourse.

The fourth is a necessity of the rational determination to one [act out of alternative possibilities] by a practical judgment of the intellect, which the will cannot resist.

The fifth is a moral necessity or necessity of servitude, arising from good or bad habits and from the presentation of objects to their faculties. For such is the nature of moral habits that, although the acquisition of them was in our power, yet when [730] our will is imbued with them, they can neither be unexercised nor be laid aside (as the philosopher rightly teaches).[18] Hence it happens that the will which is free in itself, is thus determined either to good or to evil that it cannot but act either well or badly. Hence flows the servitude of sin or of righteousness.

The sixth is a necessity of the existence of the thing or of the event, in virtue of which, when a thing is, it cannot but be.

Necessity of coercion and physical necessity repugnant to freedom
V. As there are two principal characteristics of free choice in which its essential structure consists: 1. the decision (ἡ προαιρεσις), so that what is done is done by a previous judgment of reason; 2. the willingness (το ἡκουσιον), so that what is done is done voluntarily and without coercion, the former belonging to the intellect; the latter to the will, so two species of necessity also contend with it. The first is *physical and instinctive necessity*; the other *necessity of coercion*. The former takes away the decision (προαιρεσις); the latter, however, the willingness (ἡκουσιον). For the things which happen out of physical necessity by natural agents who are by their nature determined to one [kind of actions] and without reason, cannot be judged to happen freely, i.e., by the previous light of reason. And the things which happen by force and coercion cannot be said to happen spontaneously.

About these [kinds of necessity], there is no controversy between us and our opponents. In passing, only this is to be reminded that Bellarmine (cf. *De Gratia et Libero Arbitrio*, 3.4 in *Opera* [1858], 4:332-37) and other papists slander our men when they charge them with holding that freedom from coercion is sufficient to constitute free choice, because besides this they require also immunity from physical necessity. And when they sometimes say that man is free from coercion, but not from necessity, they do not mean physical necessity, but necessity of dependence, of servitude and rational necessity. [Clearly they did not mean] physical necessity, because there was no controversy about it and it is sufficiently excluded of itself, both by the condition of the subject (which is rational) and by the acts of judging and willing (which are incompatible with it).

18. *NE* III.5, 129-132.

But the four other kinds of necessity agree with it

VI. But if these two species of necessity mentioned by us contend against free choice, it is not the same case with the others, which can exist with it and by which freedom is not so much destroyed as preserved and perfected, which can be shown for each of the four species of necessity indicated before.

First, concerning the *necessity of dependence* upon God, free choice does not exclude, but supposes it [threefoldly]. This dependence can be understood either as a moral dependence of right in reference to the divine law from which a rational creature can never be exempted; or as a physical dependence of fact as to the actual concourse of providence, by which things so depend upon God, as the highest ruler and first cause in being, becoming and operating, that they can neither be nor do anything except in dependence upon him; or [it can be understood as] a dependence of futurition as to foreknowledge and the decree, from which arise [respectively] the necessity of infallibility and of immutability. For however great the freedom of the creature may be in its operations, still they are necessary in [both of] these respects, otherwise the foreknowledge of God could be deceived and his decree changed.

VII. Secondly, the *rational necessity* of a determination to one [act out of alternative possibilities] by the practical intellect [does not destroy free choice]. For since the will is a rational appetite, such is its nature that it cannot but follow the ultimate judgment of the practical intellect [731]; otherwise it could seek evil as evil and be turned away from good as good, which is absurd (ἀσύστατος). For if the ultimate judgment of the practical intellect is brought so far that it judges that this object, here and now, all circumstances being weighed, is the best, and the will should be opposed to this judgment, then it would be turned away from good as good. Nor ought it to be objected that the will frequently seeks evil, because it does not seek evil as evil, but as an apparent, useful or pleasant good.

VIII. Thirdly, *moral necessity* arising from habits [does not destroy free choice]. For as the choice can be called "free" if it is devoid of habit, so it can rightly be called "enslaved" if it has been determined to a certain manner of acting by a habit. Yet, this servitude by no means overthrows the true and essential nature of freedom. Otherwise it would follow that habits destroy the will, which they rather perfect and facilitate to operate.

As moral habits are twofold: some good, others evil, so a twofold servitude is thence also born: one of righteousness in good; another of sin in evil and misery. The latter belongs to man in a state of sin, about which is John 8:34 "Everyone who commits sin is a slave to sin," and Rom. 6:17 "You who were once slaves of sin." The former [kind of servitude] characterizes him in a state of grace, about which is Rom. 6:18 "Having been set free from sin, you have become slaves of righteousness." This servitude is true freedom, as there is no more real and miserable servitude than that of sin. For he who serves sin the least does what he wills. He does by a particular inclination what he least wills by a universal inclination. For all, by a universal and natural appetite, always seek good and happiness for themselves.

IX. Hence, it is evident that the adversaries (and especially Bellarmine, ibid., 4.6, pp. 363-64) falsely charge our men with having said that choice is a slave in the state of sin, as if its freedom were destroyed by that very thing. For Scripture beforehand calls it so and indeed with a twofold limitation: (1) that the servitude should be understood not absolutely and physically, but relatively, after the Fall in a state of sin; (2) not simply about every natural, civil or external moral object, but especially about a spiritual object, which is good in itself.

In this manner the inability ($\dot{a}\delta v v a\mu\iota a$) to do good is strongly asserted, but the essence of freedom is not destroyed. For although a sinner is so enslaved by evil that he cannot but sin, still he does not cease to sin most freely and with the highest willingness. Hence Jansen in Book 3, *On the state of fallen nature*, chapter 5[19] acknowledges that Luther did not introduce the term "enslaved choice" first, but followed Augustine who had so spoken of it long before in his *Manual to Laurentius concerning faith, hope and charity (Enchiridion)*, chapter 30, and *Against Two Letters of the Pelagians* 3.8. He is angry with those of his own party who maintained that the term "enslaved choice" was unknown before Luther. Augustine [says in] *Admonition and Grace (De correptione et gratia)*, chapter 13: "Choice was free, but not freed; free of righteousness, yet a slave of sin, in which it is involved by different hurtful desires; in some more, in others less, but all in evil" and in his *Manual*, chapter 30: "Man using free choice badly, lost both himself and itself."[20]

X. Fourthly, the necessity of event [does not destroy freedom of choice]. For although whatever that [732] is, necessarily is, when it is, it, so that it could no more not be; still it is said to happen no less freely or contingently as depending upon free or contingent causes. For the certainty and truth of the existence of a thing cannot change its essence.

Sources of solution

XI. Although choice is free, this does not prevent that it is determined by God and that it is always under subjection to him. For this freedom is not absolute and independent or uncontrolled ($\dot{a}\delta\epsilon\sigma\pi\sigma\tau\sigma\varsigma$) which belongs to God alone, but it is limited and dependent. Otherwise if no faculty is free except it is in subjection to no one, either a free choice does not exist in creatures or every second cause will be the first.

XII. The will is said to be the mistress of its own actions, not absolutely and simply, as if it always depended upon itself [alone] to elicit or not elicit them. For it cannot be such in this [absolute] way, then being not in subjection to God or to the intellect. It is said relatively, with regard to imperate acts by which it governs inferior potencies; not with regard to elicited acts which cannot properly be said to be under the control of the will, since they are the

---

19. Cornelius Jansen, *Augustinus* (Louvain, 1640; repr. Frankfurt am Main, 1964), vol. 3, *De statu naturae lapsae*, 5:441-46.

20. *De correptione et gratia* XIII, 42 (*MPL* 44, 942); *Enchiridion* IX, 30 (*MPL* 40, 246).

very command of the will by which it governs the acts of other faculties subjected to itself.

XIII. The will can be viewed either in relation to the decree and concourse of God or in contradistinction to the intellect. In the former sense, it is rightly said to be so determined by God that it also determines itself (because, as was seen before, God so moves creatures that he leaves their own motions to them). But in the latter sense, it cannot be said to determine itself, because it is determined by the intellect whose ultimate judgment of practical intellect it must follow.

XIV. If the will is always determined by God, it can be called his instrument in a popular sense. In this way, the relation of instrument is attributed in Scripture to wicked men when they are called the *axe*, the *hammer*, the *rod of God*. But not in a philosophical and proper sense in which an instrument denotes an agent which has within itself no principal causality and has such a nature as to produce an effect more noble than itself (as the heat of the sun, which is inanimate, produces living animals). For the will does not produce an entity nobler than itself and does not cease to be the principal cause; if not absolutely, still in its own genus (to wit, of second cause).

XV. Although the will can oppose the theoretical judgment of the intellect or the absolute and simple judgment of the practical intellect; whither pertain those words of Medea in the Poet—"I see the right and approve it too, and still the worse pursue,"[21] yet it can never oppose the relative and ultimate [practical] judgment.

XVI. In the first sin, the will of Adam did not follow the first and absolute judgment of the intellect by which it judged that the fruit must not be eaten, because God had prohibited its use under penalty of death (Gen. 3:3). Rather it followed the relative and ultimate judgment by which it is said that *the woman saw the fruit of the tree to be good to her for food and judged it to be desirable to the eyes* (v. 6), viz. according to the deceitful promise of Satan that they would be like God.[22] [733]

XVII. In the sin against the Holy Spirit, the will indeed opposes the judgment of the practical intellect, namely the first relative judgment.[23] Otherwise it could not be said to be committed against conscience and the knowledge of the truth. Nevertheless it is not repugnant to the ultimate relative judgment, in which the flesh, all things here and now being considered, judges that the gospel should be denied and Christ forsaken.

---

21. "The Poet" is Ovid and the citation is from Ovid, *Metamorphoses* 7.20-21, Loeb Classical Library 42, 43: *Ovid in Six Volumes* (Cambridge, MA: Harvard University Press, 1968), 1:342-43.

22. We have given an own translation to preserve the aspect of (Eve's) judgment.

23. For the difference between *absolute* practical and *relative* practical judgment see the commentary on the text of De Moor (7.6).

Third question: Whether the essential structure of free choice consists in indifference or in rational willingness. The former we deny; the latter we affirm against papists, Socinians and Remonstrants.

Free choice in the genus of being

I. Free choice can be viewed either in the genus of being and absolutely (as belonging to a rational being in every state); or in the genus of morals and in relation to various states (either of sin or of righteousness). In this question, we treat of it in the former sense; in the [two] following ones, we will discuss it in the latter sense.

It is not placed in indifference, but in willingness

II. Concerning the essential structure of free choice, it can be disputed: (1) κατ' ἀρσιν and negatively that we may see in what it does not consist; (2) κατα Ͽεσιν and positively that it may be evident in what it does properly consist. As to the former, the error of the adversaries must be opposed who place its essential structure in indifference. As to the latter, the orthodox truth must be established which asserts that it is placed in rational willingness (*lubentia rationalis*).

III. We contend here against the Jesuits, Socinians and Remonstrants who, following Pelagius, place the essence of free choice in indifference (ἀδιαφορα) and are wont to define it as "the faculty by which all requisites for acting being posited, the will can act or not act." Now those things without which an action cannot be performed are called requisites for action, such as the decree of God and his concourse; the judgment of the mind; and other circumstances which belong here.

Statement of the question

IV. Hence it is evident that it is not inquired here concerning indifference in the first act or in a divided sense, i.e., with respect to the simultaneity of potency (*simultas potentiae*), which is called passive and objective indifference. [So the question is not] whether the will, considered absolutely in its natural constitution and the requisites for acting being withdrawn, is determinable to various objects and holds itself indifferently towards them. For we do not deny that the will of itself is so related [to its objects] that it can either elicit or suspend the act, which is the freedom of exercise and of contradiction or can be carried to each one of opposite [acts], which is the freedom of contrariety and of specification. We also confess that the will is indifferent as long as the intellect remains doubtful and uncertain whither to turn itself.

But the question is about indifference in the second act and in a compositive sense, i.e. with respect to the potency of simultaneity (*potentia simultatis*), which is called active and subjective indifference. [So the question indeed is] whether the will, all requisites for acting being posited [734]; for example, the decree of God and his concourse; the judgment of the practical intellect, etc. is always so indifferent and undetermined that it can act or not act. This is pretended by our opponents in order that its own freedom may be left to the will. We deny it.

Freedom does not consist in indifference

V. First, such an indifference to opposite [acts] is found in no free agent, whether created or uncreated: neither in God, who is most freely good indeed, yet not indifferently, as if he could be evil, but necessarily and immutably; nor in Christ, who obeyed God most freely and yet most necessarily because he could not sin; nor in angels and the blessed, who worship God with the highest willingness and yet are necessarily determined to good; nor in devils and reprobates, who cannot but sin, although they sin freely. So neither the constancy and immutability of the former in the good destroys, but perfects their freedom; nor the inextricable obstinacy and firmness of the latter in evil prevents them from sinning most heinously and so deserving the heaviest punishment.

VI. What can be objected here?

1. Whether divine freedom has another nature than ours? We answer that the more perfect the freedom of God is than ours, the farther his freedom must be removed from indifference, which is not so much a virtue as rather a defect of freedom.

2. Whether Christ, although he never sinned, still was not absolutely unable to sin, nor was it repugnant to his nature, will or office to be able to sin? Episcopius and other Remonstrants have not blushed to put forth this blasphemy. We answer that it be far from us either to think or say any such thing concerning the immaculate Son of God whom we know to have been holy (ἄκακος), undefiled (ἀμίαντιος), separate from sinners; who not only had no intercourse with sin, but could not have both because he was the Son of God and because he was our Redeemer, who if he would have been able to sin, he would also have been able not to save us. Nor if he was able to be miserable, he would for the same reason be able to be a sinner. Misery for a time is not opposed to his most holy nature and contributed to the execution of his office because he was bound to pay the punishment of our sin and so to bear it by suffering. But he could not deserve it.

3. Whether the freedom of the saints on earth and in heaven is different? We answer that since the essential structure (*ratio formalis*) of freedom must be the same with respect to its essential parts (*quoad essentialia*) [for both], if the latter have a most perfect freedom without indifference, indifference cannot be said to belong to the essence of freedom.

VII. Second, the will can never be without determination, as well extrinsic determination by the providence of God, as intrinsic determination by the judgment of the intellect, as has been shown. Bellarmine himself proves this by various arguments.[24] Therefore when all the requisites for acting are posited, the will cannot still have the choice between acting or not acting. Otherwise it would neither be created, because it would not depend upon

---

24. See Bellarmine, *De Gratia et Libero Arbitrio*, 3.8 in *Opera* (1858), 4:338-440.

God; nor rational, because it would act against the judgment of reason and seek evil as evil. Nor is it an objection that it is said to be of the nature of free will to determine itself, because [735] subordinates do not contend against each other. It is indeed of the nature of the will to be determined by itself, but not by itself alone. Thus the determination of the will does not exclude, but supposes the determination of God.

VIII. Third, the volition of the highest good and of the ultimate end cannot be without the highest willingness. And yet it is not without great and unavoidable necessity: according the consent of our opponents themselves and the agreement of the philosophers, we cannot abstain from seeking (*appetendo*) the highest good because no one can bring himself to wish to be miserable. Nor can it be said that free choice is not occupied about the highest good or ultimate end, but only about the election of means. For in the appetite of the (true or false) highest good, the reason (*ratio*) of virtue or of vice is principally situated. It is necessary that freedom, without which there is no reason either of virtue or of vice, is occupied no less about the goal than about the means. Again, when certain means are offered which have a necessary connection with the end, and the will is occupied about their election, it is free in electing them, and yet it will be necessarily captured [by them].

IX. Fourth, the indifference of the will being assumed:

1. The use of prayers and exhortations is taken away, because God is prayed in vain to convert and sanctify us, exhortations are employed in vain, if whatever action of God being posited, the will cannot be moved from a state of equilibrium, and remains always in its power to convert itself or not.

2. The promises of God concerning the production of holiness and the efficacy of grace would be made vain, because he could not perform what he promised; for whatever he would perform about the will, it would always remain in equilibrium and indifference. Now how could he thus be said to give the willing and performing and so to make a new heart?

3. All our consolation is gone because in whatever manner God acts in us, we can never be certain of grace if it depends always upon the will to admit or reject it and thus to frustrate every operation of God.

4. The dominion of God over the will is destroyed, which [will] would be independent and of its own right, if all the requisites for acting being furnished, it can act or not act. So, man will be the author and principal cause of his own conversion, not God, because all the operations of grace being supplied, the will always shall be in equilibrium, nor is determined by any other than by itself.

Freedom is placed in willingness

X. Since, therefore, the essential structure of freedom is not placed in indifference, it cannot be sought elsewhere than in rational willingness, by which man does what he pleases by a previous judgment of reason. Thus necessarily two things must be joined here together to its constitution: 1. the decision (τὸ προαιρετικον), so that what is done is not done by a blind impulse and a certain animal instinct, but by decision (ἐκ προαιρεσεως) and the previous light of reason and the judgment of the practical intellect; 2. the willingness (το ἐκουσιον) so that what is done may be done spontaneously and freely and without coercion. Hence the philosopher calls it "the willing preference" (ἐκουσιον προβεβουλευμενον), Ethics III.2.[25]

XI. That this is the essential structure of free choice is plainly gathered from this that it suits with all [free agents], solely and always [suits with free choice]. Thus there is no free agent (either created or uncreated) in which these two [736] characteristics are not found; nor for a time only, but always, so that this rational willingness being posited, freedom is posited; while, if rational willingness is removed, freedom is taken away as well.

Hence, it follows that it is an inseparable adjunct of the rational agent, attending him in every state so that he cannot be rational without on that very account being free; nor can he be deprived of freedom without being despoiled also of reason. This also proves that free choice absolutely considered and in the genus of being can never be taken away from man in whatever state he may be. If this is denied by some to man in a state of sin, it ought to be understood not so much physically and absolutely as morally and relatively: not so much with regard to the essence of free choice as with regard to its powers, as will be shown afterwards.

Sources of solution

XII. The principle of election can be in its own nature indifferent and undetermined in the divided sense—as to the first act and the simultaneity of potency; but not in the compositive sense—as to the second act or the potency of simultaneity. To be free, election ought to enjoy an immunity from coercion and physical necessity; but not from the extrinsic necessity of dependence upon God and the intrinsic one of determination by the intellect. And so far is the determination to one [act], made by reason, removed from taking away free election, that it rather makes it perfect. For free choice therefore elects this or that, because it is by a judgment of the intellect determined to it.

XIII. That which is of an instinctive nature, not knowing itself, does not have a reason of vice or virtue; but only that which is of a rational nature. Sin is called natural not as nature is opposed to free choice, but as nature is opposed to grace. A place is granted for obedience or disobedience even without indifference and with a determination to one [kind of actions], as in Christ who was immutably determined to obey the Father and in the devils who were necessarily determined to disobey him, yet still sinning most freely and worthy of the severest punishment. The nature of obedience is not placed in this—that man can obey or not obey; but in this—that man obeys freely and without coercion by previous reason.

XIV. So far is the use of exhortations and commands from being taken away by our opinion, that it is rather the more strongly asserted. For if it is certain that

---

25. *NE* 127 ("the voluntary ... what has been reached by prior deliberation").

the will is determined by the intellect, the intellect must first be persuaded before it can influence the will. And yet how can it be persuaded except by reasons and exhortations? Although a compliance with the exhortation is impossible by us without grace; still not the less properly can it be addressed to us because it is a duty owed by us.

XV. In order to grant a place for reward or punishment, it is not necessary that there should be indifference in the will to either of two opposites. It suffices that there be a spontaneity and willingness depending upon a judgment of reason, such as there is in all men.

6.3 Structure of the Text

Turrettini's *locus* on free choice can be summarized as follows:

1. The term "free choice" in theology (question 1)
   a. A legitimate theological concept in Christian theology (theses 1-4)
   b. Its signification: a mixed faculty of intellect and will (theses 5-7)

2. The compossibility of freedom and necessity (question 2)
   a. The issue:
      i. Remonstrants and Pontificians deny any compossibility (theses 1-2)
      ii. Orthodox distinguish between compatible and incompatible kinds of necessity
   b. Common distinction of freedom (thesis 3)
   c. Sixfold distinction of necessity: (theses 4-9)
      i. Physical necessity
      ii. Necessity of coercion
      iii. Necessity of dependence on God
      iv. Rational necessity
      v. Moral necessity
      vi. Necessity of event.
      The first two are incompatible with freedom, the latter four rather perfect it

3. The essential structure of free choice (question 3)
   a. The issue discussed negatively: the essential structure of freedom is not properly defined by indifference (theses 1-3)
      i. Distinctions in indifference (theses 4-5)
      ii. Arguments against definition of freedom by indifference (theses 5-9)
   b. The issue discussed positively: the essential structure of freedom is defined rightly by rational spontaneity (theses 10-11)

4. The accidental features of statebound freedom (question 4)

5. The virtues of the heathen (question 5)

In this commentary we offer an interpretation of Turrettini's views on freedom of choice in the state of sin (*locus* X) and we will proceed by following Turrettini's division in five questions. (Questions 4 and 5 were not translated, and are not addressed in this commentary.) After establishing the usefulness of the term "free choice" in Christian theology, he focuses on the question of whether freedom belongs to the intellect or to the will as functions of the human mind (q. 1). Further, a series of distinctions in the concept of necessity safeguards the fact that freedom has a structural level that is essentially given, as a human being is connected to God by way of the inner ontological make-up of his human nature (q. 2). Turrettini proceeds by discussing the right definition of free choice (q. 3). All these questions are dealt with in a structural way, and only in the fourth and fifth question is sin being put into the picture: didactically as part of the context in which freedom is being discussed in the system of *loci*; ontologically as the factual determination of the relationship between God and man in the state of sin. Here, Turrettini addresses the question: how does decision-making, especially in relation to what is really good, operate in a human being that lives in a state of denial of God (q. 4)?

6.4 Freedom and Necessity

Since the combination of freedom and necessity may appear counterintuitive, not only in our time, but apparently also at least for Turrettini's opponents, it is useful to provide clarification on the issue involved. So after having established that there is such a thing as the legitimate use of the term "free choice" in Christian doctrine in the first question,[26] Turrettini starts his second question by distinguishing between different kinds of freedom, as well as different meanings of the term "necessity."

Basically, Turrettini argues, *necessitas* and *libertas* are not to be judged prematurely to be incompatible, since both necessity and liberty or freedom may mean a range of things.[27] So, Turrettini starts his discussion on the relationships between necessity and freedom by discussing various definitions and distinctions in both concepts. He distinguishes between six kinds of necessity, each of which is then discussed in regard to freedom.

It is noteworthy that Turrettini acknowledges the distinctions in freedom, made by Bernard of Clairvaux and Peter Lombard, for these were adopted by the entire later medieval tradition, and were also transferred into Reformed theology.

---

26. Turrettini does not only give reasons for using the term "liberum arbitrium" in Christian doctrine, but he also points to the orthodox understanding of the term as the only legitimate one, for he says: "Nam ut quoad rem postea demonstraturi sumus, nos longe verius Adversariis liberum arbitrium stabilire: Ita scripta Nostrorum abunde docent, nos nomen hoc bene intellectum haudquaquam repudiare." (X.1.iv).

27. X.2.ii: "[...] opponitur Orthodoxa veritas, quae statuit, Non omnem necessitatem pugnare cum libertate, Nec omnem etiam cum ea subsistere, sed aliquam cum ea esse ἀσύστατον, aliquam vero cum ea amice conspirare, quod supra jam obiter observatum VIII.1." See also VIII.1.v about the liberty of Adam before the Fall.

We encounter them also in Calvin and Luther—usually depicted as tough adversaries of "free will."[28] The distinction is put as follows:

Libertas a necessitate, cannot be lost, since it is given with the nature of man

Libertas a peccato	lost by sin	restored by grace
Libertas a miseria	lost by sin	restored by glory

Discussing the compatibility of freedom and necessity, Turrettini at the outset makes clear that only the first kind of freedom is involved.

The first meaning of *libertas* belongs essentially to human beings. This is an important observation, for it means that this freedom cannot be taken away from a human being. It would be removed, however, by necessity in the sense of physical necessity (we shall call this necessity [1]), or by coercion (necessity [2]). So, these two types of necessity conflict with freedom.

The other two types of freedom will be addressed in section 6.7 below, as this freedom from sin and misery has to do with the redemptive process of the four different states of mankind.

There are four other kinds of necessity, Turrettini argues, which do not take away freedom. These kinds of necessity are quite harmless to freedom; they even preserve liberty, as Turrettini says. They are, respectively, (3) necessity of dependence on God; (4) necessity of the last judgment of the practical intellect; (5) necessity arising from habits; and (6) necessity of the event. Why is it that only two types of necessity are repugnant to freedom while four concepts are said to safeguard freedom? As he will point out later, a nuanced and balanced view on the relation between freedom and necessity is needed against the opponents who understand indifference as belonging to the very core of free choice. Indifference the way the opponents take it does indeed exclude more types of necessity. So, in order to challenge the understanding of the essentials of freedom, Turrettini has to be clear about the relationship between necessity and freedom as understood by the adversaries.

A clear sky with respect to the compatibility of freedom and necessity is needed for advancing the definition of free choice and its application in the various relationships between God and man (the various "states," e.g., the state of grace, the state of sin, the state of glory). Therefore, Turrettini gives in four paragraphs (quaestio 2, articles vi, vii, viii and x) a consistent account of the way orthodoxy understands:

---

28. See the discussions by Vincent Brümmer and Paul Helm in *Religious Studies* (a similar discussion appeared in Dutch between Brümmer and A. De Reuver in *Theologia Reformata*); Dewey Hoitenga in his *John Calvin and the Will* (Grand Rapids: Baker Academic, 1997); and the more subtle approach in *The Bondage and Liberation of the Will: A Defense of the Orthodox Doctrine of Human Choice against Pighius*, ed. A.N.S. Lane, trans. G.I. Davies, Texts and Studies in Reformation and Post-Reformation Thought 2 (Grand Rapids: Baker Academic, 1996).

God's providence and concurrence preserving human free will (necessity [3])
Human rationality as essential to free choice (necessity [4])
Human being as impossible to be conceived without having any habits, or
    acting in a vacuum of habits (necessity [5])[29]
The factual history of the world (necessity [6])

The last type of necessity does not bother freedom ultimately, because there is
no way of conceiving the choice, once made, as being necessary.[30] We could
characterize all four types of necessity that are compatible with free choice by
saying that they are related to the faculty of free choice, as its "requisites," by way
of a strict implication, since any free choice *entails* determination by God, the
practical intellect, the habitual structure of the soul, and the existence of the
actual set of states of affairs. So, we can formulate the relation between free
choice and all the things requisite for its operation as follows:

(1) It is necessarily so that if all requisites for acting are present, then the
    action takes place.[31]

Not only divine predestination, providence and concurrence have been under
suspicion as compelling free choice in a causal deterministic way, but also the
rational determination by the practical intellect was thought to jeopardize
freedom, although Turrettini himself does not seem impressed by accusations of
determinism. In the next section we will focus on the seemingly problematic
relation between will and intellect as arising from the Turrettinian mixture of
faculties. It is perhaps useful to point out here that "to determine" in scholastic
usage often simply means "to assign a truth-value to a proposition." For example,
if a scholastic author claims that the truth of a future contingent proposition is
determined, mostly all that is meant is that it has a truth value, in distinction from
lacking it (being neither true nor false). The content we often hear in

---

29. "Quoad necessitatem moralem, quae oritur ex habitibus; Nam ut voluntas libera potest
dici, si est habitu vacua: Ita serva recte dicitur, si per habitum ad certum agendi modum fuerit
determinata. Quae servitus tamen veram et essentialem libertatis rationem haudquaquam evertit;
alias sequeretur habitus desturere voluntatem, quam perficiunt potius et facilitant ad
operationem. Hinc sit ut duplices sunt habitus morales, alii boni, alii mali; duplex etiam inde
nascatur servitus, alia justitiae in bono, alia peccati in malo et miseria" (X.2.viii).

30. This is one important way the maxim "what is, when it is, is necessarily" was read. There
are other interpretations, which to our mind are ruled out by Turrettini's explanation of it, and
also by his use of the simultaneity of potencies, on which is more below. The full text reads here:
"Nam etsi quicquid est, quando est, necessario est, ita ut non possit amplius non esse; non minus
tamen libere vel contingenter fieri dicitur, prout a causis liberis, vel contingentibus pendet: quia
certitudo et veritas existentiae rei, non potest essentiam ejus mutare" (X.2.x). Especially the last
part of the sentence is interesting, for here Turrettini indicates that the essential properties of an
entity cannot be changed by coming into existence. Therefore, an entity cannot start as
contingent and end up as necessary.

31. In formula, if we take "action" to mean "volition": $N\ (raWp \rightarrow aWp)$. Note that by
characterizing the types of necessity (3)-(6) together as having the structure of formula (1), we take
them as being implicative necessities, rather than absolute necessities. This is also expressed by
Turrettini, when he speaks of hypothetical necessity in the case of divine determination (X.2.vi).

"determined" is "could not be but so-and-so." This necessitation element, however, is only attached to the meaning of "determined" in a basically non-Christian, Aristotelian paradigm.[32] Even if we keep in mind that a "determination" may mean in this context that God performs his eternal act by which all creaturely states of affairs exist, nothing deterministic has happened. God assigns a truth value to propositions. In section 6.5 below, we will address more forms of determinism.

6.5 Will and Intellect

The way Turrettini treats the relation between will and intellect as psychological powers reminds of the way he defines theology in the first *locus* as a science:

> Theology does not lose its unity although it may be called partly theoretical, partly practical. Any science is called one not by a simple and absolute unity ...,
> but by an aggregative unity which is termed the unity of collection ... Thus the image of God is one although it embraces newness of mind and of the affections; and free will is one, although it resides in the intellect and will. [33]

This quotation indicates that he does not feel uncomfortable with a combination, as an *unitas collectionis*, of two different concepts into one, like the concept of theology as a mixed science, the concept of *Imago Dei* as a combination of mind and affections, and also free choice as a mixture of both intellect and will.

Both his remarks on the determination by the ultimate judgment of the practical intellect (*judicio comparato & ultimo intellectus practicus*), as well as his remarks on the unity of theology like the unity within free choice point to the understanding of the *subjectum* of free choice. In other words: where do we have to locate, psychologically speaking, the faculty of free choice?

Free choice consists in the marriage (*conubium*) of intellect and will (X.1.iv). With respect to the free act of choice, it belongs to the will, and considered from the point of judgment or choice it resides in the intellect. Since it is possible to consider free choice under two aspects, free choice resides in both the intellectual and the volitional powers of the human soul. However, as Turrettini says, it is not easy to determine the exact subject in terms of a faculty as the seat of free choice. As a mixed faculty, free choice is a power with both intellectual and volitional

---

32. Here, "Aristotelian" is not taken in the very diluted sense in which the entire era of scholasticism may be labeled "Aristotelian," but in the stronger sense of "historical Greek Aristotelianism." See also the introduction in *RS*. More on this conflation of truth and necessity, e.g., in *CF*, and for an explicit discussion of it in a seventeenth-century context, see *RM*.

33. "Non perit Theologiae sua unitas licet dicatur partim theoretica, partim practica; quia scientia quaevis una dicitur, non unitate simplici et absoluta, quae unitas numerica et individualis dicitur, quasi esset una et simplex qualitas v.g. albedo in pariete; sed unitate aggregativa, quae dicitur unitas collectionis, quatenus scilicet multi speciales habitus conflantur et ordinantur ad unum totalem scientiae habitum constituendum. Sic Imago Dei una est, licet novitatem mentis et affectuum complectatur, et Liberum Arbitrium unum, licet in intellectu et voluntate situm sit" (I.2.xiv).

aspects. [34] He explains these aspects by discussing the relations of free choice to both intellect and will, and uses scholastic language for spelling out a relation between two terms (or *extrema*, as they called them) between which the relation exists. The intellectual component of free choice relates to the will as the latter's basis and the volitional component to the intellect as the former's source, which once more indicates that will and intellect are very closely related (q. 2, iv). The rational soul is able to produce three mental acts, i.e., will, knowledge and choice. The close relationship between intellect and will points to the cooperation of both faculties for producing an act of choice. The operation of free choice necessarily presupposes the operation of both intellect and will.

Intellect and will are inseparable at the ontological level, since it is impossible to conceive of a being entailing either *intellectus* or *voluntas* and missing the other faculty. In Turrettini's terminology: there is no (intrinsic) real distinction between will and intellect. On the other hand, he holds to an extrinsic distinction with respect to the different objects offered to the faculties. So, depending on the objects worthy to be considered by either the intellect, will or faculty of free choice, there is an extrinsic distinction between intellect and will. For example, if the possibility of cycling to school is offered to the rational soul, then the intelligibility of the possibility addresses the intellect, and the desirability addresses the will. Both will and intellect cooperate in bringing about a particular choice, though the will keeps primacy in free choice and has the nature to determine itself; otherwise it would not be a *free* choice. [35]

The question of the will's *determination* by the rational judgment of the intellect is consistent with the previous remarks on the ontological relation between intellect and will. If it is the case that acts of the intellect are to be integrated with the set of requisites that are to be supposed by any free act of choice, then it is necessary that the practical intellect plays a determining role in the process of deciding.

The intellect, in a Turrettinian sense, is able to produce three different intellectual acts: a theoretical *intelligere*, an absolute practical *intelligere* and a "comparative" or ultimate *intelligere*. In Turrettini's conception of intellect there is a volitional moment involved with respect to the judgment of practical intellect. The ultimate judgment of the practical intellect does not coincide with the theoretical judgment, or the absolute practical judgment, but depends on other circumstances than just the assignment of truth values (theoretical intellect), or moral judgments in general (absolute practical intellect). The ultimate judgment is the ultimate judgment, not of what is to be done in general, but of what is to be done here and now, in this situation. Turrettini provides the example of Adam,

---

34. Turrettini strongly asserts that *liberum arbitrium* is a not an act or habit, instead of a faculty: "Ut in anima praeter animae essentiam tria tantum occurunt, facultas, habitus, actus, vulgari notione arbitrium actum mentis notat; Sed hic nec actum, nec habitum significat proprie, quod et ab homine separari possint singuli, et eum ad unum duntaxat contrariorum determinent: Sed facultatem (...) rationalem ex qua boni vel mali non sumus quidem, sed esse possumus per illius actus et habitus" (X.1.vi).

35. X.3.vii: "esse de ratione voluntatis liberae, ut seipsam determinet (...) sed non a se sola; sic determinatio voluntatis, non excludit, sed supponit determinationem Dei."

which shows that the relationship between absolute and ultimate judgment itself involves an act of will.

It is important, moreover, to emphasize that we are discussing a *practical* judgment, which is by definition related to something we need to know in order to do something with it, not something to which we know only as such, i.e., not related to action. We read in q. 3, xvi that Adam's absolute judgment is that the fruit must not be eaten because God had prohibited it, but the ultimate judgment, in which other factors *including desirability*, are taken into account, is that it must be eaten. The will acts upon the desirability, and therefore the ultimate judgment accounts for an element of will.

In sum: since the will is already active in the process toward an ultimate practical judgment, the fact that the ultimate practical judgment itself is necessarily followed by the will does not necessitate the will in a deterministic sense.

6.6 Structural Freedom

After having established that determination and necessity do not coincide with coercion, Turrettini wants to argue in the third question that the true nature of free will expressed in a formal definition[36] does not consist in indifference, but in rational willingness (*lubentia rationalis*). The first important point which we should address is the correct understanding of the concept of indifference. Turrettini distinguishes between two different types of indifference, of which he rejects the second, called active indifference, for all rational beings, created or uncreated, finite or infinite. The first type of passive indifference is explicitly acknowledged. We shall come back to it at length below.

The third question in this *locus* of the *Institutes* differs from the fourth in a structural way. The third question points out the essential structure of freedom (*genus entis*) against the accidental application in a particular state (*genus moris*) which is covered in the fourth question. The essential freedom "is always the same everywhere in every state of man" (q. 4, ii). So, we have to understand the third question as an overall picture of freedom which is to be transferred to all states in which a man can possibly be situated. Turrettini's question, then, is whether the overall picture of freedom embraces indifference.

Generally speaking, Turrettini rejects the positive answer as given by his opponents, but we must bear in mind that the concept of indifference is not used in the same way by orthodox and adversaries. Indifference can mean two things, according to Turrettini. His explanation of these two meanings of indifference is of great importance for the model in which he turns out to think, so we must look carefully at this explanation. Turrettini draws parallels between two series of distinctions applicable to the concept of indifference:

---

36. A formal or essential definition (*ratio formalis*) differs from a notification of all essential properties of a certain object; "able to laugh," for instance, is an essential property of a human person, but does not belong to its formal definition.

(2) In first act or in the divided sense, as a simultaneity of potencies, which is called passive and objective (*Actu primo seu in sensu diviso, quoad simultatem potentiae, quae passiva & objectiva dicitur*).

(3) In second act or in the compounded sense, as a potency of simultaneities, which is called active and subjective (*Actu secundo seu in sensu composito, quoad potentiam simultatis, quae activa & subjectiva dicitur*).

Only (2) is adopted by Turrettini, while (3) is rejected (but accepted by his opponents). We shall address each pair of distinctions, starting with that of the simultaneity of potency *versus* the potency for simultaneities. To start with the latter: a potency for simultaneities regards two simultaneous, i.e., synchronous, objects of will, which can be willed. Now if by these objects of will are meant contradictory objects, it is clear that they cannot be willed simultaneously. That is to say that such a potency cannot exist. For example, a person cannot will to simultaneously sit and run. No person has such a potency. However, a potency itself can be simultaneous with another potency, even if the objects of the potency are contradictory. For example, the potency to sit can exist simultaneously with the potency to run.[37]

Perhaps the explanation of our distinction by the Hispanic Roman Catholic theologian Diego Alvarez (Dominican; d. 1635) is illuminating. In his work *De auxiliis divinae gratiae*, which was used by Turrettini and affirmatively cited with regard to divine concurrence,[38] he places the distinction between "*simultas potentiae*" and "*potentia simultatis*" clearly within a synchronic-contingent framework:

> Therefore free choice has not only before it is determined to one act simultaneously the potency by which it freely can produce the contrary act, but also at the very instant (*in ipso instanti*) in which it is determined by God and determines itself to that very act. But it has not the potency to have simultaneously the contrary act, for two contrary acts cannot be simultaneously in the same potency, but only successively. This is the origin of the distinction between the simultaneity of the potency and the potency of simultaneity, generally accepted by Theologians and Metaphysians. For in free choice there is a potency to performing this or that, or its opposite, since the fact, that it performs a certain act, does not destroy the free faculty and potency which it has

---

37. Cf. also III. 12.xxi: "It is one thing for a thing to be able to be done or not to be done (i.e., for a thing to be possible, or not to be future hypothetically); another for a thing to be able to be at the same time future and not future. The former denotes only the simultaneity of power, inasmuch as the thing could be done or not; the latter implies the power of simultaneity, because it is supposed that something could at the same time be and not be. Contingency applies to the former mode, not to the second which is absurd." ("Aliud est rem posse fieri vel non fieri, id est, rem esse possibilem, vel non esse futuram ex hypothesi; Aliud rem posse esse simul futuram et non futuram: Prius notat tantum simultas potentiae, quatenus res potuit fieri vel non fieri; Posterius infert potentiam simultatis, quia supponitur, aliquid simul posse esse et non esse. Contingens dicitur primo modo, non secundo, qui est ἀσύστατος.")

38. VI.4.v; cf. also IV.10.iv; but see VI.13.xvi.

to perform the contrary act if it wills, or to not-perform it. [...] But there cannot be a potency of simultaneity to contrary or contradictory acts, since they cannot simultaneously be in the same being.[39]

The "generally accepted" *simultas potentiae* is here the synchronic power by which free choice at the same instant of time (*in ipso instanti*) in which it elicits a certain act, can freely produce the contrary act.[40]

The second pair of distinctions Turrettini makes use of is that *between in actu primo* and *in actu secundo*—once again a common scholastic distinction. "In the first act" points to an analysis in which one distinguishes between the faculty itself, as for instance the ability or power to choose (*liberum arbitrium*), and the operation of the faculty in question in a particular act of choosing. The first level, so to speak, is that of the *possibility* of acts as given by the structure of the faculty itself. The second level concerns particular acts. The order between *in actu primo* and *in actu secundo* is a structural or logical order, i.e., concerning structural moments, and not temporal succession. If this were not already common scholastic usage, we would be able to infer from the parallel distinction of potencies that a "structural" reading is meant.

The third distinction, the one between a divided sense (*in sensu diviso*) and a compounded sense (*in sensu compositionis*) stems from the modal analysis of sentences. Aristotle's example which became a paradigm in medieval analysis of modal notions was the sentence: "It is possible that Socrates sits and runs." The signification *in sensu diviso* was taken to mean "Socrates sits and it is possible that Socrates runs," while the analysis *in sensu composito* yields the meaning: "It is

---

39. Didacus Alvarez, *De auxiliis divinae gratiae et humani arbitrii viribus et libertate, ac legitima ejus cum efficacia eorumdem auxiliorum concordia* (Cologne: P. Henningius, 1621; 1st ed., Rome, 1610), lib. 4, cap. 14, n. 3, 116-117: "Unde liberum arbitrium creatum, non solum antequam determinetur ad unam actum, sed etiam in ipso instanti, in quo determinatur a Deo, et se ipsum determinat ad eundem actum; simul habet potentiam, qua potest libere producere actum contrarium, non tamen habet potentiam ad actum contrarium simul habendum; nam duo actus contrarii simul in eadem potentia esse non possunt, sed solum sucessive. Hinc habuit ortum illa distinctio communiter a Theologis et Metaphysicis recepta de simultate potentiae, et potentia simultatis; est enim in libero arbitrio simultas potentiae ad operandum hoc vel illud, et eius oppositum: nam per hoc, quod operetur unum actum, non destruit[ur] liberam facultatem, et potentiam, quam habet ad operandum actum contrarium, si velit, vel non operandum: et similiter per hoc, quod non operetur talem actum, non amittit potestatem operandi illum actum; non tamen ex libero arbitrio, nec esse potest potentia simultatis ad actus contrarios, vel contradictorios: nam hi simul in eodem esse non possunt. Ad hoc igitur explicandum deseruit illa distinctio sensus compositi, et divisi, qua utuntur communiter Doctores, ut supra visum est."

40. The *simultas potentiae* reminds of the *potentia realis* of Duns Scotus (cf. *Lectura* I 39, 51; *Ordinatio* I 39, 16). Cf. Alvarez: "[...] in libero arbitrio simul esse potentiam ad opposita; non autem esse in illo potentiam ad opposita simul habenda. [...] Hoc sub aliis terminis explicare possumus, si dicamus cum Capreolo, in libero arbitrio esse simultatem potentiae ad opposita, non autem potentiam simultatis; id est, potentiam ad opposita simul habenda" (ibid., lib. 2, cap. 11, n. 1, 235-236. The *simultas potentiae ad opposita* corresponds to Scotus' *potentia ad opposita pro eodem instanti* (= *potentia realis*, synchronic potency: Mp & M-p); and the *potentia ad opposita simul habenda* corresponds to Scotus' *potentia ad opposita simul* (= M (p & -p), which is to be rejected) (cf. *Ord.* I 39, 16).

possible that Socrates both sits and runs," which is contradictory.[41] It is important to see that our sentence in the divided sense can still have two readings, one in which we assign different moments of time to the sitting and running of Socrates, and another in which we assign the same moment to them (the latter being, by the way, exceedingly un-Aristotelian). We then obtain

(4) Socrates sits at t1 and it is possible that Socrates runs at t2,

which could be called the diachronic reading, and

(5) Socrates sits at t1 and it is possible that Socrates runs at t1,

which accordingly is called the *synchronic* reading. These readings were well-known from later medieval periods onwards.[42]

Turrettini utilizes the scholastic distinction between *in sensu composito* and *in sensu diviso* in the synchronic, Scotist reading. Not only can we point to passages in his work in which a diachronic reading would make no sense, but it is also clear from the parallel with our simultaneity of potencies/potency for simultaneities distinction.[43]

The final distinction between passive or objective and active or subjective indifference again contrasts the will in itself with its act. The will does have passive or objective alternativity apart from its actual willing. The term passive stresses the absence of a volitional act, whereas it is called objective to affirm ontological alternativity. In its actual willing, however, the will is no longer indifferent, but decided, so active or subjective indifference does not apply.

We conclude: only an ontology that pays full attention to synchronic alternatives can make sense of the distinction *simultas potentiae* and *potentia simultatis*. Simultaneity of power connected with *in actu secundo* and *in sensu diviso* leads to an ontology of synchronic contingency.

Turning back to our analysis of "indifference": we now can see that Turrettini accepts the indifference to opposites at the first structural moment entailing the

---

41. See for the development of the analysis of modal sentences: *MMPh*, ch. 4, and Simo Knuuttila, "Modal Logic," *CHLMP*, 347-348.

42. For example, we could point at the discussion of it by Molina and Suárez in the early seventeenth century, who were both influential. See Eef Dekker, "The Reception of Scotus' Theory of Contingency in Molina and Suárez," in: *Via Scoti: Methodologica ad mentem Joannis Duns Scoti. Atti del Congresso Scotistico Internazionale*, ed. Leonardo Sileo, (Rome: Antonianum, 1995), 445-454.

43. There are places in which Turrettini speaks about the compounded and divided sense in an eternity context, which of course is evidence for the fact that it can be used synchronically. For example, III.12,xx: "Non est ἀσύσατον idem dici possibile et impossibile simul, sed κατ' ἄλλο κια ἄλλο; possibile respectu potentiae seu causae secundae, in se considerata et in sensu diviso, et impossibile secundum quid, ex hypothesi decreti et praescientiae Dei. Ita possibile fuit Christum non crucifigi, si Deus voluisset, et impossibile quod ergo in sensu composito et supposito Dei decreto de futuritione rei est impossibile non fieri, tamen in sensu diviso et seposito eo decreto, possibile esset non fieri." Cf. also IV.5.18; IV.12.6; VI.5.6. Synchronic contingency or structural possibility is explained at greater length in, for example, *MMPh*, ch. 4, and *CF*.

possibility of opposites in the divided sense and understood as *simultas potentiae*. He points to the difference between the level of the mere potency of the faculty and the level of the concrete acts of the faculty. Indifference in the first act is basic without taking into account the requisites for operation; indifference in the second act, however, is seen as indifference after having posited the requisites for acting.

Connected to our first sense of indifference we find the well-known terminology of freedom of exercise, which is also called freedom of contradiction, and of freedom of contrariety, also called freedom of specification. An extended explanation of these terms is found in our commentary on Junius and on Gomarus, elsewhere in this volume.[44] We only note here, in addition, that it is helpful to see that Turrettini connects these terms to the first meaning of indifference, and not to the second. It is not so clear in some of his opponents, who make use of the same terminology, whether or not they use it in that first sense.

So the view Turrettini deliberately rejects is the understanding of indifference in the second sense, as if it were possible that the will is indifferent at every moment with respect to any act provided that the requisites for acting are present. Given our analysis in terms of compounded and divided sense, we are now in a position to deal more precisely with the rejected sense of indifference. Turrettini argues that the opponent holds:

(6) It is possible that, all requisites for action being in place, a person still can will something else than that which relates to the requisites.[45]

Let us take an example in which the above can be applied to divine concurrence. Consider Peter's freely chosen act of speaking. Take, moreover, the views of Molina as representative of the position claimed in (6). Molina tells us that, although the influence of the human faculty of choice depends for its existence on the divine general concurrence,

this general concurrence is intrinsically indifferent as to whether it is followed by a volition to speak or a volition not to speak, or by any other act of the faculty of choice; and it is by the faculty of choice itself, as a particular cause, that this general concurrence is channelled to a specific type of act (*determinatur ad speciem actus*).[46]

---

44. Compare sections 3.5.3, 4.4.

45. Or, in formula: M (RaWp et a-Wp). See especially q. 3, ix, item 4. Note that still a different reading of proposition (6) can be entertained, namely: RaWp et Ma-Wp. That interpretation Turrettini would of course not reject.

46. Molina, *Concordia*, pars III, disp. 53, membr. 3, n. 7 (ed. Rabeneck, 387): "Itemque generalis concursus indifferens est ex se ut sequatur volitio aut nolitio locutionis aut aliquis alius arbitrii actus ab arbitrioque ipso tamquam a particulari causa is concursus generalis determinatur ad speciem actus" (trans. Freddoso, 243). Cf. also pars VII, art. 4-5, disp. 1, membr. 7, n. 23 (ed. Rabeneck, 508): "Nos autem non dicimus concursum Dei universalem determinare voluntatem ad consensum, sed potius per influxum particularem liberi arbitrii concursum Dei universalem

So it seems that Molina would affirm:

(7) It is possible that God gives concurrence to the act of speaking, and there is no act of speaking (or the creature does not speak).[47]

In other places Molina even seems to consider (7) (and perhaps also (6)) as an indispensable requirement for human liberty. We should keep, however, firmly in mind that Molina's (and others') notion of concurrence is quite different from that of Turrettini. While Molina works with *general* concurrence, Turrettini has a *specific* concurrence in mind.[48] So, it depends on the type of concurrence whether or not (7) is compatible with Turrettini's denial.

The problem for Turrettini is that such a general concurrence would yield the indifference of an autonomously free creature, able to choose from a situation of balance, having even divine concurrence at its disposal, and directing even that to wherever it likes. That type of freedom we may call, after Turrettini, *equilibristic* freedom, and is strongly rejected by him. The will is not floating around, and indifference must not be understood as equilibrium because even God and angels lack indifference as *equilibrium*.

Equilibrium as moral indifference is not available for any rational creature, but indifference as part of the most basic structure of the faculty of free choice is not denied at all by Turrettini. It is rather proposed as belonging to the essence of freedom, and therefore part of the "rational willingness," in which concept Turrettini presents his own position. By the notion of willingness the spontaneity is expressed, i.e., a person acts freely when it acts without compulsion. It is a rational willingness if it is a choice on the basis of the practical intellect.

6.7 Statebound Freedom

In the previous section we saw that Turrettini considered human free choice in several structural moments. In the first structural moment one could speak about freedom of indifference, since the faculty of free choice is able to direct itself to opposites. Regarding the actual functioning of free choice in time (considered in the final act at the second structural moment), the essence of freedom is more properly defined by rational spontaneity (*in genere entis*). Now, Turrettini moves to what he calls "free choice *in genere moris*," which is necessarily linked with a particular state (*status*) an individual occupies at a particular moment in time.

It is impossible correctly to conceive freedom of choice without consideration of the state man is in. A state (*status*) describes the relation between God and man, and Turrettini joins the tradition in distinguishing between four states. At first the state of innocence in which Adam was able to sin and not to sin (*posse*

---

determinari ad speciem actus voluntatis, prout voluntas potius influxerit ad volendum quam ad nolendum vel e contrario aut ad volendum potius hoc obiectum quam illud."
47. In formula: M (gCaWp et a-Wp). gCaWp = God gives concursus to aWp.
48. Cf. also VI.4.v.

peccare et non peccare); secondly the state after the Fall and before conversion (*post lapsum et ante conversionem*) in which Adam was not able not to sin (*non posse non peccare*); thirdly the state after the Fall and after conversion (*post lapsum et post conversionem*) in which Adam was able not to sin (*posse non peccare*); and finally the state of glory (*status gloriae*) in which Adam is not able to sin (*non posse peccare*).[49]

The fourth question deals with the freedom of man in the state of sin which is to be considered as the second state; after the Fall and before conversion. In this state man has turned his back to God, so it is not only impossible on account of the state man is in that he pleases God but from his own stand against God it is also irrational. Turrettini denies that man in the second state is able to please God by responding properly to his will, and holds that man in the second state is inclined to sin. Since freedom is not repugnant to four forms of necessity, including *necessitas moralis*, Turrettini is able to argue that freedom in a state of sin is not repugnant to *non posse non peccare*.

Freedom considered in the first act (*in actu primo*) as we have seen is a formal potency to opposites which in itself does not contain any material contents. The distinction between formal freedom and material freedom appears in Turrettini's text as the distinction between free choice in the genus of being and absolutely, that is in itself (*libero arbitrio absolute quoad naturam in genere entis*), which was treated in question 3, and free choice in relation to an actual state, and the powers of free choice in the genus of good and bad. So, in question four free choice in the state of sin is considered (*liberum arbitrium relate quoad statum peccati, & vires ejus in genere moris*). As we have seen in the previous paragraph the material contents of freedom are defined by the state man is in. Formally, the will is free to opposites in the first act; materially being in the state of sin it does not belong to the contents of freedom not to sin.[50]

Not all human choices in the state of sin are qualified by sin, as Turrettini says, but only the spiritual and supernatural objects are excluded from the material contents of freedom in the second state. Free choice in the second state is morally distorted by way of moral necessity.

It is noteworthy that Turrettini provides a good example of the way Scripture functions in this fourth *quaestio*. Not only does he discuss quite a variety of passages, but he does it in an exegetically responsible way, given the apparatus at his disposal. We can therefore see this extended discussion of scriptural passages as a contra-indication for the view that the Reformed scholastics used Scripture only for proof-texting without further exegetical ado.

---

49. VIII.2.ix.

50. See for this usage of "material" and "formal" Eef Dekker and Henri Veldhuis, "Freedom and Sin: Some Systematic Observations," *European Journal of Theology* 3 (1994): 153-161. Turrettini himself uses the terms "*formalis*" and "*materialis*" the other way around: "Non quaeritur de potentia seu facultate naturali voluntatis, a qua est ipsum velle vel nolle, quae potentia prima vocari potest, et principium materiale actionum moralium. Haec enim semper in homine manet, et a brutis per eam distinguitur: Sed de dispositione ejus morali ad bene volendum, quae potentia secunda, seu principium formale dicitur illarum actionum: nam ut a potentia naturali fluit *to* velle; ita a dispositione morali *to* bene velle" (X.4.iv).

By way of conclusion: Although Turrettini holds to essential freedom of choice when it comes to the nature of free choice (*libero arbitrio absolute quoad naturam in genere entis*) consisting in indifference *in actu primo* and spontaneity or *lubentia rationalis*, materially speaking the boundaries of freedom are given by the state (*status*) which describes the relation between God and man. Against his adversaries, the older and newer Pelagians, Turrettini holds with orthodoxy that: "Although human free choice is always in man as an essential property, no powers to do the good are left." [51]

6.8 Evaluation

Turrettini is not an innovator of theology in the Reformed hall of freedom. The common ideas of essential and accidental freedom, freedom from contrariety and from contradiction, freedom from nature and from necessity, are present in his work in the same theological vigor as we have seen already. When we place Turrettini among the authors we have discussed this far, two elaborations in the Turrettinian account of human freedom are nonetheless strikingly fresh if not creative. These features do not mark Turrettini as an original theologian in the sense the he developed an idiosyncratic personal theology, but point to a remarkable characteristic of scholastic theology that is rather neglected in previous research on the issue at hand. Scholastic theology is both ecumenical and contextually relevant.

The first Turrettinian distinctive is his expanded discussion on necessity in which he develops an even more nuanced view on the relation between necessity and freedom than we have seen in the previous texts. Freedom is a balanced state of mind that is both the result of man's ontological position of rational creation in the realm of being, as well as the consequence of man's moral standing towards God. The position of man as created being necessarily implies a threefold dependence on God's benevolent willing and acting, in its ethical dimension (God as the ultimate law-giver), its epistemological dimension (God as the most privileged being with respect to knowledge) and its metaphysical dimension (God has his own will and course of action). Furthermore, human freedom depends on man's standing (*status*) towards God, either as righteous or as sinner. Two ontological conditions complete the picture of necessity: the human will is dependent upon the factual reality (things are as they factually are) and his inner constitution of a rational being (willing p implies a rational judgment accordingly). The entire discussion on necessity focuses upon the consistency of necessity with true freedom.

The second Turrettinian distinctive is his nuanced rejection of indifference in human willing. Turrettini introduces a multi-layered concept of *indifferentia* in order to distinguish between the rights and wrongs of his opponents. God wills indifferently indeed, but indifference needs to be understood as independence. Against his nominalist opponents, Turrettini stresses that God's indifferent—read:

51."Licet liberum hominis arbitrium semper in homine quoad essentialia manere statuant, nullas tamen in eo ad bonum vires superesse censent" (X.4.viii).

independent—willing is "the greatest proof of God's perfection."[52] Although indifference in this sense is rightly being attributed to God, indifference is "found in no free agent, whether created or uncreated: neither in God, ... nor in Christ ... nor in angels and the blessed ... nor in devils and reprobates."[53] Indifference does not only mean "independence," but is also used in the framework of alternative willing. Here Turrettini moves conceptually very carefully between a necessitarian idea of willing on the one hand and an extreme nominalist idea of willing on the other hand. Every act, so argues Turrettini, consists of two moments (see section 6.6 above). In the first state of actualization (*in actu primo*) the will has indifference in the sense of the potency to opposites at the same moment in time (*simultas potentiae*). In the second state of actualization, however, the will does not have indifference in the sense of having opposite potencies at the same moment in time (*potentia simultatis*). In the second structural moment, the human will is not indifferent.[54]

Turrettini's precise distinctions in the concepts of necessity and indifference show that he is a true representative of the Golden Age of Reformed scholasticism. Following the developments in the Genevan Academy he did not pass over the issues of his day, for instance the introduction of Cartesian philosophy in his home town.[55] He dealt with relevant issues in his day, using sources and figures of thought drawing from the broad tradition of Catholic theology. His contribution to this volume is that he reminds us of the dynamic continuity of scholastic methodology in the history of Christian theology.

---

52. III.14.vi.

53. X.3.v.

54. So the Turrettinian semantics consist of three concepts of indifference. Turrettini distinguishes first between (1) indifference as independence and (2) independence as alternativity, and second between (2a) alternativity in the first and (2b) alternativity in the second structural moment. Only God has indifference as independence (1); and free entities share indifference as alternativity in the first structural moment (2a).

55. Martin I. Klauber, "Theological Transition in Geneva. From Jean-Alphonse Turrettini to Jacob Vernet," in: *Protestant Scholasticism: Essays in Reassessment*, ed. R. Scott Clark, (Carlisle: Paternoster, 1999), 256-270; and Michael Heyd, *Between Orthodoxy and the Enlightenment: Jean-Robert Chouet and the Introduction of Cartesian Science at the Academy of Geneva* (The Hague: Martinus Nijhoff, 1982).

7

Clear and Distinct Freedom

A Compendium of Bernardinus de Moor (1709-1780) in a Cartesian Context

7.1 Introduction

Bernardinus de Moor (1709-1780) studied theology at Leiden, where Johannes à Marck (1656-1731) was one of his teachers.[1] De Moor had a close relation with his teacher, and a few months before his death, à Marck asked him to continue his work in the same way.[2] After serving as pastor for several years, he was called first to Franeker (1744) and then to Leiden (1745) as a professor of theology. He then fulfilled the wish of his teacher with his huge, six-volume *Continuous Commentary on à Marck's Compendium of Christian Theology*.[3]

Probably, De Moor used à Marck's *Compendium* (1686) to instruct his students, because his *Commentary* contains the content of his lectures.[4] Alternatively, he may have used a convenient summary of the extensive *Compendium*, which à Marck had prepared for his students, and which was very popular as a textbook.[5] He does not explain the *Compendium* by using the whole text of à Marck, but he cites only the most important definitions, and subsequently elaborates them.

Besides his systematic interest De Moor also tried to stimulate the practice of piety and recommended the works of Ames and Voetius in this respect. He was an irenic character, who collaborated peacefully with his theological colleagues at Leiden University, though they did not share his "Voetian" approach.[6] He

---

1. De Moor studied in Leiden from 1726 till 1730, while à Marck held the professorate till his death in 1731. Wesselius was another teacher of De Moor. See about De Moor: D. Nauta, "Moor, Bernhardinus de," in *BLGNP* (Kampen: Kok, 1986), 3:273-276.

2. Cf. Preface to the first part of De Moor's *Commentarius perpetuus*, 2, 3.

3. Bernardinus de Moor, *Commentarius perpetuus in Joh. Marckii compendium theologiae christianae didactico-elencticum* (Lugduni Batavorum: apud Johannem Hasebroek, 1761-1771).

4. Johannes à Marck, *Compendium theologiae christianae didactico-elencticum* (Leiden, 1686). D. Nauta states that De Moor's lectures formed the substance for the *Commentarius*, ("Moor, Bernhardinus de," 275).

5. Johannes à Marck, *Christianae theologiae medulla* (Leiden, 1690). The book had a sixth edition in 1742; the Dutch translation of 1705 also had many reprints.

6. It is a strange fact that secondary literature on Dutch Church History tends to portray the Voetian party as "stubborn and aggressive" as soon as they clearly defend their position and as "dull and mug" as soon as they display an irenic spirit. De Moor has befallen the latter fate, though he clearly took a position in controversies and could stand for his point. Nauta gives several examples of his independent spirit.

participated in the whole of the church, as his activities show. During his professorate in Leiden he was also preacher in the city, and in this function also presided in the synod of South Holland in 1752.

The *Commentary* gives an all-round description of theology. Theology is described in thirty-four *loci*, each of which starts with a description of the terms (*nomina*) used in Scripture or in theological reflection and then proceeds to a definition of the given topic. After a short introduction, De Moor respectively treats the *object* of theology (God and his works) and the *subject* (man in his four states).[7]

The *Commentary* has the character of an extensive and comprehensive handbook for theology. The rise of such theological handbooks, which present an overview of the whole of systematic theology, reflects the consolidated position of theological education and Reformed universities. Apparently, there were enough good systematic monographs and treatises to refer to, and now the primary task was to lend an overview of the clearest expositions for each theological topic.

This might also explain the differences between the discussion of free choice by the previously treated authors and the text of De Moor. While they extensively argue their case, he (relatively) briefly mentions his own position and the alternative views of opponents. Next to a brief argumentation he cites a host of authors, both to clarify the Reformed position and to prove the position of others.

The huge work of De Moor has no separate *locus* on free choice. Instead, free choice is explicated in the course of an extensive theological anthropology, in which the main faculties of the human soul, intellect and will, are profoundly discussed. The *Commentary* follows the structure of the *Compendium* of à Marck in this respect. The lack of a distinct topic can be explained by the context in which à Marck and De Moor wrote. By now, Descartes and the theologians inspired by him had replaced the Arminians as the prime opponents for Reformed theology. Therefore free choice is no longer the primary issue of theological anthropology, but the nature of the human soul and its faculties, intellect and will, is. This is reflected in the treatment of faculty psychology, which is mainly distinguished from Cartesian anthropology.

Consequently, a separate *locus* on free choice is lacking. Instead, important digressions on free choice are made in various *loci*. The most convenient one to clarify the position of De Moor is in *locus* thirteen, dealing with the general nature of man.

7.2 Translation of the Texts

In XIII.13, De Moor treats the nature of the human soul.[8] Primarily explicating human *faculty psychology*, he also discusses human freedom. Two parts of this

---

7. First, the cognitive *principle* of theology (the medium by which true knowledge of God is obtained) is treated in I.12-33, then the object in I.34-XII, whereas the subject is discussed in XIII-XXXIV (a roman number signifies the locus; an arabic number refers to the paragraphs in the loci). The *Commentary* follows the *Compendium* in its division of loci and paragraphs.

8. In fact, he starts already with this in paragraph 11, but first explicates what the soul is not (κάτ' ἄρσιν) before saying positively (κάτά θεσιν) what the concept really signifies.

section are selected, one about the relation between intellect and will and the other about the definition of freedom. Since the *Commentary* comments on the *Compendium* of à Marck, the commented text is given first.

7.2.1 The Compendium of Christian Theology of John à Marck, Chapter XIII, §13

XIII.13:[9] The judgment now is either theoretical, or practical, and the last one again absolute or comparative, which the will in her action is rightly said always to follow, hence it is called blind. [...][10] And freedom belongs to man in both these faculties, which is not to be extended in a Pelagian fashion to self-empoweredness (αὐτεξουσιοτεσα), independent of the Creator, and absolute indifference, which does not even belong to God himself, but is constituted by rational willingness, which is opposed to a necessity of coercion and a natural necessity, Phil.1:4, 1 Cor. 7:36, 2 Cor. 8:3, 9:7 etc. And this freedom can in no state or case be lost by man, unless man ceases to be human, although the incapacity towards the good can take away the possible appetite of this good, in which sense the Church Fathers have said that free choice is wounded and lost in the state of sin.

7.2.2 The Continuous Commentary by Bernardinus de Moor, Chapter XIII, §13

XIII.13[1045]:[11] [...] The judgment of the intellect is either *theoretical*, by which I judge about the goodness, honesty or evil of a thing, considered in themselves: fornication, theft and the like is a sin; or the judgment of the intellect is *practical*, by which I judge about that which I must do or flee. This practical judgment is in turn either *absolute*, by which, if I consider something in itself, abstracted from the other circumstances, I judge that it should be done or omitted, or *relative*, by which I compare the honest good with the useful and the pleasant good, comparing my duty in general with the specific circumstances, in which I am. And in this way it is often the case, that although somebody judges theoretically and absolutely that something is good and should be followed, still on the basis of the relative practical judgment he judges the same thing to be neglected at this moment. And the other way round, he can judge that a thing is generically bad and must be fled, and still the pleasure or profit which one hopes to gain, may induce the mind to strive for it. He can judge that it is decent on the Lord's day to go to church and that therefore it is his duty to go to church, but in

---

9. Johannes à Marck, *Compendium theologiae christianae didactico-elencticum*, caput XIII, §13, 272.

10. Remarks about conscience and will follow.

11. Bernardinus De Moor, *Commentarius perpetuus,* pars secunda, Caput XIII, § 13 (XIII.13), 1041-1057. De Moor provides a few additions to this text in his *Supplementum Commentarii perpetui in Johannis Marckii Compendium theologiae christianae didactico-elencticum* (Leiden: Luzac et van Damme, 1774) and his *Epimetron Supplementi Commentarii perpetui in Johannis Marckii Compendium theologiae christianae didactico-elencticum* (Leiden: Luzac et van Damme, 1778). We will mark each addition. In the third part of his *Commentarius perpetuus,* he also presents additions to the second part, but not to this selected text.

order not to offend worldly people, in whose company one finds oneself and of whom he fears the hatred or mockery more than God, he can judge that he should neglect for himself that duty for this moment. [...][12]

And this relative and ultimate judgment of the intellect on what is to be done, is said rightly, according to our AUTHOR [à Marck], to be always followed by the will. For (1) unless the will wills that which the intellect or reason dictates, at the very moment at which it dictates it, just as reason offers it to be willed and unless the will follows the relative and ultimate judgment of the intellect, this rational faculty of the human mind could correctly be called brute and irrational, for it would work not only without ratio and intellect, but also [1046] against reason. (2) Experience confirms this sufficiently for everybody: nobody wills something unless for that moment at which he wills it, he has estimated, that is, judged, that it should be willed in that way. So, as long as the vacillating judgment doubts, the ambiguous will remains also suspended.[13] When judgment errs, the will also is dragged away soon in willing wrongly.

An objection from sins against conscience is not valid. Such sins are committed against the absolute judgment about our duty concerning an honest good, not against the ultimate and relative judgment about the useful and the pleasant good, which judgment is certainly followed.

For this reason some used to say that the will is *blind*, according to our AUTHOR. But it can be doubted if this is done correctly. The will would be called blind, when it does not perceive the objects it wills. But (1) since the same mind is the principle of both intellection and volition, as I say with the very learned De Vries, *Determ. pneumatol.* sect. ii, cap. iv, §12: the mind is not correctly called blind, since insofar as it is willing, it is not understanding.[14] (2) Blindness names a defect (*privatio*). This only applies to a subject naturally capable of the opposite habit, while the others can be only called with a negation (*negatio*) not seeing. But the spiritual sight of the mind belongs to the intellect— whose task it is to see spiritually, that is, to understand and perceive—not to the will. Also for this reason we are not correct, if we ascribe spiritual blindness to the will. But without absurdity it can be said about the will that it does not see, that is, perceive, as well as of the intellect that it does not will.

Thus, we can also ask, whether the will correctly is said to be determined by the final judgment of the intellect. But this question in turn would have been more important, if intellect and judgment had been faculties, really distinct from each other and from the mind, and not only modally. Yet, it is one and the same

---

12. Another example follows.

13. The term "ambiguous" should be read literally here: able to go two ways. It is suspended but able to go two ways.

14. Gerard de Vries (1648-1705) was in 1674 appointed as professor of logic and metaphysics in Utrecht. From 1685 till his death, he also held an extra-ordinary chair of theology. De Moor cites his *De natura Dei et humanae mentis determinationes pneumatologicae* (Utrecht : Joh. Van de Water, 1687). This book and De Vries' *Exercitationes rationales de deo, divinisque perfectionibus* (Utrecht: Joh. Van de Water, 1685) contained a fundamental critique on Cartesian philosophy. See about De Vries: Wiep van Bunge, "Vries, Gerard de (1648-1705)," in *DDPh II*, 1052-1055; W. J. Fournier, "Gerardus de Vries," in *BLGNP*, 1:417.

rational mind, which, when it judges something to be willed, determines itself to will that thing. The mind judges freely that this or that is to be sought, and because it judged thus, it freely determines itself to seek and obtain that thing. But if the faculty of both intellect and will are here considered as mutually distinct, the will cannot properly be said to be *determined* by the intellect, but to *follow* the intellect, in such a way that the previous judgment of the intellect is followed by the inclination of the will. The intellect is in relation to the will as a light, which the will, being enlighted, follows. See De Vries, *loc. cit.* §11. Compare Voetius, *Disputationes Selectae* I, 835-847.[15] [...] [16]

[1050] *And freedom belongs to man in both these faculties.*[17] We ask, whether freedom pertains to the will only, or also to the intellect? It is not worthwhile to treat this point again at length, for, as I said above, the faculties of intellect and will are not really separated from each other, nor from the mind itself, and the actions of both are connected to each other by a tight necessity, such that the mind is acting upon the same things in *understanding*, when it is occupied in [1051] cognition and judgment of these things; and in *willing*, when it is drawn to love or hate toward them. This according to Aristotle's *Ethics*, book VI, chapter 2, "What affirmation and negation are in thinking or understanding, pursuit and avoidance are in desire or appetite."[18] And thus correctly, free choice also pertains to intellect and will simultaneously: to the intellect because of the choice (*arbitrium* or προαιρεσις), to the will because of the freedom (*libertas*). Thus it is either the appetizing or appetitive intellect, in which way it is especially referred to the intellect, or the intelligent or intellective appetite, in which way it is principally referred to the will, according to Aristotle, *loc. cit.*[19] [...][20]

That freedom (*libertas illa: liberum arbitrium*, ἐλευθερα προαιρεσις, as the Peripatetics said): (1) should not be extended in a Pelagian fashion to a self-empoweredness (αὐτεξουσιοτητα), independent of the Creator. The Platonists designated free choice with the term αὐτεξουσιος and from their school that word crept into the writings of the Greek Fathers, who lived before Pelagius. For the

---

15. G. Voetius, "Appendix secunda ad disputationes de creatione," *Sel. Disp.*, 1:831-850. De Moor mentions the questions, which Voetius discusses here about the relation of intellect and will, but without supplying the answers.

16. The pages 1048-1050 contain a treatment of the conscience as part of the intellect, the will and its object (the good) and an extensive refutation of the Cartesian opinion, that the will extends itself further than the intellect, being in principle infinite. In his *Supplementum* De Moor also makes a statement against Spinoza.

17. This is a sentence of à Marck, on which De Moor comments.

18. ὅπερ ἐν διανοιαι καταφασις και ἀποφασις, τουτ' ἐν διωξις και φυγη. Compare *NE*, 177. In VI.2 Aristotle treats the virtues of the intellect, which together with the (moral) virtues of the character form the virtues of the soul according to Aristotle.

19. De Moor uses for free choice respectively the terms νους ὀρεκτικος, *intellectus appetens seu appetitivus* and ὀρεξις διανοητικη, *appetitus intelligens aut intellectivus*.

20. De Moor adds a comment on Locke in his *Supplementum*, 83: "Disputing against Locke, who judges the question, 'whether the will of man is free?' to be not less ridiculous, than that one, 'whether virtue is not a square?'; see Buddeus, *Theol. mor.*, part. i., cap. I, sect. iv, §11, 94, 95." Here, De Moor cites Johann Franz Buddeus, *Institutiones theologiae moralis* (Leipzig: Thomas Fritsch, 1723). Buddeus (1667-1729) was a Lutheran, who was famous for his encyclopedic knowledge.

expression "being of one's own power" (*suae potestatis esse*)—what the Greek word means—can be explained in a sane sense, namely by posing that the human will is always subordinated to the divine will. However, as that word does not induce by an innate force the glory to God in man, it will at least easily lead to these impious thoughts. Therefore, this word is seen by the Greek Fathers as being too proud, even where we must conclude about them that they judged themselves too proudly about the freedom of man, which is caused by a Platonic ferment. [...][21]

We purport that only for God it is true to be of his own right, in such a way that he absolutely not does depend on anyone, or is able to depend; therefore, only he is really self-empowered: man, on the other hand, always is constituted under power and guidance, namely of God, Is. 10:15, Dan. 4:35. [...][22]

(2) If an independent self-empoweredness (αὐτεξουσιοτης) does not fit man, his free choice surely cannot consist in absolute indifference. After Pelagius, the Jesuits, Socinians and Remonstrants have purported this, according to whom free choice is that faculty, by which, all requisites for acting being posited, the will can act or not act. See Spanheim, *Hist. Eccles.* V and those places which occur in this volume [of De Moor], VI.11, X.10,17 and XV.26.[23] So, we prove our position with the following arguments:

1. Since the requisites in man for acting are God's decree and his infallible foreknowledge stemming from this decree and his predetermining concourse, as well as the judgment of the intellecting mind [1052], man cannot be said to act or not act, when these requisites are present. For:

   (a) Thus the will would become truly independent, and God in his decree and knowledge as well as in his providential operation would become dependent, in which way the difference between Creator and creature is removed, even the complete order of things wholly inverted. Although it is proper to the will to determine itself, yet always in a subordinate way towards the determination of the divine will, under which, as first cause, all things stand, Eph. 1:11, Prov. 21:1.

   (b) By that absolute indifference, the will would also become brute and irrational, for then it could not only act without, but also against reason. Yet, we see on the contrary that there is a nexus between the twofold

---

21. Clemens of Alexandria and Origen are quoted.

22. De Moor applies for God and man respectively the terms αὐτεξουσιος or ἀνυπευθυνος and ὑπεξουσιος or ὑπευθυνος (*sub potestate et directione constitutus*). In his *Epimetron,* 41, De Moor remarks that Stoic Philosophy errs partly here, as noted by Leland, *De Nuttigheid en Noodzakelijkheid van de Christelijke Openbaring* 2ᵉ deel H.IX, 212-222. The book of Leland, *De nuttigheid en noodzaakelykheid van de christelyke openbaaring, aangetoond uit den staat van godsdienst in de oude heidensche weereld* (Utrecht: Abraham van Paddenburg, 1771), was a translation of Leland's *The Advantage and Necessity of the Christian Revelation* (London, 1764). John Leland (1691-1766), an English nonconformist divine, especially debated with deists in England and this work also has apologetic intentions.

23. Frederick Spanheim, *Summa historiae ecclesiasticae a Christo nato ad seculum XVI* (Leiden, 1689). Other passages of De Moor are consulted and will partly recur in the commentary on the text.

faculty of the rational human mind, because the will in its determination always follows the foregoing light and judgment of the intellect. And thus, the indifference, which belongs to the will with respect to many objects in the first act and in the divided sense, when the requisites for acting are not yet posited, does not belong at all to the will in the second act and in the compounded sense, when the requisites for acting are posited.

2. If absolute indifference were part of the essence of free choice, it would obtain in all rational entities. But indifference towards good or bad can neither be attributed to the most holy God, who is unable to deny himself, nor to Christ, free from all possible sins, nor to the confirmed angels and the saints in heaven, 2 Tim. 2:13, Heb. 4:15, Ps. 103:20, Heb. 12:23. The demons certainly do not stop sinning most freely, although they cannot not sin.

3. If the indifference of the will were posited, that would remove the use of prayer, for God is begged in vain to convert and sanctify us, if it always remains in the power of man to convert himself or not, whatever action of God being posited. In this way also the promises of God are in vain, by which he promises effective grace, a new heart, etc., since God cannot warrant these infallibly. Also our consolation from the everlastingness of the divine promise is removed, and so our perseverance in the state of grace, for these are rendered uncertain by the indifference of the will. Steph. Gaussenus, *de Studii theol. Ratione*, p. 53, 54: "In the question on freedom of choice the first truth is this, that we have free choice in every state, and they who say otherwise, speak improperly. Man used his free choice in the state of innocence towards the moral good, because the mind judged that moral good to conduce himself. After sin, he used the same towards evil, because the mind did not know the things of God, nor did it judge these things as being expedient for himself. So when the mind fluctuates between good and evil, both being supplied with equal strong reasonings, not until it is sufficiently clear, which reasons are most convincing, free choice wavers indifferently between good and evil; therefore, they do very wrong, who assume that the essence of free choice is placed in indifference. For we understand that indifference proceeds accidentally from ignorance, as clearly, as two times two is four."[24]

Positively, therefore, freedom is to be constituted in rational willingness [*lubentia rationalis*], by which man does what he wills, through a previous judgment of reason. Two things concur here at the constitution of freedom:

---

24. Etienne Gaussen (d. 1675; Stephanus Gaussenus) became professor of philosophy in the academy at Saumur in 1651 and in 1665 became professor of theology in Saumur. Saumur had a progressive reputation, to which Gaussen actively contributed. De Moor cites from the first part of his *Quatuor Dissertationes theologicae*: I. De studii theologici ratione. II. De natura theologiae. III. De ratione concionandi. IV. De utilitate philosophiae in theologia. V. De recto usu clavium (Saumur 1670). Bayle called it the best manual for the study of theology of his time, which is reflected in its many reprints (7th ed. in 1790). See E. Barde, "Gaussen, Etienne," in Philip Schaff, Samuel Macauley Jackson et al., *New Schaff-Herzog Encyclopedia of Religious Knowledge* (New York: Funk and Wagnall, 1908), 4:437.

1. The choice (το προαιρετιχον), to secure that that which happens, does not happen by a blind impulse and a brute instinct, but from ὁ προαιρεσις, from a deliberated plan and counsel, preceded by the light of reason and by the judgment of the practical intellect. And in this way [1053] the rational freedom is the opposite of a *natural necessity*, which obtains in the operations of the beasts.

2. The willingness (το ἑχουσιον), to secure that that which happens, happens spontaneously and willingly. [...].[25] By το ἑχουσιον the necessity of coercion is excluded, which is a power exerted by an external principle on him who struggles against it, and which completely opposes that which is voluntarily done, so that even he who does something coactedly, is not so much doing something as undergoing it—and the will can never be coacted. Coercion can indeed obtain in the *imperate* actions of will, that is, in the external actions, which follow upon the order of the will; but coercion cannot at all obtain in *elicited* acts, in the internal acts themselves of willing, which are always free. Not only do they originate from an internal principle, which acts are called spontaneous—for also the beasts are called spontaneous causes of their own acts, since they come to act by an internal principle—but also brought forth by an internal rational principle, acting from the judgment of reasoning and the decision (*placitum*) of the will. Thus freedom of man is called rational spontaneity.

   Neither can it be proved from actions which are called mixed, that the will works in a certain way partly free and partly coacted: as when for instance a sailor experiences himself to be in danger of life and shipwreck by an arising storm, unwillingly (*invitus*) throws his merchandise overboard, which he casts in the sea, what he would not have willed to do if he would have been in different circumstances: what he now, however, even willingly (*sponte*) does to save his life and his ship. Truly it must be said that this action is really both free and voluntary, because it is accepted upon a preceding election, in which someone chooses to undergo a lesser evil in order to escape a bigger one; although such an action is joined with a willingness to the opposite.

So, these two things constitute the freedom of the will, το προαιρετιχον and το ἑχουσιον. This freedom of man (1) is founded in Scripture. [...)][26] (2) The rational willingness is supposed in all teachings, warnings, promises, threats; which all together would be in vain, if man did not have rational willingness, by which he determines himself in acting. (3) That in this rational willingness, or in ὁ προαιρεσις χαι το ἑχουσιον consists the real essence of freedom, we may conclude from this, that only this kind of freedom belongs to *all* free agents, created and uncreated, and *only* to free agents, and *always*, in contrast with other forms of freedom, which in some entities or cases are accompanied by willingness only, or which are forms of freedom falsely supposed to belong to free agents only.

---

25. Texts of Aristotle's *Nicomachean Ethics* are cited in Greek.
26. Here, several biblical passages are discussed.

This rational willingness does not conflict (1) with the necessity of dependence [1054] on the divine will, which rather as a first cause excites and precedes the will to act freely; (2) nor does it conflict with the rational necessity of following the judgment of practical intellect, unless the will were to remove rationality; (3) therefore it does not conflict with moral necessity either, which in man in the Fallen state, unable to do good, removes also the possible appetite of this, even so that fallen man cannot naturally produce any spiritual good, gracious to God—unless we would want from the powerless, slavish and dead man, who has even to be generated or to be created, to expect such works, of which the one God keeps the glory for himself. [...][27] Thus man is physically free, but morally and especially with regard to spiritual goods he is a slave, and he sins necessarily, as will be shown at large in chapter 15, § 26, at which place we also shall teach against Amyraldus and Venema, that this moral impotence of fallen man towards good can also be called with a sound sense, *physical and natural*.[28] But this moral necessity to sin and the impotence (ἀδυναμια) of fallen man towards good does not conflict with the rational willingness. This willingness, in which the essence of freedom consists, is so natural for man, that it can in no case or state be lost by man, unless together with rationality itself. It follows that, although man in fallen state is so sold to evil, that he cannot not sin, still he does not stop sinning most freely and with the greatest willingness, from προαιρεσις and ἐκουσιον, which is sufficient to speak of freedom. It can thus be affirmed in truth, that every man always has free choice, also in the Fallen state. Nevertheless, with respect to the spiritual good it can be affirmed that free choice is wounded and lost, while willing that good is not free for the sinner. [...][29]

7.3 Structure of the Text

A short survey of the structure of this section from De Moor's commentary can be given by mentioning the themes of à Marck on which he successively comments:

1. Definition of the soul
   a. The two faculties of the soul
      i. The functions/operations of the *intellect*: perception and judgment
         1. theoretical judgment
         2. practical judgment (absolute and comparative)
      ii. Relation between intellect and will concerning practical judgment*
      iii. Specific operations of the intellect: conscience and memory (/recollection)
      iv. The functions/operations of the *will*: desire or rejection
         Discussion of the alleged infinity of the will

---

27. Various bible passages are cited.

28. In XV.26 (Part 3, 231-233), De Moor elaborates the systematic point, but only mentions Amyraldus and Venema, without giving references or citations.

29. Various authors are cited; mainly Augustine, but also Turrettini, *Institutio*, loc. X.i, ii, iii; and in the *Epimetron* also Jonathan Edwards in the Dutch translation of *A Careful and Strict Inquiry into the Prevailing Notions of the Freedom of the Will*.

b.   Human freedom: not consisting of independence or absolute indifference, but of rational spontaneity*

c.   The affections of the soul

The first selected text of De Moor is taken from his treatment of the functions of the intellect and deals with the judgment of the intellect.[30] Especially, the relation between intellect and free choice is important here. The part about human freedom makes up our second selection. While commenting on these basic texts of XIII.13, references will be made to other parts of his work when necessary. The relation between free choice and God's intervention in the human sphere is for instance discussed in the extensive *locus* on providence (X), while the impact of sin upon free choice is treated in the topic about the sin of man (XV).

In this commentary we offer an interpretation of De Moor's systematic position. Because he speaks about different degrees of human freedom (in relation to each of the four states), first the fundamental distinction between essential and moral freedom has to be elucidated (section 7.4). We will proceed by following De Moor's explication of faculty psychology with respect to intellect and will and their mutual relation (respectively addressed in sections 7.5-7.7). Then the stage is set for a confrontation between De Moor's conception of free choice and opposing views on human freedom (sections 7.8, 7.9), which is finally settled by looking at the compossibility and juxtaposition of various types of necessity with freedom (section 7.10). We will conclude with a summary (section 7.11).

7.4 Essential and Accidental Freedom

The "continuous commentary" starts with an overview of the whole work. In this explanatory index, De Moor promises to treat anthropology first in general (*in genere: natura*), after which human nature is considered specially (*in specie status quadruplex: institutus, destitutus, restitutus, constitutus*).[31] The essence of human nature is always present in its four different states, which are distinguished by their accompanying accidental differences.[32]

---

30. The selected parts are marked with an asterisk.

31. The four states correspond to the Augustinian distinction of man in the state "before the Fall," "after the Fall," "of grace" and "of glory." See for instance Augustine's *De correptione et gratia*, XII 33, 34.

32. The terms "essential" and "accidental" are not to be taken as a value judgment, as if they connote the importance of its referents, but they mean to indicate respectively that something is given with the nature of an entity or is not an inherent trait of it, though it still might be an important feature of concrete entities. Sinfulness or justice is an accidental aspect of human beings, according to Reformed theology, but still an important one. At the outset of his anthropology, De Moor makes the same point with slightly different terms. He distinguishes the essential parts of man, body and soul, and their union, but also the (accidental) adjuncts of the fourfold state: XIII.2, 984, 985: "Hominis *essentiam* hac complectitur definitione: creature ex corpore organico etc. quae definitio a. generis loco nos adscendere docet ad primam hominis originem, dum dicitur creatura. b. differentia specifica nobis exponit hominis a. materiam et formam seu partes ejus essentiales, corpus animamque cum utriusque unione; b. finem creationis [...] c. ceu adjunctum hominis praecipuum, quadruplicem

This distinction parallels the one between essential and accidental freedom.[33] The essential freedom of man is given with human nature and exists in each state. Moreover, each state is distinguished by a different kind of accidental freedom in virtue of the accidental qualifications of each state. Before explaining these states and the accompanying sorts of freedom, De Moor deals in *locus* XIII with the general nature of man, in the course of which he also discusses the basic freedom man has in every state. The discussion of freedom occurs in the course of an elaborate theological anthropology. Accordingly, the term "freedom" has a specific connotation, which should not be misinterpreted by generalized intuitions about what freedom is.

In order to understand the distinction between essential and accidental freedom, some remarks about the terms "freedom" and "will" might be appropriate. In scholastic theology, the will is related to goodness like the intellect is related to truth. Just as the intellect aims at truth, the will strives for good things. This understanding of the will as longing for the good is decisive for the Reformed conception of freedom. Precisely in this respect, however, a distinction must be made between alleged and real goodness. Essentially, human beings always long for what they suppose to be good. Yet, the problem of sin is that humans aspire after things they only imagine to be good. Since human will is not necessarily drawn to righteousness, accidental freedom applies in relation to the objective good.

Now, accidental freedom considers human freedom in a normative sense as moral freedom. In each state, the accidental freedom is measured in moral terms as the power to do the good. Instituted, man had the power not to sin, destituted he did not have the power not to sin, restituted he has the power both to sin and not to sin and constituted he does not have the power to sin.[34] Believing that a sinner is not in pursuit of good, De Moor cannot call him free, though he clearly thinks sin is by free and deliberate choice. Consequently, a sinner does have essential freedom in the sense of liberty viewed in relation to an alleged good, apart from the aspect of real goodness in the object.

Essential freedom is implied in the consideration of the potency of *willing*. The will is thus viewed in respect to the willing *subject*. Moral freedom on the other hand designates the potency of good or *rightly willing* (that is, in accordance to an objective norm). The will is thus viewed in respect to the desired *object*.

---

ipsius statum considerat." After having defined the essence, he mentions the four states as "adjuncts"; that is, they are not essential, but accidental.

33. De Moor does not explicitly mention this distinction, but it is underlying his discussion and needs to be clarified in order to understand his terms as the "essence of free choice" and the "loss of free choice in the state of sin."

34. These moral stances are explained subsequently in *loci* XIV, XV-XVI, XVII-XXXIII and XXXIV. *Loci* XIV and XV are especially important, in which De Moor deals respectively with the first state of man, also explaining in which sense man is the image of God (*De primo statu integritatis humanae et spectante huc, tum imagine Dei, tum foedere operum*), and the second state after the Fall (*De peccato hominum*).

(1) *Essential freedom* is a structural concept, given with human nature itself, consequently being present in all different states.

(2) *Accidental (moral) freedom* is a normative concept, related to the goodness of the desired or rejected object, consequently being different in the subsequent states of man's existence.

This distinction between essential freedom and moral freedom is also related to the one between the (essential) faculties and (accidental) habits of the soul.[35] In the process of a volitional act, De Moor argues, three aspects can be considered.[36] To produce an act, the essence of the soul is equipped with a *faculty*, which is in a certain *habit* to produce *acts*. The faculty of the will is a potency or power to produce volitional acts or actions. Besides this essential potency, man in reality is in a certain accidental state: this is designed by the term "habit." A habit is not an additional potency which changes the original faculty of the will, but it is the *same* will considered in its concrete disposition. Even if man does not act, he is in a certain disposition. "*Habitus*" is the substantive of the verb "*habere*" like "*scientia*" from "*scire*." It is possible to have knowledge without practicing it, or to love someone while not actually loving the other. The habit of love stays when the act is missing. Ethically a person is qualified as much by the habit as by the act. The accidental state of man is thus designated by the term "habit"; this habit reveals itself in actual acts. Before De Moor elaborates on the four kinds of accidental freedom, he first discusses in this chapter the freedom of man in the genus of nature. This essential freedom is discussed in the context of faculty psychology, to which we now turn.

7.5 The Faculties of the Soul

The soul[37] is a spiritual substance,[38] which has two *faculties*: intellect and will. By these faculties the soul can both act through the body outside itself and produce immanent acts.[39]

---

35. Again, De Moor does not explicitly mention this, but it is presumed in his discourse.

36. The distinction of faculty, habit and act also applies to the intellect, but that is of no account with respect to freedom.

37. A Marck has a dichotomous anthropology (body and soul); he states that the biblical language in speaking sometimes of the soul and sometimes about the mind (or spirit) in fact refers to the same spiritual substance. De Moor also uses the words *anima* (soul) and *mens* (mind) interchangeably.

38. This is directed against Descartes, who assumed the soul to exist in mere thought, and thus—in the view of de Moor—to be an accidental act and not something which has substantive self-existence.

39. The internal acts are called elicited acts, whereas the external acts are called imperate actions. This distinction applies only to the will, because the intellect has no power to produce something externally. In XIII.13, 1050, De Moor therefore only speaks about the (immanent) elicited act of the will (*actus eliciti voluntatis*) and the (externally directed) imperate act of the will (*actus voluntatis imperatos*). De Moor does not distinguish the terms "acts" and "actions," but for the sake of clarity, we shall use "act" for the internal operations and "action" for the external ones.

De Moor stresses the intimate connection between intellect and will: "Those faculties are not really distinguished from one another and from the essence of the mind, but only modally."[40] A real distinction exists between two independent things, whereas a modal distinction points to various ways in which one and the same thing exists. The same human spirit both understands and desires: "Thus the intellect perceiving something is the mind itself, which understands: the desiring will is nothing else but the mind, which strives and wills."[41]

(3) Intellect and will are (only *modally* distinct) functions of the one mind (soul).

7.5.1 The Judgment of the Intellect

In discussing the operations of the intellect, De Moor distinguishes four different operations: the acts of perception, judgment, conscience and memory (the latter is in fact a specified form of conscience which deals with the past). We shall deal here only with perception and judgment, because conscience and memory are not intimately related to free choice.[42]

Whereas Turrettini and Gomarus used the term "intellect" in a stricter sense (connoting primarily the judgment), De Moor uses it in a wider sense, also including perception. This has to be explained as a result of the Cartesian debate, whereby more attention was given to epistemology and the trustworthiness and certainty of our knowledge. Perception does not mean sense-perception here, but is used to signify the result of it: the representation of the objects in the mind. This perception of things happens through the active apprehension of the intellect: the intellect creates a concept (*notio*) of the perceived objects.[43] Descartes' concept of the mind can be summarized by the metaphor of a mirror, which passively gets an impression of its objects.[44] He reckoned only perception to the intellect, and referred judgment to the will. More important, perception deals with "clear and distinct" ideas, and cannot err. Mistakes originate therefore from prejudices of the will, and knowledge can be perfect, if the judgment of the

---

40. XIII.13, 1042: "Facultates hae à se invicem et à mentis essentiae non distinguuntur realiter, sed modaliter tantum."

41. XIII.13, 1042: "Intellectus itaque res percipiens est ipsa mens intelligens: voluntas desiderans nihil aliud, quam mens appetens volensque."

42. Although they certainly have to do with ethical aspects of free choice (such as responsibility), they do not influence the understanding of his concept of free choice as such.

43. XIII.13, 1042: "Per intellectum homo percipit [...] per apprehensionem simplicem nempe, quae est actio animae intelligentis, rem quampiam per conceptum a se formatum praesentem sibi sistentis: sive repraesentaminis rei a mente facta formatio, quatenus per eam rei repraesentatae redditur conscia." ("By the intellect man perceives, namely through a simple apprehension, which is an act of the understanding soul, by which any thing is made present for itself through a self-formed concept: or an image is formed from the thing to be presented, in as far by it the represented thing is made conscious.")

44. Compare for this contention and an influential critique: Richard Rorty, *Philosophy and the Mirror of Nature*, 9th ed. (Oxford: Blackwell, 1996), esp. 45, 46.

will only assents to "clear and distinct" ideas. De Moor dismisses this idea, and extensively argues that judgment belongs to the intellect.[45]

The judgment adjusts the truth of the notions of perception and their connections,[46] but there is also judgment about what we have to do. Like Turrettini, De Moor distinguishes this judgment in theoretical and practical, the latter again in absolute and relative. "Theoretical" should not be interpreted in the modern sense: as abstract speculation opposed to concretely doing something. Rather, it means the consideration of something in itself, without respect to my task or possible use of it. So De Moor explains the theoretical judgment as the judgment "by which I judge about the goodness, honesty or evil of a thing, considered in itself: fornication, theft and the like is a sin."[47] The practical judgment is likewise the reflection on the goodness of something with respect to my duty or to the profitableness for me. Now the goodness is not considered in itself, but with respect to my action: the judgment is "practical, by which I judge about that which I must do or flee."[48] This is either an absolute judgment, "by which I judge that generally (apart from other circumstances) this has to be done or left,"[49] or a relative one "by which I compare the honestly good with what is useful and pleasant, my duty in general with the specific circumstances, in which I am."[50] De Moor offers the following example: going to church on Sunday. My judgment about it is threefold:

1. Theoretical judgment: going to church on Sunday is good.
2. Absolute practical judgment: it is my duty to go to church on Sunday.
3. (Final) relative practical judgment: This Sunday I would rather stay home: because I fear the mockery of worldly people (in whose company I am), I judge it better to avoid their comments by staying home, than to risk offense by going to church.

This example shows that the intellect with respect to actions always judges according to a certain goal. The choice reflects which priorities I have. I can

---

45. In this context he does not further explain his reservations toward Cartesian thought, but most Reformed scholastics deny that evidence is a criterion for truth. By situating truth in perception and charging judgment only to assent to it, when it is evident, Descartes is far too optimistic about epistemology. According to the Reformed, the task of judgment to judge about the truth of perceptions is far more problematic, because evident perceptions need not be true and uncertain perceptions can yet be true.

46. XIII.13, 1044: "judicium est actio animae intelligentis, plures notiones aut ideas unientis aut sejungentis." ("The judgment is an act of the understanding soul to join or reject many notions or ideas. Thus, judgment is closely related to perception and has to do with forming a reliable image of reality.")

47. XIII.13, 1045: "judico de rei bonitate, honestate, turpitudine in se considerata; feortationem, furtum etc. esse peccatum."

48. XIII.13, 1045: "judico de eo quod mihi faciendum vel fugiendum sit."

49. XIII.13, 1045: "quo si rem aliquam in se considero, abstracte ab aliis circumstantiis, judico eam faciendam vel omittendam esse."

50. XIII.13, 1045: "quo bonum honestum comparo cum utili et jucundo, officium meum in genere cum circumstantiis peculiaribus, in quibus versor." De Moor calls it also *judicium comparatum et ultimum*.

profess that going to church is good, but in fact believe that being respected by all people is a greater benefit: in the case of a conflict between those two a judgment will prefer the (seemingly) most important one.

1. Theoretical judgment	(Truth-)judgment about goodness of an action
2. Absolute practical judgment	Judgment about my duty of the action in itself
3. (Final) relative judgment	Judgment about my duty in these circumstances

Scheme 10: De Moor on the judgment of the intellect

In explaining the relative practical judgment, De Moor uses a common distinction between different kinds of goodness in things, which he repeats in his treatment of the will.[51] The honest good (*bonum honestum*) is the goodness of a thing considered in itself; the useful good (*bonum utile*) is the goodness of a thing with respect to its profit for me; and the pleasant good (*bonum jucundum*) is the goodness of a thing with respect to its pleasantness for me. This distinction explains why I can judge in general that going to church is good, while still not doing it in this particular situation. My absence in church reveals that I expect the pleasant good to be gained by staying home to be greater than the honest good of doing my duty.

(4) The judgment of the intellect decides which is the best thing to do.

(5) The judgment considers not only the goodness of the action itself, but also our gain by it (profit or pleasure).

7.5.2 Intellect and Will

Next, à Marck's *Compendium* states about the will: "By the will however, (man) desires or rejects objects, and he does this always under the appearance of the good, whether in truth or seemingly."[52] Just as the intellect is directed to the truth, the will is directed to the goodness of objects. Thus man is essentially a seeker of the good, and his will is the faculty by which the soul is "made fit to incline itself to the enjoyment of a thing which is to be pursued or conserved, of which the intellect has judged that it is good."[53]

It is important to understand the relation between intellect and will in order to appreciate De Moor's conception of free choice. De Moor states that the will always follows the last practical judgment, which at first glance seems to imply

---

51. XIII.13, 1045 and 1048, respectively.

52. XIII.13, 1048: "Per voluntatem autem appetit vel aversatur objecta, illudque prius semper agit sub specie boni, vel veri vel apparentis."

53. XIII.13, 1048: "Est nimirum voluntas ea mentis humanae facultas, qua ea apta nata est semet inclinare ad consequendam vel conservandam fruitionem rei, quam intellectus bonam esse judicavit."

that free choice is dictated by the intellect. The modal distinction between the faculties, which really form the same mind, prevents such dictation: "Besides, even the operations of both faculties are to such a degree mutually connected, that the mind, when it judges about things and truths, at the same time also wills to judge, and when it wills an object, at the same time also judges the same thing to be desirable."[54] Thus judgment and volition are independent acts (they cannot be reduced to each other, but are both essential), which nonetheless always go together: they are both produced at the same time.

De Moor discloses this "independent-interwovenness" between intellect and will in the answer on a next question about this topic: "If you inquire nevertheless, which of these faculties is to be said first *in order*, it has to be answered that these two faculties are indeed *temporally* simultaneous, because they do not really differ; they are also *naturally* simultaneous, because they are the soul itself which has the power to extend itself in those two ways: *in (structural) order*, however, the intellect is first, if you consider the actions of those faculties, because the intellect is the guide of the will."[55]

According to De Moor, the intellect is *structurally* prior because it has a guiding task for the will. The intellect first judges about the goodness of the objects, and then the will can reasonably choose the good as good. So this structural priority should not be explained in the sense that the intellect dictates what has to be done, after which the only function of the will is to execute this judgment.[56] Such an interpretation overlooks the fact that intellect and will have the same *goal*: striving for the good.[57] This common goal of intellect and will shows in two ways the primacy of the will.[58]

First, this goal is fixed by the will as the ultimate end of all acts or actions. Since everything good is measured according to this goal of the will, the judgment about the goodness of things depends on the ultimate goodness which the will longs for. Here the distinction between means and end is crucial.[59] The means are chosen in order to attain the end. The *judgment* about the goodness of the means depends on which end is *willed*.

---

54. XIII.13, 1042: "Utriusque facultatis etiam operationes adeo secum invicem sunt connexae, ut dum judicat mens de rebus et veritatibus, simul etiam velit judicare, et dum vult objecta, simul etiam eadem volenda judicet."

55. XIII.13, 1042: "Si quaeras interim, quaenam harum facultatum dicenda sit *ordine* prior? Dicendum est, duas has facultates esse quidem simul *tempore*, dum non differunt realiter; simul quoque *natura*, dum sunt ipsa anima potens se duobus hisce modis exserere: *ordine* tamen priorem esse intellectum, si spectes ad actiones harum facultatum, quia intellectus est dux voluntatis." Italics are from De Moor (and always his, unless explicitly mentioned).

56. This would be an Aristotelian or Thomistic position, in which the judging function of the intellect reduces the will to "executioner" and no free choice is left.

57. The threefold judgment with respect to action has to do with the goodness of an action, as the (apprehended) good is the goal of acting. See section 7.4 above.

58. De Moor does not explicitly speak about this priority, but in our opinion clearly presupposes it. In the debate with the voluntaristic Cartesians, De Moor did not have to argue the priority of the will, but interpreting the relation between intellect and will differently, he discusses that point.

59. See the text of Gomarus, and the commentary in section 4.4 on the distinction between means and the goal and the parallel relation between free choice and will.

Second, this goal also discloses the priority of the will by the fact that the intellect can only *show* means to attain the end, but that the will has to *choose* them to attain it. Fundamentally, the goal of striving for the good is only reached by the will: the intellect(ing mind) can only show how it is to be reached, but the will(ing mind) tries to reach it itself by longing for it and doing what is necessary to get it. De Moor therefore calls the intellect quite appropriately "the guide of the will": it shows her the way, but the will has to reach it herself.

Although the will thus has the primacy, in structural order the last practical judgment is prior to the will. Here, De Moor also cites à Marck with approval: "and this relative and ultimate judgment of the intellect in what is to be done, is said rightly (...) to be always followed by the will."[60] The term "follow" (*sequi*) is distinguished by De Moor from "determine" (*determinare*).

He approves that the will *follows* the ultimate practical judgment. Two arguments and a reply to an objection are put forward. First, without following the ultimate practical intellect, the will would be irrational. Whereas the intellect would judge something to be good, the will still chose something different, and so seeks evil as evil. Secondly, daily experience shows that one only wills something if one has judged that it should be willed. Sin against conscience is not a legitimate objection, because then the relative judgment decides something different than the absolute, but still the will follows the relative judgment.

Next, De Moor deals with the question whether it can be rightly said that the will is *determined* by the ultimate practical judgment. His reply is that such a question would only make sense if the intellect and the will would be really (*realiter*) distinct. As separate actors, the independence of the will would be threatened if it were determined by the intellect. However, those faculties are only modally (*modaliter*) distinct: "it is one and the same rational mind, which, when it judges something to be willed, determines itself to will that thing."[61] The mind both judges and wills, and it would be utterly foolish, if it were to judge one way, but to choose the other. The will makes an independent choice, but does not have the slightest reason to incline itself to something different than the judgment advises. It is one and the same mind, which all along has the same goal.

Thus, the question is not very important according to De Moor, but when those faculties are (modally) *distinctly* considered, the will cannot properly be said to be determined by the intellect, but to follow it.[62] The will makes its own choice (*inclinatio*), and therefore the expression "determine" does not fit, but the choice of the will is in accordance with the last judgment, and it can be fittingly called to follow the judgment. The function of the intellect is compared to a light, which

---

60. XIII.13, 1045: "Et hoc judicium comparatum et ultimum intellectus ... in agendis merito dicitur voluntas semper sequi."

61. XIII.13, 1046: "Nunc una eademque anima rationalis quando quid volendum esse judicat, ad hoc volendum semet ipsam determinat."

62. XIII.13, 1046: "Si vero facultas utraque intellectus et voluntatis distincte a se vicem hic considerantur, voluntas proprie non debebit dici ab intellectu determinari, sed intellectum sequi; adeo ut praevium intellectus judicium sequatur voluntatis inclinatio."

gives it the same role as when it was metaphorically called the guide of the will.[63] The will, being enlightened by the intellect, follows the light of its judgment.

We can summarize De Moor's discussion of the relation between intellect and will as follows:

(6) Intellect and will are modally distinct, independent-interwoven faculties of the soul.

(7) The will has a logical primacy, since it longs for a goal, the intellect discerning the means to attain it.

(8) In acting, the judgment of the intellect has a structural priority, since an object must be understood in order to be chosen by the will.

(9) Whereas the intellect is a *guide* which the will *follows*, the intellect does not *determine* the act of the will.

7.6 Freedom as Autonomy or Absolute Indifference

Having discussed the faculties of intellect and will, De Moor states that "both of these faculties together make up the freedom of man."[64] Because of his view on the relations of the faculties, it is natural that he concludes: "free choice pertains to intellect and will equally, you will say correctly: to the intellect viewed as choice or *prohairesis*, to the will viewed as freedom."[65] However, this power of man is still variously interpreted. To understand De Moor's own position, it is helpful first to see what he dismisses as an inadequate elucidation of free choice.

De Moor rejects the Platonic term *autexousiotès* (self-empoweredness) as an explication of free choice. This would suggest that man is independent of his Creator. Although this term was also used by the early Greek Fathers, it has a Pelagian tendency. Man is not an autonomous agent, who can act solely by his own power, but is upheld and governed by his Maker. The freedom of man is not so absolute as to make him independent of God.

(10) Freedom of choice does not consist in absolute independence from God (autonomy).

De Moor also disapproves of the interpretation from the Jesuits, Socinians and Remonstrants of free choice as *absolute indifference*. In this conception, free choice is "that faculty, by which, all requisites for acting being posited, the will can act or not act."[66] Indifference means that the will is able to act or to not-act (at the same moment of time), and in this sense De Moor does not deny that indifference is involved in free choice (see below). His point, rather, is that the will,

---

63. XIII.13, 1046: "Intellectus in ordine ad voluntatem sese instar luminis habet, quod praelatum voluntas sequitur."

64. XIII.13, 1050: "Atque in utraque hac facultate competit homini libertas."

65. XIII.13, 1051: "Atque ita quoque liberum arbitrium ad intellectum et voluntatem simul pertinere, recte dixeris, ad intellectum ratione arbitrii seu προαιρεσεως, ad voluntatem ratione libertatis."

66. XIII.13, 1051: "Facultas, quae positis omnibus ad agendum requisitis, voluntas potest agere vel non agere."

in order to will, depends on the "requisites for acting." These are specified as the decree of God, his infallible foreknowledge stemming therefrom, God's predetermining concourse and the judgment of the intellecting mind. When these requisites are posited, man cannot be said to act or not to act, but he will act in concordance with these requisites. However, the opponents of Reformed theology convey by absolute indifference that the will can choose otherwise than the requisites provide. Thus taken, free choice means that the will is completely independent and able to choose whatever it likes.

In this context, De Moor does not deny that a kind of indifference sometimes functions in the process of willing[67] but is not a perfection of freedom neither essential for true responsibility.[68] So, the essence of freedom cannot be defined by indifference. De Moor rejects a voluntaristic definition of freedom by the concept of indifference for three reasons.

Firstly, this conception of freedom is inadequate to explain human freedom on an *essential* level. It denies man's creational dependence on God and the guiding task of the intellect for the will. The first argument is thus drawn from the abiding dependence of man as a creature of his Creator. As the benevolent and omnipotent Creator, God governs all things. He also incites man to act, and man is thus dependent on God to act. When absolute indifference were granted, the order between God and man would be inverted: then God would be dependent (in his decree, foreknowledge and providential operation) on man and man independent. As men have their being in God (they exist through him) they also can only act by him,[69] if he incites them to act, permits their wicked deeds and

---

67. X.17, 472: "Qualis libertas in omnibus actionibus rationalibus creaturarum obtinet. Sed ad hanc libertatem complacentiae, qua mens tum circa alia magis ἀδιάφορα, tum circa bonum vel malum ethicum versatur; accedit in multis rebus, praesertim naturalibus, quae in sese adiaphorae censeri possunt, *libertas* quoque *indifferentiae*, seu liberae voluntatis in agendo contingentia, ut determinare semet ipsam possit, vel simpliciter ad agendum aut non agendum, vel hoc aut illo modo agendum etc. Sive priori sive etiam posteriori modo actiones creaturarum dicantur liberae, semper subsunt divinae providentiae eo, quo §10, 11 dictum est, modo." Compare X.17, 474.

68. X.17, 473: "Dicendum potius, falsum sic semper supponi *libertatis* conceptum, ceu facultatis ita *absolute indifferentis*, ut quis positis omnibus ad agendum requisitis, semper agere possit vel non agere. Sed α. talis libertas creaturae competere nequit, quin sit plane independens: nam dependentem esse, et tamen tam absolutum in suas actiones habere dominium, ut, positis omnibus ad agendum requisitis (etiam ratione illius, à quo quis dependet) agere quis possit vel non agere, aperte contradictoria sunt [...] β. *Indifferentia* in genere considerata, seu facultas agendi utrumlibet oppositorum, ad rationem formalem sive essentiam *libertatis* ne quidem pertinet; sed est hujus tantum adjunctum, et separabile quidem, imo tale quod ex se ac per se nullam *libertati* addit perfectionem: nam a. Libertas est quidem perfectio, sed constans ad optimum determinatio pariter est perfectio: nequit autem haec illi per se detrahere; consequenter neque libertati tantum per se decedit perfectionis, quantum illi decedit indifferentiae. b. Ad actionem, ut laude vel vituperio digna sit, ob rationem modo praemissam, non per se pertinet, ut sit plane indifferens, (quod clarissime in Deo paret; cujus, quia immutabilis est bonitas et sanctitas, nulla parte idcirco minor existit gloria;) cum tamen omnino istuc pertineat, ut sit libera."

69. The opponents acknowledged that man depends in his *being* on God, but explicated divine providence in such a way to make man independent in his *actions* (they viewed providence primarily as conservation, while the concursus was considered in a general sense: concursus made it possible for man to act, but it did not direct his actions). While De Moor's opponents thought this to be necessary to preserve human freedom, De Moor rejects this because God's rule over

concurs in their good deeds. God's predetermining concourse is the means by which God actualizes the goal which he wills by his decree. As the first cause, he works together with man as a second cause, and both have a certain goal. The point here is that man does what God wills (or wills to permit), but at the same time he freely does what he himself wills. In this context, De Moor does not show how man's liberty is preserved while God directs him, but this is treated in the *locus* on providence.[70] The second argument that the will has to follow the requisites for acting is that the will always follows the last practical judgment.

Secondly, this conception of freedom is also inadequate to explain human freedom on a *moral* level. De Moor draws an argument against absolute indifference from the moral stance of rational entities. Man is not the only being which has free choice. God, Christ, the saints in heaven, the angels and the devils all have free choice, but indifference toward good or bad cannot be attributed to any one of these. Because the first four are unable to sin, whereas the demons cannot but sin, they all cannot have absolute indifference. De Moor applies the concept of absolute indifference to a moral choice between good and evil. To be indifferent towards good and evil should not be hailed as freedom, but bewailed as a defect. The will should always incline itself to good and abhor evil. When it has become indifferent, it has in fact already departed from the good. Free choice has to be defined in such a way that both at an ontological, essential level liberty is granted, as well as the moral stance of essentially good entities (who cannot sin, like God) or bad ones (who cannot but sin, like demons) can be explained. Whereas the opponents' conception of liberty is based upon absolute indifference, which is very positively estimated by them, it is in fact a defect of liberty for De Moor.

Thirdly, this conception of freedom as indifference is finally inadequate to explain (God's action and) human freedom on the *soteriological* level. When God cannot exert a definite influence[71] on human existence, even he cannot really help fallen humanity when it struggles with a corrupt will. Prayer is therefore made useless: whatever action of God is posited, man always remains in the power to convert himself or (and this frightens De Moor) not. Neither can the Lord truly warrant his promises, so we are robbed of our consolation. God's effective grace is the wellspring of all consolation, but this fountain would be barred by autonomous human freedom. However, absolute indifference is not necessary to preserve real freedom for man, while De Moor's concept of free choice still leaves him the opportunity to drink from the waters of consolation.

---

man is thus hampered and he denies that this government takes away human liberty (when defined correctly as rational sponaneity and not as absolute indifference).

70. See also section 7.8 below (on necessity of dependence).

71. The Jesuits, Socinians and Remonstrants acknowledged that God can guide free choice by a moral persuasion (*suasio*), so that man sees that he should do such and such. The Reformed had diffulties with this position, because it places God's influence on man principally at the same level as fellow-creatures' influence: they can also persuade only externally, but do not internally incite man to act; this internal guidance is instead posited by the Reformed as the prerogative of God alone.

(11) Freedom of choice does not consist of absolute indifference, a concept that is inadequate on ontological, moral and soteriological grounds.

7.7 Freedom as Rational Spontaneity

The continuous commentator calls the Reformed understanding of free choice "rational willingness" (*lubentia rationalis*).[72] Two things concur here to constitute freedom: choice (το προαιρετικον), and the willingness (το ἑκουσιον). The act of free choice does not happen by a blind impulse or brute instinct, like in the beasts, but originates from a deliberate counsel, because (structurally) the judgment of the intellect foregoes. Neither is the act of free choice determined by an external agent, because free choice determines itself.

(12) Freedom of choice consists of rational willingness.
   a. Choice is based on previous, rational deliberation.
   b. Choice is self-determined.

De Moor has several arguments making the case that the essence of free choice consists of these two elements. First, he quotes Scripture to show that man does (and should)[73] freely do what he does. Secondly, in all commands, admonitions, promises and threats this human potency is assumed. When man did not have such a free choice, all these things would not make sense.[74] Thirdly, this conception of free choice fits all free agents. De Moor proves this, by showing that this conception is not too narrow, nor too broad. This conception is not too narrow, because it applies to *all* free agents (God, Christ, man, angels and demons) and *always* fits their liberty (in all states, human freedom can be explained by it). It is not too broad either, because it includes only free agents. Whereas the conception of free choice as absolute indifference was shown to be inconsistent, this notion of rational willingness agrees with the nature of all rational entities.

De Moor emphasizes that *rational* spontaneity should not be confounded with spontaneity as such (called *natural* spontaneity by others). Spontaneity as such refers to acts which originate from an internal principle (they are not externally coacted), but still it is possible that the agents do not have any choice (for instance, animals that are driven by their own instinct to eat, but do not have the choice to do otherwise). When the Reformed position is interpreted in this way, it could easily be integrated in a deterministic system. Then man can be determined (e.g., by God's providence and predestination) and have no real possibility to do otherwise, but still act spontaneously. However, rational spontaneity requires not only an internal principle which is not coacted upon but a *rational* internal

---

72. This is synonymous with "rational spontaneity" (*spontaneitas rationalis*). Elsewhere, he calls this freedom "liberty of delight" (*libertas complacentiae*), X.17, 472.

73. This refers to the imperate actions, which one can do reluctantly (for instance, helping the poor not because one feels compassion, but to do his duty).

74. In fact, this argument is also used against the Reformed position by them who deny the moral inability of man to do good in the state of sin. They state that the command to convert oneself assumes that man has the potency to do it, but De Moor does not handle that issue here.

principle, which acts on (grounds of) both the judgment of reason and the "pleasure/compliance" of the will.[75] Hereby, man always has free choice, so this is not compatible with a deterministic worldview. Man has always a real possibility to choose whichever he likes. Thus rational spontaneity grants real freedom to man and provides him with the opportunity of a real choice.

Therefore, this rational spontaneity presupposes a certain kind of indifference, though it grants no absolute indifference.[76] As was shown already, De Moor accepts freedom of indifference in a limited sense. Next to this actual freedom of indifference, he states that the will, with respect to many objects,[77] is indifferent in the first act and in the divided sense. On the contrary, in the second act and in the compounded sense, the will is not indifferent at all.[78] De Moor uses two distinctions which have the same impact.

First, the distinction between "in the first act" (*in actu primo*) and "in the second act" (*in actu secundo*) considers respectively the faculty *in itself* and the *operation* of the faculty. Considered in itself, the faculty of the will has indifference and can incline itself to opposite choices. "In the first act" indifference is acknowledged, given the possibility of acts arising by the structure of the faculty itself. In the second act, however the will is not indifferent, but inclined to one of the opposites.[79] By now, the will is not indifferent because of the habit of the mind, which tends to an ultimate goal. This distinction between the first and second act is thus a *structural* distinction in the process of acting, and not a temporal sequence of separated acts.[80]

The distinction between a divided sense (*in sensu diviso*) and a compounded sense (*in sensu compositionis*) stems from the modal analysis of sentences. Aristotle's example, which became a paradigm in medieval analysis of modal notions, was the sentence: "It is possible that Socrates sits and runs." The

---

75. XIII.13, 1053: "Obtinere potest coactio in actibus voluntatis vel voluntariis imperatis, id est, omne genus actionibus externis [...]; neutiquam in actionibus elicitis seu ipsis volendi actibus internis, qui semper liberi sunt [...] profecti a principio interno rationali, agente ex rationis judicio et voluntatis placito, unde hominis libertas dicta est *Spontaneitas Rationalis.*" This freedom pertains always to elicited acts, but not always to imperate ones. See also below, section 7.9.

76. Compare the following explanation with section 6.6 in the chapter on Turrettini.

77. In formula: aWp & M(aWq, r, s...). De Moor does not expand this indifference to all objects, because the will can have such an explicit taste or distaste for some objects that even before its volition it is not indifferent to these objects. (At least with respect to the highest good, the will is not indifferent.)

78. XIII.13, 1052: "Adeoque indifferentia, quae voluntati competit respectu multorum objectorum in actu primo et sensu diviso, sepositis requisitis ad agendum; ea neutiquam competit voluntati in actu secundo et sensu composito, positis requisitis ad agendum." In the second act and compounded sense, the will has no indifference at all (*neutiquam*). The clue to combine this assertion with De Moor's limited acceptance of freedom of indifference is the term "requisites for acting," as in that context also was stated that this freedom is "under divine providence." Compare note 67.

79. In formula: aWp ∨ a-Wp; alternatively: aWp ∨ aW-p. The denial of indifference in the "second act" or the "compounded sense" is expressed as follows: -M (aWp & aW-p).

80. De Moor utilizes the distinction to explain the relation between the impact of the "requisites for acting" on the act, but this is based upon the distinction between the faculty as such and the operating faculty. Without the "requisites," the will is not acting and thus indifferent *in actu primo*, whereas the requisites being posited, the will is acting and thus not indifferent.

signification *in sensu diviso* was taken to mean: "Socrates sits and it is possible that Socrates runs,"[81] while the analysis *in sensu composito* yields the meaning: "It is possible that Socrates both sits and runs," which is contradictory. Thus the will has indifference in the divided sense: Socrates chooses to sit, and it is possible that he chooses to run. It would be nonsense, however, to state that he also has indifference in the compounded sense: Socrates chooses to sit and to run both at the same time. Exactly because he cannot do both things at once, he has to choose one of them. So, in respect to his *possibilities* man has indifference, but in the *realization* of one of them (in which act one possibility is chosen) indifference has no place. Rational spontaneity thus lends man real freedom, and absolute indifference is neither necessary nor helpful.

In summary, free choice arises from the cooperation of intellect and will. Like the Platonic self-empoweredness (*autexousia*), absolute indifference is not an adequate explanation of human freedom. Essentially, absolute indifference cannot lend place to the independent and free guidance of the Creator, nor to the guiding task of the intellect. Further, it is unable to explain the moral situation of entirely good beings or hopelessly bad ones, who likewise possess free choice. Finally, this concept robs man of real soteriological consolation. On the other hand, rational spontaneity is a consistent conception of free choice. It supposes a qualified form of indifference and does not (like natural spontaneity) fit in a deterministic worldview.

7.8 Necessity and Freedom

The conception of free choice as absolute indifference leaves little place for a relation to necessity. As we have seen, especially necessity of dependence has to be abandoned. Rational spontaneity can afford this and other kinds of necessity, while some kinds have to be excluded in order to guarantee real liberty. Two kinds of necessity are always excluded.

In the first place, free choice excludes a *natural necessity*. Natural necessity is a kind of necessity, which arises from the nature of a being. Because it belongs to the nature of a lion to devour other animals, his chasing is subject to this kind of necessity. Man, however, is not driven by his nature, but decides on a deliberate counsel.

Neither is a *necessity of coercion* compatible with free choice. When a power exerted by an external agent compels someone who struggles against it, someone is not so much doing it, but undergoing it. The will can never be coacted in this way, that is not in its internal volitions. The elicited acts are always produced willingly, although man can be barred by others in his external volitions. For instance, a prisoner can always will to be free, but fettered in jail, he cannot

---

81. This divided sense can be interpreted diachronically (Socrates sits at one time, and it is possible that he runs another time) or synchronically (the alternative is possible at the same time). Only the latter grants real alternativity; because De Moor uses it as a structural distinction and parallels it to the distinction between *in actu primo* and *in actu secundo*, it is clear that it has to be read synchronically.

realize his internal volition by going away. So, free choice is never hindered by the necessity of coercion, though the outward realization of some choices may be prevented.[82]

These two kinds of necessity are directly opposed to the essential elements of free choice. De Moor stated that the choice (against natural necessity) and the willingness (against necessity of coercion) together provide man with free choice.

(13) Freedom of choice is inconsistent with natural necessity (instinct).

(14) Freedom of choice is inconsistent with coercion by an external agent.

Whereas the presence of these forementioned kinds of necessity would take away free choice, others are compatible with real liberty. De Moor mentions rational necessity, the necessity of dependence and moral necessity as harmless for freedom of choice.

Rational necessity is implied by the connection between intellect and will. Because free choice is made up not only by the willingness (*to hekousion*), but also by the choice (*to prohairetikon*), a deliberate counsel of the intellect is always involved. We have seen that the judgment of the intellect is temporally simultaneous with free choice, but structurally it is first. In logical order, the mind first judges and then freely inclines itself to choose the judged case.

The *necessity of dependence* exists because man always acts in dependence on his Creator. Far from removing freedom, the divine will "rather as a first cause excites and premoves the will, in order that it acts freely."[83] This rather bold and compressed statement is not further explained here, but fortunately, De Moor handles this issue again in his treatment of the doctrine of providence. His statements about the concurrence (*concursus*) of God with creatures are especially important. He defines it as: "The immediate, previous and predetermining impulse and motion in creatures to act."[84] He emphasizes that the "*previous and pre*determining" character of the impulse of God should not be taken in a temporal sense, but in a structural sense.[85] About the

---

82. De Moor also states that in mixed acts (when someone is driven by the circumstances to do what he otherwise would deplore) the will is free. It is not the case that the will is coerced externally to do what it does not will, but in this case there are two opposing interests, of which the strongest is elicited. He mentions an example: "When for instance a sailor experiences himself to be in danger of life and shipwreck by an arising storm, *unwillingly* throws his merchandise overboard, which he casts in the sea, what he would have willed not [= "nilled"] to do, if he would have been in different circumstances: what he now however even *willingly* [*sponte*] does to save his life and his ship. Truly it is said that this action is really both free and voluntary, because it is accepted upon a preceding election, in which someone chooses to undergo a lesser evil in order to avoid a bigger one; and thus, such an action is joined with willingness in [a free choice between] opposites" (XIII.13, 1053).

83. XIII.13, 1054: "Haec autem lubentia rationalis uti non pugnat cum necessitate dependentiae à voluntate divinae, quae potius tanquam causa prima excitat et praemovet voluntatem, ut liberè agat."

84. X.10, 455: "Sed consistit coöperatio divina in creaturarum omnium immediato, praevio ac praedeterminante impulsu ac motu ad operandum."

85. X.10, 455: "Operatur Deus impulsu *praevio* ac *praedeterminante*, non tamen *temporis* sed *ordinis* ratione. Non enim ita res concipienda est, ac si Deus primo temporis momento reali

pre*determining* character of this influx, he remarks: "which predetermination is not hindering however, that the powers and natural faculties of the creatures remain unharmed, nor that the spontaneous determination of the will of rational creatures does not remain free; for as God moves everything according to its nature, the natural faculties are not destroyed, but he makes them such that they can become manifest as second causes, which they could not do without the influx of the first cause."[86]

The distinction between God's agency as first cause and man as second cause is crucial here.[87] Both God and man have free choice by which they act towards their ultimate goal. God, however, also acts with his free choice through his creatures to realize his ends. In this way, God is involved as first cause in human acts. Man himself is the second act. Again, this is a structural and not a temporal distinction, and the dependence of free choice on God is explained in the same manner as its dependence on the intellect. As the will inclines itself freely according to the judgment of the intellect, it also inclines itself freely according to the impulse of the divine *concursus*. Moreover, God moves the second causes *agreeing to their own nature*, so their freedom is not destroyed. Because it belongs to man's nature to act by free choice, God causes man to act *by his own free choice* and nothing else. The determination of God is about the desired *effect* of the action of the first and second cause. When God determines the human will to this effect, man simultaneously freely determines himself to the same effect. According to De Moor, creation is not only in its existence dependent on the Creator, but also in its acting: the divine influx (in the human will) provides humans with the power to act and to determine their own wills to act.

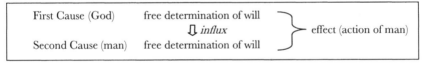

First Cause (God)	free determination of will	
	⇓ *influx*	effect (action of man)
Second Cause (man)	free determination of will	

Scheme 11: The necessity of dependence in relation to an analysis of cause and effect.

---

efficienta creaturam ad agendum excitaret; quae creatura sic mota, istaque vi externa impulsa, deinceps sequenti temporis articulo, cum aliter nequeat, operetur quoque."

86. X.10, 455: "*Praedeterminans* autem dicitur idem impulsus ac motus, quod haec sit gloria causae primae praedeterminare causam secundam a prima dependentem; [...] Qua praedeterminatione non obstante salvae tamen manent creaturarum vires et facultates naturales, nec non determinatio spontaneè libera voluntatis creaturarum rationalium: dum unamquamque rem convenienter naturae suae Deus movet, nec facultates naturales destruit, sed facit ut causae secundae has exserere queant, quod absque influxu causae primae praestare non possent."

87. X.10, 456: "Consideratio Dei ut causae primae, creaturarum ut causarum secundarum, quam hic obtinere dixi. Jam a. causa prima est primum movens in omni actione, ideo causa secunda non potest movere nisi moveatur, nec agere nisi acta à prima: absque eo Deus mere per modum concausae ageret, qualis influxus Deo est indignus [...]. 3. Revocanda insuper in mentem sunt, quae de causae primae independentia et de causae secundae dependentia a prima similiter jam sunt notata: haec enim consideratio aeque impulsum et motum creaturarum praevium et praedeterminantem ad agendum facit necessarium; dum absque eo ratio reddi non potest connexionis, qua fit ut utraque causa in eodem opere producendo concurrat."

In X,17 the issue of reconciling the freedom of creatures with divine providence (*conciliandae libertatis creaturarum et divinae providentiae*) is extensively discussed. De Moor admits it as a difficult problem, which is due to our inability to comprehend the mode in which the Creator works in our willing.[88] If it is hard to relate them, we should not deny providence in order to save freedom, nor weaken it to mere foreknowledge or permission. According to De Moor, the problem gets especially blown up by the concept of freedom as absolute indifference, which is not reconcilable with providence. However, freedom is to be defined as rational spontaneity, which does agree with divine concurrence. The necessity of dependence, caused by the divine influx of providence, is a necessity of event (*necessitas eventus*) of the effect, but still the "influxed" faculty of man determines itself, and is not forced to act against its nature.[89] As the divine concurrence does not take away the rationality of acting, neither does it destroy the willingness. Accordingly, we do not feel a divine compulsion in our concrete volitions. De Moor draws then a parallel with rational necessity: as our mind itself determines by the intellect the will, so the most wise and almighty God can act with free will of man, while preserving his willingness and spontaneity.[90]

In sections 5 and 23 of this tenth *locus*, De Moor denies that the Reformed position implies a (Stoic) fatal necessity (*fatalis necessitas*), which he sees exemplified at his time in Spinoza's followers. Because God as the first cause wills freely (and thus the result is contingent), the second causes are not moved by an absolute necessity (which does not agree with their free choice), but only by a hypothetical one (which agrees with their freedom of choice).

(15) Freedom of choice is consistent with rational necessity, i.e. the will assents to the judgment of the intellect.

---

88. X.17, 472: "Difficilem semper habitam fuisse conciliationem concursus Divini cum libertate creaturarum rationalium in harum actionibus, nil mirum est, cum modus ille, quo Causa prima operatur in voluntatem creatam, nobis plane perspectus non sit; id quod cum Dei incomprehensibilitate optime convenit."

89. X.17, 474: "Sed non pugnat cum hac libertate necessitas externa ex Causae Primae determinatione oriunda et quam dependentia nostra omnino flagitat. Nam oritur hinc quidem necessitas eventus, adeo ut ad divinum influxum facultas in homine nequeat non sese ad agendum determinare; non tamen hoc agere tenetur contra naturam suam: non adimitur per divinam praedeterminationem sua homini rationalitas, et rationalis agendi modus; non cogitur homo invitus, sese hoc vel illo modo determinare: sed Deus suaviter adeo in hominis animum insinuare sese virtute sua omnipotente novit, ut quam creaturam rationalem agere facit, faciat agere non nisi ex rationali ductu proprii judicii et plenissimo suae voluntatis lubitu. *At sic*, ut cum Vriesio loquar, Exerc. Ration. Xxv. §.16., *divina praemotio firmat nostram libertatem ac verum ei addit vigorem; quatenus nil magis libere agit, quam quod efficaciter ad libere agendum sic est determinatum, ut non-libere agere plane non possit.*"

90. X.17, 474: "Posse vero Deum sapientissimum et omnipotentem ita agere in liberam hominis voluntatem, ut salva maneat hujus lubentia et spontaneitas, dubitari nequit; cum ipsa mens nostra per intellectum determinet voluntatem, ita ut haec sequatur judicium ultimum et practicum intellectus; nec tamen quis lubenter et spontaneè voluntatem sic sequi negabit."

(16) Freedom of choice is consistent with a necessary dependence on the Creator's predetermination and impulse, since it preserves man's faculty of free, rational choice.

(17) The necessity arising from God's providence is not absolute, but hypothetical, and concerns the outcome (*eventus*) of free human acts.

The *moral necessity* arises from the habit of the will and also agrees with free choice. This kind of necessity is primarily discussed in reference to the fallen state of man and pertains to his moral freedom. De Moor's starting point is that man, as a sinner, is unable to do good.[91] Therefore, this realm is also excluded from his possible appetite. It seems that free choice is severely limited here. Nevertheless, De Moor remarks: "the rational willingness does not conflict with this moral necessity to sin and powerlessness of fallen man to do good."[92] Again our author stresses that free choice is so natural to man that it cannot be lost in any case.

How can these statements be understood? In his treatment of original sin, De Moor states that it is accompanied by a contrary habit of the will. Whereas first God was man's ultimate delight, now he has chosen a different aim. Therefore, he acts in accordance with a different habit. Remembering the distinction between essential freedom as the power of willing (what one wills) and moral freedom as the power of right willing, this moral necessity does not affect essential, but only moral freedom.[93] Acting in accordance with one's habit is not a strain on free choice, but rather a help to attain the will's own ultimate goal. When the habit is bad, moral freedom is lost by the will's own subjective inclination, yet essential freedom in no way differs!

Therefore, De Moor states: "and thus the choice of man, in the genus of being with respect to his *nature* is *free*, shows out in the *genus of morals* and with respect to the *object* to be *enslaved*. Surely, while the rational spontaneity of man remains in the determination of his will, in the genus of morals his choice is determined to vice through an inborn vicious habit in the state of sin; still it is (determined) with the highest willingness."[94] Physically—in choosing what he likes—man is thus free, but morally—in realizing what is pleasant to God—he is a slave, unless God sets him free.

De Moor argues that this moral powerlessness of fallen man to do good can also be called in a sound sense *physical and natural*. In this way, "physical and natural" should not be interpreted as "essential and belonging to the nature of man," because in the other three states in which man can be, he is not thus

---

91. De Moor argues for this thesis in XV.26, where he also explains that it applies to *spiritual* good, which is pleasing to God.

92. XIII.13, 1054: "Non tamen cum hac neccessitate morali peccandi, et ἀδυναμία hominis lapsi ad bonum, pugnat lubentia rationalis."

93. From a modern perspective a normative concept like moral freedom can easily be misunderstood, because we usually do not associate freedom with holiness.

94. XV.26, 227: "Atque sic arbitrium hominis, *in genere entis* suaque *natura liberum*, evadit *in genere moris*, et ratione *objecti, servum*. Manente nimirum hominis spontaneitate rationali in determinatione suae voluntatis, in genere moris per habitus vitiosos connatos in statu lapsus determinatur ejus arbitrium ad malum, summa tamen cum lubentia."

enslaved. Rather, it refers to the fact that the whole of humanity is born with the habit of original sin. In this sense it is natural and affects his choices so deeply that only grace can change his nature.

Thus, Bernardinus resembles his great medieval namesake who thus commented on John 8:36: "Even free choice stands in need of a liberator, but one, of course, who would set it free, not from necessity, which was quite unknown to it since this pertains to the will, but rather from sin, into which it had fallen both freely and willingly, and also from the penalty of sin which it carelessly incurred and has unwillingly borne."[95]

> (18) Freedom of choice is consistent with moral necessity; i.e., the will acts in accordance with its own habit.
>
> (19) In the state of sin, man is morally bound to doing evil, but still essentially free in doing so.

In sum: natural necessity and the necessity of coercion are opposite to free choice. On the other hand, neither the necessity of dependence in relation to God, nor the rational necessity in relation to the ultimate judgment of the intellect, nor the moral necessity in relation to the ultimate goal of the will disturb free choice.

7.9 Evaluation

In his *magnum opus*, Bernardinus de Moor provides a detailed account of Reformed theology. Though not in the fore, his conception of free choice plays an important role. His anthropology centers around four states, in which man has different moral freedom, and vital parts of soteriology (sin, grace, conversion) cannot be understood apart from his views on free choice.

De Moor's systematic account of free choice proves to be a nuanced picture of various aspects involved in free choice. Together intellect and will provide man with a freedom of choice he can never lose. The definition of free choice as rational spontaneity at the same time shows why some kinds of necessity would destroy liberty, while others do not harm it. His distinction between elicited acts and imperate actions is also helpful to understand how multiple limitations on the level of our actions still leave our willing free. In the context of faculty psychology, his analysis shows that free choice is given with man's nature and can never be lost.

In an era of early Enlightenment, the theologian De Moor did not shy away from discussion with dissident philosophers. Especially Descartes is discussed, but Locke and Spinoza also receive attention. Ironically, De Moor mentions a double enlightenment of the will, which are both more credible than Descartes' Enlightenment project of certain knowledge. First, the will is enlightened by the intellect and naturally follows its ultimate practical judgment. Against such a both faithful and rational picture, Descartes utilizes the indifference of the will to make the will independent of the intellect (and of God, the Reformed objected). The

---

95. *De gratia et libero arbitrio*, III.7, cited in *GFC*, 63.

will should be enlightened, but frequently chooses on the basis of unrational prejudices, rather than to wait for the "clear and distinct ideas" of enlighted reason. In such a model, the Reformed objected, the will gets the blame for the faults of the intellect, and a far too optimistic concept of the intellect arises. At least with respect to moral goodness, the sun of the intellect is severely darkened. Therefore, the illumining grace of God must show us the right way. De Moor persuasively argues that freedom is not clarified by the voluntaristic concept of indifference. Descartes might cherish his clear and distinct ideas, but his concept of freedom is not an improvement of the Reformed position: not only in theological respect but first and foremost philosophically it is inadequate.

For an up to date anthropology, the insights of De Moor with respect to human freedom are still relevant. Freedom functions in a rational and intentional search for the good. The denial of moral freedom in the case of sinners therefore does not debase man, but only raises his original glory. Hence, the concept of rational spontaneity presents a much nobler picture of man than the concept of absolute indifference, though the latter might seem at first sight the more attractive picture of freedom.

8

Conclusion

8.1 Summary

This volume presents six texts on the question of free choice (*liberum arbitrium*). These texts show a broad variety of time, place, genre, polemical targets and argumentation. Still, together they are representative of the development of the free choice discussion in Reformed scholasticism. Let us provide a brief survey of this development, before entering into the systematic evaluation of the presented material.

The first selected texts are by Girolamo Zanchi (1516-1590) and stand chronologically close to the times of the Reformers, Luther (d. 1546) and Calvin (d. 1564). The greatest importance of Zanchi's discussion of free choice is that he provided an overall positive treatment of this topic making clear the agenda of Reformed theology. Whereas the Reformers Luther and Calvin were justly concerned with the proper confession of justification by faith alone on the ground of God's free grace, others of their generation (Bucer, Vermigli, Hyperius, Oecolampadius) and second or third generation theologians such as Zanchi and Ursinus realized that the completeness of Christian doctrine deserved special attention. Especially questions of anthropology could not be neglected. Moreover, the Reformed emphasis on grace (culminating in the doctrine of predestination) raised the suspicion of a denial of human responsibility and freedom. It would be fatal to Reformed theology, both intellectually and religiously, if it could not refute this accusation.

A broad argumentation from Scripture and tradition (both patristic and medieval) is characteristic of Zanchi's discussion of free choice. On philological and theological grounds, he makes independent decisions on the interpretation of the crucial terms in the discussion by equating free choice and free will. Basic to his understanding of free choice is the distinction between what is natural and permanent to man and what varies according to the different states of man (before and after the Fall). In continuity with the tradition of Augustine and Anselm, Bernard of Clairvaux and the Victorines, Bonaventure and Thomas Aquinas, Zanchi holds that a will that is not free cannot be a will.

In comparison to the later authors in this volume, Zanchi's argumentation is rather rudimentary on the philosophical level. He does not discuss the questions of alternativity and contingency explicitly, although we discern the relevant conceptual structures in his teaching. In answering the objection that the infallibility of God's foreknowledge destroys human freedom, he restricts himself to elaborating the distinction between God as first cause (*prima causa*) and creatures as secondary causes (*secundae causae*). Concerning the central hypothesis of this volume, we can conclude that in Zanchi we find no explicit usage of the synchronic contingency concept.

In Franciscus Junius (1545-1602), just a generation after Zanchi, we find a far more elaborated conceptual apparatus. Contrary to Zanchi, he does not simply equate free choice and free will, but identifies an intellective and a volitional element in *liberum arbitrium*. From Junius, we have one disputation on free choice dating from his Heidelberg period, and two disputations held at Leiden University. The sequence of these disputations shows a remarkable professionalization of approaching this issue.

Junius' most significant contribution is a clear distinction between different kinds of *freedom* and different kinds of *necessity*. Characteristic of an ontology of contingency is Junius' usage of the "necessity of the consequent/necessity of the consequence" distinction. A further element of his theory of free choice is the distinction between "freedom of contrary acts" (the freedom to choose this or that thing) and "freedom of contradictory acts" (the freedom to choose or reject a certain object). Together with Junius' nuanced distinction between a structural level of possible acts and an actual level of chosen acts, his exposition suggests a synchronic conception of alternativity.

This ontological account of freedom is combined with a decidedly Reformed soteriological viewpoint. In Junius' view, man before the Fall was free in all respects. After the Fall, essential freedom of choice has remained, but the ability to do good has been lost and can only be restored by divine grace.

Franciscus Gomarus (1563-1641), the immediate, younger colleague of Junius at Leiden, utilizes mainly the same concepts and distinctions as his dear colleague, in a comparable manner. Gomarus is a distinctive representative of the new generation of Reformed thinkers, striving for a solid professionalization of theology and philosophy. Just like Junius, Gomarus specifies the objects of free choice as the means towards a goal, thus utilizing the crucial end/means (*finis/media*) tool of the medieval "will" tradition. The ultimate goal of man's life is not a matter of deliberation and choice, but is immediately given and desired. In reaction to the counter-Reformational polemist Robert Bellarmine, Gomarus states that the judgment of the intellect does not *determine* the act of the will: it only judges about the goodness or badness of a thing.

Gomarus argues that before and after the Fall man has the same essential freedom of the will. After the Fall, however, the exercise of freedom is limited to "external" or "natural" things. In moral and religious respects, man cannot do the good; nevertheless, even sinners act freely in regard to their own choice, because they consciously decide for sinful acts.

Gisbertus Voetius (1589-1676) presents himself as a grateful disciple of Gomarus. The long forgotten, recently rediscovered disputation on the freedom of the will, defended under Voetius' presidency in 1652, provides a highly technical refinement of the Reformed position on contingency, necessity, freedom and indifference. From the outset, Voetius argues against the Jesuit interpretation of free choice, which states that in spite of all the requisites for willing, the will can still choose otherwise. In the Jesuit understanding, the will is absolutely indifferent. While rejecting absolute indifference, Voetius maintains a twofold indifference as essential to human freedom: (1) freedom in respect of the object of the will: the will can choose different means in order to achieve a certain end; (2) freedom in respect of the internal operation of the will: the will is not internally determined by the intellect, but makes its own decision. Voetius argues that these two constituents of free choice are sufficient; no additional concepts as introduced by the Jesuits are needed.

In a further clarification of his position, Voetius shows that this essential freedom is not damaged by certain kinds of necessity arising from the divine decree and concursus, and from the judgment of man's own intellect. By his notion of co-causality, he explains how God's will and man's will can both on their own level determine an act. The two causes have different origins and starting points, but they end up in the same point, namely the act of the human will. Following the famous British theologian Samuel Rutherford, Voetius argues for a concrete *concursus* of God's will with the human will, instead of the Pelagianizing concept of a merely general *concursus*. By Voetius' discussion, Reformed thought on freedom receives its full conceptual and argumentative shape.

With Francesco Turrettini (1623-1687), we move from the beginning of the seventeenth century to its third quarter. Whereas the position on free choice is basically the same as in Junius, Gomarus and Voetius, the polemical scene has changed. Turrettini summarizes the substantial debates with Arminian and counter-Reformational (mainly Jesuit) theologians of the seventeenth century. His discussion of the topic results in three important qualifications. First, he gives a more elaborate treatment of the relation between intellect and will, by precisely distinguishing between the theoretical and practical judgment of the intellect. Second, he relates human freedom extensively to the different types of necessity, to the result that only implicative necessity is maintained (in a different form, the same point was made some decades earlier by Voetius). Third, he discusses the concept of "indifference," used by some opponents to establish human autonomy over against the divine decree. Just like his Dutch colleague Voetius, Turrettini rejects the concept of "absolute" indifference, but maintains the ontological "indifference" in the sense of the structural contingency of human choice.

The final stage of Reformed scholastic theology is represented in this volume by Bernardinus de Moor (1709-1780). Again we face basically the same position, while the polemical context has shifted anew. De Moor discusses the topic of free choice in the framework of a complete anthropology that explicitly reacts to the Cartesian alternative. While De Moor rejects the extreme voluntarism of René Descartes (d. 1650), he maintains the Reformed emphasis on the decisive role of the will in human action. De Moor gives a refined discussion of the theoretical and practical (absolute and ultimate) judgment of the intellect as a guide for the will. In the end, he comes back to the same point as we noted in Zanchi, but now with more conceptual clarification: God's providence does pre-determine human actions, but the necessity involved here is only a hypothetical or implicative one, that does not destroy true human freedom.

8.2 Systematic Exposition

In the scholastic Reformed doctrine of free choice, three fields of thinking are closely connected: ontology, doctrine of God and anthropology.

The systematic center is formed by a distinctive *ontology*. This ontology makes explicit the modal structures of reality in terms of necessity, contingency, possibility and impossibility. Although the sixteenth- and seventeenth-century thinkers did not dispose of full-fledged "possible world" ontology, we can plausibly explain their concepts in terms of possible worlds. In accordance with basic Christian beliefs concerning the freedom of God in creating the world, Reformed scholasticism advocates true alternativity.

We should be aware of the difference between an (Aristotelian) understanding of contingency as (temporal, diachronic) change and the (Scotist) concept of contingency as structural, modal alternativity. Whereas some phrases in the authors exposed in this volume give the impression of a diachronic understanding of contingency, we have found substantial evidence in their arguments for an interpretation in terms of synchronic contingency.

The key elements here are the statements concerning the relation of freedom and (different kinds of) necessity, the distinction between necessity of the consequent and necessity of the consequence, and the distinction between the divided and the compounded sense in which contradictory propositions are conjoined. The net result of this ontology is the statement that God is absolutely necessary, yet the events of his creation are not, since he acts contingently.

The ontology of Reformed scholasticism is mirrored by the doctrine of God and the doctrine of man, respectively. Whereas the doctrine of God was not explicitly under study in this volume, we sensed it always in the background in the Reformed discussions on the topic of free choice. Man is consistently viewed as a creature dependent on his Creator. The fundamental insight is that God is free in his actions. Just as God was free to create this world instead of a different world, he remains free in acting. God is not necessitated to know what he knows and to do what he does.

The decisive role in the doctrine of God is played by the divine will: given God's knowledge of circumstances and possibilities, he is free to choose by His will this or that possibility, and his free activity constitutes the contingency of reality. Whereas contingency holds fundamentally for God in relation to the created world, the bridge between God's acting and creaturely acting lies in the concept of dual causality. God is viewed as First Cause who brings into existence all creatures and then continues to sustain, govern and lead all things. Creatures (especially humans) are secondary causes that act in dependence on the first cause but still in the freedom suitable to their own nature. Thus, contingency and freedom are preserved in creation while God keeps together the whole course of events. Rather than violating human freedom, God's foreknowledge and decree function as the necessary conditions for human freedom.

The other half of the mirror, anthropology, is directly at stake in the discussion of free choice. We can discern different levels of anthropology that together constitute the proper understanding of free choice.

First, Reformed theology utilizes a so-called faculty psychology. Starting with the concrete acts of knowing and willing, it is asked for the potencies facilitating these actions. To be sure, these faculties are not viewed as different, independently existing substances. Rather, humankind is distinctively described in its functions of knowing (*intellectus*) and willing (*voluntas*), and on this level of abstraction the relation and co-operation between the two faculties is discussed. Over against tendencies to absolutize one of the two functions, the Reformed thinkers state that each in its own function contributes to man's acting: the intellect by knowing and judging the objects and possibilities, the will by deciding on the basis of the intellect's judgment.

Second, in addition to the general makeup of the human soul in intellect and will, the Reformed introduce historical dynamics by speaking of the different states of man: before and after the Fall, in grace and in glory. As a conceptualization of biblical salvation history, the concept of different states is crucial in understanding the kinds or degrees of human freedom. In the classic triad of natural, moral and spiritual freedom, the Fall causes a damage or loss of moral and spiritual freedom (man can no longer do the good or love God); the natural freedom, by which man's will can choose between opposites without being necessitated towards one of both, remains after the Fall. This natural freedom is essential to man, in the sense that without this freedom he would no longer be man as a rational and responsible creature. The Reformed authors treated in this volume take pains to combine the permanence of essential freedom (presupposing contingency in reality) with the disastrous slavery of sin by which man's will is bound (accounting for the factual impossibility of doing the good, since we can only do the good by loving and obeying God).

Third, building on the remaining essential freedom of choice, the Reformed discuss its relation to different kinds of necessity. The result is that human freedom does not go unqualified: man does not act out of nature, or contrary to the (ultimate) judgment of his intellect, or outside God's providence. Still, these forms of necessity obtain in terms of the necessity of the consequence by which the outcome (the consequent) is not made necessary in itself.

8.3 Objections

Possible objections against our interpretation of the Reformed doctrine of free choice can be shaped differently.

To start with, we can imagine some *historical* objections. Given the fact that Martin Luther and John Calvin rejected the concept of *liberum arbitrium* as an idle name, it does not seem plausible to find an affirmative usage of the same concept in the writings of their successors in the sixteenth till eighteenth centuries. Or, should we cherish a reversely radical discontinuity model of "the Calvinists against Calvin" in which it was only a happy accident that the Reformed scholastic theologians were unfaithful to the Reformation in their positive use of the concept of free choice? Here, we can quiet all lovers of the Reformation, but like the scholastics we have to make some distinctions.

First, it is necessary to distinguish between Luther and Calvin on this matter. In *The Bondage of the Will* (*De servo arbitrio*), Luther does indeed straightforwardly reject any positive usage of the free choice concept. Although this primarily has a religious motivation, Luther provides also a comprehensive counter-theory that amounts to the view that God is all-operative and all-determinant. All human freedom seems to be denied here.

In Calvin's *Institutes*, things are more nuanced. Despite the strong predestinarian overtones of his theology, Calvin acknowledges some freedom in the functioning of the human will and maintains the freedom from coercion as essential for man. However, against Roman Catholic interpretations of free choice as being able to do good even without grace, he decidedly resists such freedom even to the point of not deeming the term free choice suitable at all. Calvin's Reformation agenda of defending free grace led him to ignore a nuanced articulation of free choice, which made him vulnerable to the accusation of determinism by his opponents. In the long run, the ongoing debate between Reformed theologians and Catholics (apart from new developments in Protestantism itself, like the Socinians and Arminians) made it necessary to be more explicit on human freedom. Still, Calvin's ardent proclamation of grace can well be interpreted in line with the scholastic discussions of the nature and powers of free choice, in which the liberating power of grace with respect to the ability to do really and spiritually good was likewise pronounced.

Second, as already indicated in the previous remark, we can distinguish between the religious intentions behind playing down free choice and working this out in an explicit ontology. Given the context of the Reformation, it is quite understandable that Luther and Calvin combated the idea that man is free to work out his own salvation, although with divine help. The moral and spiritual consequences of sin are at stake, and in this respect the Reformers rightly teach the total corruption of man.

The further question remains, however, what happens to the essential freedom of choice: is it destroyed in the wake of the Fall, or does it remain (although radically restricted in its orientation towards the good)? The authors discussed in this volume realized that the confession of total corruption and the complete dependence on divine grace should not lead to the establishment of a necessitarian system that would in the final effect make God the author of sin. The strict distinction between essential, moral and spiritual freedom serves to find the proper balance in anthropology.

Third, it can well be argued that Luther in his ontological implications is an exception to the tradition of Christian thinking from the Church Fathers through the medievals until later Reformed theology. The distinctive Christian concept of creation does not allow for strict determinism or necessitarianism, as it would even destroy God's freedom. On theological grounds it is not recommendable, therefore, to take Luther's polemic against Erasmus as a norm for proper Reformation theology.

The rather isolated position of Luther in this respect (which is not to say that his theology is not helpful in other respects either!) is disguised by the scholastic method of *exponere reverenter*, in which Luther was taken as an "authority" of the truth of effective grace and his own statements on free choice were interpreted in the own scholastic frame of thought of the Reformed.[1]

The historical objector can continue, however. Not only viewed from the "fathers of the Reformation," but also in the light of the polemics with contemporary Roman Catholics and Arminians (to name just the most important opponents), it seems hardly credible that the Reformed scholastics could foster any positive view of free choice. Has not John Owen himself contested the "old Pelagian idol Free-Will, with the new goddess Contingency" in his *Display of Arminianism*?[2] So, when the present book, written by some innovators from the country of Arminius, defends the importance of free choice and contingency for Reformed theology, take heed!

However, the account of Owen perfectly matches our interpretation. On the one hand, it is clear that these Reformed theologians were hostile to contemporary interpretations of freedom in the sense of human autonomy. In the presented texts we find a strong emphasis on man's lasting dependence on God as the Creator and First Cause of everything. The surprising thing is, on the other hand, that they view exactly this dependence on God not as a threat to human freedom but as its ultimate warrant. Precisely because God foreknows and governs all things, man is not left to the caprices of nature, but is granted real freedom to act rationally and responsibly. In view of the defense of absolute autonomy and indifference of the human will, the Reformed scholastics did not opt for divine determinism, but for a theology of contingency and will, grace and freedom relying on God's providence. To them, it is clear that God's acts as the contingent acts of the First Cause do not destroy, but rather preserve the essential freedom of man as the second cause, who concur together in a free effect. Likewise, the structural contingency of reality is not marred by divine foreknowledge and decree, but rather constituted by the contingency of the creational and providential acts of the divine will.

Moreover, they could argue that the alternative concept of freedom as indifference was not an improvement. Rather than clarifying the actual functioning of the human will and contributing to a proper esteem of the will in a theological anthropology, it made freedom something arbitrary. The Reformed concept of rational spontaneity not only is suited better to a consistent doctrine of providence and grace, but also is more apt to clarify the reality of the

---

1. Compare section 1.3.

2. The full title of Owen's book runs: Θεομαχία Αὐτεξουσιαστική or, *A Display of Arminianism being a Discovery of the Old Pelagian Idol of Free-Will with the New goddesse Contingency, Advancing themselves into the Throne of the God of Heaven, to the Prejudice of His Grace, Providence, and Supreme Dominion over the Children of Men* (London, 1643; Edmonton: Still Waters Revival, 1989). The Greek word Θεομαχία has both the aspect of a battle between opposing gods (like in Greek mythology) and a (human) struggling or resistance against God. Seemingly, Owen expressly used this term to cover both nuances.

yearnings and longings of the human will in all its heights and depths and its connection to what we know and believe.

Similar criticisms against our interpretation can be brought forward in a more systematic way, reflecting the three main areas of our systematic exposition.

It can be doubted whether an ontology of contingency does hold. The alternative would be an ontology in which all things and events are necessary.[3] This necessity could arise either from divine pre-determination or from blind fortune. In both cases, man is not accountable for his deeds. Besides being morally and religiously inadequate, such a view of ontology can be refuted on philosophical grounds: a necessitarian ontology excludes contingency, while contingency cannot be excluded since it is in itself an essential feature of reality.[4]

How about God? If freedom and contingency do not exist for God, God himself is bound to a given state of affairs. This cannot be made consistent with the biblical and Christian picture of God who is free and powerful. It could even be argued that this would make God superfluous: if his existence and actions do not make a difference, why believe in him at all?[5]

From God's freedom, we have a fluent transition to human freedom. While we acknowledge the fundamental distinction between God the Creator and man as creature, we must state on the ontological level that if contingency exists for God, it is also structurally present in our reality. Otherwise, reality would be different for God than it is in fact. In that case the disappearance of contingency for us should be attributed to some obscure actor. Hence we cannot allow for that option. Moreover, the rejection of human freedom of all sorts (see above for the Reformed scholastic qualifications of freedom) does not fit into the biblical narrative in which man is always responsible to God.

8.4 Relevance

We also have to give a historical explanation of the neglect of classic Reformed thought on freedom in the theology of the last two centuries, at least in the proposed interpretation of this book. In brief, Reformed thought was not refuted but simply forgotten! The confusions of the political and military tensions and revolutions in the Napoleonic era and thereafter resulted in the collapse of the traditional European university and its scholastic methodology, which had flourished for six centuries: three medieval and three early modern centuries.

---

3. To be sure, this is one (important) frontier of Reformed thought. The other extreme of radical contingency thought frequently occurs in postmodern times. We would argue that the fine balance of necessity and contingency held by Reformed theology refutes this view as well. Cf. N. W. den Bok, "Scotus' theory of contingency from a (post)modern perspective: Some important developments of the notion of contingency after Duns Scotus," in: L. Sileo (ed.), *Via Scoti: Methodologica ad mentem Joannis Duns Scoti.*, 431-444.

4. For a detailed refutation of "absolute evidentialism" as an epistemological position which implies a necessitarian ontology, see *KN.*

5. Cf. the discussion between Paul Helm ("Synchronic Contingency in Reformed Scholasticism: A Note of Caution" and "Synchronic Contingency Again") and A. J. Beck and A. Vos ("Conceptual Patterns Related to Reformed Scholasticism") in *NTT* 57 (2003): 207-238.

This collapse led to a massive revolt against the basic patterns of classic Christian thought, and we note that all kinds of nineteenth-century philosophical movements (for instance idealism and romanticism, positivism and materialism, conservatism and Marxism) embrace the necessitarian way of thinking. New historical scholarship interpreted the past of Western thought in the light of ancient Aristotelian necessitarianism, with the exception of Scotism and nominalism, which were seen as one movement of arbitrary and irrational thinking. The Christian tradition was read in an Aristotelian framework with Thomas Aquinas as its primary spokesman.

Generally, Reformed theology likewise has lost its own tradition in this respect. An utterly striking example is delivered by the development of so-called *modern theology* in the Netherlands. In Germany, the historical truth of the Gospels (David F. Strauss, *Das Leben Jesu*, 1835) began to be debated on behalf of the possibility of miracles in the light of all scientific inventions of natural laws. Dutch theologians responded in various ways, but all stressing the supernatural character of Scripture and faith.

Yet, a theological movement was initiated by J. H. Scholten and C. W. Opzoomer who programmatically called themselves *modern*, because they considered it possible to advocate Christianity in a natural, non-supranaturalistic way.[6] The laws of nature were God's own thoughts by which he necessarily governs reality. Starting with a few self-evident axioms, they were confident that both a Christian theology and a philosophy of nature which agreed with scientific results could be deduced. The axioms of their foremost thinkers can be listed as follows:

a. reality is the outcome of God's universal activity;
b. God acts necessarily, and
c. God's universal and necessary causation is absolutely good, since God is essentially good.

So, the eschatological end of world history is absolutely good and everything will be right for everybody. The two first axioms were derived from the confession of God's absolute sovereignty by the Reformed tradition and the third axiom from the Christian tradition in general.

Orthodox theology massively revolted against this absolutist transformation of Christian faith and theology, because in the final analysis this transformation considered the Bible to be the fruit of ignorant antiquity and some typically Christian ingredients (incarnation, trinity, resurrection, and so on) as simple mistakes. Nevertheless, the main structural elements of the liberal way of thought, like its ontological necessitarianism and its epistemological evidentialism

---

6. Compare Karel H. Roessingh, *De moderne theologie in Nederland* (Groningen: Van der Kamp, 1914); idem, *Het modernisme in Nederland* (Haarlem: Bohn, 1922). Especially on Opzoomer, compare Wim van Dooren, *Cornelis Opzoomer. Het wezen der kennis* (Baarn: Ambo, 1990). The fundamental statement of this position is J. H. Scholten, *De leer der Hervormde Kerk in hare grondbeginselen uit de bronnen voorgesteld en beoordeeld*, 2 vols. (Leiden: Engels, 1848-1850).

of an axiomatic-deductive pattern of argumentation, profoundly influenced orthodox thinking as well.[7]

For instance, influential Dutch theologians like Bavinck and Kuyper were educated by Scholten. Evidently, they did not agree with his historical-critical view on Scripture, yet they did not refute the systematic background of it. So, the ontological necessitarism was not rebutted by making clear how divine providence is compatible with human freedom. The epistemological evidentialism of Scholten was not unmasked as untenable rationalism, but biblicistically and confessionally transformed by Kuyper: All Scripture is evidently true and historical criticism is impossible in any sense, whereas the confessions of the church have deduced the theological axioms for us out of which the whole of Christian theology can be deduced.[8]

Notably, orthodoxy did not utilize the scholastic duality of *necessary* theology and *contingent* theology typical of classic Christian thought, but merely appealed to the inerrancy of Scripture in the debate.[9] Although orthodox theologians like Bavinck and Kuyper honored their scholastic heritage, they were unable to find its adequate answer to *modern* theology.

So, the historical identity of Reformed thought as being a philosophy of contingency and will and, at the same time, a theology of grace and freedom was systematically forgotten. If the Reformed tradition aspires to survive, it has to rediscover its true identity. The explorations of this volume wish to serve this quest.

We are convinced that a renewed understanding of the Reformed tradition provides us with a promising starting point in contemporary theological and cultural debates. A reinterpretation of the Reformed heritage along the lines proposed in this volume could significantly contribute to a sound development of doctrinal topics such as predestination, grace, regeneration, and so forth. Due to the nineteenth-century interpretation into a determinist direction, Reformed orthodoxy today has lost its own apparatus to deal adequately with these issues: it is condemned to maneuver between a determinist hyper-Calvinism that leaves no room to human freedom and responsibility, and a renewed form of Arminianism that is surprisingly popular in evangelical Christianity. The tragedy of this

---

7. For this and the following paragraph compare A. Vos, "Ligt Europa in Holland? Naar aanleiding van Dr. B. Wentsel en de crisis in de cultuur van Europa," *Kontekstueel* 15 (2001): 26-35; A. Vos, "Gespleten wortels van *SoW.* Bavinck en La Saussaye," *Kerk en Theologie* 52 (2001): 213-237.

8. The original project of Kuyper's *Free University* was that the other sciences would deduce their principles from the Bible as well, after which a Christian science could deductively be developed in each discipline. Soon, this project appeared to be impossible.

9. The subject of necessary theology is the greater part of the doctrine of God in which scholastic theology argued that God as most Perfect Being exists necessarily and necessarily has certain attributes. Necessary theology also includes the implicative relations in reality (for example, if an attribute is essential for an entity, it necessarily has this attribute if it exists). Contingent theology refers to the contingent entities and contingent relations between God and reality and in reality itself. In this way, theology draws on both Scripture and general argumentation. For this reason theology was able to argue in a natural way with people who did not accept the Bible.

powerlessness is that Reformed theology has the solution to this dilemma in its own storehouse of tradition: a fully consistent theology that keeps contingency and necessity together, giving all glory to God and keeping man intact in his essential freedom.

The systematic relevance of the Reformed position on free choice lies not only in the strictly Reformed tradition of church and theology. Within the wider field, Reformed thought on freedom as presented in this volume provides an alternative to recent conceptions. For example, the movement of "open theism" owes much of its attractiveness to the presupposition that if God knows what will happen in the future, man's freedom to act is damaged or lost. The solution, in order to maintain human freedom, is to give up a significant (if not decisive) portion of God's foreknowledge.[10] As our exposition of Reformed scholastic texts on freedom shows, the idea that divine foreknowledge damages human freedom is a gross misunderstanding. It is precisely Reformed scholasticism's balanced theory of contingency that offers a third way: while there is an implicative necessity between a fact and God's knowing this fact, neither the fact nor God's knowing it are necessary in themselves. God's eternal knowledge of all future contingent events does not causally detemine these events; as the Reformed put it: God's knowledge and decree respect things in their own essential nature of being either contingent or necessary. Since foreknowledge does no harm to freedom, there is not the slightest reason to diminish God's knowledge of future things.

Finally, Reformed thought on freedom presents a position that is radically different from the modern idea of autonomy. It is understandable that, given the advocacy of freedom in the Renaissance and Enlightenment, we have learned to understand a plea for freedom as a plea for autonomy. The context of theological debates around Erasmus, Coornhert, and Arminius gives fuel to this tendency. We should not, however, be led by these associations to interpret the concept of freedom as such in terms of autonomy. The texts presented in this volume make it clear that there is real freedom, based on the structural contingency of reality as created by God, a freedom which is not taken away by God's knowledge, decree and providence nor by the other factors that constitute our choices. Still, this is a freedom that can only function in dependence on God and that can only flourish in obedience to God's good and righteous will. In recent postmodern philosophy, we see a radicalizing of contingency to the effect that "anything goes" and differences between good and bad no longer matter.[11] Seen through the lenses of biblical revelation, such autonomy is a perversion of real freedom and can never lead to worthwhile lives. Reformed theology offers an antidote to such radicalism

---

10. Open theism is presented and advocated in Clark H. Pinnock et al., *The Openness of God: A Biblical Challenge to the Traditional Understanding of God* (Downers Grove: InterVarsity, 1994); John Sanders, *The God Who Risks* (Downers Grove: InterVarsity, 1998); Gregory A. Boyd, *God of the Possible* (Grand Rapids: Baker, 2001); William Hasker, *Providence, Evil and the Openness of God* (London: Routledge, 2004). A critique of open theism is given in: John M. Frame, *No Other God: A Response to Open Theism*, (Phillipsburg, NJ: Presbyterian & Reformed, 2001); Bruce A. Ware, *God's Lesser Glory: The Diminished God of Open Theism* (Wheaton: Crossway, 2001).

11. Cf. the article by N. W. den Bok mentioned in note 3 above.

in establishing a precise balance of contingency and necessity, freedom and obligation, human responsibility and divine governance. In the pure air of God's grace and goodness, we learn to breathe again as free and responsive human beings.

Bibliography

Primary Sources

Altenstaig, Johannes. *Vocabularius theologiae Joannis Altenstaig: vocum que in opere grammatico plurimorum continentur, brevis et vera interpretatio : opus emendatum et denuo revisum ab ipso operis auctore.* Hagenau: Henricus Gran, 1516.

————. *Lexicon theologicum quo tanquam clave theologiae fores aperiuntur, et omnium fere terminorum et obscuriorum vocum, quae s. theologiae studiosos facile remorantur, etymologiae, ambiguitates, definitiones, usus, enucleate ob oculos ponuntur, & dilucide explicantur.* Repr. Cologne: Joannis Tytz, 1619.

Alvarez, Didacus. *De auxiliis divinae gratiae et humani arbitrii viribus et libertate, ac legitima ejus cum efficacia eorumdem auxiliorum concordia.* Cologne: P. Henningius, 1621.

Aquinas, Thomas. *Summa Theologica.* 2nd ed. Translated by Daniel J. Sullivan. Great Books of the Western World 17. Chicago: Encyclopaedia Britannica, 1990.

Aristotle. *Nicomachean Ethics.* Translated from the Greek (with historical introduction) by Christopher Rowe; philosophical introduction and commentary by Sarah Broadie. Oxford: Oxford University Press, 2002.

————. *Physics.* Translated by Robin Waterfield. Edited with an introduction by David Bostock., Oxford's World's Classics. Oxford: Oxford University Press, 1996.

Arriaga, Rodrigo de. *Cursus philosophicus.* Antwerp: Plantin/Balthasar Moet, 1632.

Augustine. *Christian Instruction.* Edited by John J. Gavigan, John Courtney Murray, and Robert P. Russell. 2nd ed. The Fathers of the Church 2. Washington, DC: The Catholic University of America Press, 1950.

————. *Retractationes. MPL* 32.

————. *Enchiridion ad Laurentium. MPL* 40.

————. *De civitate Dei. MPL* 41.

————. *De duabus animabus. MPL* 42.

————. *De correptione et gratia. MPL* 44.

————. *De natura et gratia. MPL* 44.

————. *De perfectione iustitiae. MPL* 44.

————. *Contra duas epistolas Pelagianorum. MPL* 44.

————. *Opus imperfectum contra secundam Juliani Responsionem. MPL* 45.

————. *Hypomnesticon. MPL* 45.

Bellarmino, Roberto. *Disputationes de Controversiis christianae fidei adversus huius temporis haereticos.* 4 vols. Ingolstadt: A. Sartorius, 1591-1596.

Bibliotheca variorium et insignum librorum, theologicorum et miscellaneorum, reverendi et celeberrimi viri D. Gisberti Voetii. 2 vols. Utrecht: Guilielmus Clerck, 1677-1679

Buddeus, Johann Franz. *Institutiones theologiae moralis.* Leipzig: Thomas Fritsch, 1723.

Calvin, John. *Institutes of the Christian Religion.* Translated and annotated by Ford Lewis Battles. Rev. ed. Grand Rapids: Eerdmans, 1994.

Clairvaux, Bernard of. *On Grace and Free Choice (De Gratia et libero arbitrio).* Translated by Daniel O'Donovan, OCSO. Introduction by Bernard McGinn. Kalamazoo: Cistercian Publications, 1988.

Episcopius, Simon. "Institutiones theologicae, privatis lectionibus Amstelodami traditae." In *Opera theologica.* Amsterdam: Ioannes Blaeu, 1650.

Ferry, Paul. *Pauli Ferrii Vindiciae pro scholastico orthodoxo, adversus Leonardum Perinum Jesuitam.* Leiden: Wiard Jelger, 1630.

Goclenius, Rudolph. *Lexicon philosophicum quo tanquam clave philosophiae fores aperiuntur.* Frankfurt, 1613; repr., Hildesheim: Olms, 1980.

Gomarus, Franciscus (Gilbertus Jacchaeus). *Disputatio theologica de libero arbitrio.* Leiden, 1602.

Jansen, Cornelius. *Augustinus.* Louvain, 1640; repr. Frankfurt am Main, 1964.

Junius, Franciscus. *Theses theologicae, quae in inclyta academia Lugduno-batava ad exercitia publicarum disputationum, praeside D. Francisco Junio variis temporibus a theologiae candidatis adversus oppugnantes propugnatae sunt.* Leiden, 1592.

———. *Opuscula selecta.* Edited by A. Kuyper. Amsterdam: Muller, 1882.

Keckermann, B. *Praecognitorum logicorum tractatus.* Vol. 3. Hannover, 1606.

Leland, John. *The Advantage and Necessity of the Christian Revelation.* London, 1764.

Limborch, Philippus van. *Theologia christiana: Ad praxin pietatis ac promotionem pacis christianae unicè directa.* Edited by Jean Le Clerc. Amsterdam: Balthazar Lakeman, 1730.

Lombardus, Petrus. *Magistri Petri Lombardi Sententiae in IV libris distinctae.* 2 parts in 3 volumes. Rome: Coll. S. Bonaventurae ad Claras Aquas, 1971-1981.

Maccovius, Johannes. *Collegia theologica quae extant, omnia.* Franeker: Ulderickus Balck, Joannes Fabianius Deûring, 1641.

Marck, Johannes à. *Compendium theologiae christianae didactico-elencticum.* Groningen: Gerhardus Nicolaus Fossema, 1686.

———. *Christianae theologiae medulla.* Amsterdam: Gerardus Borstius, 1690.

Melanchthon, Phillip, *Melanchthons Werke im Auswahl.* Vol. 2, part 1. Gütersloh: Bertelsmann, 1952.

Migne, J. P., ed. *Patrologiae cursus completus: Series latina.* 217 vols. Paris: Gaunier, 1844-1855.

Molina, Luis de. *Liberi arbitrii cum gratiae donis, divina praescientia, providentia, praedestinatione et reprobatione concordia.* Edited by Johannes Rabeneck. Societatis Iesu selecti scriptores: Ludovicus Molina. Oña/Madrid: Collegium Maximum/"Sapientia," 1953.

————. *On Divine Foreknowledge*. Part 4 of *Concordia*. Translated with an introduction and notes by A. J. Freddoso. Ithaca/London: Cornell, 1988.

Moor, Bernardinus de. *Commentarius perpetuus in Joh. Marckii Compendium theologiae christianae didactico-elencticum*. Leiden: Johannes Hasebroek, 1761-1771.

————. *Supplementum Commentarii perpetui in Johannis Marckii Compendium theologiae christianae didactico-elencticum*. Leiden: Luzac and van Damme, 1774.

————. *Epimetron Supplementi Commentarii perpetui in Johannis Marckii Compendium theologiae christianae didactico-elencticum*. Leiden: Luzac and van Damme, 1778.

Oviedo, Francisco de. *Integer cursus philosophicus ad vnum corpus redactus: in summulas, logicam, physicam, de cælo, de generatione, de anima, & metaphysicam distributus*. Lugduni: Petri Prost, 1640.

Owen, John. Θεομαχία Αὐτεξουσιαστική *or, A Display of Arminianism Being a Discovery of the Old Pelagian Idol of Free-Will with the New Goddesse Contingency, Advancing Themselves into the Throne of the God of Heaven, to the Prejudice of His Grace, Providence, and Supreme Dominion over the Children of Men*. London, 1643. Repr., Edmonton: Still Waters Revival, 1989.

Rutherford, Samuel. *Disputatio scholastica de divina providentia, variis praelectionibus, quod attinet ad summa rerum capita, tradita s. theologiae adolescentibus candidatis in inclytâ Academiâ Andreapolitanâ, [...]*. Edinburgh: George Anderson, 1649.

————. *Exercitationes apologeticae pro divina gratia: In quibus vindicatur doctrina orthodoxa de divinis decretis, et Dei tum aeterni decreti, tum gratiae efficacis operationis, cum hominis libertate consociatione et subordinatione amica [...]*. Franeker: Johannis Dhüiringh, 1651.

————. *Examen Arminianismi*. Utrecht: Anton Smytegelt, 1668.

Scholten, J. H. *De leer der Hervormde Kerk in hare grondbeginselen uit de bronnen voorgesteld en beoordeeld*. 2 vols. Leiden: Engels, 1848-1850.

Scotus, John Duns. *Quaestiones in Metaphysicam*. Opera philosophica 4. St. Bonaventure, NY: Franciscan Institute, 2005.

————. *Ordinatio* III. Civitas Vaticana: Typis Vaticanis, 2006.

————. *God and Creatures: The Quodlibetal Questions*. Translated with an introduction, notes and glossary by Felix Alluntis and Allan B. Wolter. Princeton: Princeton University Press, 1975.

————. *Contingency and Freedom. Lectura I 39. Introduction, translation and commentary by A. Vos et al*. The New Synthese Historical Library 42. Dordrecht: Kluwer, 1994.

Suárez, Francisco. *Disputationes metaphysicae. Omnia opera* 25. Paris: Vives, 1866.

Turrettini, Francesco. *Institutes of Elenctic Theology*. Translated by George Musgrave Giger. Edited by James T. Dennison Jr. 3 vols. Phillipsburg, NJ: Presbyterian & Reformed, 1994-1997.

————. *Institutio theologiae elencticae, in qua status controversiæ perspicue exponitur, præcipua orthodoxorum argumenta proponuntur et vindicantur, et fontes solutionum aperiuntur.* Editio nova recognita & multis locis aucta: cui accessit oratio de vita & obitu avthoris. Geneve: Samuel de Tournes, 1688.

Ursinus, Zacharias. *Loci theologici. Opera theologica.* Vol. 1. Heidelberg: Johannes Lancellot/Ionas Rosa, 1612.

Vermigli, Peter Martyr. *In Epistolam S. Pauli Apostoli ad Romanos commentarij doctissimi.* Basel: Petrus Perna, 1558.

————. *Loci Communes.* London: Ioannes Kynston, 1576.

Voetius, Gisbertus. *Disputatio theologica de concursu determinante, an determinabili?* 3 partes. Utrecht: Joannes à Waesberge, 1645-46.

————. *Selectae Disputationes.* Vol. 1. Utrecht: Joannes à Waesberge, 1648.

————. *Selectae Disputationes.* Vol. 5. Utrecht: Anton. Smytegelt, 1669.

Voetius, Gisbertus, and Engelbertus Beeckman. *Disputatio philosophico-theologica, continens quaestiones duas, de Distinctione Attributorum divinorum, & Libertate Voluntatis.*, Utrecht: Joannes à Waesberge, 1652.

Vries, Gerard de. *Exercitationes rationales de deo, divinisque perfectionibus.* Utrecht: Joh. Van de Water, 1685.

————. *De natura Dei et humanae mentis determinationes pneumatologicae.* Utrecht: Joh. Van de Water, 1687.

Zanchi, Girolamo. "De libero primorum parentum ante lapsum arbitrio." In *De operibus Dei intra spatium sex dierum creatis.* Book 3, chapter 3 in *Omnia opera theologica*, part 3, col. 704-710. Geneve: Samuel Crispin, 1619.

————. "De libero arbitrio in homine post ipsum non renato." In *De primi hominis lapsu, de peccato & de lege Dei.* Book 1, chapter 6 in *Omnia opera theologica*, part 4, col. 87-94. Geneve: Samuel Crispin, 1619.

Secondary Sources

Ashmann, Margreet J. A. M. *Collegia en colleges: Juridisch onderwijs aan de Leidse Universiteit 1575-1630, in het bijzonder het disputeren.* Groningen: Wolters-Noordhoff, 1990.

Asselt, Willem J. van. "De ontwikkeling van de remonstrantse theologie in de zeventiende eeuw als deel van het internationale calvinisme." In *Theologen in ondertal. Godgeleerdheid, godsdienstwetenschap, het Athenaeum Illustre en de Universiteit van Amsterdam*, edited by P. van Rooden and P. J. Knegtmans, 39-54. Zoetermeer: Boekencentrum, 2003.

————. "Natuurlijke theologie als uitleg van openbaring? Ectypische versus archetypische theologie in de zeventiende-eeuwse gereformeerde dogmatiek," *Nederlands Theologisch Tijdschrift* 57, no. 2 (2003): 135-152.

————. "The Fundamental Meaning of Theology: Archetypal and Ectypal Theology in Seventeenth Century Reformed Thought," *Westminster Theological Journal* 64 (2002): 319-335.

————. *The Federal Theology of Johannes Cocceius (1603-1669).* Studies in the History of Christian Thought 100. Leiden: Brill, 2001.

————. "Protestant Scholasticism: Some Methodological Considerations in the Study of Its Development." *Nederlands Archief voor Kerkgeschiedenis (Dutch Review of Church History)* 81, no. 3 (2001): 265-274.

Asselt, Willem J. van and E. Dekker, eds. *Reformation and Scholasticism.* Grand Rapids: Baker Academic, 2001.

Barde, E. "Gaussen, Etienne." In *New Schaff-Herzog Encyclopedia of Religious Knowledge,* edited by Philip Schaff et al. New York: Funk and Wagnall, 1908, 4:437.

Barnes, Jonathan. *The Presocratic Philosophers.* Vol. 1. London: Routledge and Kegan Paul, 1979.

Beck, Andreas J. "'Divine Psychology' and Modalities: Scotus's Theory of the Neutral Proposition." In *John Duns Scotus (1265-1308): Renewal of Philosophy,* edited by E. P. Bos, 123-137. Amsterdam: Rodopi, 1998.

————. *Gisbertus Voetius (1589-1676): Sein Theologieverständnis und seine Gotteslehre.* Forschungen Zur Kirchen- und Dogmengeschichte 92. Göttingen: Vandenhoeck & Ruprecht, 2007.

————. "Zur Rezeption Melanchthons bei Gisbertus Voetius (1589-1676), namentlich in seiner Gotteslehre." In *Melanchthon und der Calvinismus,* edited by Günter Frank and Herman J. Selderhuis, 319-344. Melanchthon-Schriften der Stadt Bretten 9. Stuttgart: Froomann-Holzboog, 2005.

Beck, Andreas J. and Henri Veldhuis. *Geloof geeft te denken: Opstellen over de theologie van Johannes Duns Scotus.* Scripta Franciscana 8. Assen: Koninklijke Van Gorcum, 2005.

Beck, Andreas J. and A. Vos. "Conceptual Patterns Related to Reformed Scholasticism." *Nederlands Theologisch Tijdschrift* 57, no. 3 (2003): 224-233.

Beeke, Joel R. "Gisbertus Voetius: Toward a Reformed Marriage of Knowledge and Piety." In *Protestant Scholasticism: Essays in Reassessment,* edited by Carl R. Trueman and R. Scott Clark, 227-243 Carlisle: Paternoster, 1999.

Bok, Nico W. den. "Human and Divine Freedom in the Theology of Bernard of Clairvaux: A Systematic Analysis." *Bijdragen, tijdschrift voor filosofie en theologie* 54 (1993): 271-295.

————. "Scotus' Theory of Contingency from a (Post)modern Perspective. Some Important Developments of the Notion of Contingency after Duns Scotus." In *Via Scoti: Methodologica ad mentem Joannis Duns Scoti,* edited by L. Sileo, 431-444. Atti del Congresso Scotistico Internazionale. Rome: Antonianum, 1995.

Boyd, Gregory A. *God of the Possible.* Grand Rapids: Baker, 2001.

Bradley, Raymond, and Norman Swartz. *Possible Worlds: An Introduction to Logic and Its Philosophy.* Oxford: Blackwell, 1979.

Broadie, Alexander. *Introduction to Medieval Logic.* 2nd ed. Oxford: Clarendon, 1993.

Bunge, Wiep van, et al., eds.. *The Dictionary of Seventeenth and Eighteenth-Century Dutch Philosophers.* Bristol: Thoemmes, 2003.

Budé, E. de. *Vie de François Turrettini, théologien genevois (1623-1687).* Lausanne: Bridel, 1871.

Burchill, Christopher J. "Girolamo Zanchi: Portrait of a Reformed Theologian and His Work." *Sixteenth Century Journal* 15 (1984): 185-207.

Burckhardt, Jacob. *Die Kultur der Renaissance in Italien.* Basel: Schwieghaufer,1860.

Calvin, John. *The Bondage and the Liberation of the Will: A Defense of the Orthodox Doctrine of Human Choice against Pighius.* Translated by G.I. Davies. Edited by A.N.S. Lane. Texts and Studies in Reformation and Post-Reformation Thought 2. Grand Rapids: Baker Academic, 1996.

Colish, Marcia. *Medieval Foundations of the Western Intellectual Tradition 400-1400.* New Haven/London: Yale University Press, 1997.

Craig, Edward. "Parmenides (early to mid 5th century BC)." In *Routledge Encyclopedia of Philosophy,* edited by Edware Craig, 7:229-235. London/New York: Routledge, 1998.

Cramer, J. A. *De Theologische Faculteit te Utrecht ten tijde van Voetius.* Utrecht: Kemink en Zoon N.V., 1932.

Cuno, F. W. *Franciscus Junius der Aeltere, Professor der Theologie und Pastor (1545-1602).* Amsterdam: Scheffer, 1896.

De Lubac, Henri, *Augustinisme et théologie moderne.* Paris: Aubier, 1965.

Dekker, Eef. *Middle Knowledge.* Studies in Philosophical Theology 20. Leuven: Peeters, 2000.

―――. "The Reception of Scotus' theory of contingency in Molina and Suárez," In *Via Scoti: Methodologica ad mentem Joannis Duns Scoti,* edited by L. Sileo, 445-454. Atti del Congresso Scotistico Internazionale. Rome: Antonianum, 1995.

―――. *Rijker dan Midas: Vrijheid, genade en predestinatie in de theologie van Jacobus Arminius (1559-1609).* Zoetermeer: Boekencentrum, 1993.

―――. "Was Arminius a Molinist?" *Sixteenth Century Journal* 27 (1996): 337-352.

Dekker, Eef and H. Veldhuis. "Freedom and Sin: Some Systematic Observations." *European Journal of Theology* 3, no. 2 (1994): 153-161.

Dooren, Wim van. *Cornelis Opzoomer: Het wezen der kennis.* Baarn: Ambo, 1990.

Duker, Arnoldus Cornelius. *Gisbertus Voetius.* Introduction by A. de Groot. Repr., Leiden: Groen, 1989.

Ebrard, Johannes Heinrich August. *Christliche Dogmatik.* Vol. 1. Königsberg: August Wilhelm Unzer, 1851.

Evans, G. R. *The Language and Logic of the Bible in the Earlier Middle Ages.* Cambridge: Cambridge University Press,1984.

Hübener, Wolfgang. "Praedeterminatio physica." In *Historisches Wörterbuch der Philosophie,* edited by Karlfried Gründer, Joachim Ritter and Gottfried Gabriel, 7:1216-1226. Darmstadt: Wissenschaftliche Buchgesellschaft, 1989,.

Fournier, W. J. "Gerardus de Vries." *BLGNP,* 1: 417.

Frame, John M. *No Other God: A Response to Open Theism.* Phillipsburg, NJ: Presbyterian & Reformed, 2001.

Frank, William A. "Duns Scotus on Autonomous Freedom and Divine Co-Causality." *Medieval Philosophy & Theology* 2 (1992): 142-164.

Goeters, Wilhelm. *Die Vorbereitung des Pietismus in der reformierten Kirche der Niederlande bis zur labadistischen Krisis 1670.* Leipzig/Utrecht: J. C. Hinrichs, 1911.

Gracia, Jorge J. E., ed., *Suárez on Individuation: Metaphysical Disputation V, Individual Unity and Its Principle.* Milwaukee: Marquette University Press, 1982.

Guthrie, W. K. C. *A History of Greek Philosophy.* Vol. 2. Cambridge: Cambridge University Press, 1965.

Hasker, William. *Providence, Evil and the Openness of God.* London: Routledge, 2004.

Helm, Paul. "Synchronic Contingency Again." *Nederlands theologisch tijdschrift* 57, no. 3 (2003): 234-238.

———. "Synchronic Contingency in Reformed Scholasticism: A Note of Caution." *Nederlands theologisch tijdschrift* 57, no. 3 (2003): 207-223.

Heyd, Michael. *Between Orthodoxy and the Enlightenment: Jean-Robert Chouet and the Introduction of Cartesian Science at the Academy of Geneva.* The Hague: Martinus Nijhoff, 1982.

Hoitenga, Dewey J., Jr. *John Calvin and the Will: A Critique and Corrective.* Grand Rapids: Baker Academic, 1997.

Hughes, George E., and Maxwell J. Cresswell. *A New Introduction to Modal Logic.* London: Routledge, 1996.

Inwagen, Peter van. "Two Concepts of Possible Worlds." In *Midwest Studies in Philosophy,* edited by Peter A. French et al., 185-213. Minneapolis: University of Minnesota Press, 1986.

Itterzon, G. P. van. *Franciscus Gomarus.* The Hague: Martinus Nijhoff, 1930.

James, Frank A. *Peter Martyr Vermigli and Predestination: The Augustinian Inheritance of an Italian Reformer.* Oxford: Clarendon, 1998.

Jonge, C. de. *De irenische ecclesiologie van Franciscus Junius (1545-1602).* Nieuwkoop: De Graaf, 1980.

Keizer, Gerrit. *François Turrettini: Sa vie et ses oeuvres et le Consensus.* Lausanne: Bridel, 1900.

Klauber, Martin I. "Theological Transition in Geneva: From Jean-Alphonse Turrettini to Jacob Vernet." In *Protestant Scholasticism: Essays in Reassessment,* edited by Carl R. Trueman and R. Scott Clark, 256-70. Carlisle: Paternoster, 1999,.

Kneale, William Calvert, and Martha Kneale. *The Development of Logic.* 2nd ed. Oxford: Clarendon, 1975.

Knuuttila, Simo. *Modalities in Medieval Philosophy.* Topics in Medieval Philosophy. London/New York, 1993.

———. "Modal Logic." In *The Cambridge History of Later Medieval Philosophy: From the Rediscovery of Aristotle to the Disintegration of Scholasticism, 1100-1600,* edited by Norman Kretzmann, Anthony Kenny and Jan Pinborg, 342-357. Cambridge [Cambridgeshire]: Cambridge University Press, 1982.

———. *Reforging the Great Chain of Being: Studies of the History of Modal Theories.* Synthese Historical Library 20. Dordrecht/London: Reidel, 1981.

Kretzmann, Norman, Anthony Kenny, and Jan Pinborg. *The Cambridge History of Later Medieval Philosophy: From the Rediscovery of Aristotle to the Disintegration of Scholasticism, 1100-1600.* Cambridge [Cambridgeshire]: Cambridge University Press, 1982.

Kristeller, Paul Oskar, and Michael Mooney. *Renaissance Thought and Its Sources.* New York: Columbia University Press, 1979.

Labooy, Guus. *Freedom and Dispositions: Two Main Concepts in Theology and Biological Psychiatry: A Systematic Analysis.* Contributions to Philosophical Theology 8. Frankfurt am Main: P. Lang, 2002.

Lalande, André, ed., "Determinisme." In *Vocabulaire technique et critique de la philosophie,* 221-224. 7th ed. Paris: Presses Universitaires de France, 1956.

Lovejoy, A. O. *The Great Chain of Being: A Study of the History of an Idea.* New York: Harper and Row, 1969.

Liddell, H. G., and R. Scott. *A Greek-English Lexicon.* Oxford: Clarendon, 1996.

Mackay, Ewald. *Geschiedenis bij de bron: Een onderzoek naar de verhouding van christelijk geloof en historische werkelijkheid in geschiedwetenschap, wijsbegeerte en theologie.* Sliedrecht: Merweboek, 1997.

Mansfeld, J. *Die Offenbarung des Parmenides und die menschliche Welt.* Assen: van Gorcum, 1964.

Meijering, E.P. *Reformierte Scholastik und patristische Theologie: Die Bedeutung des Väterbeweises in der Institutio theologiae elencticae F. Turrettins unter besonderer Berücksichtigung der Gotteslehre und Christologie.* Nieuwkoop: De Graaf, 1991.

―――. *Klassieke gestalten van christelijk geloven en denken: Van Irenaeus tot Barth.* Amsterdam: Gieben, 1995.

Molhuysen, P. *Bronnen tot de geschiedenis van de Leidsche Universiteit.* Vol. 1, 1574 – February 7, 1610. The Hague: Martinus Nijhoff, 1913.

Muller, Richard A. *Ad Fontes Argumentorum: The Sources of Reformed Theology in the Seventeenth Century.* Utrechtse Theologische Reeks 40. Utrecht: Faculteit der Godgeleerdheid Universiteit Utrecht, 1999.

―――. *After Calvin: Studies in the Development of a Theological Tradition.* Oxford Studies in Historical Theology. New York: Oxford University Press, 2003.

―――. *Dictionary of Latin and Greek Theological Terms. Drawn Principally from Protestant Scholastic Theology.* Grand Rapids: Baker, 1985.

―――. *God, Creation, and Providence in the Thought of Jacob Arminius: Sources and Directions of Scholastic Protestantism in the Era of Early Orthodoxy.* Grand Rapids: Baker, 1991.

―――. "The 'Placement' of Predestination in Reformed Theology: Issue or Non-Issue?" *Calvin Theological Journal* 40 (2005): 184-200.

―――. *Post-Reformation Reformed Dogmatics: The Rise and Development of Reformed Orthodoxy, Ca. 1520 to Ca. 1725.* 2nd ed. 4 vols. Grand Rapids, Mich.: Baker Academic, 2003.

―――. "Reformation, Orthodoxy, 'Christian Aristotelianism,' and the Eclecticism of Early Modern Philosophy." *DRCH* 81, no. 3, (2001): 306-325.

————.*The Unaccommodated Calvin: Studies in the Foundation of a Theological Tradition.* Oxford Studies in Historical Theology. New York: Oxford University Press, 2000.

Nauta, D., A. de Groot, J. van den Berg, and A. J. van den Berg, eds. *Biografisch lexicon voor de geschiedenis van het Nederlandse protestantisme.* 6 vols. Kampen: Kok, 1978-2006.

Oberman, Heiko Augustinus. *The Dawn of the Reformation.* Edinburgh: T&T Clark, 1986.

————. *The Harvest of Medieval Theology: Gabriel Biel and Late Medieval Nominalism.* Cambridge, MA: Harvard University Press, 1963.

Oort, Johannes van. *De onbekende Voetius: Voordrachten wetenschappelijk symposium Utrecht 3 maart 1989.* Kampen: Kok, 1989.

Otterspeer, W. *Groepsportret met dame.* Vol. 1, *Het bolwerk van de vrijheid: De Leidse Universiteit, 1575-1672.* Amsterdam: Uitgeverij Bert Bakker, 2000.

Pinnock, Clark H. et al. *The Openness of God: A Biblical Challenge to the Traditional Understanding of God.* Downers Grove: InterVarsity, 1994.

Plantinga, Alvin. "Modalities, Basis Concepts and Distinctions." In *Metaphysics: An Anthology,* edited by Jaegwon Kim and Ernest Sosa, 135-148. Malden, MA: Blackwell, 2003.

————. *The Nature of Necessity.* Oxford: Clarendon, 1974.

Plantinga, Alvin and Matthew Davidson. *Essays in the Metaphysics of Modality.* Oxford: Oxford University Press, 2003.

Ramelow, Tilman. *Gott, Freiheit, Weltenwahl: Der Ursprung des Begriffes der besten aller möglichen Welten in der Metaphysik der Willensfreiheit zwischen Antonio Perez S.J. (1599–1649) und G.W. Leibniz (1646–1716).* Brill's Studies in Intellectual History 72. Leiden: Brill, 1997.

Reuter, Karl. *Wilhelm Amesius, der führende Theologe des erwachenden reformierten Pietismus.* Beiträge zur Geschichte und Lehre der Reformierten Kirche 4. Neukirchen: Neukirchener Verlag, 1940.

Robinson, John M. *An Introduction to Early Greek Philosophy.* New York: Houghton Mifflin Company, 1968.

Roessingh, Karel H. *De moderne theologie in Nederland.* Groningen: Van der Kamp, 1914

————. *Het modernisme in Nederland.* Haarlem: Bohn, 1922.

Rorty, Richard. *Philosophy and the Mirror of Nature.* 9th ed. Oxford: Blackwell, 1996.

Rijk, Lambertus Marie de. *Aristotle: Semantics and Ontology.* Leiden: Brill, 2002.

————. *Logica Modernorum: A Contribution to the History of Early Terminist Logic; On the Twelfth Century Theories of Fallacy.* Assen: Van Gorcum, 1962.

————. *Middeleeuwse wijsbegeerte. Traditie en vernieuwing.* 2nd ed. Assen: Van Gorcum, 1981.

Rijk, Lambertus Marie de and P. Swiggers. *La philosophie au moyen âge.* Leiden: Brill, 1985.

Ruler, Johan Arie van. *The Crisis of Causality: Voetius and Descartes on God, Nature and Change.* Brill's Studies in Intellectual History 66. Leiden: Brill, 1995.

Rummel, Erika. *The Humanist-Scholastic Debate in the Renaissance and Reformation.* Cambridge: Harvard University Press, 1995.

Sanders, John. *The God Who Risks.* Downers Grove: InterVarsity, 1998.

Scheffczyk, Leo. "Gnadenstreit." In *Lexikon für Theologie und Kirche,* edited by Michael Buchberger, Walter Kasper, and Konrad Baumgartner,4:797. 3rd ed. Freiburg: Herder, 1995.

Schmutz, Jacob. "François Du Bois." *Scholasticon: Ressources en ligne pour l'étude de la scolastique moderne (1500-1800); Auteurs, textes, institutions,* edited by Jacob Schmutz. http://www.ulb.ac.be/philo/scholasticon/nomenD.htm#dubois (accessed April 28, 2008).

———. "Du péché de l'ange à la liberté d'indifférence: Les sources angélologiques de l'anthropologie moderne." *Les études philosophiques* (2002): 172-173.

Schreiner, Thomas R., and Bruce A. Ware. *The Grace of God, the Bondage of the Will.* Vol. 2, *Historical and Theological Perspectives on Calvinism.* Grand Rapids: Baker, 1995.

Schweizer, A. *Die protestantische Centraldogmen in ihrer Entwicklung innerhalb der reformierten Kirche.* 2 vols. Zurich: Orell, Fuessli und Comp, 1853-1856.

Southern, R. W. *Saint Anselm: A Portrait in a Landscape.* Cambridge: Cambridge University Press, 1990.

———. *Scholastic Humanism and the Unification of Europe.* Vol. 1, *Foundations.* Oxford: Blackwell, 1995.

Stegmüller, F. "Gnadenstreit." In *Lexikon für Theologie und Kirche,* edited by Josef Höfer and Karl Rahner, 3:1002-1007. 2nd ed. Freiburg: Herder, 1960.

Steinmetz, David C. *Calvin in Context.* New York: Oxford University Press, 1995.

———. *Luther in Context.* Bloomington: Indiana University Press, 1986.

Tomberlin, James E. "Actualism or Possibilism?" *Philosophical Studies: An International Journal for Philosophy in the Analytical Tradition* 84, nos. 2-3 (1996): 263-282.

Trueman, Carl R. *The Claims of Truth: John Owen's Trinitarian Theology.* Carlisle: Paternoster, 1998.

Vansteenberghe, E. "Molinisme." In *Dictionnaire de théologie catholique: Contenant l'exposé des doctrines de la théologie catholique, leurs preuves et leur histoire,* edited by E. Mangenot, A. Vacant, and É. Amann, 12:2094-2187. Paris: Letouzey et Ané, 1929.

Venemans, B. A. *Franciscus Junius en zijn Eirenicum de Pace Ecclesiae Catholicae.* Leiden: Elve/Labor vincit, 1977.

Vos, A. "Gespleten wortels van SoW: Bavinck en La Saussaye." *Kerk en Theologie* 52 (2001): 213-237.

———. *Kennis en noodzakelijkheid: Een kritische analyse van het absolute evidentialisme in wijsbegeerte en theologie.* Dissertationes Neerlandicae Series Theologica 5. Kampen: Kok, 1981.

———. "Ligt Europa in Holland? Naar aanleiding van Dr. B. Wentsel en de crisis in de cultuur van Europa." *Kontekstueel* 15 (2001): 26-35.

———. *The Philosophy of John Duns Scotus.* Edinburgh: Edinburgh University Press, 2006.

Vos, A., H. Veldhuis, E. Dekker, N. W. den Bok, and A. J. Beck. *Duns Scotus on Divine Love.* Aldershot: Ashgate, 2003.

Ware, Bruce A. *God's Lesser Glory: The Diminished God of Open Theism.* Wheaton: Crossway, 2001.

Index

near and remote, 86
"central dogma" theory, 18–19, 21–22
change, 40–41, 47
choice, 44, 98–99
    and intellect, 54–55
    and power, 53–55, 79
    as self-determined, 221
"Christian Aristotelianism," 26n35
Christian freedom, 142
Cicero, 55, 65
circumstances, 100, 105, 108, 111, 116, 120, 208
Coelestius, 71
coercion, 58, 59, 64, 67–70, 74, 99, 100, 111–12, 178, 185, 208
compounded sense of indifference. *See* divided/ compounded distinction
conceptual analysis, 27
concupiscence, 60
concurrence (*concursus*), 150, 151, 153, 155, 166, 189, 193, 196–97, 224, 225, 233
conscience, 213
consequence, 35–36
conservatism, 239
consolation, 184, 207, 220
consultation, 75, 81
contingency, 17, 31, 33–39, 47, 231, 234, 237–38
    in history of philosophy, 39–42
    and necessity, 38–39, 114
    in postmodern philosophy, 241
    of second causes, 32
contradictories, 35n55
contraries, 35n55
conversion, 109, 133, 134–35, 138, 142–43
Coornhert, 241
corruption, 104, 174. *See also* state of corruption
Counter-Reformation, 170
created freedom, 108, 119
creation, 146
creatures, 102–3
Cyrus, 149–50

D'Ailly, Pierre, 22n21
decision, 178, 208
decree, 37, 39, 87, 88, 153, 161–65, 169, 178, 179, 181, 219, 220
deliberation, 75, 81, 221
demons, 73, 207, 220
de Moor, Bernardinus, 47, 49, 113, 201–29, 233
dependence, 179

de Rijk, L. M., 16, 19n10, 24n30, 24n32, 25
Descartes, René, 202, 212n38, 213, 214n45, 228–29, 233
determination, 21, 183–84, 185, 189–90, 191
determined objects, 115
determinism, 15, 17, 18, 31, 38, 144, 221–22, 236, 237
De Vries, Gerard, 204, 205
diachronic contingency, 41, 42, 88, 89, 234
dialectic, 23, 27
discrete will, 100, 116–17
disobedience, 140
disposition, 44
disputatio genre, 96–97, 133
    authorship of, 97–98, 147n10
divided/compounded distinction, 163, 167, 193, 194–95, 196, 222
Dominicans, 17n7, 165, 174n11
Du Bois, François, 152
Duns Scotus, John, 16–17, 22, 39, 41, 156

Early Orthodoxy, 48, 51
Ebrard, J. H. A., 146
eclecticism, 26
ectype, 119
Edwards, Jonathan, 209n29
ekousios (ἑκουσίως), 65, 75, 99, 175, 208, 209, 221
election, of will, 99, 100, 107, 108, 117, 185
elenctic theology, 171
elicited acts, 84, 208, 212n39, 228, 232
ends. *See* means and ends
Enlightenment, 23n25, 137, 228, 241
Episcopius, 37, 183
epistemological evidentialism, 239–40
epistemology, 213, 214n45
equilibristic freedom, 197
Erasmus, 236, 241
Essenius, Andreas, 146, 147
essential entities, 43
essential properties, 139
exhortations, 184, 185–86
external acts. *See* imperate actions

factual necessity, 121, 123
facultas, 44
faculties, of soul, 74, 91–92, 131, 212–13
faculty psychology, 44, 202, 210, 228, 235
"faith seeking understanding," 23–24
Fall, 44, 76, 83, 89, 90–91, 104, 108–9, 120, 121, 140–41, 231, 232, 235, 236
Felix the Manichee, 70
Ferry, Paul, 151